IDEALIZATION VI:

IDEALIZATION IN ECONOMICS

POZNAŃ STUDIES
IN THE PHILOSOPHY OF THE SCIENCES AND THE HUMANITIES

VOLUME 38

The address: prof. L. Nowak, Cybulskiego 13, 60-247 Poznań, Poland.
Fax: (061) 535-535
E-mail: epistemo at PLPUAM11.AMU.EDU.PL

IDEALIZATION VI: IDEALIZATION IN ECONOMICS

Edited by
Bert Hamminga
and
Neil B. De Marchi

Rodopi

AMSTERDAM – ATLANTA, GA 1994

CIP–GEGEVENS KONINKLIJKE BIBLIOTHEEK, DEN HAAG

Idealization

Idealization in economics / Bert Hamminga and Neil B. De
Marchi (eds.). – Amsterdam – Atlanta, GA 1994 : Rodopi. – (Poznań
studies in the philosophy of the sciences and the
humanities, ISSN 0303-8157 ; vol 38)
ISBN: 90-5183-551-5 (Bound)
Trefw.: economie

Printed in The Netherlands

CONTENTS

Discussions

PREFACE

This volume had its origin in a conference held at Tilburg University, July 1-3, 1991. It was supported by the Tilburg University Department of Philosophy, CentER and the Royal Dutch Academy of Sciences KNAW.

It was the intention to bring together economists interested in the strategical backgrounds of research, economic methodologists dealing with the practical problems of the economist's work and philosophers of science. The conference was meant to be an exchange of thoughts on the idealizational nature of economic theories.

Without much difficulty, the area of economic scientific activity can be split up into a limited set of well known and accepted research lines, to which the vast majority of contemporary economic publications contributes. What one needs to know in order to be a successful participant of some research programme is usually the literature published in the past, the way in which the authors in this line of publications formulate their problems, and the kind of solutions they would like to have for their problems.

It is clear what one should do if one is to become an expert in a specific research line, and, once you are an expert, the agenda of theoretical and technical jobs is clearly visible and well specified. Internal discussions in a research line proceed orderly way, and on a technical level. It is clear in that context how one should defend and criticize and propose solutions to problems.

This comfortable order breaks down as soon as discussion takes place between experts of different research lines. The technically refined discussions are set aside and the much rougher "economists' debate" sets in.

Research lines seem flowers competing for the insects' attention. It is difficult for an economic scientist to know what to do as long as he is still in the air, his choice to land somewhere may even seem arbitrary, but as soon as he lands, he knows where to go.

What is shared by those who choose to participate in developing a specific line of research, distinguishing them from others, is (apart from a set of economic departments, regular conferences and periodicals) an *idealization*: an abstract view on real world economies that highlights some of the aspects observed, and neglects others. Central tasks of research are *analysis* (of the mathematical properties of the abstract model) and *concretization* (the successive dropping of the idealizing assumptions). Questions for this conference were: Why choose for one idealization as a starting point rather than another? What is the list of tasks once a choice is made for some specific idealization? Can there be an orderly discussion between adherents of different reseach lines, using different idealizations, and not necessarily being in the same stage of concretization? These questions were to be dealt with in a specific way, preferably by analyzing well specified examples from the real world of working economists.

This volume includes revised versions of papers presented at the conference plus a couple prepared since. It addresses three main topics, the first of which is *logical analysis of idealizational structures in economics*. An idealization is a simplified representation of the object of inquiry. The idealization abstracts from many, if not most of the known properties of the object. It is a false image, and those who use it as an idealization *know* that it is a false image.

The idealization is a small world in itself. It is described by concepts and statements. You can say false and true things about it. You can neatly model it with sets and functions. You can do formal research into its mathematical properties: some theorems hold in it, others don't. If you drop some idealizing assumptions, allowing more possibilities, different types of "species" into your ideal world, you will loose some theorems, some will be modified, others retained.

Questions: what is the structure of the idealizations that one finds in economics? For what reasons do economists regard any particular idealization as a good starting point for research? How are idealizations handled in the course of developing and refining a theory? What is the list of unsatisfactory features of an idealization that are to be improved upon?

The reader will find these topics addressed in the contributions below by Cartwright, Hoover, Walliser, Janssen, Garcia de la Sienra, Mäki, Diederich and Birner.

The second topic of the volume is *historical case studies* dealing with specific research lines. The beginning of research in new directions is usually marked by a publication (sometimes more than one) that, once research develops, becomes a "classic" in the new field that it created.

Very often, its criticism of contemporary rival approaches, its principles, and the research programme implictly advocated by its basic ideas seem *obvious*, if not *trivial* to readers in later stages of the development of the research line. It becomes harder and harder to understand what problems the earliest readers had in acquiring the new line of thought. But at the time an article that is to become "classical" was written, its points were not trivial at all. If the paper succeeds in its task of redirecting research, its points remain clear, but their original problematic character to those who have a different frame of mind, becomes more and more obscure. As one of the results, the history of the field before the "classical" publication now starts to be looked upon as a "prehistory" in which authors (now starting to count as "precursors") held bits and pieces of its idealizational ideas in rudimentary form. Idealization has done its work, including in such cases the reinterpretation of the history of the field.

Questions: what was the criticism of publications that later became "classical" of older idealizing representations of the relevant economic process? What did the old idealization look like through the eyes of those preferring the new? What did the new idealization look like through the eyes of the old? What was the countercriticism that the new approach had to overcome? How did it succeed, and in so doing, make older idealizations fade?

These processes of transition from one idealization to another can be observed in the large (the "revolutionary" periods of economics), and in the small (changes of approach within specific fields). Aspects of these problems can be found in the contributions here, by Cools, Hamminga and Kuipers, Hausman, Keuzenkamp and Jorland.

The third topic is *logical analysis of the relationships between idealizations prevalent in different research lines*. We often find adherents of rival theories opposed to each other, both claiming that the other's theory is simply a special case. Logical analysis of the relationship between the rival idealizations is something that an economist debating over the borders of his own research line does all the time. But surely it is the most difficult theoretical task an economist can assume, and a satisfactory result may not even exist in some cases. "Abstraction" means "forgetting about some things" for the time being, and analyzing the relationships between two idealizations means comparing two different sets of things forgotten for the time being, and the effect of this on theory.

It would be nice if we could assume that adherents of rival idealizations at least agreed on the complete list of relevant properties of the object of enquiry, and thus only disagreed about which of these could safely be "assumed away", as a first, second, or third approximation. But the real world of working economists seems to be more complicated.

Questions: how to model rival idealizations in such a way that rival economists would at least agree how they should be compared and what is the result of such a comparison? And, if this remote goal cannot be reached, then what is the list of obstacles? These problems are touched on in many of the contributions here, but especially exercize Balzer, Cook and Hendry, and Nowakowa and Nowak.

This gives a rough framework for approaching the individual papers, though it is hardly a proper introduction. Rather than forcing what is in fact a very wide-ranging set of papers into a mould into which they do not readily fit, we have preferred to devote the space that would otherwise have formed an introduction to sketching the models of idealization espoused by a group of well known economic methodologists: this will serve as historical background material to the papers.

Tilburg, March 1994

Bert Hamminga
Neil De Marchi

Poznań Studies in the Philosophy of the Sciences and the Humanities
1994, Vol. 38, pp. 11-40

Bert Hamminga and Neil De Marchi

IDEALIZATION AND THE DEFENCE OF ECONOMICS: NOTES TOWARD A HISTORY

ABSTRACT. Illustrates and compares the opinions of the economists J.R. McCulloch (1825), J.S. Mill (1836), K. Marx (1864), L. Robbins (1932) and M. Friedman (1953) on the problem of idealization in economics, both from a logical point of view (the structure of economic theories) and from a social point of view (idealizational methodology as a defense of theory against sceptical outsiders).

Idealization in economics has always been closely linked with abstraction. "[S]ome obscurity," Adam Smith warned his readers just before starting his analysis of price formation, "may still appear to remain upon a subject in its own nature extremely abstracted" (1976 [1776], p. 46). Smith's contemporary, Samuel Johnson, in his *Dictionary of the English Language*, makes clear that abstracted meant (as it still does) both refined, or abstruse, and general, as well as separated from everything extraneous, reduced to essentials. Johnson's *Dictionary* entries are instructive:

"ABSTRA'CTED, *part.adj.* [*from abstract.*]
1. Separated.
   That space the evil one *abstracted* stood
   From his own evil, and for the time remain'd
   Stupidly good. *Milton.*
2. Refined, abstruse.
   Abstracted spiritual love, they like
   Their souls exhal'd. *Donne.*
3. Absent of mind, inattentive to present objects;
   as, an *abstracted* scholar."

Though this is to some extent helpful, we should not forget to consult the related entries:

"*To* ABSTRA'CT *v.a.* [*abstraho*, Lat.]
1. *To* take one thing from another.
   Could we *abstract* from these pernicious effects, and suppose this were innocent, it would be too light to be matter of praise.
   Decay of Piety.

2. To separate ideas,

Those, who cannot distinguish, compare and *abstract*, would hardly be able to understand and make use of language, or judge or reason to any tolerable degree.

Locke.

3. To reduce to a epitome.

If we would fix in the memory of discourses we hear, or what we design to speak, let us *abstract* them into brief compends, and review them often.

Watt's Improv. of the Mind.

A'BSTRACT. *adj.* [*abstractus*, Lat. See the verb *To* ABSTRACT.]

1. Separated from something else, generally used with relation to mental perceptions; as, *abstract* mathematics, *abstract* terms, in opposition to concrete.

Mathematics, in its latitude, is usually divided into pure and mixed. And though the pure do handle only *abstract* quantity in general, as geometry, arithmetic; yet that which is mixed, doth consider the quantity of some particular determinate subject; so astronomy handles the quantity of heavenly motions, music of sounds; and mechanics, of weights and powers.

Wilkins's Mathematical Magick.

Abstract terms signify the mode or quality of a being, without any regard to the subject in which it is; as, whiteness, roundness, length, breadth, wisdom, mortality, life, death.

Watt's Logick.

2. With the particle *from*.

Another fruit from the considering things in themselves, *abstract from* our opinions and other mens notions and discourses on them, will be, that each man will pursue his thoughts in that method, which will be most agreeable to the nature of the thing, and to his apprehension of what it suggests to him.

Locke.

A'BSTRACT. *n.s.* [from the verb.]

1. A smaller quantity, containing the virtue of power of a greater.

You shall there find a man, who is the *abstract*.
Of all faults all men follow.

Shakesp. Antony and Cleopatra.

If you are false, these epithets are small;
You're then the things, and *abstract* of them all.

Dryd. Aur.

2. An epitome made by taking out the principal parts.

When Mnemon came to the end of a chapter, he recollected the sentiments he had remarked; so that he could give a tolerable analysis and *abstract* of every treatise he had read, just after he had finished it.

Watt's Improvement of the Mind.

3. The state of being abstracted.

The hearts of great princes, if they be considered, as it were in *abstract*, without the necessity of states, and circumstances of time, can take no full and proportional pleasure in the exercise of any narrow bounty.

Wotton."

We shall have something more to say about abstraction presently. First, however, a summary statement of our argument.

1. Idealization and attacks on political economy

Political economists, from the outset, have struggled to find coherent, consistent ways to make good on their pretensions to rise above common sense and experience, yet ultimately to give plausible, usable advice on practical matters, on policy. "Abstraction" has served the first purpose, but it has not been easy to convince sceptics of the usability of abstract truths. If abstraction in economics means simplifying *for the moment*, to gain clarity before plunging back into the complexities of the real world, that is one thing. If, however, it means treating of things which are artificial constructs, having no real existence, then it is a serious question how, and whether, one can get from the ideal to the real. Economists have at times defended procedural simplification, at times the method of strictly artificial construction. Some have even argued for abstraction as the only way to reach essential "reality". Not infrequently, the occasion of the defence, whichever way it came out, has been an immediate need to answer criticisms and provide new or more satisfactory grounds for belief in both the practical significance of economics and *also* in the need for "abstraction". This has resulted in texts that we think of as methodological, but which are in fact exercises in disciplining the thinking of errant insiders and a dubious lay public. The texts bear the marks of the particular form in which the difficulties appeared at the time of writing.

We have selected a few authors to illustrate this point: McCulloch, J.S. Mill, Marx, Robbins, and Milton Friedman; but we have no pretensions to be complete. The inclusion of Friedman is especially important because he represents an empirical line of defence that reflects an attitudinal change in economic methodology. This change occurred around the 1930s and marks a sharp departure from the defences used from McCulloch to Robbins.

2. Experimental idealization

Unlike the procedural sort of idealization, or the claim that economics dealt not in real but in deliberately artificial constructs, the new defence was both pragmatic and derived its authority from outside economics. It said simply that there is one method of science, the one already developed and tested in biology and physics. This method was thought to combine the best of pre-Newtonian insights, and the lessons of non-deterministic physics. It sought Baconian phenomenological "relations", not necessary connections or a priori truths; it was empirical, therefore, but not "naively" so (given to enumerative induction), for it employed mathematical techniques and also the new methods of statistics. All "inferences" about relations were regarded as hypotheses until tested, and the only available test was behavioral: does the hypothesis "hold", or perform better than alternatives? This, minus all frills and suppressing some well-known disputes and differences, describes the general attitude of certain of the Logical Positivists — Neurath and Kaufmann, for example — and some of the leading spirits behind the Econometric Society (Fisher certainly, Frisch and Hotelling in important respects).[1]

Recent historical studies (Morgan 1990, Epstein 1987) have traced the flowering of this attitude in the Cowles Commission program in structural estimation in the 1940s. In many ways, however, the Cowles researchers pursued a rather rigid line in econometrics, and after the 1940s there was a reversion to a more general interest in hypothesis testing, drawing directly on the work of Jerzy Neyman and Egon Pearson. The first generation of econometrics textbooks embodied their approach rather than the Cowles ideals (Lail 1993). Friedman would have no truck with Cowles methodology even in the 1940s; but as a representative of those interested in hypothesis testing he still displays some of the main features of what we are calling the new attitude.

---

[1] Morgan (1990, pp. 2-3, 55nn) draws attention to this conviction about a new method among the founders of the Econometric Society; Lail (1993) introduces the links with the Logical Positivists and traces the influence of statistical methods, particularly those due to Karl Pearson, R.A. Fisher and Jerzy Neyman and Egon Pearson.

Neyman and Pearson always insisted that their approach, which involved comparing rival hypotheses, could say nothing about truth or falsity. They were talking not about inductive inference as that had been traditionally understood by epistemologists, but about adopting a particular attitude towards the available hypotheses: an attitude of behaving "as if" one or another hypothesis were true (Lail 1993, ch.2). Nor was causation presupposed in the methods that formed the basis of their work and which had been developed in biology (*ibid.*). An agnostic approach to both truth and causation certainly marks Friedman's work, and it is striking that he problematizes "truth" precisely in a statistical-theoretic context.

We paraphrase a recent expression of Friedman's views on the latter point (interview with Hammond 1992, esp. pp. 101-102). In all strictness, one should not make a statement such as "P is *the* probability" in any case where information about the population is lacking. Such 'absolute' pronouncements presume complete knowledge. But in economics — possibly Friedman has in mind the fact of small 'samples' — even "if there be a truth, there's no way of knowing when you get it"; hence one must focus on personal beliefs, tentatively held and revisable in the light of fresh evidence.

This attitude, we would argue, infuses Friedman's work, but we confine ourselves here to his 1953 essay, where it emerges in the form of two consequences. The implications (a) of abstaining from judgements about the "truth" of one's theory and (b) of insisting on empirical evidence to assess and suggest corrections to one's *beliefs*, are clear. One then regards theory, not as a body of truths, but as an engine of analysis; and one seeks to derive empirically testable implications from the theory and to match them to data in such a way as to discriminate between alternative beliefs (Hirsch and De Marchi 1990, pp. 208, 232, 244, 259; Hammond 1992, p. 101). These themes in the essay are complemented by a third. Friedman also stresses the importance of an intermediate step between "theory" and testable implications, namely, constructing models or hypotheses. These models are idealizations. For Friedman, however, the idealizations are a means for defining and setting up mini-experiments with data. They do not lead simply to mental experiments, such as Mill and Robbins engaged in, but to empirical experimentation, sometimes using given data, sometimes using constructed data.

In the years since Friedman wrote his essay experimental idealization has evolved in surprising ways. We mention here just two of the twists that have been added to the original empirical turn.

(1) Friedman was fairly confident that, even if in principle multiple hypotheses are consistent with given evidence, often it will be possible

to formulate alternative beliefs in a form such that the test data selected can be consistent with at most one of them (see the discussion in section 5.2 below of note 11 in the 1953 essay). This may be true where we are testing for the presence of quite particular empirical effects, as in a lot of recent work on financial market data; but to be content to operate at this level also means that one is virtually abandoning any attempt to show that one's low-level empirical hypotheses are in any sense representative of a class of theoretical models, or that those theoretical models are themselves representative of general classes of underlying beliefs.[2] Even where the theorist tries to model behavior explicitly, the real purpose — at least in recent calibration models in "macro" economics — is to create an analogue to the movements displayed in real economies. The models, which embody theoretical ideals such as coherence and consistency, can be calibrated against real data, and subsequently used for simulation experiments (see, for example, Lucas' Jahnsson Lectures 1987, *passim*; cf. Hoover 1990). In either case, there is a shift away from testing "theory" to testing simply for the match between theoretically generated descriptions and particular characteristics in data. This marks a more radical separation of theory and empirical work than Friedman might have anticipated, though he ploughed the first furrow.

(2) A peculiar consequence of this shift is that discussion of general underlying convictions long held by economists, as to what characterizes agent behavior and market outcomes — rationality, and efficiency, for example — has been shunted off-stage. On-stage, a lot of attention is directed to data characteristics, at the empirical and test model level; and even if the focus is also at times on theoretical models, the explicit behavior displayed by rational agents is said to be model-specific.[3] Thus Lucas, for instance, says of "rational expectations" that it "refers to a consistency axiom for economic models, so it can be given precise meaning *only in the context of specific models*" (1987, p. 13, note 4; emphasis added). He goes on: "I think this is why attempts to define rational expectations in a model-free way tend to come out either vacuous ('People do the best they can with the information they have') or silly ('People know the true structure of the world they live in')" (*ibid.*).

This means that there is now no other context than the specific theoretical model within which discussion, about what Robbins would have thought of as basic postulates and Mill as laws of human nature,

[2] See Kim, De Marchi and Morgan (1993) for an analysis of this problem, with a case study of "tests" of the natural rate hypothesis.

[3] For an account of how theoretical, empirical and test models fit together and function in the "testing" enterprise, see Kim, De Marchi, and Morgan (1993).

is allowed. If discussion, particularly critical discussion, does take place elsewhere, that is the business of "someone else"; the philosopher, perhaps, but not the serious economist. The serious economist is exact and rigorous in the way microeconomic notions are used to shape models; and consequent about spelling out functions or "rules" for the policy game (since that is the only way to properly incorporate expectations) (*ibid.*, esp. sections II, VIII). The disgruntled "practicals" who simply appeal to "current policy *numbers*" (*ibid.*, p. 18; emphasis in original) or other economists who scoff at the notion that agents can possibly know the true model of reality, are simply not to be taken seriously.

Yet that doesn't mean that convictions held about rationality are any the less strong, and they obviously remain crucial for model-building; it just means they are not matter for discussion within economics itself. Along with, and as part of, the empirical turn, therefore, we find a retreat to unargued assertions about essential reality. The latter aspect, as we shall see, represents a return to Marx, even while Mill and Robbins are rejected.

To grasp how very odd these modern manifestations are, we need to say more about the earlier defences. As a prelude, however, we shall examine the term abstraction more closely, to help fix the two main meanings that Samuel Johnson identified: abstraction as referring to a way of obtaining something "generally" valid, and abstraction as isolating from other (extraneous) elements.

3. "Abstraction": the use of the term

When economists talk about abstraction, an "abstract theory" is often held to be "general", "generally valid" or "generally applicable". The theory applies to the set of all phenomena in the class of phenomena the theory is designed to explain.

On the other hand theories are called "abstract" because the general elements are "abstracted" from a large class of phenomena all of which individually differ from each other, as an effect of which an abstract theory does not explain any single phenomenon completely. Secondary, subsidiary factors in each individual case cause deviations from what is expected on the basis of the "abstract" theory alone. This clearly suggests that an "abstract" theory has no exact applications at all.

It is efficient and helpful to talk about what one observes in reading economics literature using a language which is familiar with some concepts that arose in the logical tradition; for example, "generality", "scope", "set", "explain", and so on. In order not to let these terms slip in implicitly we now introduce them as observation language, a tool to organize what can be seen in the economic literature.

What are (economic) words and sentences about, according to logicians? They ascribe to words and sentences *intensions*, and *extensions*, concepts originally invented by Frege who labelled them *Sinn* and *Bedeutung*. The concepts "intension" and "extension" were originally used only in connection with so-called universal terms, i.e. terms that can apply to several different objects. Thus the word "tree" designates a large set of objects – its extension – by means of its intension, which could be described as the concept created through an act of *abstraction* over the properties that all trees have in common (see Kneale and Kneale (1962), p. 318). Later, the distinction was generalized by Carnap to apply to singular terms as well (Carnap 1947). The distinction now has roughly the same import as Frege's disitinction between "Sinn" and "Bedeutung" (Frege 1952).

This reveals that logicians too talk about abstraction (in the context of *intension*). There is no reason to assume that the logician's use is identical to the economist's. We have "abstraction", "generality", "intension" and "extension". And we can apply these words to two completely different classes of things: "terms" or "words" on the one hand, and "statements", "sentences" sometimes called "hypotheses" or even "theories" on the other hand. How to use them without confusion?

Let's take the former family of applications (terms, etc.) first and construct a scheme.

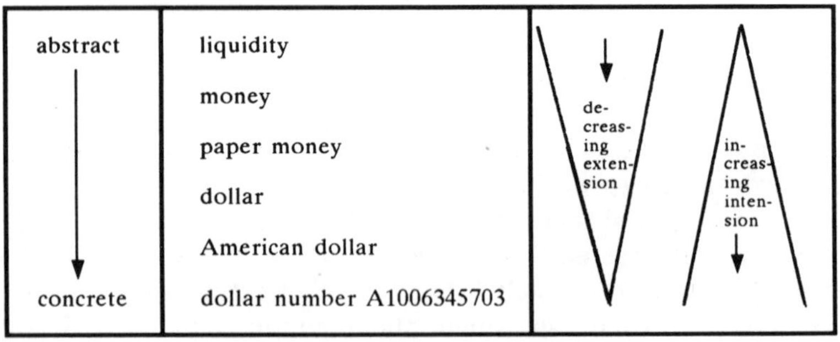

Figure 1. "Abstract" in logic

"An important rule governs the logical relationship of extension and intension [of terms]: as the extension of a series of terms increases, their intension decreases, and as the extension decreases, the intension must increase".[4] Moving from top to bottom in the scheme, the class of objects covered by the term (extension) narrows. The class of properties we need, to say what we are talking about (intension), widens.

Let us now take the second class of things we talk about: statements, etc. The *generality* of a statement hangs together with the *extension* of the concepts used in making the statements. A simple example may help: "dollar number A1006345703 is worn badly where it has been folded often" is less general than "paper money does not withstand repeated creasing".

Moreover, *derivability* between statements in turn depends on *generality*. Thus, "dollar number A1006345703 is worn badly where it has been folded often" *follows from* "paper money does not withstand repeated creasing" exactly *because* "paper money does not withstand repeated creasing" is *more general than* "dollar number A1006345703 is worn badly where it has been folded often".

Introducing another expression, the term "liquidity", we abstract from a large group of properties a very small class (intension) as a result of which the extension of "liquidity" is large indeed. In general, then, we can say that: a term A is more abstract than a term **B** if the extension of A includes that of **B**. As a result, "dollar number A1006345703 is worn badly where it has been folded often" is *less general than*, and *derivable from* "paper money does not withstand repeated creasing", *because* "paper money" is more abstract than "dollar number A1006345703".

We are now ready to pass in review the defences of an earlier generation of economic methodologists.

4. Three nineteenth century methodologists

4.1 John Ramsay McCulloch

We begin with J.R. McCulloch, follower of Ricardo and editor of Smith. McCulloch's *Principles of Political Economy*, published in 1825, was by no means the first statement on the nature of political economy, but it serves as an early and very clear example of a defence of the "science" (his word) by what we would now call the method of idealization.

McCulloch faced the problem that differences among the various exponents of political economy had generated "a disposition to distrust

---

[4] Rescher (1964), p. 26.

its best established conclusions" (1825, p. 13). He at once admonishes the doubters: is it not true of all sciences that differences of opinion exist among their practitioners? Then he makes a significant concession. There are differences among the sciences: in physics (invoking Newton), conclusions *always* apply; but the conclusions of political economy apply only *in the majority of cases* (*ibid.*, p. 14). If they do not apply to a particular case that is because some special circumstance differentiates it from the rest. But, this is not a reason to reject political economy as a whole, rather, it should send one in search of the special cause of this circumstance. The fact is that political economy deals with "man in the aggregate — with states, not with families — with the passions and propensities which actuate the great bulk of the human race, and not with those which are occasionally found to influence the conduct of a solitary member of society" (*ibid.*). In short, whereas "nothing is more common than to hear it objected to some of the best established truths in political and economical science, that they are at variance with certain facts, and that therefore they must be rejected" (*ibid.*, p. 16), this is not a charge that can be made by those who understand "the nature of the science". The sagacious observer will know how to distinguish the special circumstances that cause particular effects from those which apply in the majority of cases.

Knowledge of the "real [majority-of-cases] causes of national opulence and refinement" is to be prized, because this furnishes the statesmen "with the means of devising a scheme of administration calculated to ensure the continued advancement of the society" (*ibid.*, pp. 21-2). This rightful role of political economy is unfortunately threatened by some who, pretending to be economists, nonetheless propagate "erroneous systems", to the discredit of the science. Outsiders, who doubt because they mistake for contradicting evidence mere observations which are mis-read for lack of a sound understanding of how economic laws are to be regarded, or who are troubled by the diversities of opinion among practitioners, McCulloch encourages. In effect he invites them to place themselves among the sagacious.

The following scheme summarizes McCulloch's method of idealization.

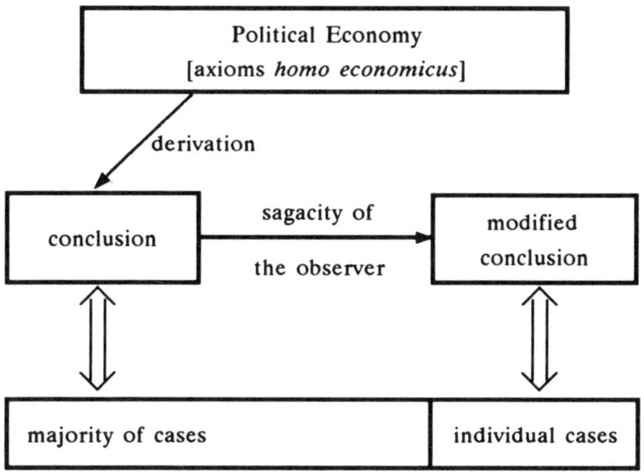

Figure 2. McCulloch's theory of idealization

4.2 John Stuart Mill

J.S. Mill published his famous essay on the method of idealization in economics under two different titles. The 1836 version reads: "On the Definition of Political Economy, and on the Method of Philosophical Investigation in that Science". The title given in his *Essays on some unsettled questions of political economy* (1844), however, alters the latter part of the original title so that it reads: "...and on the Method of Investigation Proper to It". It looks very much as if exposition for the edification of the disinterested mind had given way to a conviction on Mill's part that opponents and doubters must be confronted directly. Certainly he wanted that the essay "should become classical and of authority" (letter to a reader of a draft, in *Collected Works*, 1967, IV, p. 309).

On one level, Mill's problem was similar to the one McCulloch had faced. Outsiders, advertising themselves as "practical men", were accusing political economists of being "theorists", of employing an *a priori* method to go from invented assumptions to inapplicable conclusions. The practical men urged that those engaged in matters of such importance should stick closely to the facts. But the need for a definitive statement was felt more acutely by Mill because people like McCulloch were also doing the science no good by arguing that the laws of political economy are applicable only in the majority of cases. McCulloch's position would tend to reduce arguments about the laws of the science to a sort of counting of cases, making the outcome depend on both the knowledge held by the protagonists and also the cast they were able to put on the evidence. For Mill that was altogether too fickle a basis on which to build the science. He offered a startling alternative.

Mill acknowledged that there is an "ancient feud between what is called theory, and what is called practise or experience. There are, on social and political questions, he acknowledged, two kinds of reasoners: there is one portion who term themselves practical men, and call the others 'theorists'" (1967 [1844] p. 324). But things are not so simple, since both groups really use both theories and facts. In any case, those priding themselves on being "practical men" should know that a truth, a conclusion, must be *argued*.

Take for instance, the truth that absolute kings are likely to employ the powers of government for the oppression of their subjects. This is, Mill claims, straightforwardly provable from human nature. "Practicals" who doubt this truth would now start observing individual absolute kings, but this leads nowhere, Mill ventures. McCulloch had also used this same example, and had explicitly considered the case in which there really would be instances of absolute kings who had not oppressed their subjects, at the same time stressing that these instances would be "not enough to overthrow the principle" (1825, p. 18). Mill, however, rejects this procedure. He prefers considering the case that absolute kings had never existed, or that their behavior could not be observed, still "the conclusion would lose nothing of its certainty" (1967 [1844], p. 325).

How so? In the same manner as Euclid showed. Euclid never observed a perfectly straight line without breadth in nature. When be drew something in the sand he knew it could never really be the line about which he was thinking and speaking. Despite this, Euclid's laws were true *in the abstract*. And abstract truths give us useful information about real situations, as abstract lines do about real lines drawn in sand, roughly in proportion to the closeness of the resemblance between the supposed and the real (*ibid.*, p. 149). Hence, "[t]he conclusions of geometry are not strictly true of such lines, angles and figures, as human hands can construct. But no one, therefore, contends that the conclusions of geometry are of no utility, or that it would be better to shut up Euclid's elements, and content ourselves with practise and experience (*ibid.*, p. 327).

Having got McCulloch's false defence out of the way, Mill adopts a more conciliatory tone. Those who "distrust comprehensive thinking" and complain that economists have generalized too readily and must admit to exceptions in their so-called laws, are, it is true, using superficial and inaccurate language (1967 [1844], p. 337). But theorists themselves are not without blame. There have been economists who "predicted an actual result, when ... [they] should only have predicted a tendency to that result" (*ibid.*). There is faulty language employed on both sides, then; but the ideal to be striven for is plain: it is "one who, placed on a higher eminence of thought, comprehends as a whole what ... [those who bandy half truths] see only in separate parts; who can make the anticipations of the philosopher *guide* the observation of the practical man, and the specific experience of the practical man *warn* the philosopher where something is to be added to this theory" (1967 [1844], pp. 334-5).

Finally, Mill proposes some rules for formulating theory that will bring the ideal within reach. The problem that the "practical man" has to contend with is that, in political economy, there are always so many causes operating in any practical situation that we cannot make sense of the things we merely observe. Fortunately, however, the causes operating in political economy are laws of human nature, and we can know these laws by introspection. Moreover, the principal causes are few: a desire to improve our material situation with least effort, subject also to a preference for present over future goods, and, of course, given the existing state of knowledge. Once we know these elements accurately, "we may reason with as much certainty as in the most demonstrative parts of physics, from any assumed set of circumstances" (*ibid.*, p. 149). The assumed circumstances should bear a resemblance to real ones, otherwise the reasoner is engaged in mere trifling; but "if the assumption is correct as far as it goes, and differs from the truth no otherwise than as a part differs from the whole, then the conclusions which are correctly deduced from the assumptions constitute *abstract* truth; and when completed by adding or subtracting the effect of the non-calculated circumstances they are true in the concrete and may be applied to practice" (*ibid.*).

One key to Mill's procedure is the notion of law as tendency statement. Tendencies continue to operate even if opposed and perhaps offset in their effects by others acting counter to them. This supplants the incorrect language of laws and exceptions. It means too that to be *useful*, in the sense of *guiding* observation, abstract truth need only focus on the main causes; in Mill's words "general causes – causes common to the whole class of cases under consideration" (*ibid.*). Complete accuracy, hence applicability, which is what the policymaker needs, requires something additional, that the specific causes be added in. This supposes, of course, that causes can be added, something that Mill indeed presumes, invoking the parallelogram of forces.

These rules and exemplars do not get Mill as far as he might have hoped, as Nancy Cartwright points out in her contribution to this volume. But that is not our concern here. Our interest is in the clever way he replaces McCulloch's answer to the "practicals" with one that was completely proof against allegations of law-upending "facts", while at the same time showing the practical man how, if only he will, he might become a "true practical statesman" (1967 [1844], p. 333).

The model of idealization that stands at the center of his case, is shown in the figure below.

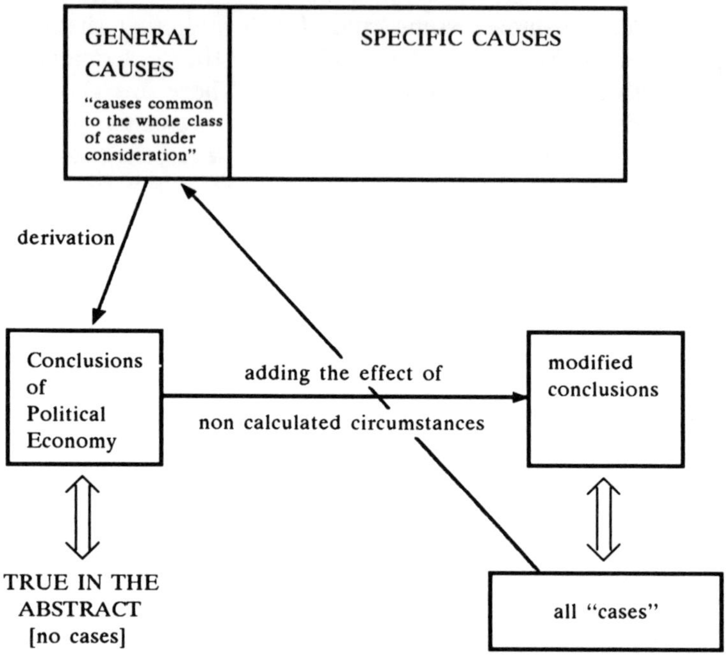

Figure 3. Mill's theory of idealization

4.3 Marx

Marx's approach to idealization has been the focus of work by Nowak (1971) and we simply offer a stripped down version of his analysis here. We should note, however, that the context of criticism perceived by Marx was very different from the one that McCulloch and Mill thought it advisable to try and deal with. Marx felt political economy was in danger, not from outside critics, but from those who took a superficial view of the nature of its laws and thought to improve their working by altering the conditions of distribution. "Utopian socialists" were his target, though that is a broad designation and could be stretched to include Owen, supporters of the Factory Acts and the Ricardian Socialists — all and any, in fact, who wanted to give the worker better conditions and a larger share of the product, even ownership of the means of production, without acknowledging that the key to righting "labour's wrongs" was to change the nature of valuation. For the root problem was not that labor had been robbed by capitalists, but that labor had been robbed of all its specificity and reduced to abstract exchange value. Owen was right to think in terms of workers owning capital, but this change had to occur at a society-wide level, not in isolated model factory-villages, since only on an economy-wide scale could one give meaning to concepts such as socially necessary labor time and social product, and restore to individual workers the freedom to pursue their personal interests in non-socially needed labor time.

At the heart of Marx's system, therefore, is a discussion of valuation. Marx's method of idealization reflects this. Instead of Mill's simple dichotomy of "general" and "specific" causes, Nowak discovers in Marx' *Capital* a complete hierarchy of "factors", describing a significance (or essential) structure:

$$
\begin{array}{ll}
(k) & H \\
(k-1) & H, P_k \\
(k-2) & H, P_{k-1} \\
\cdots & \cdots \\
\cdots & \cdots \\
(0) & H, P_k, \ldots, P_1
\end{array}
$$

"H" is the main factor, "P_k" is the second factor, "P_{k-1}" is the third, and so on. Here there are k "levels of abstraction", level k being the highest and "0" the lowest.

Marx descends (or ascends if we turn the formula upside down as some find it more helpful to do) from level k, but, according to Nowak, does not completely arrive at the lowest level in *Capital*. On level k, H, the socially necessary labour time, is the sole factor determining exchange rates between commodities. The corresponding law of value, however, is an *ideal law*, like the law of falling bodies which idealizes by supposing absence of pressure, magnetism, and other factors. This law of value presupposes the absence of a host of secondary factors $P_k, \ldots, P_1$, (differences of organic compositions of capital, profit rates, and the like).

In the world as it appears to us this ideal law has therefore no domain at all. "True in the abstract", Mill would probably say of it. Marx, however, reflecting Hegel's influence, decided to consider the law of value to be the *deepest essence* of society, discernible beneath appearances by the sagacious observor. Attaching a process to sagacity, Marx moves from level k steadily downwards (or – if you like – "up" out of the deepest essence), and at each level he describes a modified law of value, appropriate to an ever more complex, less abstract, more concrete but still imaginary world.

It seems clear that Marx and Mill were satisfied with their respective versions of idealization for close to the same reason.

In each case, the truth of the laws they adduced as belonging to political economy were protected by the method against possible counterexamples. In Mill's version, the extensions of his abstract conclusions are empty (no "cases"), and only causes common to the whole class of cases are considered. A critic adducing some case as counterexample would be advised to search for the special circumstances (counteracting causes) which must be operating in the situation in question. Marx tells the same critic that the alleged counterexample is an "appearance-phenomenon", not affecting the deep essence of reality. A claim to have found a counterexample, in the Marxian scheme, is an invitation for finding suitable modifications of the abstract law.

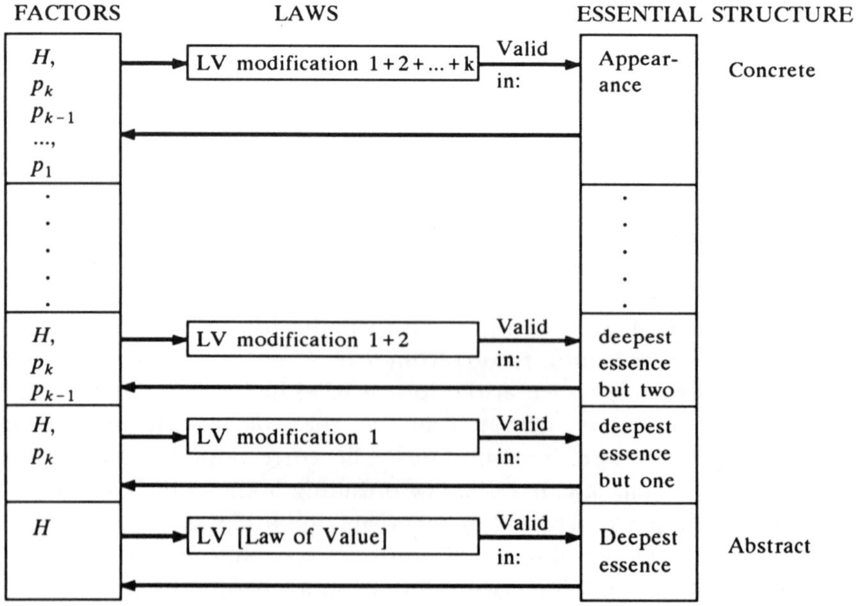

Figure 4. Marx' method of idealization according to Nowak

4.4 Some observations

We started out to try and shed some light on the notion of abstraction. The cases we looked at have turned the discussion into one of how those economists handled a particular two-sided problem: which kinds of criticism against economic theory are admissible; and how should one argue in favor of theoretical propositions?

At a fairly general level, the answers they gave look similar. When arguing in favour of theory they said: abstract theories are "generally valid"; when considering defences against criticism: abstract theories are *not* straightforwardly applicable to every individual case.

Economists — not those we looked at — have tended to use the single word "abstract" to cover both features and have thereby generated confusion about the content of this notion. But we have seen that "generally valid" meant to McCulloch that exceptions existed, whereas to Mill it meant true only of cases in which none but general causes applied; that is, true in no cases at all. This difference is important. It means, for example, that if a majority of the cases examined turned out to undermine the theory, McCulloch would have to abandon his theory. In Mill's case, however, even an overwhelming number of counter instances would not change the judgement that the laws of political economy were true in the abstract.

The greater security for theory that Mill's method buys is costly. It seems desirable in a theory that it be true in the majority of cases; for Mill to reject this line of argument puts him at risk of having his theories called abstruse in the sense of aloof, irrelevant.

Marx also rejected McCulloch's language; but he devised an even more startling inversion of common sense than Mill to defend theory. Economic laws are said to be true in the abstract, but Marx's "abstract" turns out to be a "deeper level of reality": the abstract is the essentially real. From Mill's Euclidean position we have moved to a Platonistic version of Euclid. We have already hinted at intriguing echoes of Marx's version in Lucas' methodological statements.

5. Some neoclassical defenses of the method of idealization

5.1. Lionel Robbins

Robbins wrote his *Essay on the Nature and Significance of Economic Science* in 1932, as nationalistic policies were causing world trade and output to contract literally vortex fashion and political freedoms were increasingly at risk. The book combined defences of the method of idealization, and of rationality in general and rational economic science in particular, into a case for "positive values" and human freedom.

On the surface, the problem was nothing new: "false ideas are prevalent with regard to the preoccupations of the economist and the nature and the extent of his competence. As a result, the reputation of Economics suffers, and full advantage is not taken of the knowledge it confers" (1932, p. xiv). Once again there were "practicals" and politicians abroad who, provoked to impatience with theory by the unexpected Crash and Depression, exclaimed "*Ceteris paribus* be damned", and carried with them "a substantial majority of the lay public, and a good many soi-disant economists as well" (*ibid.*, p. 123). This was as silly, said Robbins, as rejecting the laws of mechanics because "an experiment designed to illustrate them were interrupted by an earthquake". Yet this reaction was more than stupid; it was dangerous:

> in the last analysis Economics does depend, if not for its existence, at least for its significance, on an ultimate valuation – the affirmation that rationality and ability to choose with knowledge is desirable. If irrationality, if the surrender to the blind force of external stimuli and uncoordinated impulse at every moment is a good to be preferred above all others, then it is true the *raison d'être* of Economics disappears. And it is the tragedy of our generation, red with fratricidal strife and betrayed almost beyond belief by those who should have been its intellectual leaders, that there should have arisen those who would uphold this ultimate negation ... But for all those who still affirm more positive values, that branch of knowledge which, above all others, is the symbol and safeguard of rationality in social arrangements, must, in the anxious days which are to come, by very reason of this menace to that for which it stands, possess a peculiar and a heightened significance. (*ibid.*, pp. 157-58)

Robbins' defence of economics is structured in terms of an opposition between "abstraction" (1932, p. 74) and the concrete (*ibid.*, p. 117), though he prefers to contrast "general" with the "particular" or the "individual". Chapter IV is devoted to the nature of economic generalization, and it contains the core of his position. Rationality, we are not surprised to discover, is basic: "an essential constituent of our conception of conduct with an economic aspect" (*ibid.* p. 76). Rationality here means the opposite of "the blind force of external stimuli and uncoordinated impulse" (see above), and shows itself in "the schemes of valuation of the different economic subjects". Subjects have preferences; these are stable, consistent; and they incorporate a notion of indifference. We start, then, with essential concepts (rationality, expressed in the properties of schemes of valuation). Marx thought the abstract was essential but real; for Robbins the essential is instead conceptual. There are other postulates too, though these are not so much conceptual as "assumptions involving in some way *simple and indisputable facts of experience* relating to the way ... in which the subject matter of our science actually shows itself in the world of reality" (1932, p. 78; emphasis added). This experiential basis is driven home through a series of variant formulations. These postulates have "counterparts in reality"; they are "the stuff of our everyday experience"; and it is from their "existence" that "the general applicability of the broader propositions of economic science is derived" (all *ibid.*, p. 79). The postulates involved at this level are the "facts" of scarcity, and the existence of factors of production.

From the *concept* of rationality plus these *facts of experience* the propositions of economic theory are derived. These propositions, we infer, are "simple", since Robbins adds that "the development of the more complicated applications of these propositions involves the use of a great multitude of subsidiary postulates" (*ibid.*, p. 79). At the same time, since even the simple deductions carry forward the fact of "the *existence* of the conditions they assume" (*ibid.*), they thereby achieve "general applicability" (*ibid.*).

This must mean general in the sense of abstract or, of great extension (see section 3 above). Indeed, Robbins notes that "[t]he most fundamental propositions of economic analysis are the propositions of the *general* theory of value" (1932, p. 73; emphasis added; cf. p. 110), and, again in line with our interpretation, he notes that there is nothing in the general formulation of the postulate of scarcity "which warrants us in attaching it to any particular commodity" (*ibid.* p. 106). But if the particular is not straightforwardly derivable from the general, just how is the general related to the particular?

To this point, Robbins' "general" seems to have the connotation of McCulloch's true "in the majority of cases". The broad, simple, fundamental propositions of economics – these terms are used interchangeably – must cover the majority of cases, since they rest on a few postulates which are the very "stuff" of ordinary experience.

But that language is so close to the "essential constituent" designation used of the concept rational conduct that the barriers between the conceptual and the factual seem to have been taken down, and essentiality is applied to both. That which is essential cannot but apply to the majority of cases.

Here, however, while the thought may be McCulloch's, the method of reasoning is Millian, with a strong hint of Plato *via* Von Mises. Mill's laws of political economy were based, recall, on laws of human nature, the nature and truth of which was something every individual could check for themselves by introspection. Mill did not follow through on the implication that broad applicability was therefore a foregone conclusion, because he wanted to avoid the entanglement McCulloch wove for himself, namely, that a sceptic might start asking: which cases? Instead, Mill urged that, in all strictness, broad applicability meant applicable to no case in particular. That too, as we have seen in one quotation cited already, is exactly the line Robbins follows (1932, p. 106).

Thus we find Robbins cautioning that the properties of rational conduct are used "not to foster the belief that the world of reality corresponds to the construction", but "to enable us to study, in isolation, tendencies which, in the world of reality, operate only in conjunction with many others" (1932, p. 94). Just so, Mill would say (see his comments on the abstraction of man as solely a wealth-seeking individual: 1967 [1836], p. 312). The trick is to know how and when to apply such constructs. At that point many needed adjustments crowd in: subsidiary postulates, as we have seen already; and empirical studies, to provide a check on the applicability of abstract truths in circumstances that are for ever altering, to suggest which particular auxiliary postulates are needed in which circumstances, and to expose areas where theory needs to be reformulated or extended (*ibid.*, pp. 116-118). The need here is exactly for those qualities Mill described in the "true practical statesman": one who "combines ... experience with a profound knowledge of abstract political philosophy". It is false, Robbins concludes, to entertain "the hope of giving permanent and particular content to the categories of pure analysis", but by trying them out in concrete cases we may expect to refine our theoretical apparatus "as a means of interpretation and prediction" (*ibid.*, pp. 120-21).

Mention of prediction, however, introduces another twist. Mill would not have gone that far: guidance to the statesman, yes; prediction, no. We seem to be back with McCulloch, for whom the test is indeed to look at predictions and see how often the laws hold. Only Robbins doesn't really mean that. The role of empirical studies is to help ascertain applicability, not test validity. Prediction for Robbins belongs with interpretation because one cannot deny "the reality of the *necessities* they [general economic laws] describe" (*ibid.*).

Robbins' theory of idealization can be represented simply enough (figure below), but we have discovered that his defence of the method is complicated, because it introduces factual claims and the essential as if these were aspects of a single reality. Marx handled this duality by likening the succession of stages through which an idealized law is modified to ascending from the deepest essence of reality towards the world of appearances. How Robbins combined the factual and the essential is obscure. What is clear, however, is that he needed both, not because he had anything to add to Mill's method of idealization as such, but because he saw a need to defend economics against both "practicals" *and* irrationalists. Robbins basically adopted Mill's defence against the practicals; but the irrationalists were a new threat, not faced by either Mill or McCulloch. Robbins addressed the new threat by claiming the concept of rational conduct as part of the claim to significance of economics. This was in addition to the claim of general relevance for economic laws, based on their being derived from essential facts of reality. Economics, for him, exemplified in the social sphere the value of free, reasoned choice, which he contrasted with blind force and uncoordinated impulse. "The revolt against reason is essentially a revolt against life itself", he wrote; and those who choose for life must not shrink from making "the affirmation that rationality and ability to choose with knowledge is desirable" (1932, p. 157).

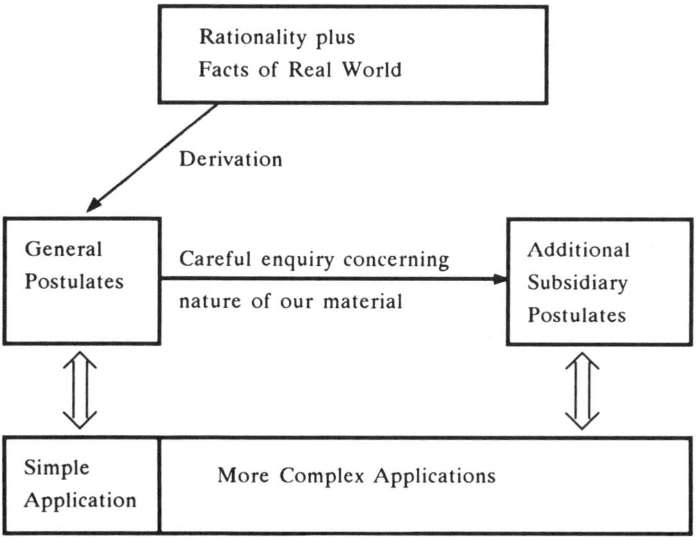

Figure 5. Robbins' theory of idealization

5.2 Milton Friedman

Robbins' affirmation that the rational theory of choice and exchange underpins social order and political freedom would have seemed perfectly appropriate to Milton Friedman, though it is not clear that he ever read Robbins' *Essay*. Nor is it clear just what provoked him to write his own essay, "The Methodology of Positive Economics" in 1953 (see interview with Hammond 1992, p. 106). Reading "below the line", among the footnotes to the essay, however, a reason is easy to find. There was a new generation of "practicals" grown up arguing, in various ways, that economic theory could not apply over an important range of cases simply because it's postulates were themselves "unrealistic". We note that the critics included Hall and Hitch (the Oxford interest rate survey); Lester, Oliver and Gordon (the marginal cost pricing versus business practices controversy); and advocates of monopolistic competition theory to fill gaps left by the monopoly and competition polar cases; but we shall not go into the debates they sparked because it is not necessary for our purposes.

Mill had answered the charge that economic laws have exceptions by saying: the theory is abstract, and as such necessarily applicable to no case at all; but it is based on a knowledge of true causes and can be filled out and complicated by adding in the effects of deliberately neglected tendencies (causes), and with careful judgement can therefore be used as a guide in interpreting real world cases. Marx's response had been to turn upside down the commonsense meaning of realistic. Robbins had reaffirmed Mill's defence, but added that there are social and political reasons to respect the rationality that characterizes economic theory, and anyway, the postulates of economics are part of the very stuff of experience; the problem, therefore, cannot lie with economic theory but must lie in the area of application, which is indeed demanding, as Mill implied.

Friedman has rejected all such defences, because all of them involve an element of essentialism, or at least claims to a knowledge of the Truth. His mature view on this is that theory which cannot be false has no value in practice. We can learn nothing from it, because we can never discover whether it is better or less good than any other; it is simply asserted to be True. Furthermore, that attitude contains the seeds of authoritarianism — the very danger Robbins hoped to guard against — because in denying that anything can ever be learned it removes the superiority of argumentation and inquiry into the facts over force as a way to resolve differences (see the interview with Hammond 1992, pp. 101-102, 110; cf. Hirsch and De Marchi 1990, p. 239). The traces of this position are readily discernible, we would argue, in Friedman's 1953 essay on positive economics.

In that essay, Friedman argued for economics to become an "objective" science (1953, pp. 4, 25), by which he seems to have meant, a discipline offering agreed-upon directives or indications for addressing real problems. The issue he had to address was how to achieve consensus, given that major barriers seemed to stand in its way. First, everyone seemed to regard economics as "within the range of his own experience and competence" (1953, p. 3). Experts, therefore, tend to be self-proclaimed, can hardly be reckoned disinterested, and speak with many voices (*ibid.*, p. 4). This would not be an insuperable problem if hypotheses in economics could be once-and-for all disproved; but that is not the situation. We test mostly on data thrown up by experience. These are uncontrolled and are therefore complex manifestations of numerous influences, both known and unknown. Such data will generally support numerous interpretations; and various conjectures as to what they mean therefore can and do live on. Some may disappear, but only for a while, before popping up again (*ibid.*, pp. 9-11).

Lacking the means to achieve consensus based on direct knowledge of what is true — an essential of the method of Mill and of Robbins, but rejected by Friedman — and being unable conclusively to disprove any hypothesis, how can we achieve consensus? First, says Friedman, let's be clear that we will not reach consensus on values; about values we can ultimately only fight or agree to differ. An objective normative economics, therefore, is beyond reach. A basis does exist, however, for a consensual "positive" economics. For, unlike value beliefs, beliefs about the economic consequences of policy changes can be subjected to the test of facts. In Western capitalistic societies basic values are not the main source of divisions; most differences about policy derive from different predictions about the economic effects of policy actions (1953, p. 5). But since we can subject our various policy beliefs to test, the way forward is clear. We must regard it as the task of economic theory to provide "a system of generalizations" capable of generating "predictions about the consequences of any change in circumstances" (*ibid.*, p. 4; cf. p. 39). The performance of these predictions can then be checked for their precision, scope and conformity with experience (*ibid.*, p. 4; cf., p. 40).

This position is laid out quite unmistakably in the early and concluding paragraphs of Friedman's 1953 essay; the rest is concerned with adding qualifications and clarifying and defending various elements making up this view. These qualifications and clarifying and defending arguments together yield a method of idealization; and we shall notice such of them, though only such, as are helpful to extracting this method. Friedman's exposition of his method of idealization, we should note, employs language that seems at times to imply links to nineteenth century methodologists, particularly McCulloch and Mill, and sometimes to twentieth century positions in the philosophy of science (realism, instrumentalism, Positivism). The text of his essay alone is not sufficient to answer questions about whether these links are real and intended, or merely reflect usages that were part of the accepted conventions for discussing methodological issues in the late 1940s and early 1950s. We sidestep those issues, but we do insist that, whatever one makes of these elements of language, they definitely were *not* used by Friedman to undergird Mill-Robbins type defences of economic theory, nor does one need more than the switch of methodological stance outlined earlier (section 1.2) to make sense of Friedman's position.

Economic inquiries into the consequences of changes in circumstances, Friedman suggests, can be thought of as sequencing through two, closely related and constantly repeated, stages. First, one constructs hypotheses; second, these are tested. The tests may suggest that a hypothesis is tentatively acceptable; or they may imply that it be "rejected" (1953, p. 8). Since, however, no conclusive disproof is possible, nor can factual evidence ever "prove" a hypothesis (*ibid.*, p. 9), we place faith in a hypothesis only if it has survived "many opportunities for contradiction" (*ibid.*). And even then, because multiple explanations for given facts can always be found, we tentatively accept only such hypotheses as (a) survive such opportunities *and* (b) perform consistently better (or less worse) than alternatives (*ibid.*).

Friedman's exposition proceeds in terms of a whole series of "twos". Not only are there two stages to inquiry in general, but two roles for theory in the construction of hypotheses (theory as language and theory as a body of substantive hypotheses: 1953, pp. 7-8), two roles for empirical evidence (to "suggest" hypotheses and to make sure in advance that a hypothesis is not out of line with the facts; and to test "validity": *ibid.*, p. 12), and two "parts" to hypotheses (a "conceptual world or abstract model" asserting that only certain forces are important; and a set of "rules" defining which facts count as proper for testing the model: *ibid.* pp. 8, 13, 14, 24). These various elements and their linkages are portrayed in the scheme below.

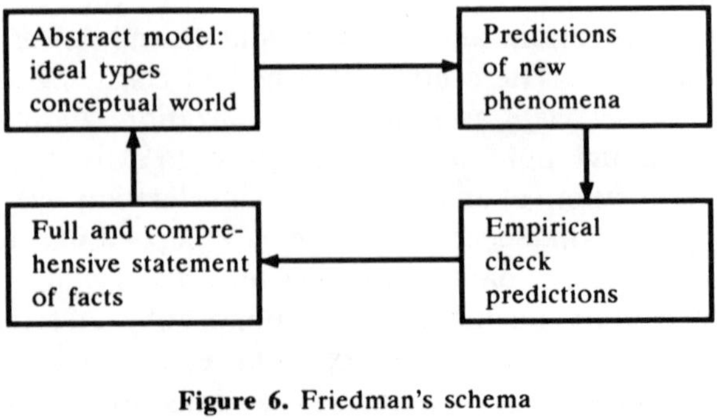

Figure 6. Friedman's schema

We start this scheme with the need for "[f]ull and comprehensive evidence on the phenomena to be generalized or 'explained' by a hypothesis" (1953, p. 12) as a reminder of the start-and-finish empirical character of Friedman's method of idealization. Theory enters even at this stage, it is true, because the investigator always imposes some sort of interpretative grid on the facts (*ibid.*, p. 34). Think of the "filing system" we call supply and demand, which we use to organize "factors" of influence and facilitate "systematic ... reasoning" (*ibid.*, pp. 7-8), or the 'organizer' known as Friedman's re-formulation of the cash balances approach to money demand, in which money along with other assets is viewed as making up a portfolio, and agents, in equilibrium, allocate demand so as to equalize expected returns from every such asset. Inventing and structuring these filing systems is the nonsubstantive, or " 'language' aspect of theorizing" (*ibid.*, p. 7). Furthermore, there is some artificiality about insisting on any "starting point" at all; for in fact "the process never begins from scratch; the so-called 'initial stage' itself always involves comparison of the implications of an earlier set of hypotheses with observation" (*ibid.*, p. 13).

The next "stage" is that of constructing hypotheses. Here abstraction of a selected group of forces deemed "important for a particular class of phenomena" (1953, p. 24) generates a hypothesis or model (at times also called a theory). Because the aim here is to deliberately isolate "from the mass of complex and detailed circumstances surrounding the phenomena to be explained" just those judged to be "common and crucial elements" (*ibid.* p. 14), the resulting hypothesis involves categories that are "ideal types" (think of perfect competition and monopoly: *ibid.*, p. 34). The hypothesis therefore is itself descriptively false (*ibid.*, pp. 14-15), and, as with Mill's abstract laws of political economy, is strictly applicable in no case at all. Friedman even invokes the difference between mathematical and real-world definitions of a line as an illustration of what abstraction entails for him. However, Friedman, unlike Mill, does not use this as a way to protect economics from counterexamples; he is not interested in safeguarding essentially true laws, but in throwing up empirically meaningful and testable hypotheses. These hypotheses are an expression of the functioning of theory as an engine of analysis, and it would be a category mistake to confuse an engine of analysis with a description of reality (cf. *ibid.*, p. 35) and to judge it as true or false rather than as fruitful and explanatorily significant (explaining much by little: *ibid.*, pp. 10, 14).

There is always some arbitrariness, Friedman warns, in the selection of a hypothesis, and in its formulation. One does not "know", but simply asserts on a tentative basis which factors are the "right" ones to isolate;

and often alternative hypotheses seem equally consistent with the evidence (1953, pp. 10, 24).

There is arbitrariness too, or at least skilled judgement, in the third "stage" of the method of idealization, where the problem is to make sure that the new phenomena predicted by the hypothesis chosen and formulated in some specific way are "about the class of phenomena the hypothesis is designed to explain" (*ibid.*, p. 13).

Friedman states that there must be "a set of rules" for doing this (*ibid.*, p. 24) as well as a specification of the correspondence between abstract and empirical entities; but he also acknowledges at once that the rules "cannot possibly be abstract and complete", "cannot be taught" and must be "learned by experience and exposure in the 'right' scientific atmosphere" (*ibid.*, p. 25). While the initial language here suggests a Friedman borrowing from the accepted (Positivistic) usages, he ends up rejecting the implied constraint of logical completeness and consistency (*ibid.*). This is in line with his insistence, concerning the 'language' aspect of theorizing, that more than logic has to be involved even there (*ibid.*, p. 7). It is consistent too, with the otherwise curious footnote 3 (*ibid.*, p. 5), in which Friedman asserts, on the authority of Gödel, "the impossibility of a comprehensive self-contained logic".

In short, his expository language notwithstanding, Friedman is at pains to infuse economic inquiry with an empirical element, or an element of informed judgement, at *every* stage. This is in sharp contrast to Mill and Robbins, for example, who start with undeniably true laws or postulates and add in complicating circumstances only when it is a matter of trying to apply correctly conclusions reached for abstract models. For Friedman, the choices of the investigator, informed by knowledge of the problems of interest, seem to be as much a part of *making* theory as of applying it.

In this connection, the long footnote 11 of the essay (*ibid.*, pp. 12-13), critical of the Cowles Commission approach to econometrics, is revealing. Friedman objects that the Cowles researchers, who distinguish between choosing a model (selecting from among all possible hypotheses a class of admissible hypotheses) and selecting a hypothesis (for them, choosing a "structure"), for reasons of statistical "identification", run the risk of unwittingly introducing different criteria at each stage, although engaged in essentially the same kind of choice.

For Friedman himself, the choice of admissible models is dictated by the problem at hand. One chooses an abstract model or hypothesis that one thinks will shed light on some real problem and *at the same time* one looks for evidence of a discriminating sort, such that it *can* be consistent with just one formulation of the hypothesis. The model is then "identified" without one's having had to jump separately through the Cowles hoops. Friedman's exposition on this point is simply a translation of the Neyman-Pearson method of testing, involving a "null" hypothesis and an alternative. In a modified version of the method two hypotheses can be compared on the basis of relative performance. This (modified) approach was applied by Friedman to his permanent income hypothesis (which he contrasted with the multiplier model of consumption) and used in the famous horse-race test he ran with Meiselman, to rule out Keynesian in favor of monetarist explanations of changes in income.

Again, in this approach, the selection of the subclass of admissible models (for example, income is 'explained' either by "autonomous" spending or by "money") and the specification of the final discriminating test versions, go hand in hand (one stage, not two). It is also independent of any need to know what the "class of hypotheses as a whole" looks like. That knowledge would be useful only if one were seeking a confirmation of completely general truth through one's testing procedures. Friedman's insistence that the choice of model reflect the problem at hand, and his insistence on a single process of shaping hypotheses so that a relative evaluation can be arrived at, both imply that he had no interest in making statements about completely generalizable truth.

We have labored this point somewhat, because it does mark a striking departure in the history of economic methodology. Henceforth the criterion "Does it work well enough; that is, for the purpose at hand?" would replace the former set of defences that had run in terms of (a) appeals to direct knowledge of true laws, (b) an asserted identity of "reality" with some deeper essence, and (c) assertions about the very stuff of experience.[5]

---

[5] McCulloch seems to stand apart in this listing. The fact is, however, that it was also part of Friedman's new methodology to insist that differences between the physical and social sciences were only a matter of degree (1953, pp. 4-5, 10-11, 40). McCulloch's defence had been that economic laws differ in kind from physical laws (hence alleged exceptions to economic laws need not require one to abandon those laws altogether, just except certain cases). Rather than mark out economics as exceptional, Friedman tended to argue that incompleteness of theory and the effect of the observer on outcomes made physical science rather like social science. All of that is consistent with Friedman's admission of the importance of choice on the part of the economic researcher and on his "Does it work well enough?" test criterion. In these things he is as different from McCulloch as he is from Mill, Marx and Robbins.

6. Concluding observations

There are three ways of dealing with counterexamples. Lakatos (1976) studied these modes intensively for a case in what he called quasi-empirical mathematics.

The first of them is called "monster barring" by Lakatos and this method consists of saying "my theory is abstract, ideal" (in Mill's sense). In so saying, one does away with the counterexample by a meta-theoretical sweep of the hand — as Mill did.

The second method is called "monster adjustment". Whereas you — erroneously — "see" a counterexample, I teach you to recognize that it is actually an example.[6] This is McCulloch's "sagacity of the observer".

The third ploy involves "lemma incorporation". In the case of theories other than the conjectures of pure mathematics, lemma incorporation could as well be called "theoretical incorporation". For us, it is Marx finding suitable modifications of the law of value by adding in additional factors.

Now monster adjustment and the theoretical incorporation of monsters involve actions of theory development. Monster barring, on the other hand, is a stipulation as to what will and what will not count as part of the conversation. Most of our 'sample' of methodologists were makers of theory as well as observers of their fellow-economists, so it is surprising that monster adjustment played as large a role as it clearly did in their defences of economics. Mill's essay, recall, was an attempt to define the nature of economics and the method proper to its investigation; that is, to set the terms for acceptable discourse. As he saw things, empirical counterexample was a category with no place in the discourse he identified as "proper". Similarly, Robbins judged that the postulates of economic theory were so much part of everyday experience as to be indisputable. In so saying, he placed any questioner of (his particular definitions of) rationality and scarcity in a category apart. By implication, they were detached, out of touch with everyday truths.

However, we must be careful. Some limits to what counts as an acceptable discourse seem inevitable. The question should be therefore, when is monster barring used to remove economics from criticism, and when is it used to refine criticism so that conversation can proceed? The Mill-Robbins exclusions had the effect of removing economics from the realm of common sense. Despite Mill's claim that the grounds of the laws of the subject are accessible by introspection, and Robbins' insistence

---

[6] Lakatos (1976), p. 31.

that they are the stuff of everyday experience, the deeper claim being made is that the conclusions of the subject are true only in a conceptual realm, in an idealized sense.

That appears to mark out Friedman as being different. He too refuses to discuss economics using the language of the assumptions "realists"; but not in order to claim that deep truths are accessible only within his own preferred discourse. Instead, he dispenses altogether with deep truth and lays down a simple — or simple-sounding — empirical test for the validity of economic hypotheses. Idealization, for Friedman, is procedural only: simplifying in order to uncover general relationships.

Friedman's approach to defending economics, we have argued, marks an empirical turn. At the same time, we have alluded to traces in the work of some more modern economists, of precisely the essentialism that Friedman rejected. To the earlier tendency to deal with dissident thinkers by labelling them confused, lacking a "proper" method, dwelling on the level of appearances only, or being out of touch with everyday truths, has been added a new variant: they are not "serious".

Dr. Bert Hamminga
Jan Evertsenstraat 18
5021 RE Tilburg
The Netherlands

Prof. dr. N.B. de Marchi
Department of Economics
Duke University
Durham NC 27708–0097
U.S.A.

REFERENCES

Carnap, R. (1947). *Meaning and Necessity*. Chicago: University of Chicago Press.

Epstein, R.J. (1987). *A History of Econometrics*. Amsterdam: North-Holland.

Frege, G. (1952)[1892]. Uber Sinn und Bedeutung. *Zeitschrift für philosophische Kritik*, NF, **100**, 25-50.

Friedman, M. (1953). The Methodology of Positive Economics. In: Friedman, M. (Ed.), *Essays in Positive Economics*. Chicago: University of Chicago Press.

Hammond, J.D. (1992). An Interview with Milton Friedman on Methodology. In: *Research in the History of Economic Thought and Methodology*, **10**, 91-118.

Hirsch, A. and N. De Marchi (1990). *Milton Friedman: Economics in Theory and Practice*. Michigan: University of Michigan Press.

Hoover, K. (1990). "Calibration versus Estimation: Standards of Empirical Assessment in the New Classical Macroeconomics". University of California, Davis. (mimeo).

Johnson, S. (1828)[1773]. *Dictionary of the English Language*. Heidelberg: Engelman.

Kim, J., N. De Marchi and M. Morgan (1993). Characteristics Testing, and Belief in the Natural Rate Hypothesis. (forthcoming) *Annals of the Journal of Econometrics*.

Kneale, W. and M. Kneale (1962). *The Development of Logic*. Oxford: Oxford University Press.

Lail, M. (1993). *The Origins and Acceptance of Econometrics.* Ph.D. Dissertation, Duke University.

Lakatos, I. (1976). *Proofs and Refutations.* Cambridge: Cambridge University Press.

Lucas, R.R., Jr. (1987). *Models of Business Cycle.* Yrjo Jahnsson Lectures. Oxford: Blackwell.

McCulloch, J.R. (1849)[1825]. *The Principles of Political Economy.* Edinburgh: Adam and Charles Black.

Mill, J.S. (1967)[1844]. *Essays on Some Unsettled Question of Political Economy.* In: Robson, J.M. (Ed.), *The Collected Works of John Stuart Mill.* Toronto: University of Toronto Press, Vol 4.

Mill, J.S. (1967) [1836]. *On the Definition of Political Economy.* In Robson, J.M. (Ed.), *The Collected Works of John Stuart Mill.* Toronto: University of Toronto Press, Vol 4.

Morgan, M.S. (1990). *The History of Econometric Ideas.* Cambridge: Cambridge University Press.

Nowak, L. (1971). The Problem of Explanation in Karl Marx's *Capital. Quality & Quality*, **5**, 2, 311-30.

Nowak, L. (1975). Idealization: A Reconstruction of Marx' Ideas. *Poznań Studies in the Philosophy of the Sciences and the Humanities* **1**, 25-42.

Rescher, N. (1964). *Introduction to Logic.* New York: St. Martins Press.

Ricardo, D. (1951)[1817]. *Principles of Political Economy and Taxation. Works and Correspondence of David Ricardo*, P. Sraffa (Ed.), Cambridge: Cambridge University Press, vol. 1.

Robbins, L. (1932). *An Essay on the Nature and Significance of Economic Science.* London: Macmillan, second ed. 1935.

Smith, A. (1976)[1776]. *An Inquiry into the Nature and Causes of the Wealth of Nations.* Glasgow edition, R.H. Campbell and A.S. Skinner (Eds.), Oxford: Oxford University Press.

Part I

General Observations on Idealization in Economics

Poznań Studies in the Philosophy of the Sciences and the Humanities
1994, Vol. 38, pp. 43-53

Kevin D. Hoover

SIX QUERIES ABOUT IDEALIZATION IN AN EMPIRICAL CONTEXT[1]

ABSTRACT. Inventarization of the main questions for research into the idealizational character of economic theories, focusing on the new classical macroeconomic research programme. It suggests a method to discriminate between rival idealized models.

Idealization as a fundamental element of scientific method is treated by Leszek Nowak (1980) as an almost entirely formal process of setting complicating conditions to their limiting values in order to isolate the essential, idealized relationship that they mask. In Theo Kuipers' (1985) discussion of the van der Waals' law, the law is seen as a step in the process of concretizing the ideal gas law. But the van der Waal's law in Kuiper's account derived from theoretical considerations. And its derivation is not necessarily motivated by empirical considerations such as the lack of fit of Boyle's law to experimental data gathered at low temperatures or high pressures. The relationship between idealized laws or theories and real-world data is one that appears not to have been fully explored. In this essay, I wish to use the new classical macroeconomics as a vehicle for exploring this relationship.[2] The new classical macroeconomics is the most unrelentingly formalized school of macroeconomic thought. Its models seem to provide perfect exemplars of idealization. Yet, from its earliest days, these models have been confronted with empirical data, and debates over how best to relate data to theory are prominent in its history.[3] It would seem, then, that the new classical economics would be well suited to the role of test-bed for conjectures on the relationship of idealization and empirical data. Despite this, shall we say, "ideal" test case, the questions raised will outweigh the tentative answers suggested in this essay.

---

[1] This paper extends my informal presentation on the problems of idealization in the new classical macroeconomics made to the conference on *Problems of Idealization in Economics*, Tilburg University, The Netherlands, 1-3 July 1991.

[2] Hoover (1988) provides a relatively complete account of new classical doctrine.

[3] Hoover (1988, ch. 8; 1991 forthcoming) discuss these debates in some detail.

The single most important document in the new classical macroeconomics is Robert Lucas's article "Econometric Policy Evaluation: A Critique" (1976). The central message of this article is that econometrically estimated macroeconomic relations (e.g., consumption functions, demand-for-money functions or Phillips curves) cannot, in general, be expected to remain invariant to changes in policy regimes. For example, since people will incorporate the central bank's money-supply rule into the process by which they form their expectations, a change in the money-supply rule would result in a change in the slope of the estimated Phillips curve.

There are at least two different interpretations of the Lucas critique. On the narrow interpretation, the problem arises – as it does in the Phillips curve example – from the existence of rational expectations, which generates an interdependence between the coefficients of different estimated equations.[4] On a wider interpretation, the omission of any relevant factor (i.e., releasing any *ceteris paribus* condition) generates a lack of invariance.[5] On either interpretation, the recommended solution is to get behind (or below) the macroeconomic relation to the so-called "deep parameters", to the tastes and technology that guide and constrain individual economic decision-makers.

Recall that the original context of the Lucas critique is the problem of evaluating policy. Policy evaluation requires quantitative advice, which in turn raises the central issue of the relationship between empirical data and the highly idealized models that are as close as the new classical macroeconomics comes to capturing deep parameters.

There have been two principal strategies for dealing with the Lucas critique within the context of the new classical macroeconomics. Each raises its own questions about the role of idealization. The first strategy is clearly exemplified in the work of Sargent (1981) and Hansen and Sargent (1980). This strategy embraces the traditional econometrics of simultaneous systems. The investigator begins with a theoretical model and derives estimatable equations from it. The new twist is to account for the effects of the rational expectations hypothesis on the interrelationships between the individual equations. Once this is done, the investigator proceeds with the usual (but now technically more complicated) methods of structural estimation.

The models that are estimated under the program of structural estimation are idealized. Typically, they are representative-agent models in which a single agent, characterized by a utility function, consumes one

---

[4] Hendry (1988) is an example of such an interpretation.

[5] Hoover (1988, ch. 8; 1992) argue for such an interpretation.

type of good during an infinite life span. The agent faces perfectly competitive product and labor markets and forms expectations rationally. The models thus idealize with respect to the heterogeneity of goods and agents, mortality, market structure, informational imperfections and so forth. Such idealization appears to be similar to Nowak's schema illustrated by Marxist economic models. Nevertheless, careful examination of these models raises the following questions.

Query One: What sort of simplifications count as idealizations?

Idealizing steps for Nowak are ones that set parameters to extreme values: zero or infinity. So, for example, in gravitational models objects are massive but dimensionless. In contrast, new classical models in particular and economic models in general often involve simplified or stylized features that result from stipulating definite values or forms, and not from removing features altogether by setting characteristics to extreme values. For example, such models often stipultate forms for utility functions: e.g., Cobb-Douglas, constant-relative-risk-aversion, or constant-elasticity-of-substitution forms. Such forms are chosen not to isolate the model from certain complicating features of reality, but to give those features a definite and tractable form. Which functional form is chosen depends in part on what issues a model is meant to address — e.g., the constant-relative-risk-aversion utility function is preferred to the Cobb-Douglas in modeling financial markets because it permits a range of values for the coefficient of relative-risk aversion rather than determining it uniquely. A second question, then, is closely related to the first.

Query Two: Is there a difference between setting aside a disturbing factor (or friction) and setting an essential factor to a stipulated value?

To illustrate the issue with a case that is not from the new classical macroeconomics, consider Baumol's (1952) model of the demand for money. Here the optimal amount of money for an individual is computed from the minimal cost of managing a financial portfolio in which there are two types of assets (money and interest-bearing bonds), costs of management related to the frequency of conversion from bonds to money, and income/expenditure flows in which identical increments to income are received at regular intervals and expenditures are made at a uniform rate. The model appears to be idealized. Yet, is the particular pattern of income and expenditure an idealization or a *stipulated concretization*? Clearly, one could always cast the issue in such a way that the pattern assumed in the model was the limit point of some sort of index of income and expenditure patterns. But the ease with which *any* pattern of income and expenditure could be placed at an extreme of index suggests that there remains a fundamental difference between this type of simplification and that, for example, incolved in assuming dimensionless points.[6]

Whether we call it an idealization or a stipulated concretization, this type of simplification abounds in new classical macromodels. The program of structural estimation typically takes the simplified models and estimates them directly using real-world data without any attempt to concretize and account for the deforming idealizations.[7] The most common test of the aptness of the model is to check whether the overidentifying restrictions (i.e., the relationships between the estimated coefficients beyond the minimum number needed to isolate them) hold. These are routinely rejected on standard statistical tests. Of course, such rejection is precisely what Nowak would expect: it is a hallmark of an idealized model that it does not accurately represent real-world data in the absence of concretizing steps.

Some new classical economists are not surprised by the failures of the program of structural estimation. These are the so-called "calibrators" (Kydland and Prescott, 1982, 1991). Like the structural estimators, calibrators use representative-agent models. They do not, however, take direct econometric tests of those models seriously, precisely because they believe that the contingencies of necessary, yet unaccounted for, concretizations would generate deformed parameter estimates that could not be expected to reveal deep structure. For the calibrator, to solve the Lucas critique, an idealized model must be *essentially* correct. Conclusions from simulating idealized models must be restricted to a range defined by the idealizing assumptions. Again, this would appear to closely parallel Nowak's view that not just any arbitrary simplification counts an idealization. Rather, an idealization is a simplification that isolates an *essential* core.

---

[6] Bert Hamminga has suggested to me that one needs to distinguish as Nowak does not between *technical* idealizations made for reasons of tractability (mathematical or statistical) and *essentialist* idealizations made to isolate the fundamental from the secondary. Clearly both sorts of simplifications occur. The issue is whether there is enough of a family resemblance between them to class them both as idealizations.

[7] Estimators of consumer demand systems take a similar approach; see Keuzenkamp (intra).

Recall that the starting point of all macroeconomics is policy analysis, and policy analysis requires quantification. Calibrators eschew macroeconomic parameter estimates, because the models are insufficiently concretized. In their place, they attempt to substitute estimates based on microeconomic studies, accounting considerations, *a priori* economic theory and informal searches of the parameter space for the "best" matching parameters on limited key dimensions. These procedures, however, raise the following general issue.

Query Three: Under what circumstances can coefficients of an empirical model be legitimately used to parameterize an idealized model?

To say that it is over legitimate poses difficulties. It seems to suppose a notion of robustness against alternative specifications that is problematic.[8] Why should the estimated coefficient representing, say, the marginal propensity to consume, be relatively invariant to misspecifications of functional form? It also suggests something like Nancy Cartwright's (1989, ch. 4) notion of causal capacities — i.e., of dispositions that are invariant in themselves, but that manifest themselves differently in different particular contexts. Cartwright's discussion in terms of linearity and orthogonality of regressors suggests a linkage with Leamer's views on robustness; yet, neither linearity nor orthogonality appear required by her more general views on causal capacities. Finally, it suggests an *essentialist* view of idealized models (i.e., idealization isolates real essences). This view is, I think, quite compatible with Nowak's account. Cartwright (1983), who regards scientific laws instrumentally, should find it harder to swallow.

If one takes the view that the point of the idealized model is to isolate the essential from the secondary deforming factors, then a purely theoretical description of the concretizing process would appear to assume rather too much. Nowak's account of Marx's economics from the idealized pure labor theory of value to the actual process of the formation of prices in the real world assumes that the ramifications of each idealizing step — or of the correlative sequence of concretizing steps — can be worked out from some principles. Similarly, Kuipers (1985) sees the addition to the ideal gas laws of the van der Waals law, deduced from theoretical principles, as a paradigm for the concretization

[8] Leamer (1978, 1983) defend such a notion of robustness. Cartwright (1991) questions its soundness.

process. And again, Cools, Hamminga and Kuipers (intra) take the simplest form of the Modigliani-Miller theorem as the idealized case and regard the theoretically understood complications of introducing taxes and bankruptcy as concretizing steps. In practice, however, we idealize — at least in the context of quantifying models — precisely because we lack a principled way of concretizing the idealized model. We generally do not know all the factors that are relevant or in just what way they are relevant. This suggests the following assertion.

> ***Assertion*: the bridge between quantified idealized models and the real world is atheoretical.**

The point of the assertion is this: if idealized laws are linked to real phenomena only through concretizing steps; and if we cannot provide all of the concretizing steps theoretically; then part of the linkage must be composed of atheoretical quantified information, something like Cartwright's (1983, Essay 6) "phenomenal laws". These phenomenal laws provide the fudge factors to match ill-fitting idealizations to data. Although, I regard this view as an assertion, I think that it can be defended through another question.

Query Four: If the assertion that the bridge between the quantified idealization and the world must be atheoretical is false, then why does the idealization have any special status?

It is sometimes argued that a Walrasian barter model is an idealization of the operation of the economy. Adding money to such a model could be regarded as a concretization. But if a complex economy could never function without money, then one might argue that the barter model distorts the *essence* of the economy. It is clear that the Modigliani-Miller theorem without taxes and bankruptcy is simpler than the theorem that accounts for those complications. Given that those complications are theoretically understood, is the simpler theorem really more of the essence?

When theoretical understanding of the implications of various complications is relatively complete, idealization would appear to be a fairly sterile formal relationship between simpler and more complicated models in nested sets. In an empirical context, however, in which the bridge to the real world is atheoretical, the idealization is in effect a substantive claim about how to take the world apart at the joints. Of course, to assert such a claim is one thing, for it to be true is quite another.

It is an adventitious fact that within the new classical macroeconomics the proponents of the program of structural estimation have, at least sometimes, favored monetary-equilibrium-business-cycle models, while proponents of the calibration program have favored real-equilibrium-business-cycle models. Both sorts of models are idealizations, yet they contradict each other at fundamental points. If the linkage between idealizations and the real world is atheoretical, and if we are committed to an essentialist rather than an instrumentalist view, we need some means of discriminating between such models.

Query Five: Can we test idealized models?

Nowak (1980, ch. 5; in press) attempts to subvert the Popperian, falsificationist approach to scientific method in part by using disconfirming instances as a source for further idealizing assumptions and further concretizations. This has the probably accidental effect of raising the initial idealized model to the status of a Lakatosian hard core (Lakatos 1970). The new classical macroeconomics provides a clear example. When Kydland and Prescott's (1982) original real-business-cycle model was quantified to best match the variance of GNP, it seemed to miss the covariance of productivity and hours worked by a large margin. Gary Hansen (1985) dealt with this disconfirmation by recognizing that the original Kydland and Prescott model idealized when it assumed continuity of the supply of labor. Hansen then showed that, if one takes a concretizing step of introducing indivisible labor (workers work fixed eight-hour days), then the model better matches the covariance. Hansen's fix, leaves the idealized core of Kydland and Prescott's model untouched. Were such a strategy also followed by proponents of the competing monetary-business-cycle models, the idealized models at the center of each program would be incommensurable, not because of incommensurability in principle, but because the strategy of idealizing disconfirming instances would mean that we would never seek a resolution to the question of which core idealization was correct.

Query Six: Is there a way to approach such a resolution?

I believe that the answer is yes. I conclude with a concrete suggestion based on linking idealization and the econometric strategy known as encompassing (Hendry and Richard 1987; Hendry 1988b).

The encompassing notion can be understood as a way of selecting between rival econometric specifications. If two specifications purport to account fully for the same phenomena, then one can apply statistical tests to see whether either is dispensable in a joint specification which nests them both. Hendry and Richard propose a framework in which the econometrician begins with a very general, unrestricted dynamic specification and searches using a mixture of theoretical insight and statistical criteria for a parsimonious representation of the phenomena as a funcion of limited set of variables. The successful parsimonious representation must possess residual errors with properties that suggest no easily remediable misspecification. For example, the errors should be mean zero, serially uncorrelated, without heteroscedasticity, and normal. Furthermore, the parsimonious specification should be a statistically valid restriction of the more general specification, i.e., it must be nested in the more general form and carry all the information carried in the general form.

Encompassing might appear contrary to the spirit of idealization/concretization. A model gains purchase on real phenomena as it becomes more concretized, more complex. An econometric specification begins general – i.e., complex – and is reduced to a simpler form. The contrariness is illusory. Econometric specifications (I have been careful not to follow the vernacular and write "model") belong to the sphere of phenomenal laws – the atheoretical relationships that I earlier asserted form the bridges from idealized models to the real world. Hoover (1994) distinguishes between *econometrics as observation* and *econometrics as measurement*. While the terminology is my own, the distinction is evident in the history of econometrics. Morgan (1990) contrasts the early econometrics of business-cycle research (an example of observation) with the early econometrics of demand curves (an example of measurement). The general-to-specific specification strategy is an observational strategy – an attempt to characterize the data rather than to measure a theoretically important parameter precisely.

Using the general-to-specific framework, I propose the following strategy for discriminating between rival idealized models.

Consider two rival idealized models. To be concrete, consider Baumol's model of the demand for money referred to above as a rival of an even simpler model in which portfolios are not managed at all. In Baumol's model, the demand for money can be written as

Model I. $$M = (bY/2r)^{0.5},$$

where M is the stock of money, b is the brokerage cost of transferring money out of bonds, Y is the level of income, and r is the market rate of interest. The rival model is simpler.

Model II. $M = Y/2.$

These models provide starkly different predictions. In Model I the elasticity of money with respect to income is 1/2: i.e., a 10 per cent increase in the level of income increases the demand for money by 5 per cent. The elasticity of money with respect to the interest rate is -1/2. In contrast, in Model II, the elasticity of money with respect to income is unity and with respect to interest is zero. Both models are idealized, and neither fits the data well on its own. Nevertheless, we may be able to choose between them in the following way:

(A) Generate a time series for the variable(s) of interest using each rival (calibrated) idealized model. E.g., for Model I, pick a value for b from microeconomic or other evidence, and use available data on Y and r to generate predicted values for M; proceed similarly for Model II.

(B) Estimate a general econometric specification for the variable(s) of interest including the generated time series. E.g., estimate a model for money of the following form:

$$M_t = \sum_{t=1}^{n} \alpha_j M_{t-j} + \sum_{t=0}^{n} \beta_j Y_{t-j} + \sum_{t=0}^{n} \delta_j r_{t-j} + \sum_{t=0}^{n} \varphi_j Z_{t-j} +$$

$$+ \mu \mathrm{MI}_t + \tau \mathrm{MII}_t + \epsilon_t,$$

where MI is the time series generated from Model I, MII is the time series generated from Model II, Z stands for all other relevant variables, ϵ is a residual random error, and t is a time index. The lag length n is chosen empirically to insure that the ϵ possess the requisite statistical properties to indicate adequate specification.

(C) Conduct a general-to-specific specification search to form a parsimonious representation of the specification in B with the restriction that both predicted time series always be retained in the final specification.

(D) Use standard statistics to test for the possibility of omitting each of the model-based predicted time series in turn and jointly.

If one model but not the other cannot be omitted from the final specification, then it clearly dominates the other. If neither can be omitted, both apparently carry information essential to the idealized model, which should be helpful in reconstructing a more suitable model. If both can be omitted, then the idealization exercise was not empirically helpful: either a different sort of model, or a different level of theoretical concretization would appear to be needed.

The new classical macroeconomics presents many examples of the quantification of apparently idealized models. Although, I have ended this essay with a concrete suggestion of how one might discriminate between rival idealized models – a task which would appear to be essential if the method of idealization is not to collapse into sterile formalism – it is clear that far more issues have been raised than satisfactorily answered. The scope for future research is obvious.

Kevin D. Hoover
Department of Economics
University of California
Davis, California 95616-8578
U.S.A.

REFERENCES

Baumol, W.J. (1952). The Transactions Demand for Cash: An Inventory Theoretic Approach. *Quartely Journal of Economics*, **66**, 546-556.

Cartwright, N. (1983). *How the Laws of Physics Lie.* Oxford: Clarendon Press.

Cartwright, N. (1989). *Nature's Capacities and their Measurement.* Oxford: Clarendon Press.

Cartwright, N. (1991). Replicability, Reproducibility, and Robustness: Comments on Harry Collins. *History of Political Economy*, **23**, 143-156.

Cools, K., B. Hamminga and Th.A.F. Kuipers (infra). Truth Approximation by Concretization in Capital Structure Theory.

Hansen, G.D. (1985). Indivisible Labor and the Business Cycle. *Journal of Monetary Economics*, **16**, 309-328.

Hansen, L.P. and T.J. Sargent (1980). Estimating and Formulating Dynamic Linear Rational Expectations Models. *Journal of Economic Dynamics and Control*, **2**, 7-46.

Hendry, D.F. (1988a). The Encompassing Implications of Feedback versus Feedforward Mechanisms in Econometrics. *Oxford Economic Papers*, N.S. **40**, 132-149.

Hendry, D.F. (1988b). Encompassing. *National Institute Economic Review*, August, 88-92.

Hendry, D.F. and J. Richard (1987). Recent Developments in the Theory of Encompassing. In: B. Cornet and H. Tulkens (Eds.) *Contributions to Operations Research and Econometrics. The XXth anniversary of CORE*. Cambridge, MA: MIT Press, pp. 393-440.

Hoover, K.D. (1988). *The New Classical Macroeconomics: A Sceptical Inquiry*. Oxford: Blackwell.

Hoover, K.D. (1994). Econometrics as Observation: The Lucas Critique and the Nature of Econometric Inference. *Journal of Economic Methodology*, **1**, forthcoming.

Hoover, K.D. (1991). Calibration versus Estimation: Standards of Empirical Assessment in the New Classical Macroeconomics. *Research Program in Applied Macroeconomics and Macro Policy, Working Paper Number 72*, Institute of Governmental Affairs, University of California, Davis, January.

Hoover, K.D. (forthcoming). Quantitative Evaluation of Idealized Models in the New Classical Macroeconomics. In: N. Cartwright and M. Jones (Eds.). *Correcting the Model (Poznań Studies in the Philosophy of the Sciences and the Humanities*, forthcoming). Amsterdam: Rodopi.

Keuzenkamp, H. (infra). What it Idealization is Problematic? The Case of the Homogeneity Condition in Consumer Demand.

Kuipers, T.A.F. (1985). The Paradigm of Concretization: The Law of van der Waals. In: J. Brzeziński (Ed.) *Consciousness: Methodological and Psychological Approaches (Poznań Studies in the Philosophy of Sciences and the Humanities*, **10**). Amsterdam: Rodopi, pp. 79-99.

Kydland, F.E. and E.C. Prescott (1982). Time to Build and Aggregate Fluctuations. *Econometrica*, **50**, 1345-1369.

Kydland, F.E. and E.C. Prescott (1991). The Econometrics of the General Equilibrium Approach to Business Cycles. *Scandinavian Journal of Economics*, **93**, 161-178.

Lakatos, I. (1970). Falsification and the Methodology of Scientific Research Programmes. In: I. Lakatos and A. Musgrave (Eds.). *Criticism and the Growth of Knowledge*. Cambridge: Cambridge University Press, pp. 91-196.

Leamer, E.E. (1978). *Specification Searches: Ad-hoc Inference with Nonexperimental Data*. New York: Wiley.

Leamer, E.E. (1983). Lets Take the Con out of Econometrics. *American Economic Review*, **73**, 31-43.

Lucas, R.E., Jr. (1976). Econometric Policy Evaluation: A Critique. In: K. Brunner and A.H. Meltzer (Eds.). *The Phillips Curve and Labor Markets*. Carnegie-Rochester Conference Series on Public Policy, vol. 1. Amsterdam: North-Holland, pp. 19-46.

Morgan, M. (1990). *The History of Econometric Ideas*. Cambridge: Cambridge University Press.

Nowak, L. (1980). *The Structure of Idealization: Towards a Systematic Interpretation of the Marxian Idea of Science*. Dordrecht: Reidel.

Nowak, L. (1991). The Method of Relevant Variables and Idealization. In: E. Eells and T. Maruszewski (Eds.). *Rationality and Probability (Poznań Studies in the Philosophy of the Sciences and the Humanities*, **21**). Amsterdam: Rodopi.

Sargent, T.J. (1981). Interpreting Economic Time Series. *Journal of Political Economy*, **89**, 213-248.

Poznań Studies in the Philosophy
of the Sciences and the Humanities
1994, Vol. 38, pp. 55-69

Bernard Walliser

THREE GENERALIZATION PROCESSES FOR ECONOMIC MODELS

ABSTRACT. When considering how economic models evolve, the main operation appearing at work is generalization, which can itself be decomposed into three basic processes, conceptually distinct although not formally independent, but more and more ambitious. The enlarging process simply consists in extending the application domain of a model without modifying its formal structure, in order to transfer its properties from one field to another. The weakening process consists in constructing a model with a less stringent specification of one or more of its assumptions, in order to account for a larger set of situations. The rooting process consists in finding out some grounding propositions which infer one or more of the model's assumptions, in order to have a deeper explanation of its properties. Each process can be logically defined and illustrated by basic examples, may be considered at different levels and gives rise to model taxonomies, and fulfills as well a formal and an empirical role.

When considering how economic models evolve in the long run, the main operation appearing at work is generalization, that is passing from local and specific models to universal and generic ones. Coupled with its inverse, particularization, it is embodied in the correspondence principle, asserting that a new theory contains the old one as a special case, valid under restrictive conditions. Generalization is very powerful in physics where always more fundamental principles are introduced, which aim at explaining an ever larger set of empirical laws, with additional assumptions. It is even more important in economics where, due to a looser relationship between theory and facts, always more general models are proposed, with hope that one specification at least will fit the data.

But the generalization operation can itself be decomposed into three basic processes, conceptually distinct although not formally independent, which are more and more ambitious and will be illustrated by many examples. The enlarging process simply consists in extending the application domain of a model without modifying its formal structure, in order to transfer its properties from one field to another. The weakening process consists in constructing a model with a less stringent specification of one or more of its assumptions, in order to account for a larger set of situations. The rooting process consists in finding out some grounding propositions which infer one or more of the model's assumptions, in order to have a deeper explanation of its properties.

As for notation, a system is composed of basic elements symbolized by "entity variables" x, and of characteristics of these elements summarized by "attribute variables" y. A property of the system may be stated under the form of an hypothesis $H(x, y, a)$ depending on all variables and including unspecified parameters a. A model is then defined by its *formal structure* S, composed of the set of all assumptions H_i, and allows to infer a set of logical conclusions C_j: $S = \{H_1, ..., H_i, ...\}$. A model is moreover provided with a *field of application* F, which gives at least the empirical counterparts of the entity variables: $x \in F$.

1. ENLARGING

a. Principles

Enlarging is a process which keeps the formal structure of a model unchanged: $S^+ = S^-$, but extends its field of application: $F^+ \supset F^-$; the inverse process is called *narrowing*. For a proposition H, narrowing implies formally to give, for the entity variables, a restricted interpretation: $\forall x, H(x, y, a) \wedge (x = \bar{x}) \Rightarrow H(\bar{x}, y, a)$. The combined process of enlarging and narrowing leads finally to an *analogical transfer* of a given formalism from one domain of application to another: $H(\bar{x}, y, a) \approx> H(\bar{\bar{x}}, y, a)$.

b. Basic examples

In physics, the law of ideal gas (Mariotte's law in France, Boyle's law in England) can be written: $pv = rT$, where p is the pressure, v the volume, T the absolute temperature and r some parameter. Enlarging first extends the field of application from gases to other fluids such as liquids or plasmas, while keeping the same attribute variables. Enlarging further widens this field to "objects" such as an economy, the "quantitative theory of money" adopting the same formal structure: $pQ = vM$, where p is the price level, Q the global production, M the quantity of money and v a parameter interpreted as the circulation speed of money.

In economics, for individual choice under uncertainty, the basic model is the "expected utility model": $V_i^k = \sum_j p_j u_{ij}^k$, where i is a material action, j a state of nature, k an agent, p_j the probability assigned to state j, u_{ij}^k the von Neumann-Morgenstern utility for k when action i is implemented and state j happens, and V_i^k the overall utility of action i for k. This model can first be enlarged to non-human agents such a pigeons or rats facing uncertain situations (Battalio-Kagel-Mc Donald 1985). It is also extended to symbolic actions such as believing or not in God, as is implicitly done in Pascal's wager argument (Elster 1979). Finally, it is applied to different states, especially in game theory, where uncertainty of a player concerns the other's preferences, the other's past actions as well as the other's future actions.

The same model may even formally be transposed to a quite different field, such as intertemporal choice, multicriteria choice or social choice. In social choice, the entity variables are subject to the following interpretation: i is always an action, j is now an agent and k is the collectivity. The preceding formula corresponds then to the Bentham rule with an adapted interpretation of the attribute variables: p_j is the weight affected to each agent, u_{ij} the utility of agent j for action i, V_i^k the utility of the collectivity for action i. As a matter of fact, other formal correspondences between both fields can be shown, for instance the formula: $V_i^k = \min_j u_{ij}^k$, which reads as the maximin rule in choice under uncertainty and the Rawls' rule in social choice.

c. Depth

The transfer from one field to another may only concern a new interpretation of one attribute variable, the entity variables being unchanged. For instance, the intertemporal utility of an agent for a decision which has effects on a sequence of periods is: $U = \sum_t \delta^t u_t$, where u_t is his utility at date t, δ his discount rate and U his aggregated utility. But, in game theory, when the game horizon is uncertain, δ may as well be interpreted as the probability that the game ends at period t (when not ended at $t-1$), the discount rate being then 1.

The transfer may more ambitiously concern an entity variable, but always taken from the economic field. For instance, a firm is assumed to maximize his profit under a production function constraint, which links the quantities of inputs and outputs. A consumer is also assumed, by a "dual" behavior, to minimize his expenditure under a constraint of minimal utility procured by his consumption basket. Taking into account the fact that the two objective functions are both linear, the optimization programs lead to supply-demand functions obeying the same Slutsky conditions.

The transfer may finally be carried out, concerning both types of variables, from other sciences like physics to economics. An analogy between an equilibrium of material bodies submitted to mutual forces and an equilibrium of economic agents seeking for mutual transactions was made very early; but if the first is governed by an hamiltonian, there is no global potential maximized in the second. However, in physics, the Ising model describes short-range interactions between neighbouring atoms which give rise to an overall similarity about their magnetic properties. Applied to economics, imitation among neighbouring agents as concerns their expectations on some variables also gives rise to a collective coordination on conventional values (Orléan 1990).

d. Taxonomy

It is then possible, for a given model, to construct a taxonomy according to its decreasing fields of application. For instance, in non-cooperative game theory, the Nash equilibrium concept between two optimizing players may be applied to two animals struggling for reproduction, to two countries engaged in arms race or to two economic agents. These economic agents may be two countries involved in international trade, the State and the economic system as macroeconomic policy is concerned, or two producers in a duopoly context. In the last case where the Nash equilibrium becomes the Cournot equilibrium, the firms may finally be taken in various industries.

In a pure economic setting, the principal-agent model describes two asymmetric decision-makers, the principal who has means of action on the agent in order to achieve his objectives, and the agent who has more information than the principal about the context in which he acts. It was applied as much to the relationship between the government and a public firm involved in the production of a public good (conditional upon a tax), as to the relationship between an employer and an employee adjusting his level of effort (conditional upon his wage). Obviously, it can be applied more precisely to specific public goods or workers.

e. Formal role

The formal role of enlarging is to start from analogous assumptions to achieve analogous conclusions. For instance, in game theory, a learning process for each player is concerned with his mixed strategies, the weight he attributes to each pure strategy being modified according to the utility he got in the preceding plays. Seemingly, an evolution process is defined in a population of players allowed with fixed pure strategies, the frequence of players being adjusted according to reproduction rules, i.e. players reproduce in proportion to the utilities they get from their interactions. The two processes are isomorphic (Maynard Smith 1982), the individual probability of using a pure strategy being replaced by the proportion of people using a pure strategy, and they seemingly converge to a nearby Nash equilibrium (called evolutionary stable state in the second framework).

Enlarging is also used inversely, in order to obtain similar conclusions from similar assumptions. For instance, the walrasian equilibrium shows interesting properties of existence, uniqueness and stability; it is the reason why it was extended to future and contingent goods, by reinterpreting the notion of good, considered now as a product delivered at some date and conditional to some state of nature (Debreu 1959). In the same vein, the walrasian equilibrium has the Pareto-optimality property; it explains why it was enlarged to the decentralization of a paretian optimum by calculating shadow prices which, should they be used by the agents, would generate a pseudo-competitive equilibrium.

In fact, many well-known formal correspondences between specific assumptions and specific conclusions are constantly used in both ways. For instance, cycles may be obtained through four main formal mechanisms. Exogenous cycles result either from external variables themselves cyclical (resonance) or from stochastic shocks which infer periodic movements. Endogenous cycles result either from differential or difference equations when some variables act with two-period delays at least, or from non linear equations which induce in particular cyclical attractors.

f. Empirical role

Enlarging has the property of defining the largest possible domain of application of a given model, and renders it more refutable, since the set of testable independent consequences increases. However, this is correct only for a well-defined class of entities, because there is no reason why a given formal model which is valid in one field would be also valid in another far-off field. For instance, the competitive equilibrium model can reasonably be extended to all sorts of material goods, such as oil, cars or toys. But it does not apply automatically to more nonmaterial goods such as labour, money or information, or even more to noneconomic activities such as marriage, crime or worship where it was nevertheless applied (Becker 1976).

In fact, enlarging and narrowing are used together to implement an application test of a model, that is to consider first its potential field of application and then to circumscribe its field of validity. This test differs from a validity test where one looks for refutability of the model in a pregiven field of application, and may even be considered as an "immunizing stratagem" able to escape refutability. For instance, the profit maximization assumption applies normally to all firms, the notion of a firm being considered as well-defined. But practically, it is tempting to restrict the field of validity to firms of a given country, a given sector or a given scale or even to a list of heterogenous firms.

2. WEAKENING

a. Principle

Weakening is a process which turns the structure S^- of a model into a weaker one S^+, in a formal sense: $S^- \Rightarrow S^+$ (and $S^+ \wedge s \Rightarrow S^-$, where s is a specification assumption); the inverse process is called *strengthening*. For an assumption, strengthening consists in specifying its formal structure, especially in giving a precise value to some parameter: $H(x, y, a) \wedge (a = \bar{a}) \Rightarrow H(x, y, \bar{a})$. The combination of weakening and strenghtening leads to define some *variant* of the initial model: $H(x, y, \bar{a}) \approx> H(x, y, \bar{\bar{a}})$.

In fact, weakening is enlarging since a weaker model has a field of application which is potentially more extended (the field F for a model is the union of domains for all values of parameters). Moreover, parameters are generally constants which appear in analytical relations, but may also be attribute variables treated as exogenous (considering a variant of a model consists then in making comparative statics). Finally, weakening is a process similar to what is called "idealization" (Nowak 1980), its inverse strengthening being similar to "concretization".

b. Basic examples

In physics, the law of ideal gas can be weakened under the form of the van der Waals law: $(p + \frac{a}{v^2})(v-b) = rT$, with the same attribute variables, but with two more parameters: a and b. If the parameters are unspecified, this law is really a weakening since one gets back to the primitive law when $a = b = 0$. But the parameters have in general specific values (depending on the gas considered) and the van der Waals law is then to be considered as a variant of the original law.

In economics, the expected utility model has different extensions, specifically the anticipated utility model (Quiggin 1982; Yaari 1987): $V_i^k = \sum_j \left[f^k\left(\sum_{l=1}^{j-1} p_l\right) - f\left(\sum_{l=1}^{j-1} p_l\right)\right] u_{ij}^k$, with the same variables (the index j being ranked in order to have decreasing u_{ij}^k). It introduces a function f^k, which deforms the probability cumulative function and gives back the former model when it is the identity function. But, for a given decision-maker, the function f^k is well defined and the two models are then competing ones. The idea behind this new model is to associate one idea to one concept, the function u^k reflecting the utility under certainty and the function f^k the aversion towards risk, whereas the two notions are collapsed in the unique function u in the primitive model.

c. Depth

Weakening first consists in giving a more general analytical form to a parametric relation while keeping the same attribute variables, the old relation appearing as an *analytical approximation* of the new one. For instance, in production theory, a linear cost function writes: $C = bq + c$, where C is the total cost, q the production, b the unitary constant marginal cost and c some fixed cost. It can be replaced by a quadratic cost function: $C = aq^2 + bq + c$, where the parameter a has a sign reflecting decreasing or increasing returns.

Weakening consists more ambitiously in introducing new explaining variables in a relation, which allows for new interpretations, the old relation appearing then as a *structural approximation* of the new one. For instance, in consumer theory, the utility of a consumer i writes $u^i(x^i)$, where x^i is his own basket of consumed goods. In order to account for "external effects", it is possible to introduce the other's consumption in the agent's utility: $u^i(x^i, x^j)$. In order to consider altruism or envy, it is even possible to introduce the other's utility in the agent's utility: $u^i(x^i, u^j)$.

Weakening consists finally in giving a new dimension to a model, in order to permit new classes of phenomena to occur, the old model appearing then as a *dimensional approximation* of the new one. A model gets from static to dynamic by introducing an explicit time dimension, and allows then for delays as well as expectations. A model with one aggregated agent may explicit two agents, and allows to formalize strategic interactions between them. A model with two agents generalizes to n agents, and allows to consider coalitions between subclasses of these.

d. Taxonomy

A taxonomy for game theory can be constructed according to alternative specifications of its assumptions, although there is a frequent opportunity to translate one category into another. Games may be split into static (normal form) and dynamic (extensive form) ones; but each dynamic game can be written under the normal form by extending the concept of strategy, and each static game is a degenerate dynamic one. Games may also be without or with uncertainty, the last category covering games with incomplete information (uncertainty on other's utility) or with imperfect information (uncertainty on other's past actions); but the first class can be reduced to the second by considering a player's "type". Finally, some subclasses of games are also defined according to the players' utility functions and possibility sets, such as symmetrical games and constant-sum games.

A taxonomy for production functions may be proposed as well, with always stronger specifications, beginning with the most general form: $q = f(k, l)$, where q, k and l are quantities of product, labour and capital. In a first step, the function f is assumed (or not) to be homogeneous at order one, reflecting constant scale returns. In a second step, function f may be written parametrically as a CES (constant elasticity of substitution) function: $q = [\alpha k^{\varepsilon} + (1 + \alpha)l^{\varepsilon}]^{1/\varepsilon}$. In a third step, different values of ε lead to a linear function (with perfectly substitute goods): $q = \alpha k + (1 - \alpha)l$ (when $\varepsilon = 1$), a setsquare function (with complementary goods): $q = \min(k, l)$ (when $\varepsilon = -\infty$) or a Cobb-Douglas function (with substitute goods): $q = k^{\alpha} l^{1-\alpha}$ (when $\varepsilon = 0$). In a last step, a Cobb-Douglas function can be further specified by giving a precise value to α.

e. Formal role

The main role of weakening is to infer weaker conclusions from weaker assumptions, in order to make possible new effects. In consumer theory, when the utility function of a consumer is "separable", each good is normal, i.e. its demand is decreasing with its price; but when the utility function is no more separable, some goods may be inferior, i.e. their demand is increasing with their price. In decision theory, when the intertemporal utility function of a decision-maker is time-invariant, his behavior is dynamically consistent: what he intends to do today for tomorrow is always optimal tomorrow; but when the utility function evolves due to past actions (in addiction for instance), the phenomenon of dynamic inconsistency arises.

Weakening is also used to deduce weaker conclusions from weaker assumptions, especially in order to avoid "negative" results. In social choice theory, it is not possible to aggregate individual preferences in a collective preference with respect to reasonable conditions (dominance, independence, non-dictatorship), when the individual preferences are unrestricted (Arrow 1951); but aggregation becomes possible when these preferences are single-peaked. In game theory, it is not possible to make players cooperate in the prisoner's dilemma when the game is finitely repeated; but cooperation gets possible when the game has an infinite horizon or when the game shows incomplete information.

Finally, assumptions and conclusions are adjusted as close as possible to obtain "positive" results, but if it is rather easy to obtain sufficient conditions for a given consequence, it is far harder to obtain necessary and sufficient conditions. The competitive equilibrium notion leads usually to multiple equilibrium states; but the equilibrium gets unique if the goods are gross-substitute, a sufficient condition defined on the total net demand. The consumer's optimization program leads to a demand function obeying the Slutsky conditions; but this necessary condition is also sufficient, for each demand function obeying the Slutsky conditions can be derived from an optimization program with a relevant utility function.

f. Empirical role

When a model gets weakened, it is less refutable because it has more degrees of freedom and allows then for a larger set of phenomena inside a given class of consequences. However, at the same time, it suggests original classes of consequences which can be confronted to the facts. For instance, the Phillips macroeconomic relation writes: $w = f(p, u)$, where w is the wage level, p the price level and u the unemployment in a given economy. It was weakened under the form: $w = f(p, \tilde{p}, u)$, where $\tilde{p}$ is the expected price level, and naturally fits the data more easily, even if it suggests to test the influence of the new variable.

In fact, weakening and strengthening are used together to implement an estimation test of a model, that is to consider first a general structure of the model and to specify then its constituting relations. This test differs again from a validity test, since it postulates that one specification at least will be selected through the data, the impossibility to refute the model being considered as an "immunizing stratagem". For instance, an export function of a country is written: $X = aQ + b\frac{p}{p'} + cQ' + d$, where X, Q and p are exports, production and price level of the country, Q' and p' stand for production and price level of foreign countries. One value of a, b, c, d fits the data at best, but this is true only because the relation is considered as stochastic.

3. ROOTING

a. Principle

Rooting is a process which gives new foundations to a model through a whole set of antecedent hypothesis $T\{K_1, ..., K_i, ...\}$, such that $T \Rightarrow S$; the inverse process is called *sprouting*. For an assumption, sprouting consists in justifying it through deeper assumptions, related to the same entity variables, but introducing possibly new attribute variables and different parameters: $K_1(x, y_1, a_1) \wedge K_2(x, y_2, a_2) \wedge ... \Rightarrow H(x, y, a)$. The combination of rooting and sprouting leads to alternative models grounded on analogous principles: $K_1(x, y_1, a_1) \wedge K_2'(x, y_2', a_2') \wedge ... \Rightarrow H'(x, y', a')$.

In fact, weakening can be considered as a special case of rooting when the explaining hypotheses of a given assumption consist in a weaker assumption and a specification assumption. Moreover, rooting can be coupled with weakening in order to infer weaker models from weaker explaining hypotheses. Finally, the rooting process is very similar to the explanation principle, and uses the formal function of any model backwards, in order to find out assumptions leading to given conclusions.

b. Basic examples

In physics, the law of ideal gas is considered as a macro-law which can be derived from micro-principles of statistical mechanics. More precisely, gas molecules are in a given state characterized by usual attributes (position, speed); they form a statistical population described by the frequence of molecules in each state; moreover, each macro-variable (volume, pressure, temperature) is directly linked to the global state of the gas system. The micro-properties of the gas lead then to a macro-relation between macro-variables through the aggregation process.

In economics, the expected utility model has been grounded on a set of axioms introduced by von Neumann and Morgenstern (1944). The idea is to consider the preference relation of an agent over a set of lotteries, a lottery being defined as a probability distribution on a set of outcomes. Four axioms are defined either on the lotteries themselves (bayesian composition) or on the preference relation on them (weak order, continuity, independence). Under these axioms, there exists a utility function on outcomes such that the decision-maker prefers a lottery to another if and only if its expected utility is higher.

c. Depth

Rooting may consist only in deriving a given relation from former ones, especially when inferring the reduced form of a model from its normal form. For instance, consider the consumption function: $C_t = \mu R_t + \nu R_{t-1}$, where the present consumption C_t of an agent depends on his present and past revenues, R_t and R_{t-1}. It may be inferred from another consumption function: $C_t = \alpha \tilde{R}_{t+1} + \beta$, where the present consumption depends now of the future expected revenue $\tilde{R}_{t+1}$, and from an adaptive expectation model: $\tilde{R}_{t+1} = \gamma R_t + \delta R_{t-1}$, where expected revenue depends on its past values. The relation between observable variables is in fact explained by relations including "hidden" variables, expectation in the preceding example and utility in the next one.

Rooting may more ambitiously derive a relation from a set of principles, especially when a macro-function is deduced from micro-behaviors. For instance, an aggregate consumption function $C = f(p, R)$, where C is the total consumption, p a price level and R the total revenue may be obtained from three elements. First, each consumer i defines his consumption c_i by a utility maximizing program, depending on prices p and revenue r_i; the distribution of the revenues r_i in the population is given; plain additive functions relate the global consumption and revenue to the individual ones.

Rooting may finally give to some model axiomatic foundations, but only a few genuine axiomatics are already proposed in economics, mainly in individual and social choice theory. For instance, in cooperative game theory, if two players are able to obtain a set of couples of cardinal utilities (u_1, u_2), the Nash solution indicates that they should choose the one which maximizes $(u_1 - \bar{u}_1)(u_2 - \bar{u}_2)$, where $\bar{u}_1$ and $\bar{u}_2$ are the minimal utilities they can always obtain. This rule is grounded on four axioms: individual and collective rationality, independence and symmetry.

d. Taxonomy

If it is not possible, as before, to construct a taxonomy by particularizing progressively a given assumption, it is nevertheless possible to use the deduction principle to define successive models, each grounded on the preceding one. For instance, axioms for choice under uncertainty lead, as already seen, to the expected utility model. Now, in a non-cooperative game where all players are allowed with this model and consider as their uncertainty space the others' actions (as well as their crossed beliefs on them at all orders), the Nash equilibrium concept may be justified (Bernheim 1986; Tan-Werlang 1988). It is enough to assume that it is common knowledge that the players are rational, hold common priors and play independently.

In fact, rooting is combined with weakening along two orthogonal dimensions (deducing horizontally, specifying vertically) in order to derive the most empirical propositions from the most theoretical models. For instance, the rational decision model describes a decision-maker optimizing an objective-function under constraints, and induces a behavior function where his actions depend directly on exogenous conditions. Applied to a consumer, the utility function depends only on the consumed goods and the linear budget constraint is parametrized by prices and revenue, giving rise to a demand function. Going one step further, if the utility function is specified as a Cobb-Douglas one, the resulting demand function is a Stone one.

e. Formal role

The formal function of rooting is first to propose several alternative explanations to a given model, grounded sometimes in contradictory sets of assumptions, as can be seen in the relation between real wage and labor productivity. In the neo-classical model, the wage being exogenous, the profit-optimizing firm fixes its production level in order to equalize the labor productivity to the wage. In the efficient wage model, the wage is fixed by the firm in order to induce a high effort from the worker, that is to adjust his productivity. In the signaling model, the productivity is exogenous, but the firm fixes the wage according to the worker's training, which it assumes to increase his productivity (the worker choosing in fact his training conditional upon his productivity).

Rooting permits even more to suggest, for a proposition, several (non-comparable) explanations situated at different depth levels, as can be illustrated by the walrasian allocation of goods for consumers (assumed to be unique). The competitive model applied to the whole economy gives directly such an allocation, through the endogenous fixation of walrasian prices. The fix-price model, when prices are exogenously settled at walrasian values, leads to the same allocation; but the walrasian model is not a special case of the fixed price model since the former treats the prices as endogenous. The oligopoly model, when the number of firms grows to infinity, achieves the same allocation with prices being again endogenous; the walrasian model is then truly a limit case of the oligopoly model.

It is even possible, for two distinct propositions (p_1 and p_2), which are directly justified by two models ($S_1 \rightarrow p_1$, $S_2 \rightarrow p_2$), to exhibit crossed explanations of one proposition by the other model ($S_1 \wedge s_2 \rightarrow p_2$, $S_2 \wedge s_1 \rightarrow p_1$). Among choice models, the optimizing model leads to an optimized action and the satisficing model (Simon 1969) leads to a "satisficed" action. But, a satisficed action may also be justified by an optimization model with a well-adapted objective-function or even a meta-optimization model trading off direct utility and processing costs (Mongin-Walliser 1988). Conversely, an optimized action may be sustained by a satisficing model when the aspiration levels are high enough, or even by a bounded rationality learning process where the aspiration levels are adjusted to past results (Walliser 1989).

f. Empirical role

Rooting a model renders it apparently more refutable since the deeper assumptions on which it is grounded can eventually be directly tested if they contain no theoretical concepts. However, these assumptions are sufficient although not always necessary, and it is only in the last case that they constitute true new consequences of the model. For instance, autoregressive expectations of a representative agent in an economic system can be grounded on an autoregressive structure of the system itself and on the rational expectations hypothesis. But this last hypothesis cannot be tested directly (except in a weak form) and even if it were, it is not at all necessary to justify autoregressive expectations.

In fact, rooting and sprouting are used together in order to revise a model once it is refuted. In a first step, one tries to find out which grounding assumptions have to be called into question, even if the problem may be indeterminate according to the Duhem-Quine thesis; in a second step, the disputed assumptions are replaced by weaker or alternative ones, in order to deduce a new model. For instance, when observing non competitive prices on a market, one or several competitive market conditions must be unsatisfied: perfect information, unconstrained transactions, exogenous prices (a condition stemming itself from a more profound one, i.e. numerous agents). Original equilibrium notions can be defined by alleviating each of the conditions: asymmetric information, fixed prices or imperfect competition (oligopoly).

* * *

The generalization operation and its three components was precedingly studied in its syntactic aspect, but it also has a more profound semantic dimension which should be examined more carefully. It surely can be asserted that any change in a model reduces in last instance to a combination of some sort of generalization and specification. But, enlarging or weakening a model modifies sometimes drastically its interpretation, since old concepts get different meanings, old relations gain modified readings, new notions are introduced and new properties emerge. In the same way, among the infinite possibilities of weakening or rooting a model, only a few are really considered as conceptually relevant by the scientific community, as regards their originality, fertility or potential empirical validity.

The generalization operation was also analyzed in a rather static and abstract framework, and more has to be said about the concrete historical process leading to a successful generalized model. A senior researcher often publishes a seminal article which, based on the rooting process, reveals some unformulated assumption or axiomatizes a well-known model. Younger economists write afterwards consolidation articles which, resting on the weakening process, give several distinct specifications to the hidden assumption or alleviate the new axiom system. Finally, less theory-oriented scientists propose more informal articles which, grounded on the enlarging process, examin whether the new framework applies more or less metaphorically to the primitive field as much as to new ones.

Bernard Walliser
C.E.R.A.S.
Ecole Nationale des Ponts et Chaussees
28 Rue des Saint-Peres
75007 Paris
France

REFERENCES

Arrow, K. (1951). *Social Choice and Individual Values.* (*Cowles Foundation Monograph*, **12**). New York: Wiley.

Battalio, R.C., J.H. Kagel and D.N. Mc Donald (1985). Animal's Choice Over Uncertain Outcomes: Some Initial Experimental Results. *American Economic Review*, **75**(4), 597-613.

Becker, G. (1976). *The Economic Approach to Human Behavior.* Chicago: University of Chicago Press.

Bernheim, B.D. (1986). Axiomatic Characterizations of Rational Choice in Strategic Environments. *Scandinavian Journal of Economics*, **88**(3), 473-488.

Debreu, G. (1959). *Theory of Value*. New York: Wiley.

Elster, J. (1979). *Ulysses and the Sirens*. Cambridge: Cambridge University Press.

Maynard Smith, J. (1982). *Evolution and the Theory of Games*. Cambridge: Cambridge University Press.

Mongin, P. and B. Walliser (1988). Infinite Regressions in the Optimizing Theory of Decision. In: B. Munier (Ed.), *Risk, Decision and Rationality*. Dordrecht: Reidel, pp. 435-457.

von Neumann, J.O. Morgenstern (1944). *Theory of Games and Economic Behavior*. Princeton: Princeton University Press.

Nowak, L. (1980). *The Structure of Idealization. Towards a Systematic Interpretation of the Marxian Idea of Science*. Dordrecht: Reidel.

Orlean, A. (1990). Le rôle des influences interpersonnelles dans la détermination des cours boursiers. *Revue Economique*, **41**(5), 839-868.

Quiggin, J. (1982). A Theory of Anticipated Utility. *Economic Behavior and Organization*, **3**, 323-343.

Simon, H. (1969). Theories of Decision-making in Economics and Behavioral Science. *American Economic Review*, **59**(3), 253-283.

Tan, T. and S. Werlang (1988). The Bayesian Foundations of Solution Concepts of Games. *Journal of Economic Theory*, **45**, 370-391.

Walliser, B. (1989). Instrumental Rationality and Cognitive Rationality. *Theory and Decision*, **27**, 7-36.

Yaari, M. (1987). The Dual Theory of Choice under Risk. *Econometrica*, **55**, 95-116.

Poznań Studies in the Philosophy of the Sciences and the Humanities
1994, Vol. 38, pp. 71-100

Steven Cook and David F. Hendry

THE THEORY OF REDUCTION IN ECONOMETRICS

ABSTRACT. Analysis of a number of types of reduction to be used in 'general to specific' modelling in econometric methodology. Specification of measures for the loss of information resulting from every type of reduction. Based upon this analysis, the formulation of criteria for model design in econometrics.

1. Introduction

The theory of reduction plays several related roles in econometrics. First, it seeks to offer an explanation for the origin of empirical models. An initial reaction is that no such 'explanation' is needed: surely models are derived from an underlying theoretical framework and estimated in the best possible way from the most accurate and reliable data, so that empirical econometric models are just quantitative representations of theory models with data-based numerical parameter values? Our answer to that (rhetorical?) question is simply 'no' – and this paper amplifies that answer. Empirical models differ fundamentally from theoretical models; they arise as reductions of the mechanism that generated the economic outcomes under study, given the measurement process; and they can be arbitrarily designed to manifest certain properties (*i.e.* achieve certain design criteria such as white-noise, homoscedastic residuals). As such, their links to the originating or concluding theoretical model may be much more tenuous than is often believed.

Second, the theory of reduction also explains the properties of empirical models: that is, why estimated counterparts of theories may have 'wrong signs' or may suffer predictive failure. It does so in addition to, but as an integral part of, explaining their origins. Further, the main concepts of econometrics arise as measures of 'no loss of information' about parameters of interest during reduction. Such concepts include innovation errors, common factors (see Sargan 1980), cointegration (see Engle and Granger 1987 and Banerjee *et al.* 1993), Granger non-causality (see Granger 1969), exogeneity (see Engle *et al.* 1983), invariance (see Frisch 1938, Haavelmo 1944 and Aldrich 1989), and encompassing (see Mizon 1984 and Hendry and Richard 1989). Consequently, reduction theory provides a taxonomy of information sets relevant to model evaluation, thereby relating model selection criteria to the basic null hypotheses of test statistics for 'no loss of information'. A model which suffers no loss of information relative to a class of empirical models based on common information will be able to account for the results of rival models and this concept of encompassing provides a limit to model reduction: invalid reductions will lead to a failure of encompassing. In turn, encompassing is linked to the notion of a progressive research strategy *via* a sequence of models each of which builds upon the findings of its predecessors. By explaining the origins and properties of empirical models and clarifying their evaluation, we arrive at the third role for the theory of reduction, as a prompt for an econometric methodology.

When relating reduction theory to econometric methodology, we must stress that the theory is unrelated to Fisher's notion of data reduction (see Fisher 1922), although both are related to 'general to specific' modelling. *Model* reduction is something that must occur no matter what approach is adopted, whereas Fisher was concerned with *data* reduction, deriving an instrument to summarize the information in a given data set. A key implication of model reduction theory is that all empirical models are designed. Sometimes this is only implicit (*e.g.* when a modeller 'corrects' a specification problem: see Mizon 1993) and such implicit model design strategies are criticized here in favour of an explicit approach which seeks to exhaust the available information. An empirical model which satisfies all the design criteria is said to be congruent with the evidence. One possible route to developing congruent models is general to simple modelling, which is interpreted here as an empirical correspondence of reduction, and is closely related to Fisher's data reduction notions: indeed, concepts of sufficiency arise naturally and are related to both congruence and encompassing.

Congruence is an operational criterion in that the information taxonomy entails a unique condition for 'no loss of information' from each reduction, and hence empirical measures of non-congruence can be constructed. Thus, in practice, subject to sampling vagaries, someone scrutinizing a given empirical model over an historical epoch can ascertain whether or not it is congruent with the existing evidence (for some pre-assigned confidence level). If the concept had meaning, then a 'true' (in the three senses of truth, whole truth and nothing but the truth) model would have to be congruent with 'correct' data, so a non-congruent model must be false (or the data incorrect – or both).

However, a congruent model need not be true (in any of the three senses). Thus, congruence is necessary for 'truth' and there are necessary conditions for congruence in turn. For models based on indirect sense data, there do not seem to be sufficient conditions which determine whether or not an empirical model is true, although there are many necessary conditions. We will argue in favour of replacing a search for truth, which cannot be ascertained in economics, by a search for congruent encompassing empirical models which have a consistent and comprehensive theoretical interpretation. This is not an instrumentalist approach since we require the empirical models to have invariant parameters of interest which characterize real entities and reveal the structure of economic behaviour.

Since practical models are inevitably false (*i.e.* are reductions with loss of relevant information compared to the economic mechanism), there may exist potential problems of contradictions. However, such difficulties must afflict non-congruent models even more, so no additional loss appears to arise from restricting modelling to congruent representations. It may be thought that congruent empirical models will be difficult to obtain: unfortunately, such is not the case. Hendry and Starr (1993) show that for a given sample, an empirically congruent model (one which satisfies all of the criteria given the data) can be constructed even if the mechanism has non-constant parameters, non-constant distributions and non-independent errors. Thus, genuine testing for congruence must utilize new information.

The concept of an empirical model plays a central role in the analysis. The term is a technical one and does not correspond to the usage whereby it connotes 'no theoretical basis' (such as a trend line for example, although such a model may be an empirical model in our sense). Rather, consider a theoretical specification of an economic relationship: to illustrate, we take the simplistic claim that consumption is a linear function of income:

$$(1) \qquad c = \alpha + \beta i + u,$$

where u denotes random perturbations of (1) unconnected with income. In (1), the theoretician has in mind that:

$$(2) \qquad \frac{\partial c}{\partial i} = \beta$$

which is deemed to hold in some abstract theory. In the actual economy under study, the behaviour of its individual agents will interact to determine some outcome for consumption and an associated outcome for income (as flows over some time period, say quarters of a year). The statistical agencies of that economy will measure its activity and publish some numbers for the constant-price magnitudes of consumption and income denoted $\{c_t^0, i_t^0\}$ (^{0} denoting observed magnitudes) and from a sample of such numbers (over $t = 1, ..., T$ say), the econometrician will seek to estimate an equation of the form:

$$(3) \qquad c_t^0 = a + bi_t^0 + e_t,$$

where $\{e_t\}$ represents the deviations from the linear relation. Imagine drawing an infinite number of observations from the given mechanism with a fixed measurement process, then the limit of (3) is the empirical model. Succinctly, the empirical model is the population representation of the theoretical postulate under the data generation process (abbreviated to DGP). Thus, estimated empirical models are reported in applied economics journals.

This paper is concerned with the status of (3). The thrust of the argument is that the similarity of (1) and (3) is misleading, and specifically the 'equality' signs denote very different relationships. In (1), given (2), the theorist has formulated a theory with a causal link (or functional dependence) from the right-hand side to the left, which we may write more clearly as:

$$(4) \qquad c \leftarrow \alpha + \beta i + u,$$

so that a change in i of d induces a change in c of βd. Assume for a moment that such a claim is in fact false and no direct link exists in the economy under study. In particular, let $\beta = 0$. Nevertheless, (3) may be well behaved, with a non-zero value for b (perhaps due to common shocks or indirect links). We should write (3) as:

$$(5) \qquad c_t^0 \rightarrow a + bi_t^0 + e_t,$$

to emphasize that it is a decomposition of c_t^0 into two components: a part that is 'explained', namely $a+bi_t^0$, and a part that is not, namely e_t. Such a decomposition is always possible, independently of the truth or falsity of (1), and holds by construction of e_t. We could write:

$$(6) \qquad e_t \equiv c_t^0 - a - bi_t^0,$$

to stress the fact that the disturbance is a derived entity, defined by the specification of the model given the DGP. We return to this issue after establishing that all empirical models are reductions of the DGP, with derived disturbances which can be designed to achieve pre-assigned criteria.

Previous papers on reduction theory additional to those already mentioned include *inter alia* Hendry and Richard (1982, 1983), Gilbert (1986), Hendry (1987), Florens, Mouchart and Rolin (1990), Ericsson, Campos and Tran (1990) and Hendry (1993). The next section provides a brief discussion of econometric methodology; section [3] presents the statistical formulation of the DGP; section [4] considers the preliminary operations; section [5] analyzes the first major group of reductions and section [6] the second group; section [7] relates the analysis to a number of general modelling issues; [8] reinterprets the main concepts of econometric modelling; section [9] considers empirical model design, and [10] develops the information taxonomy. Section [11] concludes.

2. General to Specific Modelling and Econometric Methodology

The main aim of any proposed econometric methodology must be to provide valid inference, which is why great weight will be placed on congruence herein. For valid inference, it is not enough just to add a stochastic error term to an economic theory model. The recent interest in econometric methodology started towards the end of the 1970s, as the result of dissatisfaction with the prevailing (albeit implicit) textbook methodology which adopted a 'simple to general' modelling approach (see e.g. Pagan 1987 and Hendry, Leamer and Poirier 1990). This can be understood as follows: develop a theory model, add a disturbance term, collect data, run some regressions till a good representation of the theory is obtained, use a minimal amount of diagnostic testing, and conclude by confirming the original theory. Should any misspecification be found, generalize the model to overcome it. This approach is implicit in many textbooks. However, because of the distinction between experimental and non-experimental data, economic data being of the latter kind (see Wold 1969), the problem with adopting this approach is that the experimental design given by the economic theory is different from the statistical experiment giving rise to the data (see Spanos 1986). Therefore, at the outset of a modelling exercise it is not enough to use theory information alone: it is important to capture all of the probabilistic and statistical information available in the data set. It is upon this notion that general to specific modelling is based.

In theory, one starts with the DGP which gives rise to the data, defined by the economic mechanism and the measurement system.

In a non-experimental discipline such as economics, the DGP is a complicated, unknown function which is unlikely to be discovered. Modelling is therefore viewed as a series of transformations from the DGP, with some being 1-1 but others being potentially costly reductions.[1] The stages at which information may be lost can be clarified by explicitly stating the series of reductions. As each reduction shrinks the information set, elements of the real world are excluded – against which the model can be tested.

In practice, however, analyses are conducted within a framework defined by the Haavelmo distribution rather than the DGP (after Haavelmo 1944, who drew the attention of economists to the need to model in terms of joint distributions: see Spanos 1986 and Hendry, Spanos and Ericsson 1989). This is the joint distribution of the observed random variables over the entire sample period, which provides the most general description of the probabilistic information in the data and links the DGP to probability theory. Despite the emphasis at this stage on statistical information, economic theory is also used to decide which set of variables to include in the analysis. A statistical model is then derived using probabilistic assumptions related to the memory, homogeneity and distributional properties of the process. This statistical model comprises a consistent set of probabilistic assumptions designed by the modeller, and the design is a reduction from the Haavelmo distribution using both economic theory and the structure of the observed data. In contrast to the textbook approach, it is not assumed that the theory model and the statistical model coincide. Instead, econometric modelling is an attempt to relate the theory model to the probabilistic structure of the data, summarized by the statistical model. Thus, the nature of the observed data plays a major role in the derivation of the statistical model, in the context of which the estimable model will be analyzed. Statistical adequacy is achieved when the probabilistic assumptions related to the random variables giving rise to the observed data are tested and not rejected. A glance at the chapters on heteroscedasticity (non-constant error variances) and residual autocorrelation in most econometrics textbooks will reveal that this principle is recognized, but at the wrong point: after the modelling exercise has finished rather than at the outset.

Once a statistically adequate, or congruent, empirical model has been derived then theory based restrictions and reparameterizations can be introduced. These will be important to avoid a data-specific model – to be informative, theory should not be data specific. The parameters of the

[1] Because the DGP is unknown, some of the manipulations of it will also be unknown. These statistical manipulations of the DGP are things about which, for the most part, economic theory is silent.

statistical model need not coincide with the theoretical parameters of interest. The restriction or reparametrization of the statistical model is to obtain an approximation to the DGP in terms of the theoretical parameters of interest, and this empirical econometric model must be statistically well defined. If it has been tested against all sources of information and not rejected, we have a congruent empirical model. Should this model also be able to explain the findings of other models, we have a congruent encompassing model.

Encompassing is a practical concept confronting the problem of rival specifications, which is a serious difficulty for econometrics where most data sets can support different theories. Even if the same theory is used, there is scope for alternative representations since economic theory has little to say about the precise specification of an econometric model. Many investigators might analyze the same data set and because of the nature of economic data, it is easy to derive apparently useful models if minimal counterfactual evidence is sought. However, even if such a naive confirmationist stance is not taken and models are hazarded to potential rejection against all possible sources of information in a Popperian style (see Popper 1959, 1963), more than one specification may still be derived for any given data set. Should alternative specifications have been confirmed within their own framework (that is upon sample evidence) they need to be taken outside of it to face tests against each other. This is important since otherwise we merely have a test of the modelling exercise – rather than the model – because all features of the model to be tested can be satisfied by design (see Hendry and Starr 1993). By viewing models as reduced recombinations of the DGP, they are susceptible to comparison even if their theory models are not. It is at this stage of model comparison that we step outside of the usual confines of econometrics. Parsimonious encompassing (when a nested model encompasses the nesting model) is reflexive, anti-symmetric and transitive, so a partial ordering is created across models. This sustains progression in modelling and forges a possible link with Lakatos' (1974) methodology of scientific research programmes. Encompassing can also be related to progress by viewing encompassing models as sufficient statistics, since given the encompassing model, rival specifications are essentially redundant (see Aldrich 1992).

Encompassing also reflects the fact that econometric modelling is not a once and for all activity. Over time, it is anticipated that 'better' models will be derived with the use of more information in the form of improved economic theory and statistical techniques and the availability of more, and better quality, data. The imperfect nature of economic data is notorious. Not only are they mis-measured and available only after some delay, but often there are no suitable empirical counterparts for central theoretical variables. Nevertheless, models found to be congruent on one particular data set are often found to be congruent on the revised data set (see for example, Baba *et al.* 1992).

3. The Statistical Formulation

The analysis begins with the complete set of random variables U_T^1 relevant to the economy under investigation where $U_T^1 = (u_1, ..., u_T)$, defined on a probability space (Ω, F, P), where Ω is the sample space, F the event space, and P an appropriate probability measure. The assumption that economic events are measurable does not seem unreasonable: indeed Schumpeter (1933) went so far as to argue that economics was inherently the most quantitative of the sciences since its measures arose from the ordinary business of life! The $\{u_t\}$ are not just the data to be analyzed in the investigation, but also comprise all the potential data from the economic mechanism under study, so the DGP operates at the level of U_T^1. Thus, the vector u_t comprises details of every transaction of every agent at time t in all the regions of the geographical space relevant to the analysis.[2] Obviously, U_T^1 is unmanageably large, and many of its components are either unobserved or so badly measured as to be unusable.

The assumption that the behaviour of $\{u_t\}$ can be characterized by a joint distribution function is much more tenuous, although Haavelmo (1944) presented a powerful case for its generality. We make that assumption here, and write the joint distribution function $D_U(\cdot)$ of $\{u_t\}$ as:

$$(7) \qquad D_U(U_T^1 | U_0, \psi_T^1) \text{ where } \psi_T^1 \in \Psi \subset \Re^k,$$

so that ψ_T^1 denotes the $k \times 1$ vector of parameters (entities which are independent of the realizations of the random variables) which need not be constant (allowing for transient effects and structural change), and is an element of a subset of k-dimensional real space, and U_0 denotes the initial conditions. $D_U(\cdot)$ denotes the density function (assumed continuous, which again is a non-trivial requirement), and the $|$ denotes that the realizations are conditional on the given values of U_0 and ψ_T^1.

---

[2] Since many of the u variables are not observed, the term data is not strictly applicable to u_t. The issue of measurement error will not be discussed here.

Operationally, models arise by a sequence of reductions from $D_U(\cdot)$ to a final empirical model. These reductions are organized here into three groups. Some of the stages are not uniquely ordered, as there is no logical requirement for some to precede others, but it is irrelevant in which order they are investigated since the resulting reduced model does not depend on the path taken. We begin with some necessary preliminaries which do not in fact entail any reduction in the information content.

4. Data Transformations, Aggregation and Parameters of Interest

First, we map U_T^1 one-one onto a new set of transformed variables W_T^1: $U_T^1 \leftrightarrow W_T^1$. Some of the W_T^1 are measured aggregates to be analyzed, but the vast majority are disaggregates or other aggregates which are either unobserved or are deemed to be irrelevant. However, all information is retained and nothing is eliminated. To calculate the aggregate of a given variable $\{u_{it}\}$ for N agents and T time periods, the mapping is from $\{u_{1t}, ..., u_{nt}\}$ to $\{\Sigma_i u_{1t}, u_{2t}, ..., u_{nt}\}$, which is the set $\{w_{kt}\}$. For example, aggregate quarterly consumers' expenditure at time t in the U.K. is the total flow over that quarter of the sum of all individual consumer's expenditures across all final consumers' goods and services throughout the U.K.

The important effect of aggregation transformations arises from their impact on the parameter vectors of the untransformed and transformed densities:

$$(8) \qquad D_U(U_T^1 | U_0, \psi_T^1) = D_W(W_T^1 | W_0, \varphi_T^1)$$

where $\psi_T^1 \in \Psi$ and $\varphi_T^1 \in \Phi$ with $\varphi_T^1 = f(\psi_T^{1})$. The transformed density $D_W(\cdot)$ of W_T^1 has a possibly different distribution function, albeit one which is a function of $D_U(\cdot)$. Individual decision variables often behave erratically over time, and need not be normally distributed. However, from the central limit theorem, the aggregate of a large number N of individual random variables from a non-normal distribution will be approximately normal so one benefit from analyzing aggregates is that they are closer to normal random variates. The transformation from U to W also affects the parameter space, so Ψ is transformed into Φ. The new parameters in φ may be more or less interpretable than the old, and fewer or more may be constant than in ψ.

Functional form transformations also alter the parameters and can induce or lose constancy. This is true even of monotonic transforms: with integrated processes (economic variables which require differencing to become stationary), taking logs of positive variables can remove heteroscedasticity (see Ermini and Hendry 1991).

Most econometric analyses involve models which are characterized by parameters of interest. Such parameters might be the marginal propensity to consume; the government's impact on rates of inflation from changing its deficit; the interest elasticity of the demand for money; or some functions of tastes and technology. Denote the parameters of interest by $\mu \in M$ and assume that they are identifiable (in the sense of uniqueness of the parameterization: see Koopmans 1950 and Hood and Koopmans 1953). Usually, μ is believed to be invariant to an interesting class of interventions. Such parameters can only be a conjecture in a theoretical model of the DGP. For example, there may not be a marginal propensity to consume for any agents or any society, however many theories postulate its central role or data analyses claim its determination. Nevertheless, we believe that such constructions do exist, because (*e.g.*) the aggregate marginal propensity to consume apparently can be altered by changing taxes. Moreover, a substantial number of econometric relationships persist through time, perhaps because human behaviour usually evolves slowly relative to the time-span of econometric studies. Just as there is no sufficient condition for the truth of an empirical model so we cannot verify that parameters of interest exist to be discovered.[3]

Parameters of interest motivate and structure a study and faster progress seems likely if the postulated parameters reflect salient and constant features of reality. Parameters which prove to be constant empirically are naturally of interest; we comment on potential invariance below. Economists use economic theory to suggest parameters of interest. Economic concepts and models are an essential component of our cognitive structure, and it is difficult to think about economic events without invoking aspects of existing theory. Its consistency and generality

[3] Historically, considerable progress has been made searching for parameters of interest that present knowledge suggests do not exist (see e.g. Mason 1977 and Losee 1980). As examples, seeking phlogiston to explain combustion led to the discovery of some of the principles of modern thermodynamics; searching for an 'integer' theory to explain chemical weights led to isotopic theory and later to an improved atomic theory of chemical behaviour; alchemy, which was an abortive attempt to transduce base metals into gold, was a precursor of chemistry (see Hendry 1980). These examples involved searching for entities that we now believe do not exist, but nevertheless were productive of scientific development.

endow it with considerable power as a first-order description of individual economic behaviour in relatively static circumstances. However, theories are drastic abstractions which only focus on some of the salient phenomena and consider these in isolation from other potential influences. Even at their best, they must be incomplete and idealized descriptions. Basing parameters on such theories raises the issue of mapping theoretically based entities, which are explicitly cognitive in nature, on to empirically based entities, which are functions of physically existing quantities. Several correspondence conditions are involved:

(a) between latent theory-variables and the corresponding empirical data constructs (*e.g.* from permanent income to some measured values thereof);

(b) between theory decision time periods and the empirical time intervals (*e.g.* from '*t*' to months or quarters);

(c) between a theory's *ceteris paribus* assumptions about everything not included in the theory model, and the actual irrelevance in practice of the excluded influences;

and:

(d) between the constants of the theory model and the coefficients of the empirical model.

Earlier writers such as Frisch (1938) and Haavelmo (1944) were concerned about these four correspondence problems, and although technical developments in econometrics and economic theory have alleviated some of their original concerns, there remains a gap between an abstract theory of an unrationed inter-temporal optimizing individual agent and an empirical model of aggregate behaviour. Other sources of information and forms of reasoning than just economic theory are obviously admissible in formulating and analyzing parameters of interest.

The final step prior to any actual reductions is to isolate that subset of information from W_T^1 which is believed relevant to the parameters of interest. Both theory and past evidence play important roles in this selection, which is the precursor to the largest reduction — due to marginalization. Partition W_T^1 into the two sets $W_T^1 = (X_T^1 : V_T^1)$. The objective of this partition is to ensure that everything about μ can be learnt from analyzing the X_T^1 alone, so that W_T^1 is not essential to the analysis. While the choice of the elements to include in X_T^1 is based on conjecture — as in any science — the final model will be testable, which will provide evidence on the adequacy of the partition selected. In any practical application, V_T^1 will not be fully specified and its contents are usually defined by default, as everything not explicitly included in X_T^1.

An investigator's value added depends on thinking of parameters μ that are in fact interesting, in that they correspond to constant behavioural propensities, and of the data set that will deliver those parameters of interest when properly analyzed. Theoretical reasoning is frequently of help in doing so, despite being neither necessary nor sufficient, but how one discovers useful knowledge remains an art rather than a science. In any event, given the specification of μ and the choice of X_T^1, the next step is to reduce $D_W(\cdot)$ in (8) to manageable proportions by concentrating the analysis on X_T^1 and marginalizing with respect to the remainder of W_T^1, then factorizing the resulting density to allow coherent inference.

5. Marginalizing, Sequential Factorization and Conditioning

There is no unique order for marginalizing and sequentially factorizing and the path we follow is the easier in terms of analytical derivations. To marginalize the joint density in (8) with respect to all the elements of V_T^1 involves the following density factorization:

$$(9) \quad D_W(W_T^1|W_0, \varphi_T^1) = D_{V|X}(V_T^1|X_T^1, W_0, \Lambda_{aT}^1)D_X(X_T^1|W_0, \Lambda_{bT}^1).$$

We eliminate V_T^1 by discarding the conditional density $D_{V|X}(V_T^1|X_T^1, W_0, \Lambda_{aT}^1)$ in (9), while retaining the marginal density $D_X(X_T^1|W_0, \Lambda_{bT}^1)$. This operation corresponds to throwing away the data on V_T^1, although that data was probably not actually collected (so 'throwing away' is a logical rather than a physical issue). Henceforth, an investigation only concerns the marginal (joint) distribution of the X_T^1 as a function of their parameters Λ_{bT}^1, and the initial conditions W_0 of the DGP. Thus, $D_X(\cdot)$ is no longer the DGP, merely the general joint distribution under consideration, and so it constitutes the Haavelmo distribution for the analysis.

A necessary condition for not losing information from the reduction is that μ must be a function of Λ_{bT}^1 alone, $\mu = g(\Lambda_{bT}^1)$ say: it must be possible to learn μ from Λ_{bT}^1, without there being any information about μ in Λ_{aT}^1. A second condition is that there must be nothing to learn about Λ_{bT}^1 from Λ_{aT}^1 (otherwise information is being ignored) so that $(\Lambda_{aT}^1 : \Lambda_{bT}^1) \in \Lambda_a \times \Lambda_b$. It is valid to discard V_T^1 only if everything of relevance can be learnt from analyzing Λ_{bT}^1 alone.

In econometrics, the problem of invalidly marginalizing with respect to relevant V_T^1 is often called 'omitted variables bias'. There is deemed to be a set of parameters of interest μ such that if all the relevant variables are not included, then the resulting parameter estimates are biased, or perhaps inconsistent, for μ. However, the key issue is not that biased or inconsistent estimates of μ are obtained, but that the wrong parameters are calculated. Instead of estimating μ, a different parameter vector α, say, is estimated which is mistakenly interpreted as μ. This accounts for so-called wrong signs: having marginalized the problem with respect to whatever variables are omitted, the correct parameter is no longer obtained.[4]

An important implication is that μ may have been a constant function of $\varphi_T{}^1$, yet when the distribution (7) is factorized as in (9), $\alpha = h(\Lambda_{bT}{}^1)$ might depend upon time. Consequently, if the wrong marginalization is chosen, constant parameters might not be discovered even if the relevant aspect of the world had constant parameters in an appropriate formulation: the difference made by a more informative analysis from the joint density may be between a useful and an unhelpful analysis.

Reduction by marginalization is complicated because it is difficult to write down what function $\Lambda_{bT}{}^1$ is of $\varphi_T{}^1$ in order to analyze the preservation, or loss, of constancy. That issue will be clearer after sequential factorization. Assume that we can learn everything required about μ from X_T^1 via $\Lambda_{bT}{}^1$ by analyzing $D_X(\cdot)$ in (9). To create an innovation process for statistical inference, factorize X_T^1 as follows:

$$(10) \quad D_X(X_T^1|W_0, \Lambda_{bT}{}^1) = \prod_{t=1}^{T} D_X(x_t|X_{t-1}{}^1, W_0, \lambda_{bt})$$

$$= \prod_{t=1}^{T} D_X(\varepsilon_t|X_{t-1}{}^1, W_0, \lambda_{bt}).$$

This factorization of the joint distribution of X_T^1 into sequential distributions generates a mean innovation error process $\varepsilon_t = x_t - \mathsf{E}[x_t|X_{t-1}{}^1]$, where $\mathsf{E}[\cdot]$ denotes an expectation, so by construction $\{\varepsilon_t\}$ satisfies $\mathsf{E}[\varepsilon_t|X_{t-1}{}^1] = 0$, and hence is not predictable from the entire history of x. An immediate implication is that $\mathsf{E}[\varepsilon_t|E_{t-1}{}^1] = 0$ where $E_{t-1}{}^1 =$ $= (\varepsilon_1, ..., \varepsilon_{t-1})$, hence $\{\varepsilon_t\}$ is also white noise (unpredictable from its own past).

[4] Here we are concerned with the logical issue and assume that sampling issues are not germane.

However, $\{\varepsilon_t\}$ will only be an innovation against W_{t-1} if the marginalization in (9) involved no loss of information. If so, $\mathsf{E}[\varepsilon_t|X_{t-1}^1, V_{t-1}^1] = \mathsf{E}[\varepsilon_t|X_{t-1}^1]$ and hence, conditional on X_{t-1}^1, V_{t-1}^1 does not Granger-cause x_t (see Granger 1969 and Engle *et al.* 1983). This requirement reveals the stringency of the marginalization condition in (9). The parameters of interest will be recovered only if, conditional on the variables retained, the variables omitted from the analysis actually are irrelevant – which is an all too obvious statement.

We also deduce the weaker necessary condition that $\mathsf{E}[\varepsilon_t|V_{t-1}^1] = 0$ if sequential marginalization is to be valid. It is probably at the marginalization stage that most empirical research goes wrong, by over-enthusiastic elimination of potentially relevant variables. In part, this may be due to the practice of commencing from simple models which are generalized only after rejection on diagnostic tests; in part, it may depend on assuming the empirical validity of some *ceteris paribus* clause in a theory model; and in part, it may be the result of beliefs about the information content of time-series, the prevalence of collinearity and identification problems, and the virtues of parsimony. After conducting many empirical studies, we consider the most likely cause of predictive failure in applied research to be a change in the data properties of a relevant, but omitted, variable.

Despite most econometric theory being based upon the assumption of stationary time series, many economic variables appear to be non-stationary. In particular, many variables seem to be integrated, that is require differencing to become stationary. Stationary series can also be derived by combining integrated processes which are said to be cointegrated. Another important reduction is then the elimination of linear combinations of integrated, but not cointegrated variables, since the nature of integrated processes leads to invalid inferences which suggest the presence of relationships between variables when none actually exists: these are the 'nonsense relationships' of Yule (1926) and the 'spurious regressions' of Granger and Newbold (1974). Integrated processes can be expressed in terms of cointegrated and differenced variables without loss of information, but with a reduction in the dimension of the parameter vector, so a gain in parsimony and coherent inference results from doing so (see Phillips 1991 and Hendry and Mizon 1993).[5] At the completion of these two operations, all

[5] When variables are left in an integrated form, many inferences will remain valid, but it may not always be clear which tests require conventional and which require Dickey-Fuller critical values (see Dickey and Fuller 1979, 1981, Sims, Stock and Watson 1990 and Banerjee *et al.*, 1993). We assume that a mapping to a set of differenced and cointegrated variables has been achieved but will not modify the notation to reflect this.

variables will be non-integrated, and a conventional statistical analysis can be implemented.

Much applied econometric research concerns explaining one set of variables given another set. To analyze this, partition x_t into two sets of variables: $x'_t = (y'_t : z'_t)$ where the y_t are endogenous and the z_t are non-modelled. Factorizing the sequential density of x_t in (10) into a conditional and a marginal density associated with y_t given z_t, and z_t respectively yields:

$$(11) \quad D_X(x_t | X_{t-1}^1, W_0, \lambda_{bt})$$
$$= D_{Y|Z}(y_t | z_t, X_{t-1}^1, W_0, \theta_{at}) D_Z(z_t | X_{t-1}^1, W_0, \theta_{bt}).$$

Then z_t is weakly exogenous for μ if: (i) $\mu = f(\theta_{at})$ alone; and (ii) $(\theta_{at}, \theta_{bt}) \in \Theta_a \times \Theta_b$.

Under the conditions in (i) and (ii), there is no need to analyze the marginal distribution $D_Z(z_t | X_{t-1}^1, W_0, \theta_{bt})$ of z_t in (11) to efficiently analyze μ. The problem can be reduced to only analyzing the conditional distribution $D_{Y|Z}(y_t | z_t, X_{t-1}^1, W_0, \theta_{at})$ of y_t given z_t, thereby increasing the robustness of inference to incorrect formulations of $D_Z(\cdot)$, as well as reducing the cost of the analysis. More importantly, the model selection problem is greatly simplified by valid reductions. Valid contemporaneous conditioning is especially useful when θ_{at} is constant and θ_{bt} is not. This step is almost the converse of marginalizing, in that we now discard the marginal distribution, and retain the conditional. However, exogeneity has been a contentious issue in econometrics. Above, the role of Granger non-causality was in justifying marginalizing but Sims (1972) defined exogeneity in terms of Granger non-causality, confounding issues of marginalization with those of conditioning: Granger non-causality is neither necessary nor sufficient for weak exogeneity (see Engle *et al.* 1983).

6. Constancy, Lag Truncation and Functional Form

The next reduction concerns the time homogeneity of the process through the constancy of its parameters. At this stage of reduction, the formulation in (11) is virtually vacuous, since there are potentially as many parameters as data points. To progress with empirical modelling, some assumptions are needed about the homogeneity over time of the process being observed, since little can be learnt from analyzing data drawn from a process which differs at every point in time. Consider the extreme case of parameter constancy:

$$(12) \qquad \boldsymbol{\theta}_{at} = \boldsymbol{\theta}_a \quad \text{where} \quad \boldsymbol{\theta}_a \in \Theta_a,$$

so that $\boldsymbol{\mu}$ is a function of $\boldsymbol{\theta}_a$: $\boldsymbol{\mu} = f(\boldsymbol{\theta}_a)$. This is a large reduction when it is valid, and some such reduction is essential if progress is to be made in empirical modelling.

By taking the parameter vector $\boldsymbol{\theta}_a$ as constant, regime changes must be modelled. The discovery problem is to establish which function of the x_t delivers the constant $\boldsymbol{\mu}$, or alternatively expressed, how to find the constancies of the DGP. There is an intimate link between how the data are modelled and the reasonableness of assuming that the corresponding parameters are constant. Here, some care in our language is essential. The assumption of constant parameters does not preclude such features as technical progress, learning, regime shifts, adaptation, changing shocks and so on. What it does require is that such factors are modelled as functions of more basic parameters that are constant. Equation (12) then applies to these basic parameters. The choice of formulation is an empirical issue, open to evaluation, which depends on appropriately modelling learning and adjustments, making sensible decisions about functional forms and the inclusion of relevant variables, as well as on the structure of the unknown DGP. If (12) captures constant features of the DGP in a parsimonious way then it is useful; but nothing guarantees in any given instance that it will do so.

When the constancy reduction is valid, the full sample conditional density in (11) becomes:

$$(13) \qquad \prod_{t=1}^{T} D_{Y|Z}(y_t|z_t, X_{t-1}^1, W_0, \boldsymbol{\theta}_a) \quad \text{where} \quad \boldsymbol{\theta}_a \in \Theta_a.$$

Unfortunately, the model in (13) remains non-operational even with constant parameters, because the history retained in X_{t-1}^1 increases with the sample size, so the model dimension diverges. Hence we need another reduction to capture the model forms conventionally adopted, namely lag truncation.

The relevance of history declines in processes with limited memory, and suggests a possible reduction by fixing the extent of the history of X_{t-1}^1 in (13) at n periods:

$$(14) \qquad D_{Y|Z}(y_t|z_t, X_{t-1}^1, W_0, \boldsymbol{\theta}_a) = D_{Y|Z}(y_t|z_t, X_{t-1}^{t-n}, W_0, \delta).$$

The concept that sustains this reduction is that $\{\varepsilon_t\}$ in (9) remains an innovation process despite the information reduction. Invalid exclusions will generally induce a non-innovation error because of the limited retention of the history of the process. Thus, in empirical research, examine the residuals to see whether the limited memory assumption is valid for any given choice of n. This simply requires checking that the error remains an innovation against all the available information.

Constancy, functional form and distributional assumptions are intimately related. A functional form reduction affects the form of the distribution $D_{Y|Z}(\cdot)$. It would be convenient to choose simple functional forms for y_t and z_t and their retained history that simultaneously induced constant parameters and made $D_{Y|Z}(\cdot)$ correspond approximately to a normal distribution. Then the conditional relationship would be linear, so such a reduction would entail a linear model in the transformed space of the appropriate functions of y_t and z_t. However, it is difficult, and sometimes impossible, to think of a function with the properties that satisfy all these requirements.

To implement the reduction, map y_t into $h(y_t) = y_t^*$ and z_t into $g(z_t) = z_t^*$, denoting the resulting data by X^*. Assume that y_t^* and z_t^* make $D_{Y|Z}(\cdot)$ approximately normal:

$$(15) \qquad D_{Y|Z}(y_t|z_t, X_{t-1}^{t-n}, W_0, \delta) \simeq N(y_t^*|z_t^*, X_{t-1}^{*t-n}, W_0, \gamma).$$

When (15) holds, we obtain a linear model for y_t^* in terms of z_t^*; otherwise, linearity is an additional reduction (after suitable transformations), which may not deliver a useful model in practice.

7. Derived Models

Providing the history retained in (15) is adequate to create an innovation error, the parameter of the reduced conditional density will remain γ. Actual historical time may matter for non-stationary processes, especially following major wars, but even that effect should fade as time increases. Many empirical models have the property that after transformations and modelling regime shifts, the variables are nearly stationary, and initial conditions do not have a large affect. Henceforth, we suppose this holds, so that under the above assumptions the model takes the form:[6]

---

[6] Moving-average error representations are not excluded in principle but in practice are well approximated by autoregressions of the same lag length: see Hendry and Trivedi (1972) and Hendry (1977).

$$(16) \qquad A(L)h(y_t) = B(L)g(z_t) + \varepsilon_t \quad \text{where} \quad \varepsilon_t \sim N(0, \Sigma_\varepsilon),$$

and $A(L)$ and $B(L)$ are polynomial matrices of order n in the lag operator L.

The complete sequence of reductions leads to a vector autoregressive distributed lag model in the variables in $h(y_t)$ and $g(z_t)$, although the lag length n might need to be long to ensure an innovation error. The resulting model is the conventional formulation adopted in econometrics precisely because we asserted at each reduction stage that the relevant conditions were valid. A major point of reduction analysis is to highlight the conditions necessary to sustain models like (16). Below, we will consider the obverse issue of evaluating (16) for relevant losses of information against the various reduction steps, but before doing so, we comment on (16) and its derivation.

First, if no z_t are present, (16) is a vector autoregression (VAR) in the space of $h(y_t)$, so all the reduction restrictions apply equally to that class. Second, innovation errors do not exclude models with autocorrelated errors, namely if they have common factors in their lag polynomials (see Sargan 1980, Hendry and Mizon 1978, Mizon and Hendry 1980). Such reformulations are simplifications, so that autoregressive errors are a restriction on a model, not a generalization. Third, there are four possible interpretations of (16) for scalar $h(y_t)$: whether it is a regression equation; a behavioural plan; a contingent plan; or a least-squares approximation (see Hendry and Richard 1982). Given the validity of every reduction, (16) is all of these except a behavioural plan, which is excluded by the assumption that z_t is weakly exogenous for μ. More importantly, we confirm that ε_t is a derived and not an autonomous process, being defined by:

$$(17) \qquad \varepsilon_t = A(L)h(y_t) - B(L)g(z_t).$$

Consequently, $\{\varepsilon_t\}$ is what data collection agencies call 'everything not elsewhere specified'. The only condition under which $\{\varepsilon_t\}$ can be regarded as autonomous is that there is no loss of information in any reduction required to obtain (16) from (8). In that case, $\{\varepsilon_t\}$ is the DGP error process, which makes all the reductions vacuous — (16) must also be the DGP. Otherwise, $\{\varepsilon_t\}$ is created by the reductions. That is a vital insight, because if $\{\varepsilon_t\}$ is derived and entailed by the reductions, different error processes must result from different reductions. Thus, some reductions correspond to more informative empirical models than others. Since the error is inevitably derived, it is a human artefact susceptible to design. Without an assumption of omniscience, empirical models are designer creations in econometrics, designed according to criteria specified by their proprietors (see Hendry 1987). The issue is not whether models should be designed, but how they should be designed, and hence how the gap between theory and empirical evidence should be bridged.

For any claimed empirical model, we can reverse the reduction process and consider the loss of information from each reduction. This will clarify the status of that empirical model, and cast light on the primary concepts of econometric analysis.

8. Econometric Concepts and Information Loss in Reduction

The specific conditions needed to validate each reduction provide a natural measure of the loss of information from that reduction stage. Reviewing these, almost every major econometric concept arises as a measure of when there is no information loss from the associated reduction. It is convenient to consider the concepts in the order of the reductions in [4]-[7].

(a) Aggregation entails no loss of information on marginalizing with respect to disaggregates when the retained information comprises a set of sufficient statistics for the parameters of interest μ.

(b) Transformations *per se* entail no associated reduction but introduce the concept of parameters of interest, and the notions that parameters should be invariant and identifiable.

(c) Data partition is a preliminary, but decisions about which variables to include and which to omit are fundamental determinants of the success of empirical modelling.

(d) Marginalizing with respect to v_t is without loss providing the remaining data are sufficient for μ, whereas marginalizing without loss with respect to V_{t-1}^1 entails both Granger-non-causality for x_t and variation-free parameters.

(e) Sequential factorization involves no loss if the derived error process is an innovation relative to the history of the random variables, and via the notion of common factors, reveals that autoregressive errors are a restriction and not a generalization.

(f) Integrated data systems can be reduced to stationarity by suitable combinations of cointegration and differencing, allowing conventional inference to be applied to more parsimonious relationships.

(g) Conditional factorization reductions lead to no loss of information relative to the joint analysis when the conditioning variables are weakly exogenous for the parameters of interest.

(h) Parameter constancy is a direct reduction, and relates to invariance as constancy across interventions which affect the marginal processes.

(i) Lag truncation involves no loss if the error process remains an innovation despite excluding some of the past of relevant variables.

(j) No specific concept is associated with functional form reductions. It is hard to characterize the conditions defining no loss of information from such approximations: for example, taking logarithms of log-normally distributed variables generates normally distributed variates, involving no loss.

The derived model is a reduction of the DGP, so is nested within that DGP and its properties are explained by the reduction process: knowledge of the DGP entails knowledge of all reductions thereof, although in practice, the mathematics of any given reductions might be tedious. When that property holds for any two models (so knowledge of the first entails knowledge of the other), the first is said to encompass the second. Since all models are reductions of the DGP, they are potentially comparable to see which encompasses which.

Whether the model encompasses the DGP is the issue of parsimonious encompassing. If it does, then no loss of information occurred from the entire reduction sequence, and in that sense, parsimonious encompassing characterizes a valid limit to model reduction.

Since we can reinterpret many of the main concepts that have arisen separately in econometrics in terms of reductions involving no loss of information, reduction theory has excess content. The theory arose as an explanation for the origin of empirical models and the associated 'problems' approach to empirical econometric modelling. It is a bonus that it integrates and clarifies many previously established concepts. There is further excess content to come, once we have discussed model design both as an implicit and an explicit process.

9. Model Design

Consider a model designed by one process from the spectrum of possible modelling methods — from theoretical assertion to data mining. Another investigator could attempt to evaluate that model by retracing the entailed reductions, and checking whether there was any loss of information against a more general formulation. At this juncture, we could branch in either one of two directions, both of which are facets of the theory of reduction.

The first is implicit design, or the symptomatology approach to econometrics, which comprises testing for problems like autocorrelation, heteroscedasticity, omitted variables, multicollinearity, non-constant parameters etc., and correcting these problems as they are ascertained. One should indeed be concerned about such problems, but it is unclear whether the problems are worse than the supposed cure. From reduction analysis, if a set of variables y_t is selected to be explained by another set of variables z_t using a limited history, then the derived error will not in general satisfy many of the assumptions that are conventionally made. Consequently, problems are likely to arise — all reductions are imposed merely by writing down a model like (17), although empirical model formulation is not always viewed that way.

All too often, empirical practice embodies a methodology of implicit design, whereby diagnostic tests are used as selection criteria in model building, successively extending a model to remove each significant test rejection by assuming the validity of the ostensible alternative hypothesis of the corresponding test. Once models are built according to such criteria, it is meaningless to test the models using the same criteria. The drawbacks of simple general modelling are established in Hendry (1979) and Mizon (1993) *inter alia*.

The converse approach is one of explicit model design which seeks to mimic reduction theory in practical research by employing the concepts in [8] to minimize the loss due to the reductions selected. It commences from a statistical model corresponding to the Haavelmo distribution, also called the general unrestricted model (GUM). This is the most general, estimable, statistical model that can reasonably be postulated initially, given the present sample of data, previous empirical and theoretical research, and any institutional and measurement information available. By estimable is meant that its parameters can be uniquely determined from the evidence. The GUM is also formulated to contain the parsimonious, interpretable and invariant econometric model at which we hope to end. For example, in analyzing consumers' expenditure, the GUM might comprise the current values and *n* lags of each of logs of consumption, income and past wealth, perhaps involving the decomposition of wealth into liquid and illiquid assets and debt; interest rates, measures of demographic structure including family size; indices of taxation structure and major financial innovations; and so on. Allow from the outset for everything that might matter (at least logically, if not necessarily empirically), but structured by a theoretical analysis — the GUM is not the mindless repository of the contests of some large socio-economic databank. Then investigate whether and how this initial general model can be reduced without significant loss of information about the parameters of interest.

The primary role of the GUM is to define the innovation process in the statistical analysis and to determine the variance of that innovation process, a variance such that no other model on the same data could do any better. While the GUM is itself a reduction of the DGP, it ought to be able to account for previous results from analyzing the same data set, so the GUM should encompass pre-existing evidence.

Once an empirical econometric model has been constructed by reduction from the GUM, how can its validity be evaluated? Answering that question will clarify the model building process, and deliver the second bonus from the theory of reduction: a taxonomy of evaluation information that is exhaustive. The taxonomy corresponds to the reduction process, but followed in the opposite direction. Thus, we now consider the information losses that might have occurred at each reduction stage, and classify potential information losses in terms of the taxonomy. In this context of evaluation, the same concepts recur as discussed in [8] above, but related to notions of testing, rather than designing, models.[7]

10. A Taxonomy of Evaluation Information

Partition the data X_T^1 used in modelling into the three information sets:

[a] past data;
[b] present data;
[c] future data.

This partition is based on the old adage that the past is immutable; we live in the present; and the future is uncertain. We will check the

[7] Although it is fuzzy at the boundaries, the dichotomy we have in mind is that between the contexts of discovery and evaluation proposed by Herschel (1830).

immutability of the model in the past, the validity of it in the present, and the uncertainty of it into the future. To do so, the data set is written in the following factorization: $X_T^1 = (X_{t-1}^1 : x_t : X_T^{t+1})$, where the classification into past, present and future is relative and changes with t.[8] Other available information includes:

[d] theory information (often the source of parameters of interest and a creative stimulus);

[e] measurement information (price index theory and data accuracy etc.); and:

[f] data of rival models (which could be analyzed into past, present and future in turn).

Evaluation proceeds by formulating a null hypothesis corresponding to a valid reduction for the corresponding information set, with the associated concept in [8], then constructing alternatives against which to test the model. The following null hypotheses correspond to the above classes of information:

[*a*] *Past data*

To check that a model is valid against the past, the null hypothesis is that its error is a homoscedastic innovation against the available information. Testing that there is no loss of information against the past is equivalent to testing that the ignored information is constantly irrelevant over time. A model with a homoscedastic, innovation error against the data history leaves nothing for that past to explain, so the model is historically comprehensive.

[*b*] *Present data*

For validation against present data, the contemporaneous conditioning variables z_t given X_{t-1}^1 will be valid only if z_t is weakly exogenous for the parameters of interest μ. Since there is no loss of information when z_t is weakly exogenous for μ, the validity of the model in the present maps one-one on to the concept of weak exogeneity, and the relevant evaluation test is for the null hypothesis of weak exogeneity.

[*c*] *Future data*

For future data, the concepts are constancy and invariance, where the latter requires that the parameters stay constant despite changes in the $\{z_t\}$ process (within a class of interventions). Aspects of invariance are testable using recursivity combined with super exogeneity and encompassing to check on the critique of empirical models for economic policy due to Lucas (1976) (see Engle and Hendry 1993 and Favero and Hendry 1992).

---

8 All of the information sets require dating in a general framework since theories evolve over time, as do measurement systems such as national accounts.

[*d*] *Theory information*

Important aspects of theory information are to specify and identify the parameters of interest, and hence define the formal model specification. The other main concept here is theory consistency, so that there is no evaluation conflict between the model and the theory interpretation. Many over-identified empirical models, corresponding to different ostensible parameters of interest, could be consistent both logically and statistically with a given theory. However, this issue of observational equivalence is of little practical relevance in worlds with regime shifts.

[*e*] *Measurement information*

For measurement information, the primary concepts are accuracy of observations and data admissibility. A model is data admissible if its predictions automatically satisfy all known data constraints. Inadmissible models are logically inconsistent with the data even though that does not necessarily entail that they are poor empirical representations: for example, the heights of individuals are approximately normally distributed even though height must be positive. Inaccurate data could seriously impugn an empirical model.

[*f*] *Rival models*

Since all empirical models are reductions of a common DGP, rival models on a common data set are comparable by retracing the reduction process far enough to find the process from which they were all reduced. Thus, while models may be non-nested relative to one another, all models are nested in the DGP. In the evaluation context, encompassing requires a model to act like a pseudo-DGP with the property that it can explain all the findings in the analysis.

Encompassing ensures that there is no loss of information in the reduction as a whole. Parsimonious encompassing occurs when the finally selected model encompasses the initial unrestricted model, in which case the reductions are valid empirically. When the final product is a valid, simplified and interpretable econometric model of the statistical mechanism, it goes beyond corroboration (as measured by satisfying various tests – some of which may have low power relative to the GUM) to account for and predict the results of other models without actually estimating them. Encompassing, therefore, is both entailed by reduction theory and explains when to stop a reduction sequence namely, when a simplification cannot encompass the general model: beyond that point, important information is lost.

The six main design criteria are:

[a] homoscedastic innovation errors;

[b] conditioning variables weakly exogenous for the parameters of interest;

[c] constant, invariant parameters of interest;
[d] theory consistent, identifiable structures;
[e] data admissible formulations on accurate observations; and
[f] encompassing rival models.

Models which satisfy the first five information sets are congruent: by analogy with one triangle which matches another in all respects, the model matches the evidence in all measured respects. A congruent encompassing model satisfies all six criteria.

11. Conclusion

The theory of reduction seeks to explain the origin and status of empirical econometric models. It does so by deriving models from a postulated data generating process which compounds the economic mechanism and the measurement process under study. The derivations involve transformation, marginalization and conditioning from the postulated unknown joint density of the outcomes through to the final empirical econometric model. The properties of the model are entailed by the DGP and the reductions, given the form suggested by prior theoretical analysis.

Because empirical models are entailed by reductions, they are human artefacts susceptible to design. That implication must affect the methodology of empirical modelling, and implicit design methods were criticized in favour of an explicit design approach which mimicked the reduction process in empirical implementation.

Reduction theory, however, does more than merely explain the origin and status of empirical models and highlight that they are derived entities. The main concepts of econometrics, independently evolved over more than 60 years of research, are shown to correspond to the notion of 'no loss of information' from various reductions. Moreover, an exhaustive taxonomy of information sets arises naturally, and links both design in the context of discovery and testing in the context of evaluation to reduction, interpreting these as different directions of movement along the reduction path, the one simplifying, the other backtracking to check on the first's validity.

The taxonomy provides six basic (composite) criteria of design and evaluation, as against a vast range of possible alternatives. A congruent model is one which satisfies the first five criteria on the measures selected; an encompassing model is one which can account for the results obtained by rival models of the same phenomena. Thus, encompassing also transpires to define the limit to reduction in terms of parsimonious encompassing where the simplified model must still explain the results of the initial general model which nests rival empirical explanations. Parsimonious encompassing is transitive, anti-symmetric and reflexive so defines a partial ordering over empirical models, which appears to subsume previous ordering criteria. In separate papers, it has been established that all six criteria can be satisfied in practice by design (see Hendry 1987, 1993).

Nevertheless, a congruent model is not necessarily true: an innovation is relative to its information set but may be predictable from other information. Thus, a sequence of congruent models could be developed, each of which encompassed all previous models. Satisfying all six criteria thereby sustains a progressive research strategy. Moreover, true models, if such can be conceived, must be congruent with accurate data, so it is useful to exclude non-congruent models. Further, congruency or its absence can be ascertained from the available evidence (subject to the usual *caveats* about incorrect test rejection decisions) and so provides an operational criterion, unlike truth in an empirical science. An important methodological implication of this paper, therefore, is the potential advantage of substituting the joint requirements of encompassing and congruency as operational criteria for empirical modelling instead of nearness to 'truth' as the decision criterion.

New problems are bound to arise from doing so. For example, later models reveal that earlier models were non-congruent, and hence false. Arguing from false propositions can generate contradictions and the apparent ability to prove any desired proposition: is there a danger of such an outcome here? We believe the answer is negative, since empirical models are not simply sets of propositions, but are combinations of data. In particular, a model could be non-congruent by being incomplete rather than inconsistent with reality. This is an important problem in a statistical subject since 'true' statements can be incomplete. For example, if two stationary variables y and x are jointly normally distributed, then y is also marginally normally distributed with a constant mean. However, it is also true that y is conditionally normally distributed with a mean that varies with x. And neither statement need be the whole truth.

Have we therefore ended with a 'sophisticated instrumentalism'? Certainly, we are treating econometric analysis, and indeed any scientific approach, as an instrument with which to understand reality. But the products are not judged merely by their forecasting prowess — indeed that is neither necessary nor sufficient to justify model choice (see Clements and Hendry 1993). Rather, the correspondence between the claimed invariant parameters of the empirical model and actual behavioural propensities or structures will determine the genuine explanatory power of the results (see e.g. Cartwright 1989).

The role of econometrics in economic science is the subject of a separate analysis in Hendry (1993) which seeks to establish the ability of the present framework to sustain tests between rival theories (as opposed to models). This builds on Hendry (1988), Favero and Hendry (1992) and Boland (1989), using encompassing to exploit mutual contradictions between theories each of which claims invariance to changes in non-modelled processes. Since some parameters can be changed, yet others remain constant, we believe that the resulting empirical models go well beyond mere tools whose realism is irrelevant.

Steven Cook and David F. Hendry
Institute of Economics and Statistics and
Nuffield College
Oxford OX1 1NF
United Kingdom

REFERENCES

Aldrich, J. (1989). Autonomy. *Oxford Economic Papers*, **41**, 15-34.

Aldrich, J. (1992). Explaining the Findings of Other Models' – On Encompassing and the Encompassing Principle. Mimeo, Southampton University.

Baba, Y., Hendry, D.F. and Starr, R.M. (1992). The Demand for M1 in the USA, 1960-1988. *Review of Economic Studies*, **59**, 25-61.

Banerjee, A., Dolado, J.J., Galbraith, J.W. and Hendry, D.F. (1993). *Co-integration, Error Correction and the Econometric Analysis of Non-Stationary Data*. Oxford: Oxford University Press.

Boland, L. (1989). *The Methodology of Economic Model Building*. London: Routledge.

Cartwright, N. (1983). *How the Laws of Physics Lie*. Oxford: Clarendon Press.

Cartwright, N. (1989). *Nature's Capacities and their Measurement*. Oxford: Clarendon Press.

Clements, M.P. and Hendry, D.F. (1993). Towards a Theory of Economic Forecasting. Forthcoming in: C. Hargreaves (Ed.), *Non-stationary Time Series Analyses and Cointegration*. Oxford: Oxford University Press.

Dickey, D.A. and Fuller, W.A. (1979). Distribution of the Estimators for Autoregressive Time Series with a Unit Root. *Journal of American Statistical Association*, **74**, 427-431.

Diskey, D.A. and Fuller, W.A. (1981). Likelihood Ratio Statistics for Autoregressive Time Series with a Unit Root. *Econometrica*, **49**, 1057-1072.

Engle, R.F. and Granger, C.W.J. (1987). Co-Integration and Error Correction: Representation, Estimation and Testing. *Econometrica*, **55**, 251-276.

Engle, R.F. and Hendry, D.F. (1993). Testing Super Exogeneity and Invariance in Regression Models. *Journal of Econometrics*, **56**, 119-139.

Engle, R.F., Hendry, D.F. and Richard, J-F. (1983). Exogeneity. *Econometrica*, **51**, 2, 277-304.

Ericsson, N.R., Campos, J. and Tran, H-A. (1990). PC-GIVE and David Hendry's Econometric Methodology. *Revista De Econometria*, **10**, 7-117.

Ermini, L. and Hendry, D.F. (1991). Log Income *versus* Linear Income: An Application of the Encompassing Principle. Mimeo, University of Hawaii at Manoa.

Favero, C. and Hendry, D.F. (1992). Testing the Lucas Critique: A Review. *Econometric Reviews*, **11**, 256-306.

Fisher, R.A. (1922). On the Mathematical Foundations of Theoretical Statistics, *Philosophical Transactions of the Royal Society*. A, **222**, 209-368.

Florens, J-P., Mouchart, M. and Rolin, J-M. (1990). *Elements of Bayesian Statistics*. New York: Marcel Dekker.

Frisch, R. (1938). Statistical versus Theoretical Relations in Economic Macrodynamics. Mimeo University of Oslo.

Gilbert, C.L. (1986). Professor Hendry's Econometric Methodology. *Oxford Bulletin of Economics and Statistics*, **48**, 283-307. Reprinted as Chapter 13 in: C.W.J. Granger (Ed.), *Modelling Economic Series: Readings in Econometric Methodology*. Oxford: Oxford University Press.

Granger, C.W.J. (1969). Investigating Causal Relations by Econometric Models and Cross-Spectral Methods. *Econometrica*, **37**, 424-438.

Granger, C.W.J. and Newbold, P. (1974). Spurious Regressions in Econometrics, *Journal of Econometrics*, **2**, 111-120.

Haavelmo, T. (1944). The Probability Approach in Econometrics. Supplement to *Econometrica*, Vol. 12.

Hendry, D.F. (1977). On the Time-series Approach to Econometric Model Building. In: C.A. Sims (Ed.), *New Methods in Business Cycle Research*, Minnesota: Federal Reserve Bank of Minneapolis, pp. 183-202.

Hendry, D.F. (1979). Predictive Failure and Econometric Modelling in Macroeconomics: The Transactions Demand for Money, Chapter 9 in: P. Ormerod (Ed.), *Economic Modelling*. London, Heinemann Education Books, pp. 217-242.

Hendry, D.F. (1980). Econometrics: Alchemy or Science? *Economica*, **47**, 387-406.

Hendry, D.F. (1986). On the Credibility of Econometric Evidence. Walras-Bowley Lecture, 1986 Meeting of the North American Econometric Society.

Hendry, D.F. (1987). Econometric Methodology: A Personal Perspective. Ch. 10 in: T.F. Bewley (Ed.), *Advances in Econometrics*. Cambridge: Cambridge University Press.

Hendry, D.F. (1988). The Encompassing Implications of Feedback versus Feedforward Mechanisms in Econometrics. *Oxford Economic Papers*, **40**, 132-149.

Hendry, D.F. (1992). Assessing Empirical Evidence in Macro-econometrics with an Application to Consumers' Expenditure in France. In: A. Vercelli and N. Dimitri (Eds.), *Macroeconomics: A Survey of Research Strategies*, 363-392. Oxford: Oxford University Press.

Hendry, D.F. (1993). *Dynamic Econometrics*. Oxford: Oxford University Press.

Hendry, D.F., Leamer, E.E. and Poirier, D.J. (1990). A Conversation on Econometric Methodology. *Econometric Theory*, **6**, 171-261.

Hendry, D.F. and Mizon, G.E. (1978). Serial Correlation as a Convenient Simplification Not a Nuisance: A Comment on a Study of the Demand for Money by the Bank of England. *Economic Journal*, **88**, 549-563.

Hendry, D.F. and Mizon, G.E. (1993). Evaluating Dynamic Econometric Models by Encompassing the VAR. In P.C.B. Phillips (Ed.), *Models, Methods and Applications of Econometrics*. London: Basil Blackwell, pp. 272-300.

Hendry, D.F. and Richard, J-F. (1982). On the Formulation of Empirical Models in Dynamic Econometrics. *Journal of Econometrics*, **20**, 3-33.

Hendry, D.F. and Richard, J-F. (1983). The Econometric Analysis of Economic Time Series. *International Statistical Review*, **51**, 111-163.

Hendry, D.F. and Richard, J-F. (1989). Recent Developments in the Theory of Encompassing. In: Cornet, B. and Tulkens, H. (Eds.), *Contributions to Operations Research and Econometrics. The XXth Anniversary of CORE*. Cambridge, Mass.: M.I.T. Press, 393-440.

Hendry, D.F., Spanos, A. and Ericsson, N.R. (1989). The Contributions to Econometrics in Trygve Haavelmo's 'The Probability Approach in Econometrics'. *Sosialokonomen*, **11**, 12-17.

Hendry, D.F. and Starr R.M. (1993). The Demand for M1 in the USA: A Reply to James M. Boughton. *Economic Journal*, **103**, 1158-1169.

Hendry, D.F. and Trivedi, P.K. (1972). Maximum Likelihood Estimation of Difference Equations with Moving Average Errors. *Review of Economic Studies*, **39**, 117-145.

Herschel, J. (1830). *A Preliminary Discourse on the Study of Natural Philosophy*. London: Longman & Partners.

Hood, Wm.C. and Koopmans, T.C. (Eds.) (1953). *Studies in Econometric Method*. Cowles Commission Monograph 14. New York: John Wiley.

Koopmans, T.C. (Ed.) (1950). *Statistical Inference in Dynamic Economic Models*. Cowles Commission Monograph 10. New York: John Wiley.

Lakatos, I. (1974). Falsification and the Methodology of Scientific Research Programmes. In: Lakatos, I. and Musgrave, A. (Eds.), *Criticism and the Growth of Knowledge*. Cambridge: Cambridge University Press, pp. 91-196.

Losee, J. (1980). *A Historical Introduction to the Philosophy of Science*. Oxford: Oxford University Press.

Lucas, R.E. (1976). Econometric policy evaluation: a critique. In: Brunner, K. and Meltzer, A.H. (Eds.), *The Phillips Curve and Labor Markets*. Amsterdam: North-Holland (Carnegie-Rochester Conference Series on Public Policy, vol. 1), pp. 19-36.

Mason, S.F. (1962). *A History of The Sciences*. New York: Collier Books.

Mizon, G.E. (1984). The Encompassing Approach in Econometrics. In: Hendry, D.F. and Wallis, K.F. (Eds.), *Econometrics and Quantitative Economics*. Oxford: Basil Blackwell, pp. 135-172.

Mizon, G.E. (1993). Empirical Analysis of Time Series: Illustrations with Simulated Data. In: de Zeeuw, A. (Ed.), *Advanced Lectures in Quantitative Economics*, **II**. New York: Academic Press.

Mizon, G.E. and Hendry, D.F. (1980). An Empirical Application and Monte Carlo Analysis of Tests of Dynamic Specification. *Review of Economic Studies*, **47**, 21-45.

Mizon, G.E. and Richard, J-F. (1986). The Encompassing Principle and its Application to Testing Non-Nested Hypotheses. *Econometrica*, **57**, 657-678.

Pagan, A.R. (1987). Three Econometric Methodologies: A Critical Appraisal. *Journal of Economic Surveys*, **1**, 3-24. Reprinted as Chapter 6 in C.W.J. Granger (Ed.), *Modelling Economic Series: Readings in Econometric Methodology*. Oxford: Oxford University Press.

Phillips, P.C.B. (1991). Optimal Inference in Cointegrated Systems. *Econometrica*, **59**, 283-306.

Popper, K. (1959). *The Logic of Scientific Discovery*. New York: Basic Books.

Popper, K. (1963). *Conjectures and Refutations*. New York: Basic Books.

Sargan, J.D. (1980). Some Tests of Dynamic Specification for a Single Equation. *Econometrica*, **48**, 879-897.

Schumpeter, J. (1933). The Common Sense of Econometrics. *Econometrica*, **1**, 5-12.

Sims, C.A. (1972). Money, Income and Causality. *American Economic Review*, **62**, 540-552.

Sims, C.A., Stock, J.H. and Watson, M.W. (1990). Inference in Linear Time Series with some Unit Roots. *Econometrica*, **58**, 1035-1056.

Spanos, A. (1986). *Statistical Foundations of Econometric Modelling*. Cambridge: Cambridge University Press.

Wold, H.O. (1969). Econometrics as Pioneering in Non-experimental Model Building. *Econometrica*, **37**, 369-381.

Yule, G.U. (1926). Why do we sometimes get nonsense-correlations between time-series? A study in sampling and the nature of time series. *Journal of the Royal Statistical Society*, **89**, 1-64.

Poznań Studies in the Philosophy of the Sciences and the Humanities
1994, Vol. 38, pp. 101-116

Maarten C.W. Janssen[1]

ECONOMIC MODELS AND THEIR APPLICATIONS

ABSTRACT. Discussion of idealization and concretization in economics. Fully concretized economic models are claimed to be principally beyond reach. Observed phenomena can, however, be explained on the basis of tendency laws, provided that the assumptions made in those models are consistent with the information we have about the economy or, if not, that replacing these assumptions by others that are consistent with our information should not make a significant difference for the results of the analysis under investigation.

At first economic textbooks might give the non-economist the impression that economic models are fairly complicated. Advanced mathematical techniques are commonly employed in the profession. For those who cannot resist a closer look, the impression of having to do with the most advanced of all social sciences might quickly make room for dissatisfaction, however. Economic models turn out to examine the interrelationships between only a very limited number of variables. From this perspective, a central task for further research seems to be to make economic models even more complicated by introducing variables which probably also have an influence on the question that is studied. Indeed, Nowak's model of scientific development is in this line. Roughly speaking, Nowak (1980) argues that the sciences start with simple models that abstract (Nowak uses the term *idealize*) from counteracting forces. Subsequent steps involve introducing more and more realistic assumptions that replace the abstractions one has started with. Nowak employs the term *concretization* for replacing *idealizational statements* by conditions that obtain in nature. When all idealizational statements are removed a fully concretized model is obtained.

It is beyond dispute that *if* it is reasonable to expect that fully concretized economic models could be obtained within the not too distant future, considerable research efforts should be devoted to this

[1] The author thanks Paul Dumouchel, Dan Hausman, David Hendry, Theo Kuipers, Philippe Mongin, Robert Nadeau and Jacques Vromen and participants to the Tilburg conference and the seminar in Applied Epistemology in Université de Québec à Montréal (April 1992) for raising substantial questions and for making valuable suggestions.

end. However, it is not difficult to find throughout the history of economic thought leading economists who have expressed their doubts about whether we can ever expect to have fully concretized models at our disposal. I mention John Stuart Mill's notion of *tendency laws* and his discussion of economics as an inexact science (see Mill 1836, 1843; for a clear discussion of the relevance of Mill's philosophy of economics for current discussions on the status of economic theory the reader is referred to Hausman 1981, 1992), John Maynard Keynes's rejection of the econometric method for the reason that we do not know all the relevant factors in advance (Keynes 1939); and the failure of econometrics over the past sixty years to provide the profession with stable relationships. For a more detailed argumentation that supports these doubts (and for the differences between Mill and Keynes in this respect) the reader is referred to section 3 below. In line with these doubts is the view that economists should not (primarily) strive for concretizing existing models (or tendency laws). Instead, research efforts should (also) be spent on developing more and more separate *tendency laws*. This is very much in the spirit of Elster (1989) who uses the term *mechanisms* instead of tendency laws.

Here, I take the view that although we might attempt to get more concretized models, fully concretized models will be beyond reach. One can even argue that it is a characteristic of a *model* that it always abstracts from certain entities that conceivably have an impact on the problem under examination (cf., Gibbard and Varian 1978). However abstract economic models may be, it is a fact that they are used in many applications. It is thus important to understand what assumptions are implicitly made when economic models are applied to particular situations. Two sorts of applications will be focused upon. Firstly, can economic models aid in constructing explanations for observed economic phenomena and, secondly, can economic models help us predict the future course of events?

The discussion is organized as follows. Section 1 presents a simple example that will be used throughout the paper to clarify some of the issues. Sections 2 and 3 will deal with issues concerning explanation and prediction, respectively. In the concluding section some related observations are made.

1. A very simple example

To clarify the issues which the present paper focuses upon it will be convenient to start with a simple example. The price of tomatoes (*PT*) in most West European countries in June 1991 was higher than usual for the time of the year.[2] The curious mind might like to have an answer to the question why this was the case. The answer that uniformly has been given is that the high price was due to the bad weather (*BW*) in the spring. At this point it is interesting to observe that although some abstractions seem to be involved in this story, nobody would question the "facts" that the weather in the spring of 1991 was worse than usual and that the price of tomatoes was higher than usual. The concept of "the price of tomatoes in West Europe in June 1991" abstracts from particular cities, places (market place, supermarket) and time periods. In the same way, "bad weather in the spring" abstracts from specific numbers for hours of sunshine and rain on particular days. Those abstractions seem to be unproblematic, however. Thus, the explanation given so far does not seem to involve questionable abstractions.

The above explanation is, however, incomplete unless a mechanism is specified that shows how *BW* leads to a high *PT*. At this point an economist has a large variety of options at his disposal. For example, he might say that the market for tomatoes can be described by a standard textbook model of perfect competition with an upward sloping supply curve and a downward sloping demand curve. *BW* causes the supply curve of tomatoes to shift to the north-west. Assuming that the market for tomatoes usually (and also this year) is in equilibrium, it is easily seen that this year's *PT* is higher than usual.

I think the above is *a* (not necessarily *the*) satisfactory explanation. From the perspective sketched in the introduction to this paper, it is interesting to see what kind of abstractions are involved and whether a more satisfactory explanation (or a better prediction) is given when the textbook model is concretized in some way or another. It is to these subjects that I now turn.

2. Two Types of Abstractions in Economic Explanations

The explanation for a high *PT* that is given above consists of two parts. First, it has been noted that a high *PT* might be explained by *BW*, i.e., one out of many possible[3] causal factors is chosen to explain the phenomenon

---

[2] A similar example has been studied by Hausman (1989). Many of the points I will make are related to that paper. The difference is mainly in emphasis: Hausman analyzes when certain *ceteris paribus* assumptions can be legitimately made; I am more concerned with what kind of assumptions are made when theoretical models are applied in order to give explanations and/or predictions.

[3] Mäki (1991) uses the term isolation when only a limited number of variables is explicitly taken into consideration.

under consideration (cf., Hausman 1990, pp. 170-2, on the way economists deal with the notion of causality). Second, one out of many possible mechanisms is chosen to indicate how the factor might have had an influence on the phenomenon to be explained. In the rest of this section I will discuss what kind of abstractions are involved in the two parts of the given explanation.

To begin with I take up the question whether the *mechanism* that is given abstracts from certain aspects. One has to distinguish between two cases. First, the mechanism can be *contrary to fact*, i.e., it makes assumptions that contradict the knowledge we have of the situation under discussion. Second, the mechanism might be consistent with everything we know about the situation, although due to *incompleteness* of our *knowledge* about the economy we do not know whether it is the mechanism that really governs the situation. I think it is important to distinguish between these two cases. For example, Friedman's (1953) plea for *as if* reasoning is often interpreted in a contrary-to-fact fashion, but as Hirsch and de Marchi (1990) make clear the methods Friedman uses in his positive economics fit better with an incomplete-knowledge interpretation. If Friedman's positive economics is in line with his *as if* methodology, one can argue that his methodology should also be interpreted in terms of incomplete knowledge.[4]

Let us focus the discussion by taking the example of the previous section under consideration. One of the important issues is whether in the mechanism that is provided perfect competition is assumed, and if so whether it is contrary to fact. Economists say that a market is perfectly competitive if three mechanisms (firms maximize profits, households maximize utility, and prices equate demand and supply) and two conditions (there is a very large number of firms and households, there are no transaction costs) hold. The assumption of perfect competition together with the assumptions of an upward sloping supply curve and a downward sloping demand curve is *sufficient* to show that *BW* leads to a high *PT*. The important issue then is whether somebody who questions the given explanation, for example, by arguing that there are many, but *certainly not very* many, suppliers on the market for tomatoes really makes a strong point. I doubt it. Surely, the assumption of very many suppliers is contrary to fact, but the point is that this assumption is part of a sufficient condition for the explanation to hold and is itself far from

---

[4] See also Janssen and Tan (1991). I do not claim that Friedman is right in arguing that in economics we have very little information. One can question his view that the only information we have is contained in objective data. A discussion of this issue would lead us far beyond the scope of the present paper.

being a necessary condition.[5] One could retain the same model with the alternative interpretation that suppliers just take prices as given because they don't bother to calculate the impact of their quantity decision on the market price. And this is just one of the many possible reinterpretations of the same mathematical model. It is likely that one of those reinterpretations is not contrary to fact, but instead compatible with everything we know about the economy. Thus, one line of defense for the given mechanism is to argue that an interpretation can be given that is compatible with our incomplete knowledge of the economy.[6]

A second line along which the given mechanism can be defended is the following. An economist who supports the perfectly competitive model might even grant that in the particular situation an oligopoly model is closer to "the-whole-truth". If there are many suppliers, each of them has some (small) impact on prices. One of following two cases then prevails. First, if the oligopoly model also yields the result that *BW* leads to a high *PT*, then one can argue that the fact that there is only a finite number of suppliers is apparently not essential for the relation between *BW* and *PT*. Therefore, one has good reasons to work with the simpler model, namely the perfectly competitive one. Second, if the oligopoly model does not yield the result that *BW* leads to a high *PT*, then it clearly cannot be the mechanism that relates the two variables. This argument depends on the fact that we have observed a high *PT* and that *BW* is the cause of this phenomenon (see below).

Two questions then naturally arise: (*i*) why is one interested at all in a hypothesized mechanism between *BW* and *PT* if the argument in support of a particular mechanism depends to a large extent on the empirical regularity between *BW* and *PT* itself and (*ii*) when should one be willing to look for alternative mechanisms (for example, mechanisms that are not based on the assumption of perfect competition). The first question comes down to the question why we need models (or theories) over and above empirical regularities. A first reason might be that good theories and models provide ideas for new empirical regularities. A second reason is that in economics there are hardly any empirical regularities that hold unconditionally. Theories and models can then be used to analyze (some of) the conditions under which the empirical regularities hold. This argument is further developed in Janssen (1993).

---

[5] Note that the distinction between necessary and sufficient conditions is also crucial to Boland's defense of Milton Friedman's methodology (see, Boland 1979).

[6] Of course, it is important to note that in the above example the proposed mechanism fits very well into the body of received theory. This is the major reason why one might want to defend the proposed mechanism after all.

The above discussion suggests two reasons to give up the mechanism (explanation) that is based on the perfectly competitive model: (*a*) if the model would have yielded the result that *BW* leads to a fall in *PT*, (*b*) if the model on which the resulting positive relation between *BW* and *PT* is based relies heavily on contrary-to-fact assumptions. By the latter I mean that the mechanism based on the perfectly competitive model can be retained if it is possible to give an interpretation of the model that is consistent with the available knowledge and if it is clear that bringing in more realistic elements does not destroy the positive relation between *BW* and *PT*.

The above discussion on the question whether the mechanism is based on questionable abstractions hinges crucially on the assumption that *BW* really is a cause of a high *PT*, i.e., *BW* is a proper explanation for a high *PT*. In the beginning of this section I have said that abstractions might also be involved at the level of causal factors. Here, I will turn to the question whether the given explanation abstracts from reality because it does not take other possible causal factors into account.

It is important to distinguish at least four possible interpretations of the statement "a high *PT* is explained by *BW*":

(*a*) There are no other factors that influence *PT*.

(*b*) There are other factors that influence *PT*, but those other factors take on their "usual" values.

(*c*) There are other factors and they need not take on their "usual" values in this particular case, but whenever *BW* is present, *PT* is high, i.e., *BW* dominates all other factors: $\forall t(BW(t) \rightarrow \text{high } PT(t))$, where t stands for the time period.

(*d*) There are indeed other factors and they also have an impact in this particular case and, in general, they could have been such that *PT* was low even though *BW* was present. This view is consistent with the idea that there is only a tendency for *BW* to yield a high *PT*.[7]

When economists say that a high *PT* is explained by *BW*, the statement should be interpreted in the fourth way distinguished here. What is important is that *BW* and *PT* are indeed present and that the quantitative effect on *PT* is in line with our (intuitive) knowledge of the relation

[7] A formalization of the notion of a tendency law, using non-standard logic, is given in Janssen and Tan (1992).

between *PT* and the severity of *BW*.[8] Thus, the explanation does not deny that other factors might also have had an impact on *PT* and in this sense, the explanation does not really abstract (at least not in a questionable way) from other causal factors. However, as the quantitative effect on *PT* is in accordance with our knowledge, the overall impact of the other factors should be negligible. (Of course, this might be the case for more than one factor. The fact that in many instances different economists come up with different explanations is due to the type of problem I am alluding to. The example treated in section 1, however, does not seem to be flawed by this ambiguity. The fact that nobody questions the given explanation is due to two facts: (*i*) the extent to which *PT* was higher than usual is in line with our intuition about the size of the impact of *BW* and (*ii*) there are no other factors for which this is the case).

Let us be more specific and consider that apart from the weather this year's income has also been unlike income over the past years. Furthermore, suppose that we know that there is a tendency for high levels of income to yield a high *PT*. Both a high level and a low level of income can easily be captured by the explanation given in section 1. A high level of income is not a problem, because it strengthens the tendency of *BW*: if the increase in income is small, our intuitive quantitative knowledge can be used to restrict the important causal factors to *BW*; if the increase in income is large, we can mention both *BW* and the increase in income among the causes of a high *PT* (compare the observations above on the multiplicity of possible explanations). A relatively low level of income can also be easily accommodated for *as far as explanation* is concerned. We can*not* call the low level of income the cause of a high *PT*, because we know that low income levels have a tendency to yield a low *PT*, *while a high PT was actually observed. BW* seems to be the only sensible explanation in this case. From the perspective of Nowak's model sketched in the introduction of this paper it is important to note that the possibility to give this explanation does *not* depend in any way on whether or not we have a concretized statement (as for example $PT = \alpha_0 + \alpha_1 I + \alpha_2 W$, where *I* stands for income and *W* for the weather measured in, say, days of sunshine) at our disposal. In the next section we will see that when we are concerned with prediction we do need concretized statements in cases in which two

---

8 In this paper I am primarily concerned with qualitative aspects of explanation and prediction. Of course, quantitative aspects also have a role to play. For example, given our knowledge that small changes in the weather have a small impact on *PT*, we cannot explain a big increase in *PT* by pointing at *BW*, if we know that the weather has only been a little worse than usual.

tendency laws have contradictory implications. I will argue that concretization requires quantification and that relatively stable quantitative relationships have not (yet) been obtained in economics (see also Klant 1984).

3. Some Remarks on Prediction

In the deductive-nomological model (or covering law model) explanation and prediction are dealt with in a symmetric way: whenever we can explain certain regularities or phenomena we can also predict them. In the treatment of explanation in the previous section, I have implicitly criticized the DN-model.[9] The instantiation of the DN model is presented under (*c*) of the previous section. If we would know this law to be true, then a separate treatment of the issue of prediction would be superfluous. However, I have argued that the explanation of a high *PT* is based on a tendency law (case *d*), *not* on a covering law (case *c*). Also, I have argued that the validity of the given explanation depends crucially on the fact that we already know that *PT* is high. When it comes to predicting the future we do not have this knowledge. Thus, a separate treatment of prediction is justified (cf., Cartwright 1983 on the asymmetry between explanation and prediction). Here, prediction is understood in the limited sense of forecasting the future. No account is given of ex-post prediction.

In this section I want to concentrate on two questions. First, can we predict on the basis of tendency laws only? Second, does concretization in the sense of Nowak help to make predictions in economics more accurate? The answer one might give to these questions depend, of course, on one's view on prediction. At least three different meanings of the term "prediction" can be distinguished:

(*i*) Any proposition about a future event can be regarded as a prediction. This interpretation should not bother us here. One can make a proposition about a future event without having any reason to believe that the proposition will turn out to be true, i.e., no tendency law is needed to make a prediction in this sense.

(*ii*) A prediction is a proposition about a future event which, if not true, refutes the model on which the proposition is based. This interpretation of "prediction" is too strong, in my view. It is based on the presumption that we should have a covering law at our disposal in order

[9] This is not the place to dwell upon the DN model. For some points of critique, see, e.g., Cartwright (1983) and Janssen and Tan (1991).

to predict. As covering laws are not (yet) discovered in economics, economists are not able to make predictions on this account. In particular, this account of prediction is too strong, because it neglects the fact that there are always unforeseen factors which may make the prediction become false.

(*iii*) A prediction is a proposition about a future event which, if not true, should give rise to a search for an explanation why the prediction has failed. According to this view, an unconditional prediction is an informed guess about the future state of the world.[10] As far as *scientific* issues are concerned, prediction does not deserve special attention. What is most important is that an explanation can be given why the prediction has failed.[11] In most cases such an explanation takes the form of pointing at a causal factor that has not been taken into account and a tendency law that counteracts the tendency law on which the prediction has been based.

From the above it will be clear that the answer to the first question is affirmative provided that we interpret the term "prediction" in the third way distinguished above and that we acknowledge that our predictions need not become true. From a *policy* perspective, however, it is important to know under what conditions one is able to make an "informed prediction" on the basis of a "tendency law". In the context of the tomatoes example, I want to mention two conditions. First, *BW* does not influence other factors that have a (significant) negative impact on *PT*. Second, no information about the presence of (significant) counteracting forces is available, i.e., there is no knowledge that the *ceteris paribus* condition is violated in an important way. I will argue that we can predict a high *PT* on the basis of the observed *BW* only if those conditions are met.

The first condition is in line with a condition that is frequently imposed in econometrics, namely that for a regression equation of the form $PT = \alpha_0 + \alpha_1 BW + \varepsilon$, ε is independent of *BW*. If in such a regression equation ε is interpreted as a short-hand notation for the impact of other variables, the similarity between the independence condition and the first condition imposed above becomes clear (see also Cartwright 1989 and Hoover 1990). If this condition fails to hold one of the following two situations prevails:

---

[10] I do not discuss a fourth meaning of the term "prediction" according to which a prediction is the "best" guess we can make about the future state of the world on the basis of the available information. As long as there is no agreement on how one should decide what is "best", this interpretation of the term "prediction" remains unclear.

[11] This is what Hausman (1981, pp. 373) calls the condition of excusability.

where Z is an arbitrary variable. If income I is substituted for Z the second of the two situations might be relevant (especially in an agricultural society). If the taste of tomatoes is substituted for Z the first situation might prevail (through a fall in the demand for tomatoes). Of course, knowledge of quantitative magnitudes is also relevant in this case. If we know that the impact of BW on Z and the impact of Z on PT are both much smaller than the direct impact of BW on Z, we are able to predict that PT will rise when BW has been observed. Thus, the above qualitative comments hold only in so far as factors that have a major impact are concerned.

I can be brief as regards the second condition alluded to above. First, it is important to note that a prediction is conditional on the available information at the time the prediction is made and as long as there is *no information* of other significant forces we cannot but predict on the basis of a tendency law (which is not to say that the prediction will necessarily turn out to be true). Second, if we do have information about the presence of other factors one of the following two situations is relevant (where there is no connection between Z and BW):

The second of these situations obviously does not make an informed prediction of an increase in PT impossible. If Z has a significant impact on PT and the first of the situations above prevails, it will be impossible to predict whether PT will increase or decrease when we know that the weather is bad.

If the two conditions are not satisfied and we do want to make an informed prediction, knowledge of some tendency laws is clearly insufficient. In the rest of this section I will discuss whether concretizing (in Nowak's sense) tendency laws helps to make informed predictions possible. Recall why concretization is worth considering. If one of the conditions is not met we have several tendency laws at our disposal which have contradictory implications. Suppose that in the spring of a certain year the weather has been bad and that income has also been low; the first cause having a tendency for *PT* to increase, the second one having a tendency for *PT* to decrease. In this case it is impossible to give an informed prediction of what *PT* will be. If we would have a more general relationship[12] expressing how the weather and income offset each other an informed prediction would be possible to provide. Such a relationship could be expressed in a concretized statement of the form $PT = \alpha_0 + \alpha_1 I + \alpha_2 W + \varepsilon$ (see also the previous section). This relationship can be considered a concretization of $PT = \alpha'_0 + \alpha'_1 I + \varepsilon_1$ as well as of $PT = \alpha''_0 + \alpha'_2 W + \varepsilon_2$. The important thing to note is that in cases that a concretization is called for it reguires quantification. I do not want to go too deeply into econometric issues here, but some observations need to be made.

The main question involved is that of the stability of parameters in econom(etr)ics: Does any factor that influences a certain variable has its own invariable strength or does the strength with which a certain variable carries out its influence depends on the specific circumstances? The issue is relevant because $PT = \alpha_0 + \alpha_1 I + \alpha_2 W + \varepsilon$ can be considered a concretization of $PT = \alpha'_0 + \alpha'_1 I + \varepsilon_1$ if and only if the second equation can be obtained from the first by putting α_2 equal to 0. The point is, of course, that we do not know the values of the parameters so that they have to be estimated by means of available data. Now, the estimators of α_1 and α'_1, denoted by respectively $\hat{\alpha}_1$ and $\hat{\alpha}'_1$, are equal to each other if and only if the variables *I* and *W* are uncorrelated. But this is very much like the first condition mentioned above. So, we arrive at the following situation: if *W* has a (significant) negative influence on *I*, we cannot make an informed prediction on the basis of the tendency for *BW* to yield a high *PT* and a concretization might have been useful, but in this case $PT = \alpha_0 + \alpha_1 I + \alpha_2 W + \varepsilon$ cannot be considered as a concretization of $PT = \alpha'_0 + \alpha'_1 I + \varepsilon_1$ because we do not know the values of α_1 and α'_1 and $\hat{\alpha}_1$ will not equal $\hat{\alpha}'_1$ due to the correlation between *I* and *W*.

One might argue[13] that the above argument only shows that the *particular type* of concretization considered is mistaken, not that concretization as such is less appropriate. The particular type of concretization portrays *W* and *I* as independent variables, whereas in fact, the latter

[12] Such a relationship would also be a tendency law (because still other factors are left out of consideration). To distinguish it from the simple tendency laws it could be called a compound tendency law. I have avoided the introduction of this terminology in order not to coin with new terms.

[13] Dan Hausman pointed this out to me in correspondence.

depends on the former. To do justice to this dependency, the concretization of $PT = \alpha_0 + \alpha_2 W$ should be a model of the following kind:

$$\begin{cases} PT = \alpha_0 + \alpha_1 I + \alpha_2 W + \varepsilon \\ I \quad = \beta_1 W + \nu, \end{cases}$$

where ν is also a disturbance term. Two remarks are then in order. First, Nowak's model of concretization should allow for the possibility of concretization by means of adding equations, not only by means of adding variables to *one* equation. Second, due to problems related to observational equivalence (see, e.g., Hoover 1990) there is a natural limit to the idea of concretization by means of adding equations.

In a world in which every causal factor has its own stable influence which is independent of the presence or absence of other factors, econometrics is of great use to uncover the unknown parameters (the strength with which a causal factor exerts its influence). In such a world concretization in the sense of Nowak would also be a useful method to make better predictions. Unfortunately, we seem to live in another kind of world: econometric applications themselves have revealed that for the relationships used thus far parameters have not been stable from one situation to another.[14] The fact that in economics we have not (yet) obtained relatively stable quantitative relationships is probably also the major reason why we do not find values of parameters in textbooks. In any particular situation there are many tendencies at work and the way they simultaneously produce a specific result have not yet been uncovered. Also, any situation is atypical because of the particular combination of tendencies present. In such a world, there is not much scope for concretizing tendency laws.

Here, it is useful to make some remarks on a difference between John Maynard Keynes and John Stuart Mill, which is related to the points made above. In Mill's view each tendency law specifies the (hypothetical) effect of one cause. In order to apply tendency laws, they have to be compounded. The compounding of tendency laws is, according to Mill, very much like the addition of forces in mechanics: each and every factor (cause) has its own force with which it operates. Underlying this idea is that tendencies are stable, or, in the terminology of econometrics, that there are constant parameters associated with a tendency law (cf., Mill 1967, pp. 330-1). Keynes, on the other hand, believed that the strength

---

[14] One of the reasons why I have mainly be concerned with qualitative aspects is precisely this: that we have not (yet) discovered stable parameters.

with which a particular factor operates depends on the context. In such a world, there would not exist constant parameters, which can be uncovered by econometric techniques. Whoever may be right on this point (this is a metaphysical question which we will not even try to answer here), fact is that economists have not found stable patterns between different variables.

4. Conclusions and Final Observations

In the above I have criticized the relevance of Nowak's model of idealization and concretization for economics. I have not argued that concretization is not something to be wished for, but instead that fully concretized models are far beyond reach. If this is granted it is important to understand what kind of applications we can legitimately make with existing (idealized) economic models. This is what I have focused upon in this paper. First, I have argued that we can *explain* observed phenomena on the basis of tendency laws and I have explored what kind of assumptions are implicitly made in such explanations. The most important observations in this respect have been that the assumptions made in economic models should be such that they are either consistent with the information we have about the economy or, if not, that replacing these assumptions by others that are consistent with our information should not make a significant difference for the results of the analysis under investigation. Second, I have considered two conditions that should be met in order to be able to make an informed prediction on the basis of "tendency laws": (*i*) the causal factor should not have an influence on other factors that have a (significant) negative impact on *PT*; (*ii*) information about the presence of (significant) counteracting forces should not be available. I have also considered the question whether concretizing the tendency laws helps to make informed predictions if those conditions are not met. The answer was predominantly negative, because concretization goes hand in hand with quantification and stable quantitative relationships have not (yet) been obtained in economics.

Looking at some textbooks, especially in macroeconomics in the sixties and seventies, might give the appearance that Nowak's model of idealization and subsequent concretization is more important in economics than I have admitted. But appearances can be deceptive. What one might have in mind here is the method of decreasing abstraction that is used in these macroeconomic textbooks. This is exemplified by expressions for multipliers that become more and more complicated as investment, import and export and taxes are included in the basic Keynesian multiplier model: $1/(1-\gamma)$, $1/(1-\gamma-\iota)$, $1/(1-\gamma-\iota+\mu)$, $1/(1-[\gamma+\iota][1-\tau]+\mu)$.[15] The objection I have against this procedure is the following. The implicit presumption behind the method of decreasing abstraction is that the steps that are taken subsequently bring in all the factors that are important to understand the performance of the economy as a whole. However, one does not provide any reason for why this should be so. First, it is not at all clear that the factors that are mentioned are that important after all, second, it is also not made clear how good the final model is in explaining the performance of some economies and, third, are all the important factors really included in the model? In short, unless good empirical reasons are provided, I do not see that it is a great scientific achievement to complicate multipliers in the way that is briefly described above.

Fortunately, recent journal articles that try to explain certain phenomena do not build large models. Articles try to make a specific point and a model is constructed to illustrate the point. Rasmussen (1989) is very explicit on this. Somewhat provocatively, he says

> Along with a trend towards primitive assumptions and maximizing behavior has been a trend towards simplicity, which I call "no-fat modelling". No-fat modelling is an extension of Ocham's razor and the *ceteris paribus* assumptions so fundamental to economics or, indeed, to any kind of analysis. The heart of the approach is to discover the simplest assumptions to generate an interesting conclusion: the starkest, barest, model that has the desired result. This desired result is the answer to some narrow question. Could education be just a signal of ability? ... The modeller starts with a vague idea such as "People go to college to show they're smart." He then models the idea formally in a simple way. (pp. 14-15)

The comments I have made in this paper can be seen in the perspective of this trend towards simplicity.[16] Rasmussen's observations, however, need some qualifications, I think. As emphasized in section 2 above, the conclusion in the quotation from Rasmussen need to be a true statement about the real world (as the high *PT* in West Europe in June 1991). Also, the simplest assumptions need to be consistent with our information about the situation or, if they are not, should be replaceable by assumptions that are consistent with our information without modifying the conclusion in any significant way.

---

[15] For those readers who have not read one of those textbooks, γ is the marginal propensity to consume, ι is the marginal propensity to invest, μ is the marginal propensity to import and τ is the income tax rate. Those readers might want to consult, for example, Branson (1979).

[16] The quote from Rasmussen (1989) is taken from a textbook on game theory. Most of the comments I have made in previous sections also apply to models in this field.

Finally, I want to make a remark on the relation between perfect and imperfect competition (e.g., oligopoly). In section 2 I have said that even though oligopoly is closer to "the-whole-truth" one may stick to the perfectly competitive model as long as the conclusions drawn by means of such models are in line with the information we have about the economy. The question then arises why some economists adhere to the oligopoly model even in cases in which it yields the same conclusions in terms of observations as the perfectly competitive model. From the quotation taken from Rasmussen (1989), it should be clear that the simpler model, i.e., perfect competition, should be preferred. Is this then a sign that concretization of models is important in economics? I think not. Instead, I think it is just a sign that policy considerations play an important role. It is well-known that oligopoly models have inefficient equilibria, while perfectly competitive equilibria are Pareto-efficient. Accordingly, oligopoly models provide a scope for government intervention (cf., New Keynesian models). Oligopoly models are more realistic than perfect competition models to the extent that a finite number of firms is considered. However, in other respects they are as unrealistic as perfectly competitive models and it is thus too bold a statement to claim that oligopoly models are employed because of their realisticness.

Maarten C.W. Janssen
Faculteit der Economische Wetenschappen
Erasmus Universiteit Rotterdam
Postbus 1728
3000 DR Rotterdam

REFERENCES

Boland, L. (1979). A Critique of Friedman's Critics. *Journal of Economic Literature*, **17**, 503-22.

Branson, W. (1979). *Macroeconomic Theory and Policy* (*2nd edition*). New York: Harper and Row.

Cartwright, N. (1983). *How the Laws of Physics Lie*. Oxford: Oxford UP.

Cartwright, N. (1989). *Nature's Capacities and Their Measurement*. Oxford: Oxford University Press.

Elster, J. (1989). *Nuts and Bolts for the Social Sciences*. Cambridge: Cambridge University Press.

Friedman, M. (1953). The Methodology of Positive Economics. In: M. Friedman, *Essays in Positive Economics*. Chicago: Chicago University Press, pp. 3-43.

Gibbard, A. and H. Varian (1978). Economic Models. *Journal of Philosophy*, **75**, 664-677.

Hausman, D. (1981). John Stuart Mill's Philosophy of Economics. *Philosophy of Science*, **48**, 363-385.

Hausman, D. (1990). Supply and Demand Explanations and Their *ceteris paribus* Clauses. *Review of Political Economy*, **2**, 168-87.

Hausman, D. (1992). *The Inexact and Separate Science of Economics*. Cambridge: Cambridge University Press.

Hirsch, A. and N. De Marchi (1990). *Milton Friedman: Economics in Theory and Practice*. Hertfordshire: Harvester Wheatsheaf.

Hoover, K. (1990). The Logic of Causal Inference. *Economics and Philosophy*, **6**, 207-234.

Janssen, M.C.W. and Y.-H. Tan (1991). Why Friedman's non-Monotonic Logic Defies Hempel's Covering Law Model. *Synthese*, **86**, 255-284.

Janssen, M.C.W. and Y.-H. Tan (1992). Friedman's Theory of the Consumption Function as an Example of Diagnostic Reasoning. *Economics and Philosophy*, **8**, 23-49.

Janssen, M.C.W. (1993). *Microfoundations: a Critical Inquiry*. London: Routledge.

Keynes, J.M. (1939). Professor Tinbergen's Method. *Economic Journal*, **49**, 558-568.

Klant, J.J. (1984). *Rules of the Game*. Cambridge: Cambridge UP.

Mäki, U. (1992). On the Method of Isolation in Economics. In: C. Dilworth (Ed.), *Intelligibility in Science (Poznań Studies in the Philosophy of the Science and the Humanities*, **26**). Amsterdam: Rodopi, pp. 317-351.

Mill, J.S. (1836). On the Definition of Political Economy and the Method of Investigation
Proper to It. Reprinted in *Collected Works of John Stuart Mill, vol. IV*, Toronto: Toronto University Press (1967).

Mill, J.S. (1843) [1949]. *A System of Logic*. Reprint: London: Longmans.

Nowak, L. (1980). *The Structure of Idealization: Towards a Systematic Interpretation of the Marxian Idea of Science*. Dordrecht: Reidel.

Rasmussen, E. (1989). *Games and Information*. Oxford: Basic Blackwell.

Poznań Studies in the Philosophy of the Sciences and the Humanities
1994, Vol. 38, pp. 117-133

Adolfo García de la Sienra

IDEALIZATION AND EMPIRICAL ADEQUACY IN ECONOMIC THEORY*

ABSTRACT. The problem of idealization itself can be formulated thus: *Important economic theories are defined by axioms ("assumptions") that are clearly false of the objects they avowedly intend to theorize about.* Does this fact make of economic theories pseudo-sciences? Why? At any rate, what usefulness can such theories have to know economic phenomena? The aim of the present paper is to deal with these questions by means of a real-life example taken from economic theory (consumer choice). By means of this example Musgrave's threefold distinction between negligibility, domain, and heuristic assumptions is examined in a formal and detailed way. The problem of the usefulness of formal economic theory is approached through the idea of empirical relevance, understood in terms of statistical goodness of fit.

One of the most striking features of economic theories is their containing assumptions which look (and are in fact) false even to the layman. Isn't science concerned, after all, with the knowledge of real phenomena? And how could this knowledge be expressed, except through true propositions? Indeed, many philosophers of science have denied that science is at all concerned with the knowledge of real phenomena, claiming that it is rather concerned with "saving the appearances" or "predicting the facts", where "the appearences" or "the facts" are usually taken as being nothing but given families of collected data.

In the field of economics, this view has received its most elaborated formulation in the hands of Milton Friedman, in his 1953 article "The Methodology of Positive Economics", where he defended the seemingly preposterous view that to contain false assumptions is not a-vice but a virtue of economic theories:

* I am glad to acknowledge the useful remarks made by Bert Hamminga to an earlier version of this paper.

> Truly important and significant hypotheses will be found to have "assumptions" that are wildly inaccurate descriptive representations of reality, and, in general, the more significant the theory, the more unrealistic the assumptions (in this sense).[1]

In a discussion held at the American Economic Association many years ago,[2] Paul Samuelson labeled this view 'the F-Twist' and, trying to dissociate it from Friedman's name in the hope that it was a misinterpretation of the latter's intention, reformulated it in the following terms:

> A theory is vindicable if (some of) its consequences are empirically valid to a useful degree of approximation; the (empirical) unrealism of theory "itself", or of its "assumptions", is quite irrelevant to its validity and worth.[3]

The controversy sparked by Friedman's article is enormous and continues up to the present day (Caldwell's book is almost entirely devoted to it), but I just want here to take the F-twist, and the evaluation of the same made by Musgrave (1981), as a starting point to approach the problem of idealization in economics. According to Musgrave, the F-twist has been marred "by unclarity about the status of 'assumptions' in economic theories", and then adds:

> More precisely, there has been a failure to distinguish between three different types of 'assumption', each of which makes a different type of assertion and therefore plays a different role in the theory.[4]

Accordingly, Musgrave introduces a threefold distinction among assumptions: (1) negligibility assumptions, (2) domain assumptions, and (3) heuristic assumptions. I would like in the present paper to use this distinction to address the problem of idealization in economic theory. I shall carry on the discussion in connection with a certain important economic theory, having in mind Suppes' (1962) and Stigum's (1990) methodological proposals for the analysis of the empirical adequacy of theories.

In the first section of this writing I discuss the nature of the problem of idealization in economic theory. In the second I introduce some considerations on formal methodology aimed at precisely characterizing the method of axiomatization through the definition of a set-theoretical predicate. In the third I apply this formal methodology to the theory of consumer choice, in order to discuss the problem of idealization in connection with one important example taken from economic theory. The fourth part can be seen as an attempt to check the relevance of the considerations introduced in the first section. In the last section I

---

[1] Friedman (1953), p. 14 (Caldwell, p. 149).

[2] See Samuelson (1963).

[3] Samuelson (1963), p. 232 (Caldwell, p. 189).

[4] Musgrave (1981), p. 378 (Caldwell, p. 235).

conclude trying to clarify why is idealization important in economics, even though we may (and need to) have also philosophical economic theories that are not idealized.

1. The Problem of Idealization

The ultimate goal and *raison d'être* of the science of economics is the knowledge and cognition of economic phenomena. Just as commodities are not produced for their own sake, but in order to be sold in the market, economic theories are not produced for the sake of their beauty, but to satisfy both practical and theoretical needs.

The practical needs have to do with planning and control of or within real concrete economies, like those of Mexico or Holland. This practical usefulness of economic theories brings us to the question of their *empirical relevance*, i.e. not only to the question of how can they be used to obtain specific information about parameters, measurable or otherwise, concerning an ongoing real concrete economic process, but also to the question of how reliable they are to predict the consequences of politico-economic decisions.

The theoretical needs have to do with the relevance that one theory (like decision or game theory) can have for another (like general equilibrium theory), but they also have to do with contributing to a large and encompassing view of social life, less concerned with detailed measuring of parameters than with the architectonics of a concrete social totality. It seems to me that the so-called 'problem of idealization' hardly makes any sense out of a philosophical framework that takes seriously the possibility of "concrete" or true knowledge.

Indeed, for subjective or transcendental idealism (empiricism or kantism) of the kind advocated (for instance) by some adherents of the structuralist view of theories, there is not and there cannot be such thing as the problem of idealization, because for them the object of knowledge is the model, and talk about a reality beyond the model appears as nonsensical. For the problem of idealization is a reflection of true concrete knowledge in the sphere of abstract structures; it is an awareness of the lack of truthfulness of abstract analytical models in the face of a certain acquaintance with the real structure of the world.

We can be skeptical about the possibility of accurately representing the preferences of a man by means of a continuous utility indicator, but our knowledge of human nature and history leaves no room to doubt that men have preferences regarding goods and that the range of options for the consumer has increased a lot since the Industrial Revolution, at least in industrialized countries. This *is* important relevant knowledge and no serious philosopher of economics can expect to obtain important results by questioning its objective validity. Rather, it seems to me that the interesting question has to do with the *role* of idealization in economic theory, and this is a methodological question. Can we get rid of idealizing assumptions in economic theory? Should we? Why? These are the questions that I want to address here.

The problem of idealization itself can be formulated thus: *Important economic theories are defined by axioms ("assumptions") that are clearly false of the objects they avowedly intend to theorize about.* Does this fact make of economic theories pseudo-sciences? Why? At any rate, what usefulness can such theories have to know economic phenomena?

In order to formulate this problem more precisely, consider the following argument. Since all important scientific economic theories have in fact been formulated axiomatically, we can detect for any of them a certain set of primitive terms corresponding to certain mathematical objects (that pretend to represent economic entities) $X_1, ..., X_k, Y_1, ..., Y_m$. The X's are sets and the Y's are elements of these sets or relations over them, and so these objects belong to certain types and constitute structures, i.e. objects of the form $\mathfrak{A} = \langle X_1, ..., X_k, Y_1, ..., Y_m \rangle$. And they naturally satisfy a whole bunch of sentences, grouped in the theory of the structures of this type, T. The axioms proposed by the theoreticians, as well as their logical consequences, of course belong to T, but T is equal to the set of consequences of the axioms only if these axioms are complete.

At any rate, given a set of consistent sentences on mathematical objects $X_1, ..., X_k, Y_1, ..., Y_m$, these sentences define a type of structures, precisely the type of all those structures satisfying the sentences. In certain cases, these sentences are identified with the "axioms" or assumptions of a given economic theory because somehow they are like translations of sentences about economic objects. And it is precisely at this point where the problem of idealization arises. For instance, in general equilibrium theory X_1 could be the set "of all consumers", but actually these "consumers" are just positive integers from 1 to m, and of course in the real world consumers are not numbers, but people or institutions.[5] And so on and so forth. The point is that in "modeling" economic objects as mathematical ones we are implicitly attributing to the former attributes that they in fact do not have.

[5] Of course, it is said that these numbers "stand for" agents. My point is that, in theorizing economic object in this way, we implicitly attribute to them certain dubious properties, as I try to show below.

Musgrave (1981) claims that these attributions come in the form of three types of assumptions. The *negligibility assumptions* assert that a certain factor, that *might* affect the behavior of a certain type of phenomenon (like inflation or free fall of bodies), is in fact irrelevant (like the entry of a new firm into the market, or air resistance). If this factor proves to be relevant after all in some cases, the negligibility assumption — says Musgrave — becomes a *domain assumption*, i.e. an assumption that specifies the domain of applicability of the theory (e.g. large economies, in which the entry of new firms is negligible, or massive bodies falling from a certain height). Finally, *heuristic assumptions* are assumptions made for the sake of theory-building, when one considers first a case simpler than the motivating one, and then proceeds to relax the assumptions (if that is at all possible) to approach the most difficult case. Musgrave shows how in fact Friedman considers these three cases without being aware of the differences, but I am not interested here in pursuing such an interesting line of research, only in adopting these distinctions as a starting point.

2. Formal Methodology

In order to discuss in some detail the example of consumer choice, it will be convenient to make explicit here the formal methodology that shall be used. As I suggested above, the use of the axiomatic method in economics (which is a matter of course) cannot help but produce arrays of mathematical objects ("structures") that satisfy certain conditions. This notion of structure was subjected to mathematical study for the first time by Bourbaki (1968), but Patrick Suppes is famous for having popularized its use in the realm of the sciences since the early fifties. As far as I can tell, the most convenient presentation of this notion of structure — which is the one that I follow here — is due to Da Costa and Chuaqui (1988).

If X is any set, and $\mathbf{P}(\cdot)$ denotes the power set of the set in place of the dot $\cdot$, the *universe of sets of rank n* over X, $V_n(X)$, is recursively defined as follows. The universe of sets of rank 0 is X itself, i.e. $V_0(X) = X$. For any natural number n, the universe of sets of rank $n + 1$ is $V_{n+1}(X) = V_n(X) \cup \mathbf{P}(V_n(X))$.

Also recursively is defined the set of *types of n species*. If i is a natural number between 1 and n, i is a type. If a and b are types, then both $(a, 0)$ are types. Observe that if (a, b) is a type, then $a \neq 0$.

Let $X_1, ..., X_n$ be sets and c a type of n species. The set $T_c(X_1, ..., X_n)$ of objects of type c over $X_1, ..., X_n$ is defined by means of the following conditions:

(1) If $c = i$ with $1 \leqslant i \leqslant n$ then $T_c(X_1, ..., X_n) = X_i$.

(2) If $c = (a, 0)$ then $T_c(X_1, ..., X_n) = \mathbf{P}(T_a(X_1, ..., X_n))$.

(3) If $c = (a, b)$ with $b \neq 0$ then

$$T_c(X_1, ..., X_n) = T_a(X_1, ..., X_n) \times T_b(X_1, ..., X_n).$$

We say that an object x *is of type c over* $X_1, ..., X_n$ if $x \in T_c(X_1, ..., X_n)$.

Let $X_1, ..., X_n, Y_1, ..., Y_n$ be sets and $f_1, ..., f_n$ functions such that $f_i: X_i \to Y_i$ for $1 \leqslant i \leqslant n$. The sequence f is extended to f_c for each type c, in the following way:

(1) If $c = (a, 0)$ then $f_c(x) = \{f_a(y) | y \in x\}$, for $x \in T_c(X_1, ..., X_n)$.

(2) If $c = (a, b)$ with $b \neq 0$ then $f_c(x, y) = (f_a(x), f_b(y))$, for

$$x \in T_a(X_1, ..., X_n) \quad \text{and} \quad y \in T_b(X_1, ..., X_n).$$

I leave to the reader the verification that, in effect,

$$f_c: T_c(X_1, ..., X_n) \to T_c(X_1, ..., X_n)$$

and that each $T_c(X_1, ..., X_n) \in V_k(X_1 \cup ... \cup X_n)$ for some k.

The just introduced conceptual framework is sufficient to define the crucially important notion of structur

DEFINITION 2.1.: A *system or structure* $\mathfrak{A}$ is a quadruple $\langle X, Y, t, n \rangle$ such that

(1) n is a natural number. n determines the *universe* of the system $\mathfrak{A}$, which is precisely $V_n(X_1 \cup ... \cup X_k)$, which will be the range of the variables of the language that will be introduced to express the properties of the structure.

(2) X is a finite sequence of sets $X_1, ..., X_k$, called the *basic sets* of the system. Some of them, say the first p $(1 \leqslant p \leqslant k)$, are called the *principal sets*; the others are called *auxiliary sets*. There might be no auxiliary sets.

(3) Y is a finite sequence of objects $Y_1, ..., Y_m$ and t is a sequence of types of k species $t_1, ..., t_m$ such that Y_i is an object of type t_i over $X_1, ..., X_k$, for each i $(1 \leqslant i \leqslant m)$.

The quadruple $\langle k, p, t, n\rangle$ is called the *similarity type of the system* $\mathfrak{A}$. We say that two systems are *similar* if they have the same type and the same auxiliary sets. Hence, it can be seen that a structure is constituted by sets of objects which are typical of the theory (the principal sets $X_1, ..., X_k$), and possibly by sets of numbers or other mathematical objects (the auxiliary sets $X_{p+1}, ..., X_k$). The notion of universe of sets of rank n (V_n) is used to determine the range of the variables of the language which is required to formulate the sentences of the theory: given the basic sets $X_1, ..., X_k$, there exists a natural number n such that $V_n(X_1 \cup ... \cup X_k)$ is that universe. This number can be 0, in which case the variables and quantifiers remain restricted to the union of the basic sets, but they can also be allowed to range over a wider universe, one that includes relations over the elements of the former. The objects $Y_1, ..., Y_m$ are the outstanding elements and the set-theoretical constructions (relations and functions) erected over the basic sets, and will perform as the meanings of the primitive terms, together with the basic sets themselves.

The language $L_{\mathfrak{A}}$ *appropriate* to handle the system $\mathfrak{A} = \langle X, Y, t, n\rangle$ is a first order language with identity having $\in$ as binary predicate, constants for the basic sets and the elements or constructions Y over them, as well as the constant V for the universe $V_n(X_1 \cup ... \cup X_k)$. V is the range of the variables of $L_{\mathfrak{A}}$ and its quantifiers are referred to it. A sentence φ of $L_{\mathfrak{A}}$ is *true* in $\mathfrak{A}$ if the set-theoretical proposition expressed by φ with the constants interpreted in the specified way is set-theoretically true. The definitions of the concepts of satisfaction, model and logical consequence are as usual. The expression $\mathfrak{A} \models \varphi$ is read as $\mathfrak{A}$ *satisfies* φ.

DEFINITION 2.2: Let $\mathfrak{A} = \langle X, Y, t, n\rangle$ and $\mathfrak{B} = \langle U, Z, t, n\rangle$ be systems of the same type. Then it follows that X and Y have, respectively, the same lengths k and m than U and Z. We have:

(1) The sequence $f = \langle f_1, ..., f_k\rangle$ is an *isomorphism* of $\mathfrak{A}$ over $\mathfrak{B}$ if $\mathfrak{A}$ and $\mathfrak{B}$ are similar, f_i is a bijection of X_i over U_i ($1 \leqslant i \leqslant k$), f_i is the identify function for the auxiliary sets $X_{p+1}, ..., X_k$ and, if t_j is the type c, $f_c(Y_j) = Z_j$ ($1 \leqslant j \leqslant m$). We say that two systems are *isomorphic* if there exists an isomorphism among them.

(2) A sentence φ appropriate for $\mathfrak{A}$ is *transportable* if, for any structure $\mathfrak{B}$ isomorphic to $\mathfrak{A}$, we have

$$\mathfrak{A} \models \varphi \quad \text{iff} \quad \mathfrak{B} \models \varphi.$$

It has became popular in recent times the idea that at least some scientific theories can be axiomatized through the definition of a set-theoretical predicate. In economic theory this methodology has been applied since the early fifties, as the seminal paper of Arrow and Debreu (1954) witnesses.[6] It was Patrick Suppes, however, who popularized the *dictum* that to axiomatize a theory is to define a set-theoretical predicate. This is the reason why Da Costa and Chuaqui refer to these predicates as 'Suppes predicates', a concept that they define as follows.

DEFINITION 2.3: A *Suppes predicate* is a formula $P(\mathfrak{A})$ of set theory asseting: '$\mathfrak{A}$ is a system of type $\langle k, p, t, n \rangle$ that satisfies Γ', where Γ is a set of transportable sentences appropriate to $\langle k, p, t, n \rangle$. If $P(\mathfrak{A})$, tht is, if $\mathfrak{A}$ satisfies P, then $\mathfrak{A}$ is called a P system.

Economic theory is full of Suppes predicates: 'abstract economy', 'Marxian capitalist economy',[7] 'two-person zero sum game', and so on. Of course they are also commonly used in mathematics. For the sake of the example, the reader may consider the predicate '$\mathfrak{G}$ is a group', which asserts: '$\mathfrak{G}$ is a system of type (1, 1, t, 0) that satisfies Γ', where

$$t = (((1, 1), 1), 0), 1$$

and Γ is the set of sentences

$$\forall x \forall y \forall z \; x \circ (y \circ z) = (x \circ y) \circ z,$$
$$\forall x \; x \circ e = e \circ x = x,$$
$$\forall x \exists y \; x \circ y = y \circ x = e \; .$$

The sequence X of basic sets this time contains only one: the universe G of the group. In this case there are no auxiliary sets and, therefore, $p = k = 1$. The type of the group operation, $\circ$, is (((1, 1), 1), 0), because

$$\begin{aligned} \circ \in & \; \mathbf{P}((G \times G) \times G) \\ & = \mathbf{P}(T_{(1,1)}(X) \times T_1(X)) \\ & = \mathbf{P}(T_{((1,1),1)}(X)) \\ & = T_{(((1,1),1),0)}(X) \end{aligned}$$

The type of the outstanding element is 1 because $e \in G = T_1(X)$. Finally, $n = 0$ because we want to restrict in this case the range of the variables to the group universe G.

Naturally, in the formulation of group theory, or of the theory of any other structure, every explicit mention of the parameters k, t or n is omitted, and the structure is defined only in terms of the objects X and Y;

---

[6] The authors assert there that "mathematical techniques are set-theoretical" and then proceed to define the set-theoretical predicate 'abstract economy'.

[7] See García de la Sienra (1992).

in the example, the group structure is thus identified with the triple $\langle G, \circ, e\rangle$. So much for the formal methodology.

3. The Example of Consumer Choice

Let us consider now the interesting example of consumer choice. This theory deals with the behavior of a consumer when he faces a certain price system in the market. I shall axiomatize this theory defining the predicate '$\mathfrak{C}$ is a structure of consumption'. The basic sets of this structure are the set $\mathbf{R}_+$ of nonnegative real numbers and the set of nonnegative n-dimensional vectors of real numbers, $\mathbf{R}^n_+$. The remaining objects are $P, X, u, \hat{A}$ and c^*, of types (pedantically) (2, 0), (2, 0), ((2, 1), 0), 1 and 2, respectively. Of course, a more natural way of specifying the types of these objects (actually providing a quite detailed specification of their mathematical nature) is by means of a definition like Definition 3.1. But recall before a couple of mathematical concepts. A function $f: X \to \mathbf{R}_+$ is *strictly quasi-concave* iff

$$f(\lambda x + (1-\lambda)y) > \min(f(x), f(y)),$$

for all $x, y \in X, x \neq y$ and $\lambda \in (0, 1)$. A *level set* of f is a set of the form $\{x \in \mathbf{R}^n_+ | f(x) \geqslant f(y)\}$, where $y \in \mathbf{R}^n_+$. f has *differentiable level sets in* $\mathbf{R}^n_+ - \mathbf{R}^n_{++} - \{0\}$ iff for every $y \in \mathbf{R}^n_+ - \mathbf{R}^n_{++} - \{0\}$ there exists a vector $a \in \mathbf{R}^n_{++}$ such that

$$\{x \in \mathbf{R}^n_+ | f(x) \geqslant f(y)\} \subseteq \{x \in \mathbf{R}^n_+ | ax \geqslant ay\}.$$

DEFINITION 3.1: A *potential consumer choice structure* is a system

$$\mathfrak{C} = \langle P, X, u, \hat{A}, c^*\rangle$$

that satisfies the following axioms:

(1) $P = \mathbf{R}^n_+$

(2) X is a closed convex subset of $\mathbf{R}^n_+$

(3) $u: X \to \mathbf{R}_+$ is continuous, strictly increasing, strictly quasi-concave, and has differentiable level sets in $\mathbf{R}^n_+ - \mathbf{R}^n_{++} - \{0\}$

(4) $\hat{A} \in \mathbf{R}_+$

(5) $c^* \in \mathbf{R}^n_+$.

If primitive terms formulated in this fashion are to be regarded as belonging to an economic theory, it is also necessary to specify their intended interpretation (or interpretations, for there might be more than one). In the case under consideration, $\mathbf{R}^n_+$ is taken as representing the set of all possible commodity bundles, P is the set of all price vectors, X is the set of all commodity bundles currently available to a consumer, u is a utility function representing the preference ranking of the consumer, $\hat{A}$ is the quantity of available funds of the same consumer, and c^* is the consumer's choice, i.e. the bundle of commodities actually chosen by the consumer. It must be stressed that the very possibility of providing this intended interpretation presupposes that we already have some understanding of what commodity bundles, consumers, prices, preferences and funds are. And the very typification of the primitive objects is implicitly introducing claims about these economic determinations. I shall call these claims, as well as those contained in the laws of the theory, the *fundamental claims of the theory.*

To begin with, in saying that $\mathbf{R}^n_+$ is the set of all possible commodity bundles, we are actually claiming that (C1) there may be arbitrarily large amounts of commodities and that (C4) commodities are infinitely divisible. This is an idealization if 'possibility' is taken in a physical or economic sense: If (as some versions of relativistic cosmology claim) the universe is finite, then that proposition is just false; and of course commodities are *not* infinitely divisible. The claim that (C2) P is the set of all possible price vectors seems quite correct, provided that we are willing to consider proportional vectors[8] as being essentially the same price system. This claim also presupposes that a certain monetary unit is given. The assertion that X is the set of all currently available commodity bundles means in the first place that (C3) the amounts of commodities in any available commodity bundle can be represented by means of nonnegative numbers. This assumption seems to be perfectly correct. But axiom (3) makes in addition two very substantial claims about the form of the set of available commodity bundles. Whereas we *actually know* that these sets are always finite and discrete, and that commodities are not really infinitely divisible, this axiom is claiming that (C4) any convex combination of any pair of them exists, which clearly contradicts our knowledge of the matter. The other claim, that X is closed, does not seem to add anything ontologically substantial to the previous one.

To say that (C5) u represents the utility ranking of some consumer is to say that the preference rankings of the consumers the theory deals with have very special properties, to wit, at the very least they are connected, reflexive and transitive over X. Yet, axiom (4) implicitly makes two additional substantial claims about the preferences of the

---

[8] Two vectors $x, y \in \mathbf{R}^n_+$ are called *proportional* if there exists a scalar $\alpha \in \mathbf{R}_+$ such that $x = \alpha y$.

consumer. The stipulation that u be continuous is parasitic upon the convexity of X and seems to be vacuously satisfied by any actual set of available commodity bundles, since in these sets there are no cluster points! The considerably less precise claim that (C6) to "small changes" in the vectors of commodities there correspond "small changes" in the corresponding preferences seems to be more or less true, whenever such phrases can be given an intelligible meaning. The condition that u be strictly increasing implicitly asserts (C7) non-satiability, i.e. that the consumer will always prefer a bundle contaning more commodities to one containing less. If the set X is assumed to be unbounded, this claim amounts to the assertion that the consumer suffers from *infinite lust*, a strange assertion that presupposes that men can feel lust for things like an arbitrarily large set of Cadillacs that demonstrably (on physical grounds) will never be able to exist. This seems to happen in some cases, but this is not the place to enter into the fields of ethics and religion. The strict quasi-concavity of u asserts that the utility of a convex combination of commodity bundles is always strictly greater than that of the one in the combination that has the smallest utility. This assertion is parasitic upon the convexity of X and, together with the one affirming that u has differentiable level sets, implies that (C8) the consumption bundle is unique for each price system,[9] a step required in the proof of the Fundamental Theorem of Consumer Choice (see below).

Finally, the assertion that (C9) $\hat{A}$ is the amount of available funds of the consumer seems obviously true, because such funds are always given as a certain positive amount of money.

The point to be noted is that the typifications together with the intended interpretation of the primitives are already delineating a rather bold doctrine about certain economic objects. This doctrine is completed with the introduction of the substantial axioms of the theory, those that go beyond the mere typifications to actually define the set of all models of the theory (in the present case, consumer choice structures). In order to define this set-theoretic predicate, it will be convenient to introduce two previous definitions.

DEFINITION 3.2: If $\langle P, X, \hat{A}, c^* \rangle$ is a consumer choice structure, a *consumer* is a triple $\langle X, u, \hat{A} \rangle$.

DEFINITION 3.3: Let $\Gamma(p, A)$ be the set $\{x \in X | px \leqslant A\}$. An element c of X is a *consumption bundle* iff there exists a pair $(p, A) \in P \times \mathbf{R}_+$ such that (1) $pc \leqslant A$ and (2) $u(c) = \max\{u(x) | x \in \Gamma(p, A)\}$. The consumer's *set of*

[9] Compare this with the remarks on strict quasi-concavity made by Arrow and Debreu (1954).

consumption bundles is the family $C(\hat{A})$ of all commodity bundles that are consumption bundles with respect to a pair of the form $(p, \hat{A})$.

In terms of these notions we can introduce the desired Suppes predicate.

DEFINITION 3.4: A *consumer choice structure* is a potential consumer choice structure in which the bundle of commodities chosen by the consumer is a consumption bundle, i.e. $c^* \in C(\hat{A})$.

The claim that the bundle of commodities chosen by the consumer is a consumption bundle is the fundamental law of the theory of consumer choice. It defines the concept of a "rational consumer" in quite precise terms. It constitutes also a quite substantial claim about the behavior of the consumer. According to it, (C10) the consumer in the market will purchase the commodity bundle that maximizes his utility, subject to his budget constraint.

The gist of introducing the former axioms is to enable the proof of Samuelson's Fundamental Theorem of Consumer Choice, according to which "any commodity that is known always to increase in demand when income alone rises must definitely shrink in demand when its price alone rises".[10]

4. Epistemological status of the Fundamental claims

In the previous section we identified the fundamental claims of consumer choice theory (C1-C10), i.e. those claims about the intended object of theorization (the behavior of the consumer) implicitly made by the axioms of the theory together with their intended interpretation. In the present section we shall see whether Musgrave's threefold distinction is appropriate to characterize their role in economic theory. The question is whether each of the fundamental claims (C1-C10) falls into Musgrave's classification. For the sake of easy reference here they are:

(C1) There may be arbitrarily large amounts of commodities.

(C2) P is the set of all possible price vectors.

(C3) The amounts of commodities in any available commodity bundle can be represented by means of nonnegative numbers.

(C4) Commodities are infinitely divisible.

---

[10] Samuelson (1953), p. 107; Stigum (1990), pp. 186 and 189-190. Stigum provides a detailed proof of this theorem, under the additional assumption that $X = \mathbf{R}^n_+$.

(C5) The preference rankings of the consumers are connected, reflexive and transitive over X.

(C6) To "small changes" in the vectors of commodities there correspond "small changes" in the corresponding preferences.

(C7) Non-satiability, i.e. the consumer will always prefer a bundle containing more commodities to one containing less.

(C8) The consumption bundle is unique for each price system.

(C9) The amount of available funds of the consumer is a non-negative real number.

(C10) The consumer in the market will purchase the commodity bundle that maximizes his utility, subject to his budget constraint.

Claims C2 and C3 seem to be true of actual economies. Certainly, bundles of commodities are always measured in nonnegative real (rational) numbers and price systems can always be scaled. This is the foundation of the possibility of chopping zeros from from the currency of any particular country, when inflation has made difficult the handling of the coins and bills. In economic theory, this possibility of scaling the price systems has given a basis to the adoption of the standard simplex as the set of all possible price vectors. C6 also seems to be approximately true if "small changes" is adequately interpreted. Its intuitive validity can be seen by means of nonstandard concepts. Suppose that the consumer prefers x to y. Then, an infinitestimal variation of x will still be preferred by the consumer to y. Of course, infinitestimals have no physical counterparts but the reader will accept that if sufficiently small changes do not alter the preference ranking, infinitestimal ones would alter it the less. (C9) seems to be clearly and precisely true also because the amount of available funds for any consumer at any given moment is a nonnegative real number of monetary units. None of these assumptions seems to fall in any of the drawers devised by Musgrave, since his distinction seems to be intended to hold only for unreal assumptions or for assumptions of restricted validity within the range of phenomena the theory is intended to theorize about. These assumptions seem to have full generality within such a realm.

C1 is false unless by 'possibility' it is understood conceivability in the abstract. Certainly, we are right now conceiving a bundle of three trillion Rolls Royces but perhaps it is really (i.e. economically and physically) impossible to produce ever that bundle in any feasible course of events for the history of humanity. Taken in the first sense of 'possibility', C1 is not an idealization but a true sentence asserting that it is possible to conceive any amount of commodities of any class. Taken in the physical, and therefore also in the economic sense, it is plainly false and is adopted by Stigum only to simplify the proof of the Fundamental Theorem. C1 is thus clearly a heuristic assumption, since it is only made for the sake of theory building or just to simplify the presentation of the theory; nothing seems to preclude the feasibility of adopting instead some bounded subset of $\mathbf{R}^{n}_{+}1$, even though this might complicate a little the mathematics.

C4 is also false. Not even water or sugar can be infinitely divided, even though these commodities are closer to satisfy such condition. Moreover, if current quark theory is true, *nothing* in the physical universe can be infinitely divided. Yet this assumption (which is implied by convexity) is necessary since "the convexity assumption is crucial because of its role in all the existing proofs of several fundamental theorems".[11] Hence, it is clearly also a heuristic assumption that some economists would like to eliminate.

There is dispute about the validity of C5 for actual consumers in the market. Some authors claim that transitivity is not quite true of actual preference rankings. These conditions, however, are necessary for the existence of a numerical representation (a utility) of the preferences of the consumer. Hence, it also must be placed as a heuristic assumption.

The plausibility of C7 depends of the set X on which u is defined. For the usual finite or compact sets of commodities, (in which there are points of saturation) insatiability looks plausible, a fact that popular wisdom recognizes as well established. For unbounded sets the assumption looks weird, to say the less, and can only be taken as an extrapolation; in this case it must be considered also as a heuristic assumption.

C8 says that, for each price system, there is only one commodity bundle that maximizes the utility of the consumer, subject to his budget constraint. In other words, it means that there is a most preferred consumption menu that the consumer can buy with his monetary resources. This precludes the possibility of there being many such menus that are indifferent. This assumption is not true in general and, again, since it is required in the proof of the Fundamental Theorem, it is only heuristic.

Finally, C10 is the most substantial assumption of the theory. It does not seem to be either obviously true or obviously false. Clearly, it is not a negligibility or a heuristic assumption, but the very core of the theory of consumer choice. In some sense, it can be taken as a domain assumption, namely as the one delimiting the applicability of the theory only to "rational consumers", but one of the claims of the theory is precisely that

---

[11] Debreu (1959), p. 41.

consumers in modern market economies *are* rational. To what extent they are rational can only be determined subjecting the theory to empirical tests.

Summing up, I think we can conclude the present section accepting the usefulness of Musgrave's threefold distinction, but also acknowledging the need of empirical tests to determine the extent to which "unreal assumptions" approximate to actual empirical facts. This calls for statistical methods.

5. The Role of Idealization in Economic Theory

The empirical realism of the fundamental claims of an economic theory is not altogether irrelevant to its worth, because wildly unrealistic assumptions may prevent the "consequences" of the theory from having a useful degree of approximation. Indeed, if *all* the fundamental claims of the theory are true, then the consequences of the theory *must* be exactly true, and the blame for any departure of the data from them must be put upon the data, not upon the theory. The fact is, nonetheless, that idealizations (very specially heuristic assumptions) are useful and sometimes impossible to get rid of in order to prove important theorems. Just like in other scientific domains, in economics conjectures arise (like the one that gave rise to Samuelson's Fundamental Theorem) that the economists would like to be able to prove, and the demonstration of these conjectures requires almost always the introduction of idealized assumptions.

Yet, science is not merely a matter of theory building, but also of confronting the theories with the world. This happens in the form of data collecting and organizing, in order to employ statistical methods to determine how well the theory fits the data. A detailed development of this methodology would require another paper or perhaps a book, and is also beside the point, which is only to see the relevance of idealization in this process, but it is important to stress here that there are two aspects involved in the use of statistical methods to test economic theories: a formal one and one that is not amenable to mathematical treatment.

The statistical testing of theories is a complex art that involves a phase of experimental design, on which little in general can be said from a general methodological standpoint, since that phase has to do with what Suppes calls *ceteris paribus* conditions: "Here is placed every intuitive consideration of experimental design that involves no formal statistics. Control of loud noises, bad odors, wrong times of day or season go here".[12] These considerations give rise to what Suppes (1962) calls 'models of the data', which are essentially a presentation of the experimental or observational evidence. On top of these models there is a whole hierarchy of structures constituting the bridge between the observational evidence and the theory. As Suppes puts it: "exact analysis of the relation between empirical theories and relevant data calls for a hierarchy of models of different logical type".[13] The point to be stressed in this connection is that the formal aspects of statistical testing have to do with the construction of mathematical structures, and this requires more idealizations: in fact, in addition to those contained in the theory, negligibility and more heuristic assumptions are required to simplify the mathematics and construct the sample spaces.

Hence, to the question 'Can we get rid of idealizing assumptions in economic theory?' the answer is negative because such assumptions are required both to prove interesting conjectures and to employ statistical methods. This fact does not make of economic theories pseudo-sciences, because such methods are common even to the so-called hard sciences. Insofar as the predictions of economic theories fit the data with sufficient accuracy, the theories are empirically adequate, they are reliable and are in fact used to make forecasts, and design and check economic policies.

Finally, it must be noted that it is one thing to acknowledge the usefulness of idealizations in the field of economics, and quite another to pretend that vaguer but more concrete concepts are useless. The aims of scientific economics require idealizations and sometimes very rigorous and precise concepts, but it is also possible to produce interesting and important theories that do not pretend to obtain measurements of quantities. Philosophical theories of the economy do not provide the details of economic processes, but they may provide a non-trivial, interesting comprehension of the architectonics of economic systems like the modern market economies. Positivism, of course, denies the worth of any such theory and intends to restrict itself to purely formalized (or formalizable) theories. In fact, contemporary positivism can be characterized as the effort to get rid of any concrete doctrine, to replace the imprecise concrete with abstract determinations.[14] Unfortunately for positivism, however, to get rid of concrete vague concepts is not only to eliminate the possibility of a metaphysics of economics, but also to get rid

---

[12] Suppes (1962), p. 258.

[13] Suppes (1962), p. 260. A very interesting discussion on the methodology of statistical testing, with special applications to economics, can be found in Stigum (1990). Stigum's approach is different from that of Suppes but also makes heavy use of logical techniques.

[14] This is what in its own jargon is called "the clarification of the language of science".

of *ceteris paribus* conditions, of those intuitive statistical considerations which are so important in the design of statistical tests. No wonder, then, that contemporary versions of positivism substitute simplified trivialities about the "empirical claims" of theories for the difficult and not entirely formalizable methods of statistical testing.

Adolfo García de la Sienra
Instituto de Investigaciones Filosóficas
Universidad Nacional Autónoma de México
Circuito Mario de la Cuerva, CU
04215, México DF

Centro de Investigación y Docencia Económicas
Apartado postal 10-883
01210, México DF

REFERENCES

Arrow, K.J. and G. Debreu (1954). Existence of an Equilibrium for a Competitive Economy. *Econometrica*, **22**, 265-290.

Bourbaki, N. (1968). *Theory of Sets*. Herman and Addison-Wesley, Boston and Reading.

Caldwell, B.J. (Ed.) (1984). *Appraisal and Criticism in Economics*. Boston: Allen & Unwin.

Da Costa, Newton, C.A. and R. Chuaqui (1988). On Suppes' Set-Theoretical Predicates. *Erkenntnis*, **29**, 95-112.

Debreu, G. (1959). *Theory of Value*. New Haven: Yale University Press.

Friedman, M. (1953). The Methodology of Positive Economics. In: *Essays in Positive Economics*. Chicago: University of Chicago Press, pp. 3-43. Reprinted in Caldwell (1984), pp. 138-178.

García de la Sienra, A. (1992). *The Logical Foundations of the Marxian Theory of Value*. Dordrecht: Kluwer.

Musgrave, A. (1981). 'Unreal Assumptions' in Economic Theory: the F-Twist Untwisted. *Kyklos*, **34**, 377-387. Reprinted in Caldwell (1984), pp. 234-244.

Samuelson, P. (1953). Consumption Theorems in Terms of Overcompensation Rather than Indifference Comparisons. *Economica*, **20**.

Samuelson, P. (1963). Discussion. *American Economic Review Papers and Proceedings*. May, 231-6. Reprinted in Caldwell (1984), pp. 188-193.

Stigum, B.P. (1990). *Toward a Formal Science of Economics*. Cambridge: MIT Press.

Suppes, P. (1962). Models of Data. In: Nagel, E., Suppes, P., and Tarski, A. (Eds.), *Logic, Methodology and Philosophy of Science: Proceedings of the 1960 International Congress*. Stanford: Stanford University Press, pp. 252-261.

Poznań Studies in the Philosophy of the Sciences and the Humanities
1994, Vol. 38, pp. 135-146

Izabella Nowakowa, Leszek Nowak

ON CORRESPONDENCE BETWEEN ECONOMIC THEORIES*

ABSTRACT. An analysis of the relationships between theories in terms of 'dialectical correspondence' in the sense of the idealizational theory of science. Such correspondence can be observed in the history of economic theory, though somewhat less clearly than in physics, due to the secondary influence of ideology.

1. The idealizational approach to science

Everybody knows that science applies idealization. The understanding of this fact is far from being so common. However, in recent philosophy of science there have appeared conceptions which admit the key role of idealizations in science (e.g., Barr 1971, Suppe 1972, Wójcicki 1974, 1979, Cartwright 1983, 1989 and others; cf. a review of various recent approaches to idealization in Niiniluoto 1986, 1990). According to one of these approaches which is presupposed here (cf. Nowak 1970, 1971a-b, 1972, 1980), the scientific method can be summarized as follows. The pure abstract of a given type of phenomena is formed by depriving them of some of their features, those which are considered to be secondary. What remains still contains merely the principal properties of the empirical original. If some simple formulae connecting them (idealizational laws) are valid, it is for the pure abstract alone. The idealizational statement is concretized by gradually admitting the previously neglected secondary properties and modifying its formula. The laws become more and more complicated and therefore ever closer to the empirical reality. And also the body of them in subsequent models of the increasing realism becomes larger and larger. This procedure continues until the most realistic model becomes a sufficient approximation of the given system. Whether this is the case, or not, only experience will decide.

The structure of a scientific theory *t* is thus given by a sequence of models M^k, M^{k-1}, ..., M^i, AM^i, where M^k is the most abstract model equipped with *k* idealizing conditions, M^{k-1}, ..., M^i being its subsequent

* Translation of this paper has been supported by the grant 2496 from the *Komitet Badań Naukowych*.

concretizations, finally, AM^i is an approximation of the least abstract of these models M^i to the empirical reality.

As has been shown (cf. Nowak 1971a, 1980) such is the basic structure of many typical scientific theories. There are also numerous less typical variants based on some derivative constructions — *ceteris paribus* (Patryas 1975), proto-idealizing (Brzeziński 1978, 1985), stabilizing (Chwalisz 1979, Zielińska 1981), para-idealizing (Maruszewski 1983), aggregating (Łastowski 1988), normalizing (Nowak 1991), etc.

2. The development of scientific theory in the idealizational approach to science

In a work by Nowakowa (1972, cf. also 1975a-b) a certain notion of correspondence has been proposed. According to it a new scientific theory t' gets, in comparison to the old theory t, new idealizing conditions, i.e. it becomes a more abstract conception, and at the same time t' is concretized with respect to those new idealizing conditions; as a result t'' is obtained which is an equally, or less abstract theory as the initial theory t. Let us take the simplest idealizational statements as theories. In the initial period it is claimed factually that:

$$t\text{: if } u(x), \quad \text{then} \quad F(x) = f(H(x)).$$

It turns out, however, that t is false: for some a such that $u(a)$, $F(a) \neq f(H(a))$. Then, science searches for a factor responsible for the deviation. Let it be the factor p. This means that the formula $F = f(H)$ can be kept only if it will be additionally equipped with an idealizing condition abstracting from the working of p. In other words, the following idealizational statement is put forward:

$$t'\text{: if } u(x) \text{ and } p(x) = 0, \quad \text{then} \quad F(x) = f(H(x)).$$

On the other hand, t' is an idealizational statement which is unable to explain why the deviation occurs. Therefore, a concretization of t' is necessary which says how the additional factor p influences F:

$$t''\text{: if } u(x) \text{ and } p(x) \neq 0, \quad \text{then} \quad F(x) = f^*(H(x), p(x)).$$

t'' is said to correspond with t dialectically.

For more complicated cases of the structure of theories the definition of the dialectical correspondence becomes more complicated as well (Nowakowa 1975a, chap. 3). There are some writings finding out the relation of dialectical correspondence between the historical transformations of numerous classical laws of physics (cf. Nowak and Nowakowa

1973, Nowak 1974, Nowakowa 1975a-b, Such 1978, Nowakowa 1982 etc.). In the theoretical biology Łastowski (1987) has found out the relation of dialectical correspondence between the subsequent versions of the theory of evolution.

The notion of dialectical correspondence presupposes that the compared laws assume basically similar images of the essential structure of a given magnitude, i.e. that the repertory of factors claimed to be principal for the determined variable is constant. That is why it can hardly be claimed that revolutions in science consist in making new theories that dialectically correspond to the former ones.

Paprzycka (1990) introduces the relation called, somewhat unfortunately, dialectical reduction. The relation holds between t' and t, if – roughly – the images of the essential structure of the magnitude determined in t and t' differ as to the repertories of principal factors but there is a common part in them. Due to that at least some elements of the old law are preserved at subsidiary positions in a chain of concretizations of the new idealizational structure. That is why this relation which we shall call dialectical refutation connects laws separated by a scientific revolution.

The famous Kuhnian notion of paradigm may be paraphrased on the grounds of the outlined approach as a theory whose repertory of principal factors is not questioned in a given period – called the period of normality – at all, and which is corrected by the theories dialectically corresponding to it. Scientific revolution consists in replacing one paradigm by another. Therefore, one may claim that the history of science divides into periods of normality and revolutions. In a period of normality new theories dialectically correspond to a given paradigm. This lasts up to the scientific revolution which leads to a new paradigm dialectically refuting the previous one.

The goal of this paper is to state whether this claim holds for the theoretical economics.

3. Marx's theory of reproduction

Consider Marx's theory of reproduction for capitalist (E) societies. It has already been shown that the theory in question is of the idealizational nature (Nowak 1980, pp. 25ff). It is namely based on four idealizing assumptions formulated by Marx in *Das Kapital*:

(i^1) the accumulation fund in society x equals zero;

(i^2) the value of the commodities produced in society x is constant;

(i^3) society x is composed of two classes only, i.e. the capitalists and the workers;

(i^4) society x is in total isolation (or – which is supposed to mean the same – the capitalist mode of production exists in all the societies in the world).

Because of reasons which will become clearer below, we shall confine the reconstruction of the Marxian schemes to only one of these assumptions claiming that accumulation (A) in the considered economy equals zero. Therefore, the schemes of the so-called simple reproduction: $P^i = C^i + V^i + M^i$ ($i = 1,2$; P, C, V, M stand, correspondingly, for the global product of a given sector, the constant and variable capitals in it, the surplus value created in that sector of the considered economy) can be reconstructed as idealizational statements of the form:

(M^1) if $E(x)$ & $A(x) = 0$, then $P^1(x) = C^1(x) + V^1(x) + M^1(x)$

(M^2) if $E(x)$ & $A(x) = 0$, then $P^2(x) = C^2(x) + V^2(x) + M^2(x)$

Then Marx removes the assumption $A(x) = 0$ and takes into account the fact that capitalist economy x does accumulate, i.e. utilizes a part M^c of the surplus value for an increase of the means of production and the other part M^v of the surplus value for an employment of more labour force: $0 < A = M^c + M^v$. At the same time the schemes (M^1)–(M^2) are corrected correspondingly:

(M^{*1}) if $E(x)$ & $A(x) > 0$, then $P^1(x) = C^1(x) + V^1(x) + M^1(x) + M^{1c}(x) + M^{1v}(x)$

(M^{*2}) if $E(x)$ & $A(x) > 0$, then $P^2(x) = C^2(x) + V^2(x) + M^2(x) + M^{2c}(x) + M^{2v}(x)$

The problem arises of how the theory of reproduction was evolving. Even the superficial look at the history of that theory allows to find some arguments supporting the supposition that next variants of the Marxist theory of economic growth have stood to the Marxian origin in the relation of dialectical correspondence.

4. Some expansions of the Marxian theory

One of the troubles the Marxist economists face is the fact that in Marxian schemes the economy is divided into two sectors, only. For instance, the production of arms is not a production of means of production, neither is it a production of the means of consumption. Where are the armaments to be classified? Nonomura (1953) attempts to include the production of arms into Marx's schemes. His idea is that the armaments are to be treated as a separate, the "third", sector of the economy. The reason for this is that the production of this sector is bought by the state thanks to the taxes. And the taxes form a part of the surplus value. That is why the picture of the economy adopted by Marx is too simple, and a new subject of the economic activity, the state, is to appear. Nonomura claims that Marx's schemes can be kept only under an additional simplification that eliminates the state out of the scenery:

(i^5) the taxes T^a supplied in the economy x for the armaments equal zero.

In a reconstruction, Nonomura still maintains the Marxian schemes of the simple reproduction but on the idealizing conditions (i^1)—(i^5). In our simplified formulation, Nonomura's schemes of simple reproduction take the following form:

(*N1*) if $E(x)$ & $A(x) = 0$ & $T^a(x) = 0$, then $P^1(x) = C^1(x) + V^1(x) + M^1(x)$

(*N2*) if $E(x)$ & $A(x) = 0$ & $Ta(x) = 0$, then $P^2(x) = C^2(x) + V^2(x) + M^2(x)$.

These schemes are next concretized, i.e. the correction accounting for the role of the armament expenses is introduced into the schemes of Marx. Namely, a part of the magnitude T^a is supplied to the first sector producing the means of production and the other part is supplied as wages and, in effect, spent for the means of consumption. As a result, the Nonomura's concretization of the Marxian schemes is the following:

(N^{*1}) if $E(x)$ & $A(x) = 0$ & $T^a(x) > 0$, then $P^1(x) = C^1(x) + V^1(x) + M^1(x) + T^{1a}(x)$

(N^{*2}) if $E(x)$ & $A(x) = 0$ & $T^a(x) > 0$, then $P^2(x) = C^2(x) + V^2(x) + M^2(x) + T^{2a}(x)$.

Apart from that, Nonomura adds a new statement telling what the armaments (P^3) depend upon:

(N^{*3}) if $E(x)$ & $A(x) = 0$ & $T^a(x) > 0$, then $P^3(x) = C^3(x) + V^3(x) + M^3(x) + T^{3a}(x)$.

In the next step Nonomura repeats Marxian concretization obtaining the schemes of enlarged reproduction accounting for the armaments:

(N^{**1}) if $E(x)$ & $A(x) > 0$ & $T^a(x) > 0$, then $P^1(x) = C^1(x) + V^1(x) + M^1(x) + M^{1c}(x) + M^{1v}(x) + T^{1a}(x)$

(N^{**2}) if $E(x)$ & $A(x) > 0$ & $T^a(x) > 0$, then $P^2(x) = C^2(x) + V^2(x) + M^2(x) + M^{2c}(x) + M^{2v}(x) + T^{2a}(x)$.

(N^{**3}) if $E(x)$ & $A(x) > 0$ & $T^a(x) > 0$, then $P^3(x) = C^3(x) + V^3(x) + M^3(x) + M^{3c}(x) + M^{3v}(x) + T^{3a}(x)$.

As one may notice, Nonomura's three models $\{\{(N^1)-(N^2)\}, \{(N^{*1})-(N^{*3})\}, \{(N^{**1})-(N^{**3})\}\}$ dialectically correspond to Marx's two models $\{\{(M^1)-(M^2)\}, \{(M^{*1})-(M^{*2})\}\}$.

There are numerous undertakings of the same kind in the history of Marxist economy. Kawakami (1965) states that Marx's theory of reproduction is based on a silent simplification neglecting the existence of the service sector and expands the schemes of reproduction accounting for the role played by the services in the economy. Lange (1965, p. 40ff) states that the Marxian schemes presuppose a tacit assumption claiming that the accumulation is allocated in the same sector of the economy in which it is created. He removes this simplification correcting those schemes with respect to the mutual flows of the accumulation between sectors of the economy. Nagels (1973) takes into account the role of exports and imports presenting the schemes of reproduction for the open economy. Etc. In all these cases we have to do with the relation of dialectical correspondence of a new conception to the Marxian paradigm.

5. On some peculiarity of the development of economic theories

Notice that the above examples are taken from one theoretical orientation, *viz.* the Marxist economics. It is clearly seen in many papers of this volume, notably those by Walliser, Hendry, Cools, Kuipers and Hamminga, that the same rule of dialectical correspondence governs the transformations of paradigms also within other theoretical orientations. However, it is doubtful whether the relation of dialectical correspondence ties conceptions which belong to different orientations. For instance, Jevons' theory of prices does not stand in the relation of dialectical correspondence to the Marxian theory of value because of the simple fact that the factors it refers to (the subjective utility) are quite different from those of which Marx's theory makes use (the socially indispensable time of production). In the theoretical economics there occurs thus not one scientific tradition of "normal science" organized by the relation of dialectical correspondence which is — in principle — the case in the history of physics but there occur numerous parallel traditions, each of them separately organized by the rule of dialectical correspondence. One may conjecture that this very fact has, apart from the normal cognitive reasons, something in common with the multiplicity of social interests finding their expression in the competing ideologies.

The question arises of what is the role of the relation of dialectical refutation in the history of a given economic orientation. In particular, whether the picture known of the history of physics can be seen here, i.e. that the sequence of enlargements (dialectical correspondents) of a given paradigm completes and a new paradigm appears which, first, dialectically refutes the old paradigm and, second, opens a new sequence of enlargements.

6. The theory of Rosa Luxemburg as a dialectical refutation of Marx's theory of reproduction

Not the whole history of the theory of reproduction in Marxism is composed of attempts to correspond dialectically to the Marxian origin. There was also an attempt to overthrow Marx's theory and to replace it with a basically new theory. Such an endeavor has been made by Rosa Luxemburg.

She has found out that the Marxian theory does not give an answer to the question of what are for the capitalists the reasons to make investments. Whether they will decide to allocate some fund A for accumulation, that is, to produce additionally some mass of commodities depends upon whether those commodities find a demand. If so, then the surplus value becomes the form of money and the capitalists allocate some part, A, of the surplus value to the means of production and wages. If not, then the capitalists, not having obtained the expected profit, do not accumulate and can even reduce production. Not knowing whether the surplus value will be realized, the capitalists do not have any motivation for investment decisions. However, if they in fact accumulate, then the appropriate demand (i.e. demand for A) had to appear. Where does it come from? In words of Rosa Luxemburg:

> An actual accumulation, that is, an enlargement of production, requires ... the enlargement of the effective demand for commodities. What is the source, however, of this constantly increasing demand which gives the foundation for the incessant enlargement of production in Marx's scheme? (Luxemburg 1963, p. 177)

It is Rosa Luxemburg's famous thesis that under Marx's assumptions (in particular, those of the two-class capitalist society and its isolation) it is impossible to find the source of this additional demand justifying investment decisions on the part of the capitalists. Therefore, no accumulation occurs at all. But this means that no enlarged reproduction is possible under these assumptions. Marx himself did not understand the trouble, mixing it incessantly with the question where the money indispensable for the process of production comes from (Luxemburg 1963, p. 205).

The conclusion of this criticism of Marx's theory of reproduction is that the theory is defectively constructed — its idealizing assumptions eliminate just what cannot be abstracted from if the phenomenon of enlarged reproduction is to occur at all. Marx's stratification of factors influencing the phenomenon in question is faulty — it does not contain all the principal factors for it.

Therefore Rosa Luxemburg constructs a new theory of reproduction taking into account from the very beginning both the existence of the classes of the pre-capitalist origin inside the society under consideration and of the non-capitalist environment, i.e. other non-capitalist societies on the outside. All this creates an additional demand for the capitalists which makes them possible to enlarge production. At the early stage of the development of capitalism the internal pre-capitalist social categories (the small producers, peasantry, etc.) fall victim to the capitalist made of production. For a mature capitalism, non-capitalist societies on the outside create the additional demand necessary for the enlarged reproduction. But by doing this the social environment becomes gradually more and more capitalist. This accelerated development has a limit of its own, i.e. the capitalization of the whole world. When this would happen, the breakdown of the whole world capitalist system is inevitable — there is no possibility to create an effective demand any more.

True or false, that is an interesting theory. Being formulated only intuitively, it cannot be compared with the Marxian origin precisely enough. Yet, it might be supposed that Rosa Luxemburg's theory of reproduction stands to the Marxian theory in relation of dialectical refutation. First, assumptions (i^1)—(i^2) are taken to be misleading as neglecting the factors that cannot be abstracted from and some new factors (the demand on the part of the inner pre-capitalist social classes and the outer non-capitalist societies) are posited to play the role of the principal factors. Second, some of the principal factors of the Marxian origin (C, V, M) are preserved in Rosa Luxemburg's theory.

If the pattern of physics was to be repeated, Rosa Luxemburg's theory had to replace the "old Marxian paradigm" thus opening a new series of expansions corresponding dialectically to the new paradigm. Nothing of that kind occurred. One may conjecture that it is the pressure of ideological interests that did not allow to change the old paradigm. Ideology of the increasing social-democratic and then communist movements was stimulated by the authority of Marx. Facing this all the cognitive reasons had to go out of the scenery.

7. Concluding conjectures

In so far as the above analyses can be claimed to be typical for the theoretical economics, they allow to put the following conjectures. First, the cognitive reasons underlying the development of economics are roughly the same as those working in the history of physics. In particular, they incline the economists to improve their paradigm by building new conceptions dialectically corresponding to it and, when the possibility of further expansions exhausts, the same reasons incline the economists to create the new paradigm dialectically refuting the old one. Second, those cognitive reasons are disturbed by the working of social factors mediated by the ideologies. This contributes to the fact that economic orientations multiply *praeter necessitatem*, if they may be treated as supporting, or being expressions of, influential ideologies. This, too, gives some paradigms additional support due to which they are kept even if there are cognitively good reasons to replace them with new paradigms.

To put it briefly: one may conjecture that in the history of economics works the same "logic" which is visible in the history of physics but the closeness to ideologies disturbs that "logic". Sometimes, as in the history of Marxism, it does so quite seriously.

I. Nowakowa, L. Nowak
ul. Cybulskiego 13
60-247 Poznań
Poland

REFERENCES

Barr, W.F. (1971). A Syntactic and Semantic Analysis of Idealizations in Science. *Philosophy of Science*, **38**, 258-272.

Brzeziński, J. (1978). *Metodologiczne i psychologiczne wyznaczniki postępowania badawczego w psychologii* (The Methodological and Psychological Determinants of the Research Practice in Psychology). Poznań: Poznań University Press.

Brzeziński, J. (1985a). The Protoidealizational Model of the Investigative Process in Psychology. In: J. Brzeziński (Ed.), *Consciousness: Methodological and Psychological Approaches* (*Poznań Studies in the Philosophy of the Sciences and the Humanities*, **8**) Amsterdam: Rodopi, pp. 36-57.

Cartwright, N. (1983). *How the Laws of Physics Lie?*. Oxford: Oxford University Press.

Cartwright, N. (1989). *Nature's Capacities and Their Measurement*. Oxford: Oxford University Press.

Chwalisz, P. (1979). Stałe w idealizacyjnej koncepcji nauki (Constants in the Idealizational Conception of Science). In: A. Klawiter, L. Nowak (Eds.), *Odkrycie, abstrakcja, prawda, empiria, historia – a idealizacja* (*Discovery, Abstraction, Truth, Experience, History – and Idealization*). Warszawa-Poznań: PWN, pp. 99-104.

Kawakami, M. (1965). Relations between Expanded Reproduction Schema and National Income. *The Science Council of Japan* (February) [quoted after Nagels (1973)].

Lange, O. (1973). *Teoria reprodukcji i akumulacji* (The Theory of Reproduction and Acumulation). Warszawa: PWN.

Łastowski, K. (1987). *Rozwój teorii ewolucji. Studium metodologiczne* (The Development of the Theory of Evolution. A methodological study). Poznań: Adam Mickiewicz University Press.

Łastowski, K. (1988). O wielopoziomowych teoriach naukowych (On Multi-level Scientific Theories). In: J. Brzeziński, K. Łastowski (Eds.), *Filozoficzne i metodologiczne podstawy teorii naukowych* (Philosophical and Methodological Foundations of Scientific Theories) (Poznańskie Studia z Filozofii Nauki, **11**). Warszawa-Poznań: PWN, pp. 119-42.

Luxemburg, R. (1963). *Akumulacja kapitału. Przyczynek do ekonomicznego wyjaśnienia imperializmu* (The Accumulation of Capital. A Contribution to the Economic Explanation of Capital). Warszawa: PWN.

Maruszewski, T. (1983). *Procesy poznawcze jednostki w świetle idealizacyjnej teorii nauki* (The Cognitive Processes of Individual in the Light of the Idealizational Theory of Science). Poznań: Poznań University Press.

Nagels, Th. (1973). *Reprodukcja kapitału w ujęciu Karola Marksa* (The Reproduction of Capital: Marx's Approach). Warszawa: KiW.

Niiniluoto, I. (1986). Theories. Approximations and Idealizations. In: (Eds.) R.B. Markus, G.J.W. Dorn, and P. Weingartner, *Logic, Methodology and Philosophy of Science*, **VII**. Amsterdam: North-Holland, pp. 255-289.

Niiniluoto, I. (1990). Theories, Approximations and Idealizations. In: J. Brzeziński, F. Coniglione, T.A.F. Kuipers, L. Nowak (Eds.), *Idealization-I* (*Poznań Studies in the Philosophy of the Sciences and the Humanities*, **16**). Amsterdam: Rodopi (a revised and enlarged version of the 1986 paper), pp. 9-57.

Nonomura, K. (1953). The Development of Wartime Reproduction Theories in Japan. *The Annals of the Hitotsubashi Academy*, **2** [quoted after Nagels (1953)].

Nowak, L. (1970). Analiza logicznej struktury modelu ekonomicznego (An Analysis of the Logical Structure of Economic Model). *Ekonomista*, **6**, 1231-51.

Nowak, L. (1971a). *U podstaw Marksowskiej metodologii nauk* (Foundations of the Marxian Methodology of Science). Warszawa: PWN.

Nowak, L. (1971b). The Model of Explanation in Marx's *Capital*. *Quality & Quantity* **V**, 2, 311-30.

Nowak, L. (1972). Theories, Idealization and Measurement. *Philosophy of Science*, **39**, 4, 533-47.

Nowak, L. (1974). Prawda względna, zasada korespondencji, prawda absolutna, praktyka (Relative Truth, the Principle of Correspondence, Absolute Truth, Practice). In: W. Krajewski (Ed.), *Zasada korespondencji w fizyce a rozwój nauki* (The Principle of Correspondence in Physics and the Development of Science). Warszawa: PWN, pp. 147-78.

Nowak, L. (1980). *The Structure of Idealization. Towards a Systematic Interpretation of the Marxian Idea of Science*. Dordrecht: Reidel.

Nowak, L. (1991). The Method of Relevant Variables and Idealization. In: E. Eells, T. Maruszewski (Eds.), *Probability and Rationality. Studies on L. Jonathan Cohen's Philosophy of Science* (*Poznań Studies in the Philosophy of the Sciences and the Humanities*, **21**). Amsterdam/Atlanta: Rodopi.

Nowak, L. and I. Nowakowa (1973). W sprawie zasady korespondencji w fizyce (Concerning the Principle of Correspondence in Physics). *Kwartalnik Historii Nauki i Techniki*, **1**, 33-43.

Nowakowa, I. (1972). *Zasada korespondencji w fizyce* (The Principle of Correspondence in Physics). Ph.D.-thesis. Dept. of Philosophy, Adam Mickiewicz University. Poznań.

Nowakowa, I. (1975a). *Dialektyczna korespondencja a rozwój nauki* (The Dialectical Correspondence and the Development of Science). Warszawa/Poznań: PWN.

Nowakowa, I. (1975b). Idealization and the Problem of Correspondence (*Poznań Studies in the Philosophy of the Sciences and the Humanities*, **1**, 1, 65-70).

Nowakowa, I. (1982). Dialectical Correspondence and Essential truth. In: W. Krajewski (Ed.), *Polish Essays in the Philosophy of the Natural Sciences* (*Boston Studies in the Philosophy of Science*, **68**). Dordrecht: Reidel, pp. 135-146.

Paprzycka, K. (1990). Reduction and Correspondence in the Idealization Conception of Science. In: J. Brzeziński, Fr. Coniglione, T.A.F. Kuipers and L. Nowak (Eds.), *Idealization-I: General Problems* (*Poznań Studies in the Philosophy of the Sciences and the Humanities*, **16**). Amsterdam/Atlanta: Rodopi, pp. 277-86.

Patryas, W. (1975). An analysis of the caeteris paribus clause. *Poznań Studies in the Philosophy of the Sciences and the Humanities*, **1**, 1, 59-64.

Such. J. (1978). Idealization and Concretization in the Natural Sciences. *Poznań Studies in the Philosophy of the Sciences and the Humanities*, **4**, 49-73.

Suppe, F. (1972). What's wrong with the Received View on the Structure of Scientific Theories? *Philosophy of Science*, **39**, 1-19.

Wójcicki, R. (1974). *Metodologia formalna: metody, pojęcia i zagadnienia* (The Formal Methodology: Methods, Concepts and Problems), Wrocław: Ossolineum.

Wójcicki, R. (1979). *Topics in the Formal Methodology of Empirical Sciences.* Dordrecht: Reidel.

Zielińska, R. (1981). *Abstrakcja, Idealizacja, Uogólnienie* (Abstraction, Idealization, and Generalization). Poznań: Poznań University Press.

Poznań Studies in the Philosophy of the Sciences and the Humanities
1994, Vol. 38, pp. 147-168

Uskali Mäki

ISOLATION, IDEALIZATION AND TRUTH IN ECONOMICS

ABSTRACT. Challenges the widely held view that good models must necessarily be simplifications and hence cannot be true. This is done by distinguishing between whole truth (complete description) and truth (essential description, attained by the method of isolation).

1. Introduction

In his discussion of the rationality principle, Karl Popper says the following:

> Can any model be true? I do not think so. Any model, whether in physics or in the social sciences, must be an oversimplification. It must omit much, and it must overemphasize much. (Popper 1983 (1967), p. 361.)

The same idea can be found in David Hendry's comments on the foundations of econometrics:

> I take it as self-evident that economic behaviour is sufficiently complex and evolutionary that it is not helpful to talk about economic theories being 'true' or of inferences yielding the 'correct' results. . . . By their very nature, models are inherently simplifications and inevitably false. (Hendry 1986, pp. 30-31)

Popper and Hendry seem to hold the view that any theory or model[1] is necessarily false for two reasons.

[A] A theory is false because it is a *partial* representation of the world ("it must omit much").

[B] A theory is false since it involves *idealizing* representations of aspects of the world ("it must overemphasize much"; "models are inherently simplifications").

[1] It is hoped that no major distortion is caused by not separating the notions of theory and model in what follows. In a more elaborate analysis, such a separation may be needed. Note that in the quotation above, Hendry does not make the distinction, so at least his statement does not seem to depend on it.

These convictions are naturally accompanied by the notion that a sequence of models or theories approaches the truth only if each subsequent theory incorporates more details of the object under study by relaxing one or more of the idealizing assumptions. The following passage by Alexander Rosenberg exemplifies this idea.

> The general question of how any scientific model with false assumptions, like the Bohr atom or the ideal gas, can help us understand its subject is important, and part of the answer involves the fact that such models represent stages in the succession of relatively fuller and more detailed models, in which successive restrictions are relaxed and new factors introduced. ... But explanations of the uses of economic models cannot share these considerations, because the succession of economic models have simply not reflected this sort of increasing approximation to the truth. (Rosenberg 1978, p. 680)

In what follows I wish to challenge these views. The statements by Popper, Hendry and Rosenberg seem to be based on conflating truth and the whole truth, i.e., the accurate representation of the whole of reality. I am not going to question the legitimacy of the notion of the whole truth, but rather to argue that there is a way of thinking about truth and a scientific model or theory which permits us to use the vocabulary of veracity when assessing the merits and demerits of theories which are partial and involve idealizations. My line of thinking seems to be intuitively familiar and acceptable to practising economists, as evidenced by the following statement in a popular textbook:

[C] "A model's power stems from the elimination of irrelevant detail, which allows the economist to focus on the essential features of the economic reality he or she is attempting to understand." (Varian 1990, p. 2)

The problem of the present essay is the following: Can [C] be accepted without accepting [A] and [B]? In other words, is the pursuit of nothing-but-the-truth consistent with [C]?

My point of departure is to view economic theory as an outcome of what may be termed *the method of isolation*. Any theory is bound to isolate a small slice of the world from the rest of reality. Therefore, any theory is bound to violate the whole truth. Theories typically accomplish this by violating nothing-but-the-truth as well since they involve false idealizations. The question remains whether a theory or model could be true of those items that are included in the isolated domain. My suggestion is that this possibility is not undermined by the two violations: *a theory may be true even if it is partial and involves idealizations.*

It is essential to my endeavor to understand that a typical economic theory is an extremely complex creature, both syntactically and pragmatically, a fact neglected by the application of simplistic philosophies of science. A theory has a number of elements with varying functions and formulations. It typically makes or can be used to make a number of different claims, each of which plays its own role in the creation of an overall picture of an aspect of the economy. The task of the metatheorist is to identify the various claims that an economic theory involves and to specify the roles they play. Furthermore, the metatheoretical endeavor has to be metaphysically sensitive. It has to take account of the metaphysical underpinnings of the basic categories used for formulating the claims of a theory. Only then can we hope to see clearly how truth and falsity might be attributed to different parts of a theory and how these attributions are to be assessed in the assessment of the whole theory. I hope to shed some light on this question by employing the idea of theory as an isolation. The paper develops some themes in an earlier essay (Mäki 1992a; see also 1991b, 1992b, 1993a, 1993b).

Section 2 outlines the idea of theory as an isolation, based partly on idealizing assumptions. Section 3 discusses the truth value of idealizing assumptions under various formulations. The suggestions of Alan Musgrave are commented on in this context. Section 4 considers the possibility that some key elements of isolative theories may be true even if the picture they provide is partial. Among other things, Nancy Cartwright's views are discussed in this section. The final section summarizes the argument and points out its significance for understanding the character of disagreement in economics.

2. Theory as an isolation involving idealizations

The world is infinitely rich and complex. Our concepts and theories are, at most, partial representations of very limited slices of this richness. Any theory or concept may be said to *isolate* a part or aspect of the world from all the other parts and aspects. In the domain of any conceptual representation, a small number of items are included, while a vast number of others are excluded.

There is the universe, i.e., all there is in the world. Planet Earth is a part of the universe. A cosmologist may disregard the Earth since she is interested in the larger system of galaxies. There are seas and mountains and trees and people and countries on Earth. An astronomer, however, may treat the Earth as a mass point, as a dimensionless, sealess, peopleless, etc., concentration of mass with a velocity and a location in spacetime, unaffected by the force of gravity of the other planets. There are cities in the countries. An international economist may treat countries as cityless, as spatially homogenous entities with certain resources and productivity. There are houses in the cities. An economic geographer may treat cities as houseless. There are rooms in the houses, disregarded by a painter interested in the external profile of a city. There are tables in many of the rooms, disregarded by a house architect. Some tables have apples on them, ignored perhaps by an interior designer. Most of the apples are round, some of them are red and ripe, three of them are located on a table in Rögnvaldur's house and belong to him. Rögnvaldur eats one of them today because he believes it keeps the doctor away, *ceteris paribus*. Rögnvaldur's friend, a biochemist, explains to him that apples have this capacity because they have such and such a biochemical structure, not because they are red nor because they are colored in general nor because those eaten by Rögnvaldur happened to lie on a table in Rögnvaldur's house in the city of Reykjavík.

Isolations may be classified on a number of dimensions. The distinction between what may be called *material isolation* and *theoretical isolation* is important from the point of view of economics. While some natural sciences are capable of accomplishing artificial material isolations by using experimental arrangements, most isolations in economics are theoretical in character, based on "thought experiments". While these two kinds of isolation have a similar logical character, their ontological grounds and epistemic powers are different.

Another distinction usually overlooked by philosophers of science writing on idealizations is one between what I have called *horizontal isolation* and *vertical isolation* (Mäki 1992a, pp. 324-326). Horizontal isolation is isolation at a given level of abstraction, while vertical isolation brings about a change in the level of abstraction. Isolating Rögnvaldur's apples from Rögnvaldur's table and from all the other particular apples and tables in the world or isolating the capacity of apples to keep doctors away from all the other properties of apples, are examples of horizontal isolation. Isolating the universal of appleness from the particularities of all the past, present and future apples or isolating the universal of redness from all the other properties of red apples (such as their appleness) and of other red objects, are examples of vertical isolation.

Theoretical horizontal isolation is, for the most part, based on simple *omissions*: an item is neglected without mentioning it. No explicit statements about the omitted items are put forward. Obviously, omissions imply the violation of the whole truth. They do not, and cannot, violate nothing-but-the-truth for the simple reason that they are not the sorts of entities to which truth value could be attributed. No statements, no truth value. No true or false statements are made about the gravitational pull between Earth and Mars while omitting it in the Walrasian, Austrian and Marxian theories of the economy.

Horizontal isolation may also be brought about by using *idealizing assumptions*. The very notion of idealization is ambiguous. In its most general sense, an idealization amounts to making something ideal. Being ideal, in turn, may be understood in a number of ways. In the case of qualitative accounts, there is plenty of room for different notions of being ideal. In the case of quantitative accounts, one way of understanding being ideal is in terms of parameters with numerical values 0 or $|\infty|$. An idealizing assumption can often be formulated in the general form, $p(x) = 0$, i.e., the value of a parameter is assumed to be zero. For instance, in astronomical models it is often assumed that the gravitational attraction between Earth and the other planets is zero. This is how the relation between Earth and the sun is isolated from interplanetary relations. Likewise, the relations of trade between two countries may be isolated by assuming that there are no other countries and no more than two goods to be traded.

In an idealizing assumption, unlike in an omission, the item thereby excluded is mentioned explicitly. This is often so because the items excluded by omission are not supposed to be causally relevant, whereas the items excluded by idealization are supposed to have causal relevance for the relations concerned. In a study of capital movements between Hong Kong and mainland China, interplanetary gravitation is not regarded as relevant, hence not worth mentioning, while at some stage of the study at least, it may be explicitly assumed that the amount of Japanese investment in China is nil; idealization is used because this would be expected to be a relevant variable.

Among idealizing assumptions, we may distinguish between what may be called nullifications and stabilizations. A *nullifying idealization* has the standard form $p(x) = 0$, while a *stabilizing idealization* has the form $\dot{p}(x) = 0$, whereby the rate of change of factor x is nullified. In economic theories, the assumptions of zero transaction costs and instant adjustment are nullifications, while the assumptions of the constancy of tastes and technology are stabilizations. The *ceteris paribus* assumption is a stabilizing idealization having all but the isolated items in its domain. What has sometimes been called the *ceteris absentibus* assumption is a nullifying idealization having all but the isolated elements in its domain.

Isolation is a process that can be reversed. The reverse process may be called de-isolation.[2] *Horizontal de-isolation* is a process of adding factors

[2] I am indebted to Adolfo García de la Sienra for suggesting the term 'de-isolation' to me.

without a change in the level of abstraction. Some factors are added by relaxing the idealizing assumptions that helped neutralize them. The outcome is a more comprehensive, more encompassing picture of the causal nexus behind the phenomena under consideration.

Vertical de-isolation is a matter of decreasing the level of abstraction in our representation of an aspect of the world. It is needed when trying to apply a given general theory to more particular cases. The outcome is more concrete, covering more specific features possessed by a smaller set of objects.

The necessity of distinguishing between verticality and horizontality is evidenced by the fact that in actual economic research practice, vertical and horizontal isolation and de-isolation do not have to go hand in hand in the same direction: e.g., vertical de-isolation is often accompanied by horizontal isolation. This was noticed by Haavelmo in his classic essay:

> Every research worker in the field of economics has, probably, had the following experience: When we try to apply relations established by economic theory to actually observed series for the variables involved, we frequently find that the theoretical relations are 'unnecessarily complicated'; we can do well with fewer variables than assumed a priori. (Haavelmo 1944, p. 26)

To conclude this section, a terminological remark might clarify matters. I have suggested that the relevant basic processes of scientific theorizing of interest here are isolation and de-isolation. Abstraction is a form of isolation (viz., vertical isolation), while concretization is a form of de-isolation (viz., vertical de-isolation). Idealization is a device for accomplishing isolations. Now some scholars use these terms differently. Nowak, for instance, uses the pair of terms 'idealization' and 'concretization' to characterize the two basic processes (Nowak 1980). Krajewski, in turn, uses the pair 'idealization' and 'factualization' (Krajewski 1977a, 1977b). Some methodologists of economics have adopted this terminology (Hamminga 1990; Birner 1990). It should be clear that I find such usages unnecessarily misleading.

3. Idealization and truth

By definition, *isolative theories violate the whole truth*. At most, they are representations of parts or aspects of the world. When employing idealizing assumptions, *isolative theories also violate nothing-but-the-truth*. This concerns assumptions such as that goods and factors are perfectly divisible, that prices adjust themselves infinitely fast, that transaction costs are zero, that *ceteris paribus*. They are false statements. Should one conclude from this that theories containing such assumptions are false? I do not think so. Such a conclusion would ignore the logical, pragmatic and metaphysical complexity of scientific theorizing.

Let us start with a discussion of the issue of truth in the case of idealizing assumptions of form $p(x) = 0$ or $p(x) = |\infty|$. It is often thought that genuine idealizations have to be false of their objects, i.e., that in no cases are 0 or $|\infty|$ the real values of the relevant parameters. The idealizations of a mass point, of a frictionless plane and of a rigid body in physics are genuine in this sense. In economics, the idealizations of zero transaction costs, perfect divisibility and instant adjustment are also genuine. In both disciplines, the *ceteris paribus* and *ceteris absentibus* assumptions, literally taken, no doubt are genuine idealizations. On the other hand, the assumptions that a certain market is in equilibrium (i.e., excess demand = 0), that the government budget is balanced (i.e., budget deficit = 0) and that technology remains constant do not count as genuine idealizations if they are sometimes true, even if they are false most of the time. Following Nowak (1980, pp. 190-194), such assumptions may be called *quasi-idealizations*.

Under this construction, idealizations are false statements about the world. Scientists are also typically aware of their falsity. This may be found puzzling. Why should scientists accept such assumptions in their theories? An instrumentalist may not find such acceptance problematic, but should a realist feel troubled by it? Here we need to embark on the pragmatics of theorizing. Idealizations may be used for various purposes. It is clear that some idealizations are based on considerations of formal tractability; they are there to ease mathematical derivability. The use of some other idealizations may be based on metaphysical considerations; they are made to exclude those aspects of the object that are expected to be ontically peripheral or inessential. Sometimes the use of an idealization may exemplify both purposes at the same time.

In all such cases, we cannot escape the conclusion that, from a semantic point of view, idealizations would seem to be straightforwardly false statements. The function of falsehood in science is clearly in need of clarification and justification. To begin with a terminological point, it may be of vital importance that idealizations are usually called *assumptions* rather than *assertions*. Indeed, the contents of the idealizing assumptions of a theory are not what one holding the theory would present as the assertions of the theory. Perhaps the assumptions can be rephrased so as to acknowledge this circumstance. Let us discuss an attempt at such a rephrasing.

In his insightful intervention in the assumptions controversy in economics, Alan Musgrave (1981) suggests that many assumptions that have been regarded as unavoidably false, are in fact often true statements, or at any rate that the truth of assumptions often does matter, as against the famous F-twist.[3] As examples he uses the assumptions that there is no government and that the government has a balanced budget (he also mentions the assumptions that goods are infinitely divisible, that consumers have perfect knowledge of them and that transport costs are nil).[4] In the foregoing I have dealt with such assumptions as possibly legitimately false idealizations, while Musgrave views them as ideally true statements. The explanation for this difference is that Musgrave is in fact commenting on certain special forms of these assumptions, either rephrased from a pragmatic perspective or conjoined with certain meta-level comments. He suggests that one and the same sentence may be used to make three types of assertion and may therefore play three different roles in economic reasoning. He calls them negligibility assumptions, domain assumptions, and heuristic assumptions. Let us try to see how the message of these three types can be clarified. Clarification is needed, since Musgrave is not always entirely clear about the formal identity of the three types of assumptions and thereby of the items to which truth values are to be assigned.

A *negligibility assumption* is "the hypothesis that some factor F which might be expected to affect [the] phenomenon [under investigation, say P] actually has no effect upon it, or at least no detectable effect" (Musgrave 1981, p. 378).[5] For instance, when applying Galileo's law to

---

[3] Musgrave uses unfortunate expressions when denoting the crucial attributes of economic assumptions. He talks about "unreal assumptions" and the "reality of assumptions". Now it does not seem unnatural to think of an assumption as real if someone has stated it, provided linguistic items or the items expressed by linguistic items in general are regarded as potentially real. My suggestion is that instead of 'reality' (or 'realism'), we should talk about 'realisticness' as an attribute of economic assumptions (Mäki 1989).

[4] It should be noted that the assumptions that Musgrave mentions are not all of the same kind from the point of view of the notion of idealization. The assumptions that goods are infinitely divisible and that consumers have a perfect knowledge of them appear to be genuine idealizations, statements that are necessarily false, whereas the assumptions that the government has a balanced budget and that the transport costs are nil and even that there is no government might rather be regarded as quasi-idealizations, possibly true of some cases.

[5] Jack Birner has suggested that implicit in Musgrave's characterization is a distinction between two kinds of negligibility assumptions, one concerned with the "no effect" case, the other concerned with the "no detectable effect" case. Birner suggests that the second type of negligibility assumption can be formulated in terms of approximation: the move from

[i] $(x)\ ((p_1(x) > 0\ \&\ p_2(x) > 0\ \&\ \ldots\ \&\ p_n(x) = 0 \rightarrow F(x) = 0)$

to

[ii] $(x)\ ((p_1(x) > 0\ \&\ p_2(x) = 0\ \&\ \ldots\ \&\ p_n(x) = 0 \rightarrow F'(x) = 0)$

compact bodies falling relatively short distances, the assumption that they fall in a vacuum may act as a negligibility assumption. The assumption makes the assertion that air-resistance is negligible. This assertion may be true even if those bodies do not in fact fall in a vacuum. The situation is similar with the assumption of the non-existence of the government. The statement, which we may take as an idealizing assumption and a nullifying one, albeit probably a quasi-idealization,

[G] There is no government

is, in most cases, clearly false, while in the rephrased form

[NG] The government has negligible effects on the phenomena under investigation

it may well be true. Similarly, the statement (also a quasi-idealization and again a nullification)

[B] The government has a balanced budget

is often false, while

[NB] Any actual budget imbalance has negligible effects on the phenomena under investigation

may be true. Indeed, it is relevant to ask of assumptions of type [NG] and [NB] whether they are true or false, and it is good for the theory in which they appear if they are true. Note that [NG] and [NB] as well as [G] and [B] are *statements about economic reality*. [G] and [B] are statements about the existence of "factors", while [NG] and [NB] are statements about their causal powers, viewed from a pragmatic perspective.

In a footnote to an article on idealizations, Jack Birner provides a criticism of Musgrave's treatment of negligibility assumptions (Birner 1990, p. 148, fn19). It is illuminating to reflect upon Birner's comments here. He writes that "it is not very clear whether Musgrave considers

---

involves adding the assumption that $p_2(x) = 0$ (whereby the factor denoted by p_2 is neglected) and switching from *F* to F', i.e., to what Birner says is an approximation of *F*. (Birner 1990, p. 132) This seems questionable to me. It does not seem to be clear at all that the epistemic notion of detectability is analyzable in terms of approximation. Furthermore, I am not entirely convinced that a fruitful distinction can be drawn between these two kinds of negligibility assumption. The first type of negligibility assumption (the "no effect" case) makes negligibility depend on ontic considerations, while the second type (the "no detectable effect" case) makes it depend on epistemic considerations. However, the two grounds of negligibility are functionally or pragmatically equivalent, and it might be argued that this is all that matters; the concept negligibility is, after all, a pragmatic notion.

negligibility assumptions to be idealizations or true assumptions about the irrelevance of factors". First, Birner's first option seems to be concerned with assumptions such as [G] and [B]. Here (and elsewhere) he seems to equate being idealizing with being false. The problem with this is that an assumption like [B] may well be true in many cases and yet not be an assumption about the irrelevance of budget imbalance. Second, unlike Birner, I do find it fairly clear that Musgrave considers negligibility assumptions to be of the second kind, exemplified by [NG] and [NB] (Musgrave is much less clear with the other two types of assumption). I also find it problematic to say, as Birner does, that Musgrave "does not distinguish between negligibility assumptions which are true and those which are idealizations" and that the true ones are about the "no effect" case, while the "idealizations" are about the "no detectable effect" case. Birner fails to see that negligibility assumptions of the "no detectable effect" case may be as true as those of the "no effect" case. The assumption that *F* has no detectable effect on *P* may be a true statement about the relationship between a cognitive subject and a causal relation between *F* and *P*. Part of Birner's problem may be due to conflating the distinction between the "no effect" case and the "no detectable effect" case on the one hand and the distinction between idealizing assumptions exemplified by [G] and negligibility assumptions exemplified by [NG] on the other. These are, of course, different distinctions, and the latter is far more important than the former.

Let us then move on to the second class of assumptions in Musgrave's typology. A *domain assumption* is a hypothesis about the domain of applicability of a theory: theory *T* applies only if factor *F* is absent (ibid., p. 381). While in the case of negligibility assumptions *F* is supposed to have no effect or no detectable effect on the phenomena under investigation, in the case of domain assumptions *F* may be supposed to have significant effects, and therefore the application of *T* is restricted to situations where *F* does not obtain.

Musgrave's formulation of domain assumptions is not entirely clear. He does not give any general formulation of such assumptions, and his example of the balanced budget assumption is ambiguous in this respect. It is not quite clear whether the relevant domain assumption is the statement

[DB] The government has a balanced budget

or the meta-level statement

[DB'] The theory only applies where budget imbalance is absent.

Yet, given some textual evidence, [DB] would appear to be a more promising candidate. Musgrave says that "if a domain assumption is always false, then the theory containing it can be applied to no actual situation and is in fact untestable. If governments never balance budgets, then a theory about what happens *if they do* cannot be tested." (*Ibid.*, pp. 381-382) Therefore, if we happen to value testability, then we should hope that our domain assumptions are true of as many actual cases as possible. Now this point is relevant about [DB], but not about [DB'], since [DB'] may be always true even if [DB] is always false. Thus, it seems that, for Musgrave, [DB] is a non-rephrased domain assumption to which it is relevant to assign truth values and the functioning of which is interpreted in the light of [DB']. Note that while [DB] is a statement about economic reality, [DB'] is a *meta-level descriptive statement about an economic theory or model.* Musgrave's formulations of domain assumptions seem to be different in this respect from negligibility assumptions.

Before proceeding to Musgrave's last category of assumptions, let us briefly comment on Nancy Cartwright's conception of the *ceteris paribus* clause. Cartwright formulates her views in terms of what she calls *ceteris paribus* laws. The fundamental laws of physics, she says, are *ceteris paribus* laws. She further says that they are laws "that hold only under special conditions, usually ideal conditions" and that "it would be more apt to read *'ceteris paribus'* as 'other things being *right'* " than as 'other things being equal' (Cartwright 1983, p. 45). As an example she gives Snell's law which is a statement about the angle of incidence and the angle of refraction for a light ray. Cartwright then explains that Snell's law is a *ceteris paribus* law since it "holds only in special circumstances"; namely, it is "true only for media whose optical properties are isotropic" (*ibid.*, p. 47). Cartwright says that

> *Ceteris paribus* generalizations, read literally without the *'ceteris paribus'* modifier, are false. ... On the other hand, with the modifier the *ceteris paribus* generalizations may be true, but they cover only those few cases where the conditions are right. (*ibid.*, p. 45.)

Now it is clear that Cartwright is talking about laws that involve *domain assumptions* in Musgrave's sense. The 'other things being right' clause is a generalized and encompassing domain assumption. However, not all domain assumptions, such as [DB] above, are *ceteris paribus* assumptions in the sense defined in section 2 above; that is, stabilizing idealizations to the effect that 'other things are constant'. Conversely, not all *ceteris paribus* assumptions serve as domain assumptions, for they may also serve as negligibility assumptions or as first-step assumptions, to be discussed shortly. Furthermore, not all domain assumptions are idealizing assumptions. Finally, not all idealizing assumptions are *ceteris paribus* assumptions. Cartwright's suggestion may lead to an unnecessary conflation of these types of assumptions.

Take then Musgrave's third category of assumptions. It includes what he calls *heuristic assumptions*. They should be understood in a dynamic context: they are assumptions first made and then relaxed. Here a scientist develops his theory in two stages: "in the first stage he takes no account of factor *F*, or 'assumes' that it is negligible; in the second stage he takes account of it and says what difference it makes to his results" (*ibid.*, p. 383). The assumption made in the first stage is a heuristic assumption. They might be better called *first-step assumptions*. In the terminology of section 2 above, they serve as part of the first step in the process of de-isolation. Musgrave does not provide any formulations of such first-step assumptions *per se*. His example, "Assume for the moment that the budget is balanced (we will relax this assumption shortly)" (*ibid.*, p. 386), is a different kind of formulation than [NB] and [DB]. It amounts to *making the assumption*, not to the assumption itself. Perhaps the first-step assumption in this case is a conjunction of the non-rephrased descriptive statement [B] and a *meta-level promise* that [B] is going to be temporary, that it will be relaxed in due course. In other words, what Musgrave may have in mind is the conjunction of [B] and [HB]:

[B] The government has a balanced budget.

[HB] [B] is an element in an early formulation of the theory and will be removed as the theory is developed.

Musgrave does not have much to say about the truth of heuristic or first-step assumptions. He briefly discusses Newton's inquiry into the solar system where "he first neglected inter-planetary gravitational forces by 'assuming' that there was only one planet orbiting the sun" (*ibid.*, p. 383). Musgrave then claims that "you miss the point if you object that Newton's assumption is false, because our solar system has more than one planet" (*ibid.*). This is probably supposed to be so because of the promise that the assumption will be relaxed, not because Musgrave thinks that promises do not have truth values.

Even if we miss the point if we object to [B] because of its falsehood, there should be no objection to holding [B] to be false whenever the budget is not balanced. The situation is similar to that in the case of negligibility and domain assumptions. There is the difference that while [NB] and [DB'] may be true, [HB] cannot be true in the same sense, provided it is construed as involving a promise. If it were construed as a prediction or some other kind of description of the dynamics of economic theories, it might sometimes be true. In the case of many such assumptions, it would be false, however.

Musgrave also states that Friedman's dictum that "the more significant the theory, the more unrealistic the assumptions" does not hold in the case of heuristic or first-step assumptions (*ibid.*, p. 385), but he leaves the claim unargued. In fact, I see no reason to deny that significant theories involve radically unrealistic assumptions in the sense that in the "first approximation" they provide of their objects they focus on the supposedly most crucial factor and falsely assume the other factors to be non-existent.

We may conclude that while idealizations and quasi-idealizations may sometimes be reformulated as true statements when treated as negligibility assumptions, this does not seem to be so in the case of their reformulation as domain and first-step assumptions. None of this, however, implies that the key statements of a theory cannot be true, as we shall see.

4. Isolation and truth

Consider next the issue of truth in relation to the partial character of theories. As noted already, isolation is conceptually connected to the violation of the whole truth. Every theory, model or statement of law is partial. Before embarking on the difficult task of attributing truth values to such a representation, one has to be clear about the claim that it makes. I find attractive the simple idea that partial representations are about parts or aspects of the world, and as such they may be true, i.e., nothing but true, about those parts without having to be true about other parts or all parts.

It is instructive to consider the contrast between this obvious suggestion and Nancy Cartwright's thesis in her *How the Laws of Physics Lie* (Cartwright 1983). Cartwright argues that the fundamental theoretical laws of physics are false, while the very low-level phenomenological laws may hope to be true.

> One of the important tasks of a causal explanation is to show how various causes combine to produce the phenomenon under study. Theoretical laws are essential in calculating just *what each cause contributes*. But they cannot do this if they are *literally true*; for they must ignore the action of laws from other theories to do the job. (Cartwright 1983, p. 12; emphases added.)

Cartwright here implies the view that 'literal truth' is synonymous with 'the whole truth'. She thinks that truth is violated because of the obvious fact that theoretical laws "must ignore" the action of other laws. Once we relax Cartwright's equation, it becomes possible and natural to think that theoretical laws may be true, even literally true, or approximately so, of what they are about; namely, of "what each cause contributes". The same remark applies to the following passage:

> We construct different models for different purposes, with different equations to describe them. Which is the right model, which the 'true' set of equations? The question is a mistake. One model *brings out some aspects* of the phenomenon; a different model *brings out* others. (*ibid.*, p. 11; emphasis added.)

My response to this is that the question about truth is a mistake only if truth is mistaken for the whole truth. Partial models do not capture the whole truth. But if we reject the idea that this is the only notion of truth there is, it becomes possible to think that models that "bring out" specific aspects of a phenomenon may be true of such aspects without having to be true of other aspects or all aspects.

Let us consider the partiality of representations resulting from vertical isolation. Vertical isolation leads to abstract concepts and theories, depicting items such as apples and money, not particular apples and particular pieces of money, but appleness and moneyness. Appleness may be defined as the possession of certain chromosome structure, shared by particular apples. The power to keep doctors away is a consequence of this structure. The redness of Rögnvaldur's apples does not belong to the universal of applehood, nor does their current location on Rögnvaldur's table. Appleness is an isolated partial aspect of Rögnvaldur's apples and all other apples. Moneyness may be taken to essentially involve purchasing power, common to all particular pieces of money. The color, molecular constitution and current location of the coins that Rögnvaldur gave in exchange for his apples do not characterize the universal of money. This universal is a partial aspect of all particular coins and other particular pieces of money, isolated from their other aspects.

The view that vertical isolation leads to falsehood implies that we may have true statements about particulars only, such as Rögnvaldur's apples and coins, in the richness of all their properties. Truth may be preserved if these statements are universally quantified over all particular apples and all particular pieces of money. Once they are formulated as statements of applehood and moneyness, in theoretical isolation of all particularities, they are taken to distort reality. This is the nominalist stance. It is exemplified by the following passage by Gibbard and Varian in which they build upon a distinction between a model and an applied model:

> [T]he difference between a model and an applied model is this: whereas a model speaks of entities of certain general kinds – prices, consumers, information, and the like – without saying which particular entities in the world they are, an applied model specifies the particular classes of entities it treats. The theory of the firm, for instance, is a model; when it is interpreted as talking about the cars General Motors produces, their prices, and the like, it is an applied model. . . . whereas the statements of a model are not propositions that are true, nearly true, or grossly false, the statements of an applied model are. (Gibbard and Varian 1978, pp. 667-668)

The alternative stance is realism about properties and kinds or universals in general. This view implies the possibility of having true statements about the relations between universals or quasi-universals, such as that between a certain chromosomal structure and the capacity to keep doctors away, or between prices, income, information and demand. The statements of models in Gibbard and Varian's sense might have a truth value even if they are not about particular situations.

Consider the following weak version of the invisible hand thesis:

[MC] The free market system coordinates economic activities.

Since this is a claim that seems to be implied by some economic theories, we must inquire about its precise contents and ask whether it may be true. If economists were nominalists, they would think that [MC] might be true only if formulated as

[MCn] For all particular entities *x*, if *x* is a free market system, then *x* coordinates economic activities.

If economists were realists about universals, they would be prepared to consider the truth of the following version, which makes no reference to particular entities.

[MCr] The property of being a free market system necessitates the property of being capable of coordinating economic activities.

The realist of this sort might hold the view that the law of demand or the quantity theory do not have to be formulated as universally quantified statements about particular entities and events to be potentially true. It might be that

[D] An increase in the price of a good *leads to* a decrease in the demand for it

is true about the relations between the universals of price and demand, and that

[M] An increase in the amount of money *leads to* a decrease in the purchasing power of a unit of money is true about the universal of money. Neither of these statements would have to be solely about particular cases of an increase in price or the amount of money in order to be potentially true. A nominalist would think that, to have a chance of being true, [M] would have to be construed as a generalization of particular cases of the relationship of "leading to", such as the ones reported in Friedman's and Schwartz's studies of the monetary histories of the U.S.A. and the U.K.

However, economists know that [D] and [M] have to be reformulated in order to have any hope of counting as true statements. Such vertically isolative statements unavoidably involve horizontal isolation as well. Retaining the metaphysical character of the notion of "leading to", the presence of horizontal isolation can be made clear by adding the *ceteris paribus* clause to the two statements.

[Dcp] An increase in the price of a good *leads to* a decrease in the demand for it, *ceteris paribus*

and

[Mcp] An increase in the amount of money *leads to* a decrease in the purchasing power of a unit of money, *ceteris paribus*.

The problem with [Dcp] and [Mcp] is that they may be inapplicable due to the falsity of the *ceteris paribus* clause. In this case they are vacuously true. Another reformulation involves a metaphysical revision of the notion of "leading to" by adopting the concept of tendency.

[Dt] An increase in the price of a good *tends to lead to* a decrease in the demand for it.

[Mt] An increase in the amount of money *tends to lead to* a decrease in the purchasing power of a unit of money.

These statements are about tendencies, not about actual sequences of events. If the respective tendencies are there, the statements are true, even if [D] and [M] are false.

Economists tend to measure such tendencies. Consider a simple linear demand equation

[Dt'] $q = \beta p + r$

which gives the quantity demanded as a function of price. Price is regarded as having a systematic effect on the demand, while r captures the random influences, in addition to the measurement error. Parameter β represents the price elasticity of demand. The estimation of β amounts to measuring the tendency by which price influences demand. As Cartwright says, it is assumed here that "the price has a stable tendency to influence demand, and that the tendency has a fixed and measurable strength", represented by the value of β (Cartwright 1989, p. 150). I would like to add that the fact that [Dt'] is partial and that some strong assumptions are typically made about the distribution of r does not preclude the possibility of having a true account of the strength of the tendency; that is, having the correct estimate of β. This is not to deny that there may be other obstacles to this possibility.

The necessity of reformulating [D] and [M] in terms of the *ceteris paribus* clause or in terms of tendencies is a reminder of the presence of horizontal isolation: the statements neglect a number of factors that might have an impact on the outcome. In particular, the micro stories behind such statements are partial in that they do not encompass all the causes of economic phenomena. Since causally relevant but theoretically excluded factors may enter the stage and intervene in the process under consideration, prediction is an uncertain endeavour. Indeed, it is not exceptional that the predictions of economics go wrong. Yet, the partial character of theories and the incorrectness of predictions are not sufficient to conclude that the premises of economic theories are false. Since they are representations of parts or aspects of the world, we have to ask whether they could be true or false about those parts or aspects.

Let us cite the passage from Hendry again:

> I take it as self-evident that economic behaviour is sufficiently complex and evolutionary that it is not helpful to talk about economic theories being 'true' or of inferences yielding the 'correct' results. ... By their very nature, models are inherently simplifications and inevitably false. (Hendry 1986, pp. 30-31)

Cartwright's early view of the character of fundamental physical laws is similar to that of Hendry's about economic models:

> If the fundamental laws are true, they should give a correct account of what happens when they are applied in specific circumstances.[6] But they do not. If we follow out their consequences, we generally find that the fundamental laws go wrong ... (Cartwright 1983, p. 13)

A hundred years earlier, John Eliot Cairnes expressed a view which runs counter to that of Hendry and Cartwright. Here Cairnes follows Senior and J.S. Mill even if he uses slightly different terminology. Cairnes is explicit in admitting that the outcomes inferred from fundamental theory are not true. In this he agrees with Hendry and Cartwright. But Cairnes does not agree on the claim that the fundamental premises of

[6] Here as sometimes elsewhere, Cartwright's wording is not very careful. *What happens when being applied by scientists* cannot conceivably be within the domain of the fundamental laws, while *what happens in specific circumstances as represented by the implications of the fundamental laws* might.

a theory cannot be true. He says that the conclusions of economic theory are "hypothetical", while its premises are "positively true". For instance, it is

> positively true ... to assert that men desire wealth, that they seek, according to their lights, the easiest and shortest means by which to attain their ends, and that consequently they desire to obtain wealth with the least exertion of labor possible. (Cairnes 1888, p. 62)

Indeed, the premises may be positively true even if they do not encompass all the causes and conditions which have an impact on phenomena. The set of premises is incomplete.

> But it is surely possible that the premises should be true, and yet incomplete – true so far as the facts which they assert go, and yet not including all the conditions which affect the actual course of events. (Cairnes 1888, p. 68)

In other words, the set of premises provides a partial truth at most. In short, it purports to isolate the most significant factors contributing to the outcome. Since not all causally influential factors are covered by the theory, its implications cannot be expected to match the phenomena. The factors covered by the theory in fact combine with others not included in the theory. Therefore, its implications are true "hypothetically" only. As Cairnes writes, the conclusions of both mechanics, astronomy, and economics, "when applied to facts, can only be said to be true in the absence of disturbing causes; which is, in other words, to say that they are true on the hypothesis that the premises include all the causes affecting the result" (Cairnes 1888, p. 61). Cairnes here implies that theories in these fields involve *ceteris absentibus* clauses as special cases of nullifying idealizations. This makes the conclusions of economics counterfactual or tendential statements: "... the doctrines of Political Economy are to be understood as asserting, not what will take place, but what *would* or what *tends* to take place, and in this sense only are they true." (Cairnes 1888, p. 69).

I would like to add that not only can the conclusions of economic theory be interpreted as expressing tendencies, but so can the fundamental premises themselves. In particular, the proposition that "men desire wealth, that they seek, according to their lights, the easiest and shortest means by which to attain their ends, and that consequently they desire to obtain wealth with the least exertion of labor possible" (*ibid.*, p. 62) might be taken to depict a mental tendency characterizing human beings. This seems to have been J.S. Mill's view. This also appears to be Gibbard and Varian's position concerning the modern incarnation of the above proposition. They say that "the economist's assumption of perfect optimizing behavior ... may be useful in describing the 'central tendency' of economic behavior" (Gibbard and Varian 1978, p. 670).

However, it is yet another indication of the difficulty of applying the terminology of truth to statements of tendency that they say the optimization assumption might be "useful" at most and that "of course this assumption is, strictly speaking, false" (*ibid.*). A realist about powers and tendencies would not find any insurmountable difficulty in hypothesizing that a tendency statement is true even if it is partial and non-observational.

The suggestions above imply that the attainment of truth does not presuppose a de-isolated picture of the world, either horizontally or vertically or both. This seems to diverge from the positions held within the Poznań School. Nowak thinks that what he calls the "concretization" of a theory takes it closer to the truth. Concretization amounts to relaxing the idealizing assumptions of a theory. This does not yet as such imply the rejection of the idea that isolative theories may be true of parts of reality. Krajewski's approach seems to lead to such a rejection, however. He talks about the "factualization" of idealizing theories (Krajewski 1977a, 1977b). Factualization is the same process as concretization in the Marx-Nowak terminology. Obviously,"factualized" theories are supposed to be closer to the "facts" than "idealized" theories. This terminological decision seems to reflect some sort of empiricist approach to scientific theorizing. Only empirical or observable facts are facts proper. Only "factualized" theories can hope to be true of facts, while "idealized" theories are about imaginary constructs.[7]

A realist, on the other hand, does not discriminate between facts and non-facts by using the criterion of observability or empirical character. Isolative theories using idealizing assumptions may also successfully depict facts, such as causal powers, tendencies and universals. The process of de-isolation is therefore not to be confused with factualization. Furthermore, concretization is only one form of de-isolation, namely vertical de-isolation.

We know that economists are not consistently devoted to de-isolating (or "factualizing") their theories. Many economic theories remain strongly isolative and their major idealizing assumptions fail to be relaxed. Should we adopt Krajewski's approach, this would be taken as sufficient to deny those theories the attainment of the truth.

[7] Note that Jack Birner (1990) has adopted Krajewski's terminology. He uses the pair 'idealization'-'factualization'.

5. Conclusion

I have tried to argue that isolative theories are not false because they are partial. Nor are they false because they are abstract. Nor are they false because they involve idealizing assumptions. They may be shallow because the slices they carve are not joints of the world. They may be explanatorily false because they fail to capture the most crucial explanatory features of a situation. Economists disagree as to what is true and what is false, what is shallow and what is deep, and what is explanatory and what is non-explanatory. Chronic disagreement is not sufficient for falsity either.

It follows that *de-isolation* is not the only path to the truth, even if it is needed for the pursuit of the whole truth. *Switching over to a different isolation* is sometimes needed to approach the truth about the essential aspects of an object. Such a move would exemplify what I have termed increasing *essesimilitude* (Mäki 1991a). This is precisely the kind of idea that is needed to make sense of the truth of isolative theories. When construed in terms of first-step assumptions, this idea would allow us to think of one isolative theory as a true first step, while another theory is false, or that one is closer to the truth than the other. First steps are not *merely* first steps on the way towards representing reality, rather they may be serious attempts to truly represent crucial aspects of reality.

This idea would make it possible to conceptualize some of the most fundamental disagreements in economics in terms of veracity. Indeed, economists might in fact hold rival views of true first steps rather than merely of the most useful, fruitful or convenient first steps. The notion of essesimilitude denotes a type of truthlikeness which is suggested as relevant in such cases. On the other hand, the Popperian concept of verisimilitude is fruitless for this purpose, since it suggests a measure of closeness to the whole truth.

Let us quote again the passage from Popper from which we began: "Can any model be true? I do not think so. Any model, whether in physics or in the social sciences, must be an oversimplification. It must omit much, and it must overemphasize much." Popper says that all models are *over*simplifications and that an omission of something involves an *over*emphasis on something else. Such "overly" representations are, of course, false. But there is a way in which Popper's claim can be questioned, as suggested in the foregoing. I argue that not all simplifications need to be *over*simplifications and that not all emphases need to be *over*emphases. Simplifications and emphases do their job properly if they help isolate the essential or dominant features of the research object. If they don't, they simplify and emphasize too much or too little – or falsely.

Uskali Mäki
Department of Economics
Duke University
Durham NC 27706
USA

REFERENCES

Birner, J. (1990). Idealizations and the Development of Capital Theory. In: J. Brzeziński, Fr. Coniglione, T.A.F. Kuipers and L. Nowak (Eds.), *Idealization I: General Problems* (*Poznań Studies in the Philosophy of the Sciences and the Humanities*, **16**), pp. 127-149.

Cairnes, J.E. (1888). *The Character and Logical Method of Political Economy*. 2nd ed. London: Macmillan.

Cartwright, N. (1983). *How the Laws of Physics Lie*. Oxford: Oxford University Press.

Cartwright, N. (1989). *Nature's Capacities and their Measurement*. Oxford: Oxford University Press.

Gibbard, A. and H.R. Varian (1978). Economic Models. *The Journal of Philosophy*, **75**, 664-670.

Haavelmo, T. (1944). *The Probability Approach to Econometrics*. Supplement to Vol. 12 of *Econometrica*. Chicago: Econometric Society.

Hamminga, B. (1990). The Structure of Six Transformations in Marx's *Capital*, Volume III. In: J. Brzeziński, Fr. Coniglione, T.A.F. Kuipers and L. Nowak (Eds.), *Idealization I: General Problems* (*Poznań Studies in the Philosophy of the Sciences and the Humanities*, **16**), pp. 89-111.

Hendry, D. (1986). Econometric Methodology: a Personal Perspective. In: T.F. Bewley (Ed.) *Advances in Econometrics*. Cambridge: Cambridge University Press, 29-48.

Krajewski, W. (1977a). *Correspondence Principle and the Growth of Science*. Dordrecht: Reidel.

Krajewski, W. (1977b). Idealization and Factualization in Science. *Erkenntnis*, **11**, 323-339.

Mäki, U. (1989). On the Problem of Realism in Economics. *Ricerche Economiche*, **43**, 176-198. [Reprinted in *The Philosophy and Methodology of Economics*, edited by B. Caldwell and E. Elgar.]

Mäki, U. (1991a). Comment on Hands. In: N. De Marchi, and M. Blung (Eds.) *Appraising Economic Theories: Studies in the Methodology of Research Programmes*. Aldershot: Edward Elgar, pp. 85-90.

Mäki, U. (1991b). Realism and the Nature of Theory: A Lesson from J.H. von Thünen's *Isolated State*. Mimeo.

Mäki, U. (1992a). On the Method of Isolation in Economics. In: C. Dilworth (Ed.), *Intelligibility in Science* (*Poznań Studies in the Philosophy of the Sciences and the Humanities*, **26**), pp. 317-351.

Mäki, U. (1992b). Friedman and Realism. *Research in the History of Economic Thought and Methodology*, **10**, 171-195.

Mäki, U. (1993a). The Market as an Isolated Causal Process: A Metaphysical Ground for Realism. In: B. Caldwell and S. Boehm (Eds.), *Austrian Economics: Tensions and New Developments*. Dordrecht: Kluwer Publishers, pp. 35-59.

Mäki, U. (1993b). Scientific Realism and Some Peculiarities of Economics. Forthcoming in *Boston Studies in the Philosophy of Science*.

Musgrave, A. (1981). Unreal Assumptions' in Economic Theory: The F-twist Untwisted. *Kyklos*, **34**, 377-387.

Nowak, L. (1980). *The Structure of Idealization*. Dordrecht: Reidel.

Popper, K. (1983) [1967]. The Rationality Principle. In: D. Miller (Ed.), *A Pocket Popper*. Oxford: Fontana.

Rosenberg, A. (1978). The Puzzle of Economic Modeling. *The Journal of Philosophy*, **75**, 670-683.

Varian, H. (1990). *Intermediate Microeconomics. A Modern Approach*. 2nd edition. New York: Norton.

Part II

Case Studies of Idealization in Economics

Poznań Studies in the Philosophy of the Sciences and the Humanities
1994, Vol. 38, pp. 171-188

Nancy Cartwright

MILL AND MENGER: IDEAL ELEMENTS AND STABLE TENDENCIES

ABSTRACT. This paper starts from a discussion of the opinions of John Stuart Mill and Karl Menger on idealization in economics. How can we get from studies of economic actors as ideal or quasi-ideal reasoners to policy recommendations? The focus is on the transition from the so-called "ideal" to the real (from *a priori* principles to accounts of empirical phenomena), especially when the theory of the ideal proceeds mathematically, with at best small glances at data.

1. Introduction

This paper takes up some questions about idealization raised by John Stuart Mill and Carl Menger. It is part of a larger project with a more modern orientation. Ultimately my topic is the use in economics of theories that take the rational, or partially rational behaviour of individual agents as their basis for economic theory. I worry about those theories because much of their development depends on *a priori* reasoning. In my view the principal point of economics is policy formulation. The question is the obvious one: how can we get from studies of ideal or quasi-ideal reasoners to policy recommendations? Though the problems will bear on each other, my primary concern is not with aggregation, with the question of how to get from a theory of individual behaviour to a description of society as a whole, but rather with the question of how to get from the so-called "ideal" to the real, especially when the theory of the ideal proceeds mathematically, with at best small glances to data. The issue I want ultimately to understand about these modern theories is how they can begin with *a priori* principles and hope to end with an account of empirical phenomena.

Mill and Menger are instructive. Both reject induction and attempt to produce economics *a priori*; both deduce their economic principles from the putative behaviour of ideal economic agents; and both self-consciously idealize. I will be concerned with two kinds of idealization in this paper. I will look briefly at the assumption that the agents under study are rational, and in more detail at the assumption, that these agents act purely from economic motives. The methods used in Menger's *Principles of Economics* ([1950], orig. (1871)) were defended in his *Problems of Economics and Sociology* ([1963], orig. (1883)) a dozen years later. Mill's *Principles of Political Economy* (1848) are underwritten in the *System of Logic*, especially in Book VI ("On the Logic of The Moral Sciences" (1843)), as well as in his "Definition of Political Economy" (1836). These philosophical works are the principal reason for turning to Mill and Menger. Both provide a detailed and sophisticated defense of their methods, defence of a kind that is not to be found in modern writers on the foundations of economics.

2. Two Problems for the Covering Law Account of Explanation

> We understand a concrete phenomenon in a *theoretical* way . . . by recognizing it to be a special case of a certain regularity (conformity-to-laws) in the succession, or in the co-existence of phenomena, in other words we become aware of the existence and the peculiary, the nature of a concrete phenomenon by learning to recognize in it mere exemplification of a conformity-to-law of phenomena in general. Accordingly we understand the e.g. in concrete cases increase of ground rent on the decrease of the interest of capital and other such things in a theoretical way since the pertinent phenomena present themselves to us (on the basis of our theoretical knowledge) merely as particular examples of the laws of ground rent, of interest on capital, etc. (Menger 1963, Bk 1, Ch. 2)

This passage could have been written, indifferently, by either Carl Menger or by C.G. Hempel. As it happens, it was written by Menger. But it expresses precisely the theory of the covering-law model of explanation defended by Hempel. In science we explain a concrete happening by showing it to be a special case — or exemplification — of a general law.

I have for a long time opposed the covering-law model for bits of physics, where it has been thought, *prima facie*, to apply best. So I am, not surprisingly, suspicious of its application in economics. Broadly, there are two problems with the claim that physics explains a concrete phenomenon by, as Menger says, "recognizing it to be a special case" of theoretical laws:

(1) A good many of the abstract laws we use in a physics explanation tell not what things do but what they *tend* to do. That's because much of physics works by the method of analysis: phenomena are broken into their "essential" parts. The laws describe the behaviour of the parts separately, and do not themselves cover most cases directly. Phenomena which are directly a "special case of the law" are rare, if they exist at all,

and generally occur only in highly contrived experimental settings. To explain a naturally occurring phenomenon, some kind of synthesis of the pieces must be made.

Consider the case of Coulomb's law of electrostatic attraction and repulsion. Coulomb's law says that the force between two objects of charge q_1 and q_2 is proportional to $q_1 q_2 / r^2$. Yet this is not the force the bodies experience. They are always subject in addition to the law of gravity and usually to other forces as well. We say that Coulomb's law gives the force *due to* their charge, but we need to remember that the force "due to their charge" is not the force that actually occurs. Coulomb's law, as stated, does not cover any real phenomena at all.

(2) The laws of physics tend to apply not to real, but only to fictional objects. This is a point that Pierre Duhem (*Aim and Structure of Physical Theory* [1954], orig. (1906)) makes much of in his attack on realism. Newtonian mechanics explains the motion of the earth around the sun by treating the two as point masses, not as real physical objects, or more sophisticatedly, it treats them as extended bodies but assumes they have a "centre of mass" that occupies a precisely defined geometrical point. Kelvin despised these falsehoods of Newtonian physics, which he derided as "abstract mechanics". Often fictionalization in physics is forced by the mathematics. For instance, we use equations whose solutions require that a field be defined at every point around a geometrical boundary, and preferably be zero there. Thus in experiment we often enclose the fields in an earthed copper sphere which we treat as an "ideal" conductor with no thickness, so we can take the field to be zero in the perpendicular direction everywhere on its outer surface. The need for this kind of fiction was one of the principal grounds for Poission's objections to Fourier's use of differential equations. But Poission and Kelvin replaced the theories they attacked with theories that also treat only of fictions, although of course of fictions they found far more "realistic". My general conclusion from studying cases like these is that the laws of physics are, in Menger's language, "exemplified" only in models. The relation between models and real phenomena is both problematic and highly various. Making the connection is the exciting work of applied physics and understanding what legitimates it case by case is the real undone work of philosophy of physics.

3. *A Priori* Economics

Both Mill and Menger take notice of the problems that face covering-law explanation. Mill stresses the first; Menger, the second. But in both cases, the principles of political economy they offer are subject to both kinds of problem. Menger tells us with regard to "the realm of economic phenomena" in their "full empirical reality": "Properly their can be no question of strict (exact) theoretical knowledge in general or of strict laws (of so-called 'laws of nature') in particular for them under this presupposition". But, he urges,

> What needs no less to be emphasized is the circumstance *that with this presupposition the same thing also holds true of the results of theoretical research and all the remaining realms of the world of phenomena*. For even natural phenomena in their 'empirical reality' offer us neither strict types nor even strictly typical relationships. Real gold, real oxygen and hydrogen, real water – not to mention all the complicated phenomena of the inorganic or even the organic world – are in their full empirical reality neither of strictly typical nature, nor, given the above manner of looking at them, can exact laws ever be observed concerning them. (Menger 1963, p. 58)

For this reason both Menger and Mill reject the inductive method for discovering laws in the social sciences. Mill attributes the difficulty to the great variety of causes that come together to produce a single event, so that the same combination is unlikely to occur frequently enough to provide grounds for an induction:

> The phenomena of society might not only be completely dependent on known causes, but the mode of operation of all those causes might be reducible to laws of considerable simplicity, and yet no two cases might admit of being treated in precisely the same manner. So great might be the variety of circumstances on which the results in different cases depend, that the art (that corresponds to even a perfect science) might not have a single general precept to give... (Mill 1843, p. 56)

So simple induction by enumeration is ruled out, along with much else. The most powerful method for reasoning from experience is that of the artificial experiment. But that is not available in the social sciences, not only because we do not have the power to contrive great social experiments but because, even if we could, we should suffer "both the impossibility of ascertaining and taking note of all the facts of each case, and because (those facts being in a perpetual state of change) before sufficient time had elapsed to ascertain the result of the experiment, some material circumstances would always have ceased to be the same." (Mill 1843, p. 61) So then, "We can only watch those [experiments] which nature produces" (Mill 1843, p. 61) and try to apply to them our best passive methodology, that is, "Mill's methods". Mill surveys these, from strongest to weakest, and shows that they will not serve either. All that remains is some kind of *a priori* method – of course for Mill this does not mean totally *a priori* reasoning, but rather use of evidence that we have prior to any detailed observations of complex social life.

Happily, this kind of evidence is available in political economy, since the causes it studies

> are laws of human nature and external circumstances capable of exciting the human will to action. The desires of man and the nature of the conduct to which they prompt him are within the reach of our observation. We can also observe what are the objects which excite those desires. The materials of this knowledge everyone can principally collect within himself, with reasonable consideration. Knowing therefore accurately the properties of the substances concerned, we may reason with as much certainty as in the most demonstrative parts of physics, from any assumed set of circumstanices. (*On the Definition of Political Economy* (pp. 428, 429))

Menger too opposes induction. His attack on the German historical school is well known. In large part his argument is grounded on his claim that the historicists spend their efforts laying out in detail what has actually happened, which is altogether the wrong way to go about finding exact laws. He, like Mill, will rely on *a priori* reasoning to establish the exact laws of political economy. Indeed, what I find most striking about Menger's *Principles of Economics* is that it is not a work in empirical science at all but entirely a work of philosophy. Mill at least insists on checking the results of the *a priori* method against the facts, if only to show up where we have missed something in our accounting of the initial conditions. Moreover, inductively established empirical regularities can be of real use: It is true that the knowledge of the initial arrangement of causes is almost always beyond us, so precise prediction is impossible. Nevertheless, "an amount of knowledge quite insufficient for prediction may be most valuable for guidance." (Mill 1843, Bk. VI, Ch. VI) From Menger, we cannot expect even guidance. Over half of his book on methodology is spent showing that historical information — information about the sources, background and development of real occurrences — provides neither (i) an inductive base, nor (ii) a testing ground, nor (iii) a target of prediction for the theoretical sciences. What then *is* the relation between theory and the world? With respect to prediction, the answer is given in one sentence "[O]nly the exact sciences in their *totality* are able to offer a *universal* theoretical understanding of the world of phenomena — indeed even of a single complicated phenomenon of the real world" (Menger 1963, p. 77) Failing completed social science, testing seems equally out of the question. Exact science must proceed on its own, without much help from empirical observation.

How then should it proceed? Menger proposes the same kind of analytic method that we shall see in Mill. The way for theoretical science to proceed, "essentially different from Bacon's empirical realistic induction, is the following: it seeks to ascertain the *simplest elements* of everything real, elements which must be thought of as strictly typical just because they are the simplest." It is to do so "without considering whether these in reality are present as *independent* phenomena." Indeed, "the empirical forms here under discussion, e.g., absolutely pure oxygen, pure alcohol, pure gold, a person pursuing only economic aims, etc., exist in part only in our ideas". (Menger 1963, p. 61) Here we have explicit mention of the kind of fictionalization that I worry about but that Menger not only seems to admit but seems positively to embrace. Before turning to discuss it, I want first to remark on Menger's conception of law.

Menger tells us that theoretical exact science is supposed to break phenomena into their simplest elements and then determine the laws these elements follow. But how is theoretical science to discover these laws? He doesn't say. We know we are to reject induction. One of the reasons gives a clue as to what to do instead. What is wrong with induction is that it can only show that two phenomena have been regularly associated; the claim that they are associated "in general" is "*not strictly* warranted", and nothing can help. "Strict (exact) laws" can never result from an inductive method "even if this [method] were the most perfect conceivable and its fundamental observation the most comprehensive and the most critical." (Menger 1963, p. 57)

Menger mentions Aristotle, not Hume, as having correctly recognized this fact about induction. I take it that the alternative then must be deduction. Laws about what the simplest elements do must follow simply from the identification of what they are. This Aristotelian account is supported by Menger's characterization of understanding: "We understand a phenomenon when we have recognized the reason for its existence and for its characteristic quality (the reason for it's *being* and for its *being as it is*)". (In the original, "den Grund ihres Seins und ihres So-Seins.") (Menger 1963, p. 43) It is also suggested by his remark that the simplest elements "must be thought of as strictly typical just because they are the simplest," where we have just been told that "strictly typical phenomena of a definite kind must always, and, indeed in consideration of our laws of thinking, simply of *necessity* be followed by strictly typical phenomena of just as definite and different a type." (Menger 1963, p. 60) So it looks as if one criterion for judging whether we have really found the simple elements is that we can do *a priori* science with them. Once we have a simple element, its behaviour can be figured out simply using the laws of thought. That is why Menger's *Principles*, unlike Mill's, can read like a work of pure reason.

It is important in this respect to note that Menger's concept of value, which is usually characterized as a subjective concept, is so only in one sense. The value of a good is not a feature it possesses independent of its relation to human needs. It is not, for instance, determined by its method of production. Value is characterized as "merely the importance that we first attribute to the satisfaction of our needs, that is, to our lives and well being, and in consequence carry over to economic goods as the exclusive causes of the satisfaction of our needs." (Menger 1963, p. 116) The "we" is misleading. Menger is here already making an idealization. For he does not mean the importance "we" real people each attribute to our own needs, but rather the importance attributed by "the economizing man," i.e. the importance that *should be* attributed to the need. Menger must mean this both because his chief concern about how real men fall short of the ideal economizing man is *error*, and this includes errors about the importance of our needs; also, Menger is prepared to tell us what needs are more important than others. It is controversial whether Menger actually sticks to this objective sense of "subjective" value throughout. But it is important for philosophical consistency that he do so, for reasons well rehearsed. If "value" turns out to refer to what people do value as opposed to what is valuable, then the theory of value will require empirical input, even if only, as Mill maintains, material that the economist can collect "within himself." *A priori* economics will not be possible.

4. Replacement of *Ceteris Paribus* Laws by Tendencies

Turn now to the first of the two troubles I described for the covering-law model. This is the one that Mill focuses on. The idea of a *ceteris paribus* law is well known in the history of economics, and in physics too. We might render Coulomb's law in *ceteris paribus* form: "If there were no other forces at work, the force between two charged particles would be proportional to (q_1q_2) and inversely proporional to r^2." Mill would put it differently: "Two charged particles *tend* to experience a force proportional to q_1q_2/r^2." Mill's version steers between two faulty alternatives. If we put the *ceteris paribus* clause in, we have a law which is practically useless. It covers next to nothing, since it describes what happens in only one very specific – and very uncommon (impossible ?) – circumstance. If we leave it out, then the law will no longer be true. Mill tells us about cases like these:

> We might have cautioned inquirers against too extensive *generalization*, and reminded them that there are *exceptions* to all rules. [But] the error, when there is error, does *not* arise from generalizing too extensively . . . Doubtless a man often asserts of an entire class what is only true of a part of it; but his error generally consists not in making too

> wide an assertion, but in making the wrong kind of assertion; *he predicated an actual result when he should only have predicated a tendency to that result – a power acting with a certain intensity in that direction*. (Nagel 1950, p. 438)

The advantage of the language of tendencies is that it marks what we really assume: that the behaviour we highlight is stable from situation to situation. Experiencing a Coulomb force is not only what charges do when all other sources of force are absent; it is also what they *try* to do, or what they contribute to the total effect, even when other sources are present. I try to avoid the language of idealization that is commonly used to describe these cases since it distracts from the central assumption, the one of stability Menger talks about "economizing man"; presumably this is a man engaged only in "economy", that is in "the precautionary activity of humans directed toward covering their material needs". (Menger 1963, p. 63) This is an idealization in that we study what people do in very unusual, perhaps impossible, circumstances — when they are engaged in economy. But we care about what would happen in those peculiar circumstances because we are convinced that we learn something there about what economizing activity will contribute when the full tide of life is carried on as well. Otherwise, what has the "ideal" case to do with real economic phenomena?

Mill uses a similar idealization:

> Political economy considers mankind as occupied soley in acquiring and consuming wealth; and aims at showing what is the course of action into which mankind, living in a state of society, would be impelled if that motive, except in the degree in which it is checked by the two perpetual countermotives above adverted to, were absolute rules of all their actions. (Nagel 1950, p. 420)

He also utilizes the idea we have seen in Menger of breaking phenomena into their elements. According to Mill "The method of the practical philosopher consists of two processes: the one, analytical; the other, synthetical. He must *analyze* the existing state of *society* into its elements, not dropping and losing any of them by the way." (Nagel 1950, p. 436)

But Mill is much more at pains to stress the final task, which Menger does not feel obliged to think about since he casts it outside of the domain of theoretical science.

> After referring to the experience of individual man to learn the *law* of each of these elements, that is, to learn what are its natural effects and how much of the effects follow on from so much of the cause when not counteracted by any other cause, there remains an operation of synthesis: to put all these effects together and, from what they are separately, to collect what would be the effect of all the causes acting at once. If these various operations could be correctly performed, the result would be prophecy. (Nagel 1950, p. 436)

I worry about how widely this process of analysis and synthesis can be applied. That will be the topic of the last sections. Before that I turn briefly to the second problem I described for covering laws.

5. Purely Fictional Objects

Menger talks of "absolutely pure oxygen, pure alcohol, pure gold, a person pursuing only economic aims". The last item on the list points to the first problem for covering laws, which Mill's treatment promises to dissolve. On Mill's account, in cases like this we are not trying to attribute events that really happen to causes that never occur. The ideal economizing agent is not himself the explanation but only an epistemological tool with which we construct an explanation. The explanation is an abiding tendency associated with the economic motive, a tendency to produce a certain fixed outcome whenever that motive is at work. It is of course in most real cases only a partial explanation, since countervailing tendencies must be taken into account as well. The idealization to situations where the economic motive operates purely on its own serves only to show us the nature of the tendency involved.

The case of pure oxygen, pure alcohol, and pure gold, along with the purely rational agent, are in all probability different. They, unlike an economic motive, simply aren't there to contribute to the effect. In some cases it may be plausible to suppose they are. For instance, in quantum mechanics we might first describe the energy due to just the relation between a one-proton nucleus and a circulating electron, and call that the Hamiltonian for "the pure hydrogen atom." Then we consider other structural features that describe a particular atom (or set of atoms) we want to study, write down Hamiltonians for each, and add them all together. That's like Mill's method of analysis and synthesis, and hence this case is a candidate for a tendency account.

But is the ideally rational agent like that? Menger proposes to add in the effects of error at the end, as indeed do many modern theories, in different ways. This strategy may work to produce a predictively adequate account, but I think it would be a mistake to use Mill's ideas of tendencies as a justification for it. An economic motive is something that people can have and operate from along with a number of other motives. But pure rational behaviour is not there in the first place with irrationality as a countervailing cause; nor should we think that we have within ourselves some kind of tendency to correctly-rational behaviour which is simply clouded over by inattention, miscalculation, and the like. Rationality plus some add-on correction factor should not be too readily assimilated to Mill's image of a cause acting in conjunction with a disturbing factor. That does not mean that the decomposition into purely rational behaviour plus error is mistaken as an explanatory strategy. The point is, it needs defending.

The problem of the pure fiction appears in a number of different forms throughout Menger's *Principles*. First, as I have been discussing, Menger in a sense studies the "ideally rational" economizing man since he looks not at what the economic motive leads to in people as they are socially and psychologically constructed, but rather at what behaviour this motive should lead to. Or consider his theory of exchange. Here he assumes a society in which each agent acts on his own behalf, weighing his needs for one good against another. Menger's notion of rank among commodities is equally an idealization. George Stigler complains of it: "To attempt to trace in detail the stages of production of even a simple commodity – a common pin, for instance – in the highly complex modern economy would amount to nothing less than a detailed description of economic life and history! The concept of ranks is too precise, in other words, either for our analytical powers or for our analytical requirements." (Stigler 1973, pp. 232-233)

There are a number of other examples in the *Principles* as well, as indeed in all abstract theories. I have nothing very useful to offer about how to go about "de-idealizing". Different strategies will surely be appropriate for different cases. My aim here has been only to warn that we must not too readily assimilate this problem to Mill's and assume that all the problems facing fictions reduce to the ones that face Mill's account of tendencies.

6. Stability of Tendencies versus Local Causality

Both Menger and Mill feel driven to *a priori* economics because they cannot conceive any way to infer the principles that govern the elements from the complex happenings of "full empirical reality." Generations later, one of the greatest hopes for the probability approach in econometrics, especially by its founders Ragnar Frisch and Trygve Haavelmo, was that it would be able to solve this problem. That is a different story. Here I want to talk about the inverse problem: not, "How do we get from empirical phenomena to laws for the elements?" but rather "Given laws for the elements, how do we get back to full empirical reality?" Mill took this to be possible both in physics and in economics, though not in chemistry. In chemistry, causes interact: "[T]he Concurrence of Causes gives rise to a new effect bearing no relation to the separate effects of those causes." (Mill 1843, p. 167) In physics and economics causes compose. In Mill's own words "The general idea of the Composition of Causes [is] that though two or more laws interfere with one another, and apparently frustrate or modify one another's operation, yet in reality all are fulfilled, the collective effect being the exact sum of the effects of the causes taken separately." (Mill 1843, p. 168) In physics, summing is easy.: "[T]he effect of the joint forces is the same when they act simultaneously as if they had acted one after another, or by turns." (Mill 1843, p. 70) Mill never tells us how to calculate sums for economic effects.

Summing is not all that is going on in Mill's doctrine of the Composition of Causes. He assumes as well that there are fixed designated effects to be summed. That is part of his doctrine of tendencies. The use of the term "tendency" marks two different features about how causes operate. The first concentrates on the idea of analysis. In a given cause-effect sequence, the complex initial conditions can be conceptually divided into pieces each of which makes its own special "contribution". The effect in question is made up of the separate contributions composed together. The claim that each component cause produces its designated outcome is true when interpreted not literally, but as a tendency claim. The second feature highlighted by the term "tendency" is stability: the particular kind of effect assigned as special to a cause in one situation will be the same in all others, or at least across a wide range of varying circumstances.

Correlative with the two aspects of tendency, two distinctions need to be drawn. The first is the distinction between, on the one hand, causal claims that are true, but only locally, and, on the other, tendency ascriptions that involve commitments about how a cause will operate more widely. The second is the distinction between the claim that the designated effects of two separate causes "sum" to produce the occurent outcome in a given situation. This is the case in which we say the causes compose, in contrast to the claim that the causes "give rise to a new effect bearing no relation to the separate effects of these causes," in which case we say that the causes interact.

Hume argued that the only grounds on which we can appoint one particular behaviour as the specially designated effect of a given cause on a particular occasion is the fact that that kind of effect is regularly associated with that cause on all occasions. I do not follow Hume in this conclusion, and hence I am keen to keep the two distinctions separate. What I want to take up here are questions bearing on the first distinction between causal claims that are true only locally and those that hold across various boundaries. For the moment I want to ask not "What makes Mill think that causes compose in economics, and what are the rules for composition?" but rather "What makes him think that the behaviour of economic causes is stable from one situation to others that are importantly different?"

Surprisingly, Mill gives no answer to this question. I can suggest an answer to the alternative question about why we should think economic causes compose. That has to do with Mill's methodological individualism. Mill assumes that the causes in economics are the motives of individuals, their desires and aversions; and he models motives on forces. That is why he includes "aversion to labour" and "desire for the present enjoyment of costly indulgences" among the proper subjects of political economy. "These do not merely, like other desires, occasionally conflict with the pursuit of wealth, but accompany it always as a drag or impediment." (Nagel 1950, p. 420) Notice too his use of the language of *force* and *tendency* throughout his *Principles of Political Economy*. For instance,

> Demand and supply govern the value of all things which cannot be indefinitely increased; except that even for them, when produced by industry, there is a minimum value, determined by the cost of production. But in all things which admit of indefinite multiplication, demand and supply only determine the perpetuations of value, during a period which cannot exceed the length of time necessary for altering the supply. While thus ruling the oscillations of value, they themselves obey a superior force, which makes value gravitate towards Cost of Production... (Menger 1963, p. 312)

As to stability, Mill does defend the stability of human behaviour from situations in which we might consider people acting in isolation to social situations when they interact with each other. He says, "The laws of the phenomena of society are, and can be, nothing but the laws of the actions and passions of human beings united together in the social state. Men, however, in a state of society, are still men; their actions and passions are obedient to the laws of individual human nature." (Mill 1843, p. 59) But this is not enough. We need to be assured that motives are stable in the face of other motives, not that individual behaviour is stable in the face of other individuals.

An easy way to see the problem I worry about is to look at contrasting fables or parables. The introduction of fables seems apt, for the arguments of Menger and Mill, and of Ricardo, and indeed of most of the classicals, read very much like Harriet Martineau's parables, which are supposed to teach the lessons of political economy to dutiful workers. Mill and Menger, as we have seen, move our studies from the real world to an "ideal" one; they focus on a world in which the economic motive operates entirely on its own.[1] But they must carry into this ideal world a number of other features from the real world as well, features they neither want, nor try, to specify, explicitly. Mill makes some effort in that direction when he attends to the relation between physical and economic

---

[1] For a discussion of what makes a situation ideal, see N. Cartwright, "Aristotelian Natures and the Modern Experimental Method" (Cartwright, 1993).

knowledge, concluding, "Political economy, therfore, presupposes all the physical sciences" (Mill 1836, p. 318). But I think it would be impossible to specify exactly what is and what is not presupposed. Fables succeed by using stereotypical characters, like the fox, selected for his bragadocio in the tale of the sour grapes. We focus on the features identified with the stereotype; nevertheless we have a real character in the story, with all the other characteristics we will need to derive the prescribed behaviour. That is an important aspect of how fables work. The morals describe general relations between abstract features, but the abstract features are embodied in concrete individuals.[2]

Consider two fables with contradictory morals. First:

A marten eats the grouse;
A fox throttles the marten; the tooth of the wolf, the fox. (Lessing 1759, Sec. 1)

The moral of this fable is "The weaker are always a prey to the stronger." On the other hand, "What man is there of you whom if his son ask bread will give him a stone?" (Mathew 7:9). This second parable shows that the lesson of the first fable is local. We do not learn from the wolf and the fox, the marten and the grouse, about a fixed tendency associated with relative strength across all contexts. In the context of the hunt for food, the natural effect of strength is preying; in the context of the parent-child relationship, the natural effect of strength is nurturing.[3] Of course, the whole point of the fable is to teach a lesson beyond the context of the fable itself. In the one case we are supposed to see that political relations or perhaps the relationship beween landlord and tenant may elicit effects like those between predator and prey; in the other we are meant to learn about God's concern for the people he has created. Knowing how far and where to apply a fable is part of the art.

Menger and Mill both ignore this art. For Mill, that is because he assumes that the economic motive carries a stable tendency that acts in the same way across all the complicated contexts of social and political life. There are of course contervailing causes — other motives — usually at work, but the contribution of the economic motive itself

[2] Cf. G.E. Lessing (1759) Sec. 1.

[3] One could cling to the claim that the natural effects are stable by insisting that these are cases of interaction. I think that is not a very useful way to look at it, since it priveleges one of the effects as correct and the other as abherent; and it takes attention away from the central problem of figuring out where and how far either effect can be exported. Also I think it will prove far more fruitful to think of being a parent or going hunting as contexts rather than as countervailing causes.

is always the same. The complications involve discovering the rule for summing effects, which Mill does not explicitly address, and finding out for a given case what all the countervailing causes are, a problem he makes much of.

Menger too ignores the problem. I think that's because his *a priori* economics is supposed to be genuinely *a priori*. It is supposed to use "principles of cognition" and "laws of thinking" in order to establish results that could not be otherwise:

> [W]ith the assumption of strictly typical elements, or their exact measures, and of their complete isolation from all other causative factors, [exact science] does to be sure, and indeed on the basis of rules of cognition characterized by us alone, arrive at laws of phenomena which are not only absolute, but according to our laws of thinking, simply cannot be thought of in any other way but as absolute. That is, it arrives at exact laws, the so-called "laws of nature" of the phenomena. (Menger 1963, p. 67)

Recall, Menger aims to find out for a phenomenon "den Grund ihres Seins und ihres So-Seins" – the reason for its being and for its being what it is. He is going to find out what value and exchange really are and from that, how they must behave given what they are. There can be no doubt then that wheresoever they appear, we find they behave as they must. As with Mill, the "ideal" situation of "complete isolation from all other causative factors" is only a heuristic to teach us about the "natural" effect of a cause. But unlike Mill, there can be no question of this natural behaviour failing in a radically different context, since our theoretical investigations teach us what the cause must do given what it is.

Mill is an empiricist. This kind of defense is not available to him. For an empiricist, causes must be independently identifiable; there is no behaviour that can be supposed true of them just because of what they are. That is why Mill must turn to knowledge of our own psychology to substantiate his fundamental principles. And it is why in the end he must turn to empirical experience to back up his claims that economic motives have very stable tendencies and that the causes of social phenomena compose.

Menger has a corresponding problem. Max Weber praises Menger specifically for the fact that he does not allow psychology at the base of marginal utility theory. The reason the market rates in the Berlin Stock Exchange bear out the theory so well "is because action on the stock exchange is economically rational in especially high degree". (Max Weber 1908, p. 33) According to Weber "The rational *theory* of price formation not only has nothing to do with the concepts of experimental psychology. More generally, it has nothing to do with any 'psychology' of any kind which aspires to be a 'science'..." Weber is instructive for two reasons.

First, he does like Mill take experience to be crucial; it is psychological experiment he opposes. The passage just cited continues "*which* aspires to be a 'science' *going beyond everyday experience*", and only a few pages before, he tells us just what views of common experience must be justified in order for marginal utility theory to be feasible. Second, Weber, we know, is no realist about the laws of nature. His own work develops ideal types, which indeed is the description he gives to marginal utility theory. The point is that Weber had a theory of how to construct ideal types and of what role they play in the understanding of real empirical phenomena. Menger does not, and the stab Weber makes on Menger's behalf in a few paragraphs of his discussion of marginal utility theory hardly counts as a beginning. This is the reason I stressed the point that pure fictions make big problems for the covering-law model, even though I had nothing useful to say about various solutions proposed for these problems in economics. Menger may be able to figure out merely by reasoning how things he calls *value* and *exchange* behave. But then he has a major job to justify that what we call *value* and *exchange* in the real world are examples of Menger-value and Menger-exchange, or that they behave in the same way, either exactly, or approximately, by tendency or with rough similarity to the prescribed tendencies. Menger solves the problem of the stability of tendencies by definition; but he sets an equally troublesome problem in its stead. Mill's account requires an empirical defense. The problem is that he doesn't give it, and I would caution against too optimistically assuming that the job can be done at all.

7. Conclusion

The principles of economics developed both by Mill and Menger govern individuals who operate purely from an economic motive. Yet both aim to explain real social phenomena. How can something that is real be accounted for by something that never happened? Mill offers a solution. The behaviour of the purely economizing man does not explain anything. It plays instead a methodological role. It teaches us what tendencies to associate with the economic motive. The tendency is really there whenever the motive is, and it is the tendency that serves, in conjunction with other genuinely occuring features, to explain what happens in the world around us.

I have argued that Mill's account relies on a major undefended assumption. Let us admit, for the sake of argument, that it is possible to figure out — really figure out correctly — what effects would be produced by a person operating exclusively from economic motives, either by knowledge of our own psychological natures, as Mill suggests, or by pure reason, as Menger argues. What then? In that case we would know the effects of the economic motive in one particular situation – the situation when the economic motive operates on its own. We still have to provide good reason to think that this local causal relation can be exported to different kinds of situations – that is, that the behaviour we see in this very special case is the expression of a stable tendency. That's a job that Mill does not undertake. Menger does. For him stability is easy: whatever behaviour exact theory attributes to the economic motive is behaviour it must exhibit, by necessity, and hence everywhere. But Menger's advantage is purely temporary. For he then faces the problem of defending that the thing he has chosen to call the *economic motive* is identical with anything we every identify empirically as an economic motive.

Must we take these concerns seriously? Problems with stability will clearly differ from domain to domain. But I have a very general worry that stability may be far less wide ranging than we suppose. My worries have been generated by thinking about physics and its applications. The fundamental tendencies of physics are supposed to be terrifically stable. Indeed, the laws are often advertised as truly universal. I think this claim is radically false, or at least that the evidence we have points in exactly the opposite direction. For the most part, as the social constructionists have taught us to notice, the exact laws of physics are true only of what we make. There are notorious exceptions, like the planetary motions. But these are rare. We do not measure the success of modern physics by its ability to explain the material world around us as it naturally comes; but rather by its ability to create very particular environments in which nature behaves in regular and precisely predictable ways, as in the laboratory where we put our theories to the test, or in new pieces of technology where we put them to use, like the hydrogen bomb or the laser.

We can get physics to work in the world of "full empirical reality", but we do so not by grappling directly with the world outside of the laboratory. Instead we carry the whole laboratory into the world, usually with a good sturdy shield around it, like a battery casing. We can use Superconduciting Quantum Interference Devices (SQUIDS) to detect stroke victims, but we must put both the SQUID and the victim in a Hertz box. Notoriously, we cannot predict the course of a feather blowing about in the wind.

Far from being transparently universal, the evidence suggests that the laws of physics come with great long *ceteris paribus* clauses in front. Their domains are restricted; their tendencies are highly context-constrained.

How far can they be exported? I would argue that the laws of physics can be applied to exactly those situations that resemble the well-tested models of those laws. That's why the Newtonian mechanics of point masses works for the planetary system and not for the wayward feather – the planetary system is exactly the kind of system that the laws are true of.

How far can the principles of Mill and Menger be exported, or those of the modern economic theories I mentioned at the start? None of these, of course, begin in the laboratory, but rather somewhere in the heavenly regions where pure reason can yield results. I should think that that would make it harder. I think the fundamental tendencies we have studied in physics have shown themselves to be stable only across a very narrow range of circumstances. But the range is well laid out in the standard models that every physics student learns. For the well-established theories of physics we have a detailed – and well-tested – sense of where the tendency claims established in the laboratory can be relied on outside. What similar promise do we have for various exact non-inductive theories of economics?

Nancy Cartwright
Dept. of Philosophy, Logic and Scientific Method
London School of Economics and Political Science
Houghton St.
London WC2A 2AE
United Kingdom

REFERENCES

Cartwright, N. (1992). Aristotelian Natures and the Modern Experimental Method. In: Earman, I. (Ed.), *Inference, Explanation and Other Philosophical Frustrations*. Berkeley: University of California Press, pp. 44-91.

Duhem, P. (1906). *La théorie physique: son object, sa structure*. Paris, *Bibliothèque de philosophie expérimentale; 11*, sec. ed. Paris, Riviere, 1954. Transl. of sec. ed. *The aim and structure of physical theory*. Princeton: University Press, 1954.

Lessing, G.E. (1890). *Abhandlungen über die Fabel*, Wien: K. Graeser.

Menger, C. (1871). *Grundsätze der Volkswirtschaftlehre*, Wien: Braumüller. Transl.: *Principles of Economics*. Glencoe, Free Press, 1950.

Menger, C. (1883). *Untersuchungen über die Methode der Sozialwissenschaften, und der politischen Oekonomie insbesondere*. Leipzig: Duncker & Humblot. Transl. *Problems of economics and Sociology*. Urbana, University of Illinois Press, 1963.

Mill, J.S. (1836). On the Definition of Political Economy. In: Robson, J.M. (Ed.), *The Collected Works of John Stuart Mill*, Toronto: University of Toronto Press, Vol. 4, 1967.

Mill, J.S. (1843). *A System of Logic*. London: Parker.
Mill, J.S. (1848). *Principles of Political Economy*. London: Parker.
Nagel, E. (1950). *John Stuart Mill's Philosophy of Scientic Method*. New York: Hafner.
Stigler, G. (1973). The Economics of Carl Menger. *Journal of Political Economy*, April 1973.
Weber, M. (1908). Marginal Utility Theory and Fundamental Laws of Psychophysics, *Social Science Quarterly*, **56**, 1975/6, pp. 21-36.

Poznań Studies in the Philosophy
of the Sciences and the Humanities
1994, Vol. 38, pp. 189-203

Wolfgang Balzer*

EXCHANGE VERSUS INFLUENCE: A CASE OF IDEALIZATION

ABSTRACT. The intertheoretical relation between economic equilibrium theory and a theory of social institutions is studied in reduced form, i.e. by comparing the central primitives rather than the full formal models. It is shown that equilibrium can be regarded as a limit of institutions with ever more symmetrical power relations. Economic equilibrium theory thus is shown to be an idealization of the theory of social institutions. A provisionary topology which gives substance to the notion of a limit is defined "internally", i.e. by reference to items occurring in the models only. The meta-scientific status of idealization is briefly discussed.

Some famous authors have held that an adequate account of social phenomena can be given only by a combined approach including economics, sociology, psychology, and history.[1] This idea certainly is compelling; everyone having worked with a theory applicable to social systems will have felt that some part or aspect of the real situation could be better understood from the point of view of a different theory. It then seems natural to try combining different theories in order to improve the scientific picture of the situation. The problem, however, is that we have no clear ideas what it means to "combine" different theories from different disciplines to form a "joint picture" of the real phenomenon. There is a "problem of joint application". Vague notions of complementarity occur here and then, also the notion of a caricature has been used to describe the issue. We are certainly not in a position to make general claims about how different theories can, or do, work together in modelling real systems more adequately, simply because there are very few cases in which such combination was attempted, and because in such attempts the "theories" involved were very vague.[2]

---

* I am indebted to Bert Hamminga for helpful comments on an earlier draft.

[1] The view is explicit, for instance, in Braudel (1980), it is clearly implicit in Marx's work.

[2] Like in Marx.

In this paper I want to approach the problem by studying the borderline between economics and sociology. Here is a clear cut case in which the economic idealization of a free market clashes with the real existence of institutions aiming at the distortion of that market. It seems to me that this situation is typical for the relation between disciplines of the above list. By studying it more closely we therefore may hope to get a better understanding of how different theories in the social domain relate to each other and to reality. Intuitively, the relation in the case mentioned seems to be one of idealization or concretization: if the idealizations defining a free market are taken back, and the economic theory in this way is concretized, we arrive at a more comprehensive theory including institutions and market-like phenomena. A question arising naturally in that context is whether this case fits Nowak's conceptual account of idealization.[3]

Of course, there is little sense in talking about the whole disciplines of economics and of sociology; these are bodies of knowledge too comprehensive in order to describe real phenomena. From a meta-theoretic point of view[4] real phenomena or real systems are described or modelled by scientific theories. So we have to find two theories dealing with systems of the kind of markets and institutions. In economics there is no problem of finding a rather generally accepted theory about ideal markets, which in its various different forms is called equilibrium theory. As I will not go into the full details of any of its axiomatizations here, it is not necessary to pick one particular exposition. Any reader may think of his or her favorite version.[5] On the other hand, there is at the moment no theory of institutions on which sociologists would agree in a similar way. In sociology, the leading paradigm among formally trained scientists is game theory.[6] However, no empirical application of a game theoretic model to a real life social institution has been achieved up to now.[7] Moreover, it can be argued that game theory misses, and even contradicts to, a basic feature of institutions which consists in the change of the opponent's payoff-function. While game theory assumes that the

---

[3] Expositions are found in Nowak (1980), see also Hamminga (1989).

[4] My personal meta-theory is of course the structuralist view of theories which, I think, is the most sophisticated general approach to the structure and development of theories. See Balzer, Moulines, Sneed (1987).

[5] Arrow & Hahn (1971), Debreu (1972), Haendler (1979), Hildenbrand (1974).

[6] In particular, there is the claim that social institutions can be understood as supergames. See Taylor (1976) for the technical notions.

[7] There are of course numerous abstract "applications" of the game theoretic apparatus to abstract classes of situations being defined by certain characteristic payoff functions. But by "empirical application" I mean the full-fledged confrontation of a model with empirical data gathered from a concrete situation.

payoff functions are given, the theory of institutions assumes that individuals try to change their opponents' payoff functions.[8] Therefore I prefer a theory of social institutions which I have developed myself,[9] and I will take this theory as the sociological "counterpart" to equilibrium theory. The more narrow aim then is to study the relation between general equilibrium theory and that particular theory of social institutions in order to see what the relation of idealization amounts to in this case.

The result may be summarized by three propositions. First, the case indeed exemplifies the central feature of idealization, namely that we come from one theory to the other by means of abstraction. We come from institutions to markets by abstracting from certain features present in institutions which in fact prevent free exchange. Second, we even can point out some internal criteria — criteria formulated purely in terms of the theories' vocabulary — for idealization, and for the degree in which idealization is present. Third, however, there are doubts whether Nowak's conceptual model of idealization is general enough to treat cases of this kind in a natural way.

1. Preparations

The initial image of the situation is this. We know that real markets are biased by all kinds of regulations imposed by political and other institutions. Because of this, real markets are neither free nor competitive.[10] On the other hand, we believe we can imagine various such regulations of different strength, and we can imagine that by eliminating the strongest distortion, and then step by step other, less important ones, the system will approach a free market. In other words: if we make more and more idealizing assumptions about a real exchange system we will approach a free market, a model of equilibrium theory.

In order to obtain a more substantial account we have to look more closely at the two theories modelling the system "before" and "after" the idealizations have been made. If we assume that all important distortions are imposed on the system by social institutions, we may take the system in its non-idealized form as a model of the theory of institutions. The (counterfactual) idealized system on the other hand clearly is a model of equilibrium theory. For reasons of space it is not possible to present

[8] See Balzer (1992a) for details.

[9] Balzer (1990).

[10] In the last two decades this insight found expression in an internal economic approach, the "new institutional economics". See Bardhan (1989) for a brief account.

these two theories here in full detail. Rather, I will pursue the following strategy. I will concentrate on one central primitive of each theory, and see how these primitives relate to each other. By indicating informally their central role in the respective theory, and by assuming that "other parts" of the models are not essentially affected by the changes considered the comparison is thus "reduced" to the study of these two primitives. Without offering a full-fledged formal analysis I claim that the result obtained by this "reduced" approach will also be obtained when the full models of both theories are taken into account.

At the side of equilibrium theory I concentrate on the notion of *exchange* which, informally, lies at the heart of equilibrium theory. Ironically, this notion does not function as a primitive in the usual axiomatizations. It may be easily introduced, however. Let us consider a primitive of the following format:

$$exchange(i, a, j, b),$$

to be read: "individual i exchanges with individual j commodity a against commodity b". a and b are interpreted as tokens whose description includes the kind of good as well as the quantity. This notion is closely linked to that of endowment. If we know the endowments of all individuals before the exchange, and if we have complete knowledge of the exchange-predicate then the endowment after the exchange is uniquely determined. Also, from the exchange-predicate both endowments, before and after, may be determined, provided we know the "rest", i.e. those quantities which the individuals keep in their possession without exchange. This shows that the predicate really is fundamental for equilibrium theory. If it were not for reasons of simple mathematical formalism it might have easily entered into existing expositions. To the observational basis provided by endowments or exchange equilibrium theory adds the notion of utility or preference, as well as that of equilibrium plus the well known assumptions of maximization, convexity of preferences, and clearing of markets.

At the sociological side more explanation would be necessary. One main primitive of the theory of institutions is the notion of power which is used in the following format

$$power(i, a, j, b),$$

to be read: "individual i by performing action a exerts power over individual j so that j performs action b". Again, a and b are tokens, that is, concrete actions in their historical uniqueness. This mode of actually exerting power has to be distinguished from the disposition of having power which can be understood in terms of exerting power (to have power is to be able to exert power under suitable conditions[11]), and from the means of power which are objects, roles or institutions enabling the dominant agent *i* to exert power.[12]

Very roughly, a social institution is modelled as a hierarchy of macroscopic groups among which a *status* relation is established in terms of individual exertions of power. Roughly, group **g** has higher status than group **g'** if almost all members of **g** exert power over suitable members of **g'** but not vice versa. A stronger kind of connection is obtained by requiring that almost all members of **g'** are affected in such power relations, i.e. for nearly every member *i* of **g'** there is some member of **g** exerting power over *i*. Thus on the macroscopic level, an institution consists (among other things) of a structure

$$\langle \mathbf{G}, \mathbf{s\,t} \rangle,$$

where

1) **G** is a set of groups
2) **s t** is a binary relation on **G**
3) **s t** is transitive[13] and
4) there exists a group **g** in **G** which has highest status.

Further parts of the model, like the *superstructures* which contain those parts of the intellectual representations relevant for the institution, and the *social practises* which capture the origin and development of the different types of actions in terms of which the groups are characterized, cannot be described here in detail.[14]

What is important here is to see the way in which social institutions function. An institution may be regarded as a kind of crystallized web of power relations among individuals which is stabilized in the interest of the unique group having highest status in the institution. As certain power relations are favourable for members of this group, the members are interested in having these relations legitimized and stabilized. Once this is achieved, and the institution is established, we may well see how these power relations also function as obstacles for competitive exchange. A group with high or highest status may be able to introduce all kinds of regulations which yield some extra benefit for members of

---

[11] This leads to the analysis of counterfactuals which is not seen problematic to-day. See, for instance, Lewis (1973).

[12] Compare Wartenberg (1990) for an up to date account of power.

[13] I deviate in this point from Balzer (1990), where the status relation is taken to be anti-reflexive. Anti-reflexivity in the full theory enforces asymmetries which are not compatible with the picture of equilibrium we have in exchange. If exchange is to become a "special case" of an institution this requirement therefore has to be weakened.

[14] More details in Balzer (1990).

this group. If this group is not itself engaged in business it will impose taxes or the like, if it is a group actively trading itself, it will try to protect its business against members of other groups. All kinds of taxes, subsidies, and institutional regulations and prescriptions in modern states may be seen in this way as favoring some politically more powerful group — i.e. a group the members of which can exert power over many members of other groups — at the cost of other groups. This description should be sufficient to stress the fundamental role of the above notion of power in the theory of social institutions.

2. Comparison

I will now try to compare the two theories in a "reduced" way by comparison of the two primitives: *exchange* and *power*. These notions are well suited for comparison. They have the same numbers of arguments, and two of their arguments may be taken to be the same on both sides in a straighforward way. The notion of an individual or a person is the same both in equilibrium theory and in the theory of institutions. So "i" and "j" in the above expressions may be taken to denote the same kind of entities in both predicates.

What about "a" and "b"? In equilibrium theory these denote commodity tokens, in institution theory they refer to actions. Is there a big ontological difference between commodities and actions? Certainly, under suitable circumstances, actions may pass for commodities. I may prefer action *a* to action *b*, or action *a* may have some utility for me. Conversely, it would seem odd to say that commodities are a kind of actions. But there is no invincible obstacle between the two. With a slight, and natural step of additional interpretation we may come from commodities to actions. The use of any commodity is in its consumption, and its potential use in its potential consumption or its potential to improve consumption.[15] In the present context we may well pass over from a commodity to the action of its being consumed. Under this reinterpretation, commodities may be "translated" into corresponding actions. But it is not necessary to agree on this global ontological embedding. As already stated, equilibrium theory may be rephrased such

[15] Obviously, we are not discussing deep philosophical or moral issues here. The context is an empirical theory about certain kinds of social systems and the way of individuals' behavior in such systems. Even if some persons may attach value to things like rules, truth or beauty, this does not provide a serious argument against the transition proposed, for such phenomena will very likely be eliminated in the course of the approximate application of empirical theories of the kind discussed.

that it talks about *exchange* and non-exchanged possessions instead of the usual endowments. Now exchange of commodities clearly may be described in terms of actions. Instead of saying that i and j exchange a for b, we may as well say that i performs the action "i hands over commodity a to j" and that j performs the action "j hands over commodity b to i". Of course "a" and "b" still must be verbally described, but their description usually will not contain the expression "commodity". It is natural to regard each exchange as a pair of two actions, and for this reason we may – in the present context – neglect the ontological difference and take the "commodities" in *exchange* as really being the actions performed in the exchange. Under this construal the ontology of both predicates, *exchange* and *power*, is the same. Writing

E for the set of action tokens which may be, or are, performed in a system, and
J for the set of actors present in the system,

exchange as well as *power* is a subset of $J \times E \times J \times E$. It has to be stressed that the notion of action is very comprehensive, and may be applied to such vast enterprises like the building up of an army or the sacking of a town. Thus we can say that i, the king, say, by building up an army exerts power over his neighbour-king to make him pay tribute.

If the ontology is the same for both predicates, where is the difference? We have to explain what we mean by exertion of power in order to see the difference. In the theory of institutions exertion of power has three features.[16] Let me call any quadruple $\langle i, a, j, b \rangle$ for which it holds that *power*(i, a, j, b) a *power event*. First, and rather trivially, the two actions a, b occurring in a power event have to be actually performed. If this were not the case we could not say that power *is* exerted. Second, action b has to be caused by action a at least partially from the point of view of one of the actors i or j. If there were no partial causation, both agents would say that b simply happened to be performed some time after a but without any connection. Third, and most importantly, agent j originally does not intend to perform the action b. Thus we arrive at the following characterization of power (which is not meant as a definition but as an ordinary axiom).

power(i, a, j, b) iff
(1) i performs a and j performs b
(2) i or j believes that a is a partial cause of b
(3) i intends that j should do b while j does not intend to do b.

---

[16] Compare Balzer (1990) and Balzer (1992b) for details.

To make this more precise, we may imagine the power event as comprising two instants. In the first instant, action *a* is performed by person *i*, and at some later time action *b* is performed by person *j*. Now the crucial condition is that originally, i.e. at the time when *a* is performed by *i*, *j* does *not* intend to do *b*. Thus the fact that *j* later actually performs *b* points to some internal change on *j*'s side. *j* may have come to change her intentions so that, at the later time, *j* also intends to do *b*. But sometimes this is not so: *j* performs *b* eventhough she does not intend to do *b*. Informally, we may say that exertion of power has to overcome some resistance on *j*'s side.[17] Here is a clear difference between *exchange* and *power*. In exchange, both actors intend to perform their actions, in exertion of power actor *j* (which may be called the *subordinate* actor while *i* is called the *superordinate* actor) does not intend to perform his action, at least originally he does not. This difference, once stated, must not be overemphasized. The degree of resistance is variable and may become arbitrarily small. On the other hand, being as small as we like, it still marks a difference. To see this, consider a possible objection[18] pointing out that in exchange also some resistance is overcome. The offered price being large finally overcomes the partner's "resistance" to sell. Under the usual idealizing assumptions of equilibrium theory this way of describing the situation is not satisfactory, though. The usual analysis would run as follows. The rational, potential seller, *j*, for each fixed price *p* knows whether selling at *p* increases his utility or not. If not, the seller does not intend to sell at the given price, and in the meaning of the term as used above resists the exchange. If, on the other hand, *p* is high enough, the person intends to sell, and the exchange takes place. Similar considerations apply to the potential buyer, *i*, and the particular price she offers. She will intend to exchange only if the price is below some fixed bound known to her. Looking at the situation in this way "to overcome *j*'s resistance" means to make a new, better offer which means to perform a new, different action. By the original action *a* of offering a price *p* too low, *i* does not overcome *j*'s "resistance", and no action takes place on *j*'s side. So there is no exertion of power. By the different action *a'* of offering a price high enough, on the other hand, no resistance needs to be overcome, so again there is no exertion of power.

Consider the spectrum of English verbs reaching from begging at the one end *via* asking, proposing, to exchanging in the middle, and *via* requiring, demanding to ordering at the other end. The order inherent in

---

[17] This feature has been recognized long ago, see for instance Weber (1980), p. 28.
[18] I am indebted to B. Hamminga in this point.

this list corresponds to a similar order of the actor's status with respect to the other person, the addressee. To beg means to speak from the lowest lewel, to ask for something still indicates an inferior position. In exchanging both persons are at the same level. The person who demands or orders is in a superior position with respect to the addressee. There are certainly other expressions falling into that spectrum unknown to me because of my poor English. Systematically, and independently of the particular language, the general situation may be depicted as in figure 1.

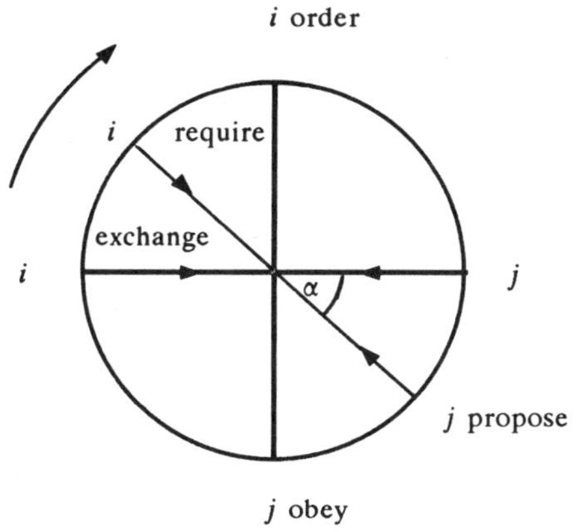

Fig. 1.

At the opposite sides of the circle we have on any line through its centre two persons *i* and *j* interacting with each other. If the corresponding line is horizontal the interaction is an exchange, if it is vertical the interaction is an exertion of power of the person "on top" over the person "on bottom". Between these two extreme positions there are infinitely many intermediary positions each being abstractly given by some specific angle α. If α ranges from zero to 90° the corresponding interaction changes from pure exchange to pure exertion of power.

We also interpret the picture as showing just different degrees of exertion of power each degree being given by angle α. Power is exerted in the highest possible degree if $\alpha = 90^o$. When α decreases power becomes less articulated. In this interpretation exchange becomes a special case of exertion of power. It is the mildest form of power, a form in which both agents are practically equal. This special case is approached "in the limit", namely when α goes to zero.

At the institution's side this limit really involves two features. First, we may look at the degree of resistance which has to be overcome on the subordinate's side. In the above characterization of *power*, condition (3) says that *j* does not intend to do *b*, but condition (1) states that *b*, is performed by *j*. Now the higher *j*'s intention not to do *b* the greater is *j*'s resistance, and the more power is exercised over *j* by *i*, if *j* actually performs *b*. A second feature is that when going to the limit the relation between the two actors becomes more symmetrical. The subordinate agent also develops an intention to the effect that the superordinate agent should do "his" action *a*, and also there is growing belief among the two that action *b* partially causes action *a*. In the limit when there is no resistance at all but an intention also on *j*'s side and when there are symmetric causal beliefs the situation is perfectly symmetric. In a power relation which is close to exchange *i*'s action *a* also may be described by saying that *i* hands over some good to *j*, and *j*'s action *b* accordingly by saying that *j* hands over some good to *i*.

Extending this relation to the two full theories we should say that equilibrium theory is not only a special case of the theory of institutions, but even is a limit case of the latter. On the macroscopic part of an institution, going to the limit amounts to changing the hierarchical structure <**G**, **s t**> in a way in which the status relation becomes "weaker". The status relation between two groups is "defined" in terms of the individual exertions of power among their members. When these power relations approach exchange they become more symmetric as just described, and thus the "difference" or "distance" in status vanishes. In the limit, status differences disappear, the groups have "equal" status in the sense of neither group being higher or lower in status than any other, and thus in a certain sense the groups "merge" into one big group (the set of economic agents).

3. Internal criteria of distance

These considerations indicate that it is not only possible to imagine a transition from an institution to an equilibrium exchange system but also to find criteria of how far the institution is away from the "economic limit" of a model of equilibrium theory. It seems possible to state the degree in which an institution differs from equilibrium in rather operational terms which even may give rise to a quantitative notion of distance.

Consider a system of agents and actions involved in power relations of a social institution. As before, agents are denoted by variables *i*, *j* and actions by variables *a*, *b*. For $r \leqslant 4$ let us say that *x occurs in the r-th position* of the *power* relation iff there exist x_1, x_2, x_3 such that x, x_1, x_2, x_3 form a complete instantiation of the *power* predicate, and x occurs in position number r of this instantiation. Consider the four projections of the *power* predicate

SUPERORDINATES (*power*)	=	the set of actors occurring in the first position of *power*
SUBORDINATES (*power*)	=	the set of actors occurring in the third position of *power*
ORDERS (*power*)	=	the set of actions occurring in the second position of *power*
OBEDIENCES (*power*)	=	the set of actions occurring in the fourth position of *power*.

If the system is close to an exchange model the first two sets should be similar in the sense of having a similar number of members, and the same should hold for the last two sets. For in exchange the "exertion of power" inherent in the superordinate's action *a* is balanced by an "exertion of power" inherent in the subordinate's action *b*. Whenever *i* exerts power over *j* in the weak sense of exchange, and thus *i* is in SUPERORDINATES (*power*) and *j* in SUBORDINATES (*power*), it is also the case that *j* exerts power over *i* in this weak sense, and thus *j* is in SUPERORDINATES (*power*) and *i* in SUBORDINATES (*power*). We may take the difference in number of members of both sets as a first component of a measure of difference or distance between *power* and *exchange*. If the difference is great, i.e. if there are many more persons in SUBORDINATES (*power*) than in SUPERORDINATES (*power*), then *power* is far away from *exchange*. It is clear that such a difference cannot be expected between ORDERS (*power*) and OBEDIENCES (*power*) because every action of ordering usually has its counterpart of obedience and *vice versa*. So these two sets will be similar in number also for the *power* relation. There is, however, a second component of the distance measure. In institutions the "upper" groups have relatively few members, but their members exert power over many members of the "lower" groups. Thus the *power* relation in a "normal" institution — where there is a strong status hierarchy — exemplifies a big difference in the number of members of SUPERORDINATES (*power*) and SUBORDINATES (*power*), as already pointed out. On the other hand the numbers of ORDERS (*power*) and OBEDIENCES (*power*) are the same or similar. So few superordinate agents perform many orders, and many subordinate agents each perform an obedient action. This means that — on the average — each superordinate agent performs many different actions of ordering while every subordinate agent performs few actions of obedience — at least much less than a superordinate agent's orders. So the difference in numbers of elements of the sets ORDERS (*power*) and SUPERORDINATES (*power*) also yields some indication of how far the *power* relation is away from exchange. The larger this difference, the more orders are performed by each superordinate agent, the stronger the power structure, and the more distant is the system from exchange.

We may define a first, admittedly rough, measure of distance of a *power* relation from exchange by the sum of these two differences. Perhaps this is not the ultimate word on comparing the two notions. The point however is that it is defined in purely instrinsic terms; it refers to the *power* relation and to nothing else.

It may be objected that this picture of asymmetries is not in accordance with democratic states which certainly should be included in the analysis of institutions. The objection would point to the fact that in a democracy each voter exerts power over members of the ruling group by voting. Here the second feature of my analysis of power comes into play: the believed partial causation of action *b* by action *a*. Even if I would admit that the actors' beliefs are not so important so that what really counts are the "real" causal connections (whatever this means), the point is that in voting the causal connection is very partial — of the order of one to many millions, as we know. Given that all empirical theories apply only approximately such a small connection will be completely submerged in the blurs used to fit the data to a model. Therefore, the connection does not really count. To put it differently, and straight: on my analysis the voter in a large democracy does not exert power.[19]

If we replace "*power*" in the definition of the above four sets by "*exchange*" we obtain four new sets which also may be used in the comparison. By summary the following propositions seem to spring from the previous discussion (where "similar" means "similar number of elements").

SUPERORDINATES (*power*) and SUBORDINATES (*power*) are not similar;
SUPERORDINATES (*exchange*) and SUBORDINATES (*exchange*) are similar;
ORDERS (*power*) and OBEDIENCES (*power*) are similar;

[19] I admit that these brief remarks do not exhaust the issue of democratic institutions. There still is the possibility that the voters develop some joint intentions and joint beliefs, and exert power on this "joint" level. An analysis of this is certainly highly important, but still missing. Compare Tuomela (1992) and other work of Tuomela mentioned there for a sophisticated and fruitful approach to joint intentions and beliefs.

ORDERS (*exchange*) and OBEDIENCES (*exchange*) are similar;
SUPERORDINATES (*power*) and ORDERS (*power*) are not similar.

Of course, this is not a complete list.

4. Idealization

Going to the limit in a sequence of *power* relations which converges (in the sense induced by the distances just defined) to an *exchange* relation may well be rephrased by saying that abstractions or idealizations are made in the transitions at each step. My analysis has made precise which features are abstracted or idealized away. In the "real" systems — the institutions with their status hierachy — there are asymmetrical *power* relations. Asymmetry is present in the form of resistance on the subordinate's side, and in differences in the numbers of persons acting as superordinates and as subordinates. When we idealize these asymmetries we come to exchange. In realistic terms: when we counterfactually assume that there is no resistance of the subordinates where really is, and that there are equal numbers of agents on "both sides" where there really are not, then our system looks like a model of equilibrium theory.

It is not a bold hypothesis to claim that equilibrium theory will turn out as an idealization of the theory of institutions. The essentials have been discussed. A model theoretic account involving the full models of both theories would not add much to the picture.

The question however is not to evaluate whether such idealizations are useful or admissible. They occur in all branches of science, prominently in physics, and therefore may well be taken as legitimate scientific procedures. The meta-theoretic question is about the general structure of idealization, and of the role of idealization in science. I want to close with brief comments on both points.

The general structure of idealization was first modelled by Nowak,[20] his account has stimulated much of the present work on the subject. His model is formulated in terms of transitions of axioms from one stage to the next where the axioms in the less idealized stage contain some non-zero parameters the convergence of which to zero indicates that the idealized stage is approached. Application of the model to a concrete case thus presupposes that those features which are "idealized away" will be expressible in the theory by means of a number. The situation in our example seems favorable. We managed to define some numerical

[20] Nowak (1980).

measure of "distance from exchange" which in principle can be made a part of the theory of institutions.

But such a procedure does not seem to be very natural. Intuitively, the measure of distance is not a part of any of the two theories. It is — and was introduced — only as a means for comparing them. A more natural account of idealization would leave this measure external and describe the transition to the limit by means of a converging sequence of models. This idea may be worked out along the lines formally proposed by D. Mayr.[21] The general situation which is exemplified by the case before us is that Nowak's model grasps what is basic to idealization but at the cost of using a rather restrictive formalism which may be improved in the way indicated.

As regards the role of idealization in science I have two remarks.[22] First, we speak of an idealization only when we have some idea of which features exactly are neglected in the idealized picture. If we assume that scientists are clever enough to include all features they think are relevant into their models, we are forced to conclude that idealization can only be detected when a better theory has occurred. Only when we know better we may point out the deficiencies of the idealized theory. This view is confirmed by the development of the natural sciences. Second, materialists will tend to understand idealization as leaving out of consideration some of the true features of the system. Since we have no other access to truth than by our best theories the postulate of an independent reality is strongly metaphysical and does not seem to have many defenders now.[23] Both remarks point to the role of the notion of idealization as a means of becoming aware of, and to "measure", scientific progress, and I take this as its main role.

Wolfgang Balzer
Institut für Statistik und Wissenschaftstheorie
Universität München
Ludwigstr. 31
80539 München
FRG

---

[21] Mayr (1981).

[22] I admit that these remarks are based more on the history of the natural sciences than on that of economy. Hoover's contribution to this volume provides a somewhat different view which seems to prevail in econometrics. However, the issue cannot – and should not – be settled in the present state because this will require a precise explication of idealization which includes the process of confrontation of data and model (and thus the process of parameter estimation).

[23] Of course, the premiss in this sentence is also metaphysical, but "it's" metaphysics is more advanced than materialism.

REFERENCES

Arrow, K.J. and Hahn, F.H. (1971). *General Competitive Analysis*. San Francisco: Holden-Day.

Balzer, W. (1990). A Basic Model of Social Institutions. *Journal of Mathematical Sociology*, **16**, 1-29.

Balzer, W. (1992a). Game Theory versus Power Theory: A Critical Comparison. In: T.E. Wartenberg (Ed.), *Rethinking Power*. Albany: SUNY Press, Chap. 4.

Balzer, W. (1992b). A Theory of Power in Small Groups. In: H. Westmeyer (Ed.). *The Structuralist Program in Psychology: Foundations and Applications*. Seatle: Hogrefe & Huber, pp. 191-210.

Balzer, W., C.U. Moulines, and J.D. Sneed (1987). *An Architectonic for Science*. Dordrecht: Reidel.

Bardhan, P. (1989). The New Institutional Economics and Development Theory: A Brief Critical Assessment. *World Development*, **17**(9), 1389-95.

Braudel, F. (1980). *On History*. Chicago: University of Chicago Press.

Debreu, G. (1972). *Theory of Value*. New Haven: Yale University Press.

Haendler, E.W. (1979). *Logische Struktur und Referenz von mathematischen ökonomischen Theorien*. Dissertation, University of Munich.

Hamminga, B. (1989). Sneed versus Nowak: An Illustration in Economics. In: W. Balzer and B. Hamminga (Eds.). *Philosophy of Economics*. Dordrecht: Kluwer, pp. 247-265.

Hildenbrand, W. (1974). *Core and Equilibria of a Large Economy*. Princeton: University Press.

Lewis, D. (1973). *Counterfactuals*. Cambridge: Cambridge University Press.

Mayr, D. (1981). Approximative Reduction by Completion of Empirical Uniformities. In: A. Hartkämper and H.-J. Schmidt (Eds.), *Structure and Approximation in Physical Theories*. New York: Plenum, pp. 55-70.

Nowak, L. (1980). *The Structure of Idealization. Towards a Systematic Interpretation of the Marxian Idea of Science*. Dordrecht: Reidel.

Taylor, M. (1976). *Anarchy and Cooperation*. London: Wiley.

Tuomela, R. (1992). Group Beliefs. *Synthese*, **91**, 285-318.

Wartenberg, T.E. (1990). *The Forms of Power*. Philadelphia: Temple University Press.

Weber, M. (1980). *Wirtschaft und Gesellschaft*. Tübingen: Mohr.

Poznań Studies in the Philosophy of the Sciences and the Humanities
1994, Vol. 38, pp. 205-228

Kees Cools, Bert Hamminga, Theo A.F. Kuipers[1]

TRUTH APPROXIMATION BY CONCRETIZATION IN CAPITAL STRUCTURE THEORY

ABSTRACT. This paper supplies a structuralist reconstruction of the Modigliani-Miller theory and shows that the economic literature following their results reports on research with an implicit strategy to come "closer-to-the-truth" in the modern technical sense in philosophy of science.

> "These and other drastic simplifications have been necessary in order to come to grips with the problem at all . . . Having served this purpose, they can now be relaxed in the direction of greater realism and relevance, a task in which we hope others interested in this area will wish to share"[2]

Introduction

In 1982 one of the authors published a structuralist theory of truth approximation (Kuipers 1982). The main ideas were the following. According to the naive structuralist approach theories can be represented as sets of structures. Point of departure is a set *Mp* of structures of a certain similarity type, called the potential models or conceptual possibilities. The target of theorizing is some unknown subset. In proper empirical contexts the target set is the set of empirical possibilities. In other contexts (such as applied mathematics and pure economic theory) the target set may be the set of conceptual possibilities in which a certain interesting theorem is valid. A theory is now conceived as the combination of some subset *X* of *Mp*, together with the claim that *X* in fact coincides with the target set.

The core of the naive structuralist theory of truthlikeness is based on the following ternary relation of theorylikeness: theory *Y* is closer to theory *Z* than theory *X* is to *Z* if *Y*-*Z* is a subset of *X*-*Z* and *Z*-*Y* is a

[1] We are indebted to Wolfgang Balzer for helpful comments on an earlier draft of this paper.
[2] Modigliani and Miller (1958) p. 296.

subset of Z-X.[3] This transforms into naive truthlikeness by substituting for Z the target set of empirical possibilities.

The naive definition has many attractive aspects, among others, it has not the famous shortcomings of Popper's original definition of truthlikeness. However, it is also immediately clear that the naive theory cannot cover cases were similarity between structures plays a crucial role, as is normal, in particular in quantitative cases. One important type concerns theories which are improved by concretization. The theory of gases of Van der Waals is an improvement of the so-called ideal theory of gases, by accounting quantitative factors related to the volume and mutual attraction of molecules. Hence, a satisfactory definition of refined truthlikeness, i.e. on the basis of an underlying structurelikeness relation, should contain concretization to the true theory as a special case and should reduce to the naive one when the notion of structurelikeness is trivial.

After a first failing attempt at a refined definition (Kuipers 1987), recently has been construed a satisfactory refined definition (Kuipers 1992).[4] In the final section of that paper it was shown that the refined definition could deal with concretization in general and the Van der Waals example in particular. Moreover, it was indicated that it could deal with elementary and complex forms of concretization in the context of validity research. The main point of the present paper is to show under what conditions and in what sense the theory of Kraus and Litzenberger (1973) about the capital structure of firms is a concretization of the theory of Modigliani and Miller bringing us closer to a provable interesting truth about the actual financing behavior of firms.

In Section 1 we present an informal exposition of the crucial results in capital structure theory. The first author was also the one who suggested to elaborate this example as a possible case of truth approximation by concretization. Although it would have been more easy to take an example from general economics, e.g. the case of international trade (Hamminga 1983), an example from financial economics has the additional advantage that it illustrates the formal kinship of theory structure and development in business economics and other applications of neoclassical equilibrium theory. In Section 2 the second author gives a structuralist reconstruction of the relevant theories. This reconstruction is required in order to be able in Section 3 to deal with the relevant theories as sets of structures and to enable the easy checking of some crucial logico-mathematical claims. An independent merit of Section 2

---

[3] Where "Y-Z" denotes the set of all elements of Y that are not in Z.

[4] For a much shorter version vid. Kuipers (1992a).

is that it provides an exemplification of the claim that not only theories in general economics (e.g. Janssen 1989, Janssen and Kuipers 1989), but also in financial economics can be made transparent by structuralist reconstruction. Finally, in Section 3 the third author explains in some detail what the example illustrates: economists attempt to approach interesting truths by concretization, and they may well succeed in this. In general, truthlikeness research attempts to explicate what working scientists always implicitly assume, but most philosophers like to make suspect.

Section 1

The First Three Steps in Capital Structure Theory

1.1. Introduction

"How do firms choose their capital structure?" is one of the most important issues in corporate finance — and one of the most complex. The "capital structure" is the ratio between debt (money borrowed by a firm at a fixed interest rate), and equity (money invested in the firm by shareholders that own the firm, have full posession of its assets and profits, and thus are the residual claimants)[5] Corporate finance is part (the other part being investment theory) of financial economics, which is a branch of applied micro economics and therefore based on neoclassical utility theory. In additon to standard utility theory assumptions, in corporate finance it is assumed that the goal of a company is to maximize shareholders' wealth (= utility) i.e. maximize the market value of equity.[6,7] Given the above mentioned goal of the firm, the answer to the question "How do firms choose their capital structure?" can be rephrased as "Which capital structure maximizes the value of the firm?" or "Can the value of the assets be increased by an optimal financing policy of the firm?".

---

[5] The term 'capital structure', more broadly defined, refers to the way in which a firm finances its assets, it not only denotes the relative quantities of debt and equity, but also warrants, trade credit, convertibles, leases, etc. For simplicity we shall assume that the capital structure only consists of debt (money borrowed from banks or bondholders) and equity (stocks or shares).

[6] For reasons of brevity we will hereafter speak of "value" in stead of "market value".

[7] By definition, the value of the firm equals the value of equity plus the value of debt. And, since the value of the debt does not change because it is assumed to be risk free, maximizing the value of the equity (= shareholders' wealth) is equal to maximizing the value of the whole firm.

In 1958 Franco Modigliani and Merton Miller wrote their seminal paper on the issue of the optimal capital structure. Although for some decades the paper has been the subject of intense scrutiny and often bitter controversy, and Franco Modigliani once stated that "I must confess that ... my two articles with Miller on corporate finance are written with tongue in cheek, to really make fun of my colleagues." (Klamer 1983, p. 125). Most of these controversies can now be regarded as settled: the essential results of the paper have overcome. Moreover, the results, often called the MM propositions, have spread beyond corporate finance to the fields of money and banking, fiscal policy and international finance (for examples, see Miller 1988). And finally, the scientific community has recognized the importance of the paper by awarding both authors the Nobel Prize in economics (Modigliani in 1984 and Miller in 1990).

Proposition I of MM has become the first step in capital structure theory and is sometimes called the 'nothing matters' or 'irrelevance' theorem. It states that, as an implication of equilibrium in perfect capital markets, the value of a firm is independent of its capital structure (that is, its debt/equity ratio). In proving this proposition they used a then-novel arbitrage argument, which is now common throughout finance. The second step was also made by MM, first in their 1958 paper, but corrected in Modigliani and Miller (1963). It says that, when corporate taxes – interest payments are tax deductible – are introduced in the model, 100% debt financing is optimal. The intuition behind this being that the more debt, the less taxes a firm pays, and therefore the more money – thus value – is left for the financeers (shareholders and debtholders) of the company. This result was extremely puzzling, since in real world one never observes firms with 100% debt financing. The third step in capital structure theory was first suggested by Baxter (1976) and later formalized by others. Now, bankruptcy costs are introduced. These costs consist of payments that must be made to third parties other than bond- or shareholders when the firm goes bankrupt, such as trustee fees, legal fees, costs of reorganisation, etc. These "dead weight" losses associated with bankruptcy cause the value of the firm to be less than it would have been otherwise, namely the value based on the expected cash flows from operations. And since the change of going bankrupt is higher when a firm is financed with more debt, there are costs involved with debt financing. The tradeoff between the tax advantage of debt and bankruptcy costs associated with debt results in an optimal capital structure, the so called balancing theorem.

To summarize, in a perfect world – without taxes of bankruptcy costs – the debt/equity ratio is irrelevant for the value of the firm (theorem A). When the imperfection of corporate taxes is introduced, 100% debt financing is optimal, i.e. maximizes the value of the firm (theorem B). Finally, when also bankruptcy costs are taken into consideration, there is a cost to debt financing and an interior solution for the optimal capital structure emerges; a debt/equity ratio somewhere between 0% and 100% maximizes the value of the firm (theorem C). Theoretically, it would also be possible to consider a world with only the imperfection of bankruptcy cost (and no corporate taxes), in which case 100% equity financing would be optimal (theorem D).

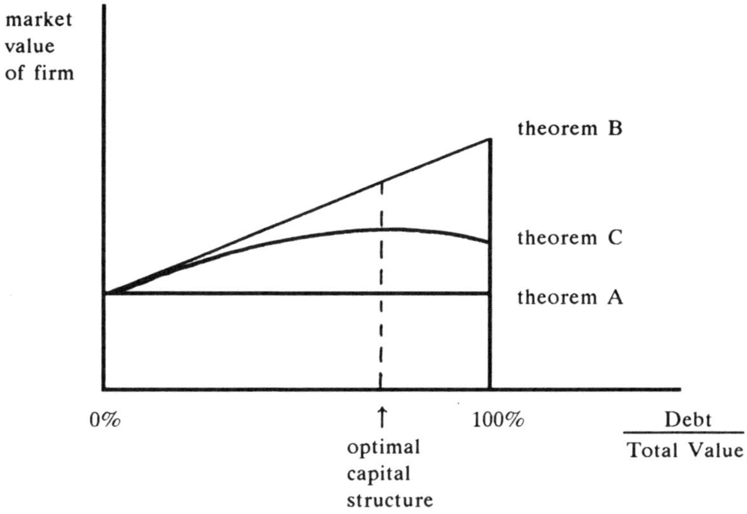

Figure 1. Optimal capital structure

Now, let us go more into the details of the famous MM "Proposition I"

1.2. Modigliani and Miller's "nothing matters", theorem A

The value of the firm equals the net present value, *NPV*, of future expected cash flows (that is: net receipts of money after deduction of all cost exept interest payments). The *NPV* of a T-period 'project' can be written as

$$NPV = \sum_{t=0}^{T} \frac{CF_t}{(1+r)^t} \ ,$$

where CF_t, is the cash flow on time t and r is the required rate of return or discount rate. r is determined by the time value of money (the risk free interest rate[8]) and the riskiness of the expected cash flows, CF. In case of a perpetuity (i.e. an infinite, constant stream of cash flows) the NPV can be written as

$$NPV = \frac{CF}{r}.^{9}$$

An unlevered firm is a firm that has no debt, in other words, it is financed with 100% equity.

When V^U is the value of the unlevered firm and assuming perpetuities $V^u = CF/\rho$, where CF_t, $t = 1, 2, \ldots$ denote the operating cash flows generated by the firm each year and ρ is the rate of return required by the shareholders. How the question is, *given* the level and riskiness of the operating cash flow, when debt is introduced, is there a certain amount of debt D^* that would maximize the value, V^L, of such a levered firm (by definition $V \equiv E + D$, where E is the value of equity and D the value of the outstanding debt).

By using an arbitrage pricing argument, Modigliani and Miller showed that the value of the firm, V^L, is independent of the ratio D/E (then it follows immediately that $V^L = V^U$). This is known as Modigliani-Miller (MM) Proposition I: "The market value of any firm is independent of its capital structure and is given by capitalizing its expected return at the rate ρ appropriate to its risk class" (MM 1958, p. 268). This "nothing matters" theorem is denoted theorem A and the arbitrage argument MM used to prove their Proposition I can be summarized as follows. Using the same notation as MM, V_1 is an unlevered firm (only equity) and V_2 has some debt in its capital structure, X is the total annual return (cash flow), r is the interest charge, D is the market value of debt and S is the market value of equity.

Then: $V_1 = S_1$ and the income available for the stockholders equals X_1

$V_2 = S_2 + D_2$ and the income available for the stockholders equals $X_2 - rD_2$

---

[8] This is a remuneration for providing money without any risk, the value of which is determined by inflation, time preference of consumption and other factors.

[9] This can be proven as follows. Let $CF/(1+r) = a$ and $1/(1+r) = x$. We now have $NPV = a(1+x+x^2+\ldots)$ (1). Multiplying by x gives $xNPV = ax+ax^2+\ldots$ (2). Substracting (2) from (1) gives $NPV(1-x) = a$. Now substitute for x and a and rearrange: $NPV = CF/r$.

Now consider an investor holding s_2 dollars' worth of the shares of firm 2, representing a fraction α of the total outstanding stock, S_2. So, the investment, αS_2, gives the investor a return of

$$(1) \quad Y_2 = (X - rD_2).$$

Now, suppose the investor sells his αS_2, worth of company 2 shares and buys an amount $s_1 = \alpha(S_2 + D_2)$ of the shares of company 1. He can do so by utilizing the amount αD_2 realized from the sale of his initial holding, and *borrowing an additional amount*, αD_2, on his own account. This gives him a fraction $s_1/S_1 = \alpha(S_2 + D_2)/S_1$ of the shares, and therefore earnings, of firm 1. Taking into account the interest payments on the personal debt, $r\alpha D_2$, the return, Y_1, is given by

$$(2) \quad Y_1 = \frac{\alpha(S_2 + D_2)}{S_2} X - r\alpha D_2 = \alpha \frac{V_2}{V_1} X - r\alpha D_2$$

Since in both cases ((1) and (2)) the same amount of money has been invested, in equilibrium both investments should give the same return, Y_1, Y_2. Comparing now (1) and (2) we see that as long as $V_2 > V_1$ we must have $Y_1 > Y_2$, so that it pays owners of firms 2's shares to sell their holdings, thereby lowering S_2 and hence V_2; and to acquire shares of firm 1, thereby raising S_1 and thus V_1. MM conclude therefore that levered companies cannot command a premium over unlevered companies because investors have the opportunity of putting the equivalent leverage into their portfolio directly by borrowing on personal account. The possibility to borrow on personal account is a crucial element in the proof of the theorem and has become known as 'homemade leverage'.

A similar line of reasoning is followed for the other possibility, namely that the market value of the levered firm V_2 is less than V_1 (MM 1958, p. 270).

It is important to realize, that the MM Propositions only hold in an ideal, perfect, world, which has become known as the MM world. MM implicitely or explicitly assumed that:

1. Capital markets are frictionless.
2. Firms can lend at the risk-free rate (riskless debt).
3. Individuals can also borrow and lend at the risk-free rate.
4. There are no costs to bankruptcy.
5. Firms only issue two types of claims: risk-free debt and (risky) equity.
6. All firms are assumed to be in the same risk class.

7. There are no taxes.
8. All cash flow streams are perpetuities (i.e. no growth).
9. Corporate insiders and outsiders have the same information (i.e. no signalling opportunities).
10. Managers always maximize shareholders' wealth and do not expropriate in any way other stakeholders of the company (i.e. no agency costs).
11. Contracts are complete and can always be enforced.

What happened between June 1958 and today is that each of these assumptions has been relaxed in order to study the effect of every single imperfection on the MM results. The driving force behind this 'theory development' is the gap between theory and practice. Especially with respect to MM 1 the gap was immense. All real world debt-equity ratios vary within a certain range of, let's say, 60% to 20% debt. In fact, MM themselves ended their 1958 article with inviting others to study the relaxation of assumptions: "These and other drastic simplifications have been necessary in order to come to grips with the problem at all.", followed by the curtain line of the paper "Having served their purpose they can now be relaxed in the direction of greater realism and relevance, a task on which we hope others interested in this area will wish to share." (MM 1958, p. 296).

Essentially, ever since June 1958, theoretical papers on capital structure have been concerned with relaxing one or more assumptions. The form it has taken in the last decade, however, is to introduce new techniques (e.g. game theory) and new imperfections (e.g. incomplete contracts), which only implicitly or without realising were assumed to be absent before. The first step, however, was taken by MM themselves in their 1958 paper, but corrected in MM (1963).

1.3. Modigliani and Miller with corporate taxes, theorem B

In MM (1958) the first imperfection was already introduced: corporate taxes (Modigliani and Miller made a technical correction in 1963). The important thing about corporate taxes is that interest payments are tax deductible. MM (1963) showed that when corporate taxes are included, the value of the levered firm is equal to the value of an unlevered firm plus the present value of the tax shields associated by debt: $V^L = V^U + \tau_c D$, where τ_c is the corporate tax rate. In this way the capital structure that maximizes the value of a firm consists of 100% debt. This result we call theorem B; a corner solution where full debt financing is optimal.

In 1963 MM again used an arbitrage argument, similar to the one in 1958, to prove 'Theorem B'. Following their own line of reasoning, their 1963 proof can be summarized as follows. Using the same notation as MM,

X is the (long-run average) earnings before interest and taxes generated by the currently owned assets of a given firm in some stated risk class, τ is the marginal corporate tax rate,

X^{τ} is the after-tax return,

R is the interest bill, equals rD in the 1958 notation, and

ρ^{τ} is the rate at which the market capitalizes the expected returns net of tax of an unlevered company in a certain risk class.

Then $X^{\tau} = (1 - \tau)(X - R) + R = (1 - \tau)X + \tau R$.

This suggests that the after-tax return consists of two components: (1) an uncertain stream $(1 - \tau)X$; and (2) a sure stream τR. Therefore, the equilibrium market value of the combined stream can be found by capitalizing each component separately. More precisely, the market capitalizes the expected returns net of tax of an unlevered company in a certain risk class at rate ρ^{τ}, i.e.

$$\rho^{\tau} = (1 - \tau)X / V^{u} \quad \text{or} \quad V^{u} = (1 - \tau)X / \rho^{\tau} .$$

And since r is the rate at which the market capitalizes sure streams, r is the appropriate discount rate for the tax shield τD.
Then we would expect the value of levered firm with a permanent level of D to be

$$(3) \qquad V^{L} = \frac{(1-\tau)X}{\rho^{\tau}} + \frac{\tau R}{r} = V^{U} + \tau D$$

(MM 1963, p. 436-7).

Modigliani and Miller show that if (3) does not hold, investors can choose a more profitable portfolio by switching from relatively overvalued to relatively undervalued firms.
Suppose first that unlevered firms are overvalued, i.e. $V^{L} - \tau D < V^{U}$. An investor holding m dollars of stock in the unlevered firm has a right to a fraction m/V_U of the eventual return, i.e. $Y_U = (m/V_U)(1-\tau)X$.

Consider now an alternative portfolio obtained by investing m dollars as follows: the portion $(\{S_L / (S_L + (1 - \tau)D\}) \cdot m$ is invested in the stock of the levered firm, S_L, and the remaining portion, $(\{(1 - \tau)D / (S_L + (1 - \tau)D)\} \cdot m)$ is invested in its bonds (= debt). The stock component entitles the investor to a fraction $\{S_L / (S_L + (1 - \tau)D)\} \cdot m$ of the net profits of the levered firm, which equals $\{m / (S_L + (1 - \tau)D)\} \cdot \{(1 - \tau)(X - R)\}$. And the holding of the bonds yields $\{m / (S_L + (1 - \tau)D)\} \cdot \{(1 - \tau)R\}$. Hence the total return from the alternative portfolio is $Y_L = \{m / (S_L + (1 - \tau)D)\} \cdot \{(1 - \tau)X\}$ and this will dominate the uncertain income Y_U if, and only if, $S_L + (1 - \tau)D \equiv S_L + D - \tau D \equiv \equiv V_L - \tau D < V_U$.

Thus, in equilibrium, V_U cannot exceed $(V_L - \tau)D_L$, for if it did investors would have an incentive to sell shares in the unlevered company and purchase the shares (and bonds) of the levered company.

A similar line of reasoning is followed for the other possibility, namely that the market value of the levered firm, $(V_L - \tau)D$, is less than the value of the unlevered firm, V_L. (See MM (1963), p. 427-8).

Theorem B was even more irrealistic than MM without taxes. There exists not a single firm which is voluntarily financed with 100% debt. Therefore the process of relaxation went on and in the beginning participants in the research programme were mainly looking for disadvantages of debt financing in order to come up with an internally optimal capital structure.

From MM theory it follows directly that the debt/equity ratio is irrelevant for the value of the firm, no matter the risk class. Hence assumption 6 was relaxed without theorem A or B being effected.

The factor that, intuitively, one would guess will alter the 100% debt corner solution will probably be the relaxation of the risk free debt assumption. In real life, when leverage (debt financing) increases debt becomes more risky since the chance that not all debt obligations can be met increases and debtors will therefore ask for a higher interest rate. Consequently, one would maybe say, since more money has to be paid to debtholders, that the value of the firm will decline if the debt/equity ratio rises. However, the introduction of risky debt does *not* change the MM propositions; it has no impact on the value of the firm. Stiglitz (1969) first proved this result, using a state preference framework, and Rubinstein (1973) provided a proof, using a mean-variance approach. Therefore, the introduction of risky debt cannot, by itself, be used to explain the existence of an optimal capital structure with a debt-equity ratio between 0% and 100% (a so called "interior" solution).

1.4. Bankruptcy costs, theorem C (an interior solution)

As we have seen, in a world without transactions costs risky debt does not affect on the value of the firm. However, when bankruptcy costs are taken into account, things are beginning to look differently.[10] Baxter (1967) was one of the first to suggest the existence of an internal optimal capital structure, based on bankruptcy costs: "If, ..., bankruptcy involves substantial administrative expenses and other costs, and causes a significant decline in the sales and earnings of the firm in receivership, the total value of the levered firm can be expected to be less than that of the all-equity company.". Since then, more sophisticated treatments have been offered by Kraus and Litzenberger (1973), Scott (1976) and Kim (1978).

When bankruptcy costs are considered, the value of the firm in bankruptcy is reduced by the fact that payments must be made to third parties other than bond- or shareholders. Trustee fees, legal fees, and other costs of reorganization or bankruptcy are deducted from the net asset value of the bankrupt firm and from the proceeds that should go to bondholders. Consequently, these "dead weight" losses associated with bankruptcy may cause the value of the firm in bankruptcy to be less than the discounted value of the expected cash flows from operations. This fact can be used to explain the existence of an interior optimal capital structure: theorem C.

1.5. Later developments

The next step in capital structure theory was the introduction of personal taxes (Miller 1977). Miller showed that, again, a "nothing matters" situation arises when you combine corporate and personal taxes. Since capital gains (equity income) are not taxed, but interest is taxed at the personal level, for the investor, who ultimately determines the market value of a company, there might even be a tax *disadvantage* to debt financing. Then, a new strand of literature was started by the famous Jensen and Meckling (1976) paper. They introduced the so called *agency theory* in the world of corporate finance, which relaxes the assumption of no conflict of interest between different parties, especially management, shareholders and debtholders. In particular, managers do not always act in the interest of the shareholders and consequently the goal is not always to maximize the value of the company. The paper shows that, based on these agency problems and without assuming taxes or

[10] It should be stressed that only bankruptcy *costs* but not bankruptcy *risk* can explain an optimal mix of debt and equity, because the bankruptcy *risk* is reflected in the higher interest rates when risky debt is introduced into the model.

bankruptcy costs, an optimal capital structure can be explained. One year later Ross (1977) introduced the existence of asymmetric information in capital structure theory. Assuming that managers have more information about the expected returns of the company than outside investors, he argued that greater financial leverage can be used by managers to signal an optimistic future of the firm. In the same year Leland and Pyle (1979) used the existence of asymmetric information to show that the firms value if positively related to the fraction of the owners stake in the company and therefore the firm will have greater debt capacity and use greater amounts of debt.

Since the late seventies, until the late eighties, virtually all research concerning capital structure issues has been concerned with agency and/or asymmetric informational issues. Since the middle of the eighties, interrelations between financing and investment decisions (e.g. Titman 1984) and capital structure choices in relation to takeovers (e.g. Harris and Raviv 1988) have been studied. Most recently, the assumption of comple contracts is relaxed. Instead, contracts are assumed to be on-complete, i.e. they don't specify precise provisions for every conceivable future event (e.g. Cools and Zon 1992). And apart from the theoretical literature hundreds of papers try to empirically test all the different capital structure theories.[11]

Section 2

Structuralist reconstruction of the relevant theory

2.1. Interesting theorems

This section displays the logical skeleton of "A State-Preference Model of Optimal Financial Leverage" by Kraus and Litzenberger (1973). As usual in theoretical economics, the strategy of model construction is focused on an interesting theorem (Hamminga 1983). Here, what is to be derived is a theorem on how the value of (debt plus equity of) a firm depends on the proportion of debt in that value. Modigliani and Miller

---

[11] This started with a paper of Franco Modigliani and Merton Miller in the *American Economic Review*, June 1958.

(1958, 1963) used a plausible model to arrive at implausible, and therefore intriguing theorems: the proportion of debt has no influence at all on the value of the firm if corporate tax is nonexistent, and should be 100% if corporate tax exists. The model of Kraus and Litzenberger based on a state preferance approach, could explain the existence of an optimal solution between 0% and 100%.

2.2. *State preference*

The "state preference" approach consists of assuming a set J of all conceptually possible end-of-period "states of the world" j. In every single possible state of the world j there is a fixed and given return X_{fj} for every firm f, a given tax rate T_j and given bankruptcy cost C_{fj} ($C_{fj} = 0$ for firms f that survive in state j).

It is a one period analysis. The return (earnings before interest and taxes) X_{fj} of firm f in state j is identical to the end-of-period market value of firm f. If you would know what state j would be realized you would have no problems of uncertainty. Hence, the problem of uncertainty solely consists of investors not knowing what state will be realized, and having different probability beliefs concerning $j \in J$.

A "market expectation" about the states $j \in J$ is negotiated among investors by assuming tradeable "primitive securities" Π_j, which can be thought of as "lottery tickets" yielding 1$ if state j occurs and nothing if $j' \neq j$ occurs. The equilibrium price P_j of Π_j could be derived from 1) probability beliefs of investors concerning state j 2) their time preference for holding money, 3) their risk aversion and 4) their utility functions (Arrow 1969, Debreu 1959). Kraus and Litzenberger do not perform this derivation, but take P_j, $j \in J$ as given, exogenous variables. Any other security bought by an investor can now be identified with a definite number of lottery tickets Π_j for every state j (since investors are assumed to know the return of every security in every state).

2.3. *Potential models (conceptual framework)*

Now we are ready to specify wat structure a thing x should have in order to be a conceptual possibility in the language that Kraus and Litzenberger have chosen for their theory.

x is a *potential debt equity market system with corporate tax and bankruptcy cost* ("x is a *DETCp*") iff (if and only if)

$$x = \langle J, F, \Psi, \mathbf{R}, \Pi, D, X, T, C, P, Y, Z, B, S, V, \rangle$$

The symbols J, F, Ψ, $\mathbf{R}$, denote elementary sets. Their meanings are

J	the set of states of the world j
F	the set of firms f in the market system
Ψ	the set of primitive securites
$\mathbf{R}$	the set of real numbers

The symbols Π, D, X, T, C, P, Y, Z, B, S, V, denote functions:

Π: $J \rightarrow \Psi$ yields the primitive security Π_j that has a return of 1\$ if state j occurs, and 0\$ in any state $j' \neq j$.

D: $F \rightarrow \mathbf{R}^+{}_D$ yields the debt of firm f, a promise to pay a fixed amount D_f, irrespective of the state that occurs, a nonnegative real number

X: $F \times J \rightarrow \mathbf{R}^+{}_X$ yields the return of f in state j, the end of period value of f, a real number X_{fj}, negative in case of bankruptcy.

T: $J \rightarrow \mathbf{R}_T{}^{[0,1]}$ yields the tax rate over X in state j, a real number T_j in the closed interval [0,1].

C: $F \times J \rightarrow \mathbf{R}^+{}_C$ is the bankruptcy cost C_{fj} of f in state j, zero if the firm survives in state j.

With the help of the primary functions Π, D, X, T, C, the secondary functions P, Y, Z, B, S, V, are defined.

P: $\Psi \rightarrow \mathbf{R}^+{}_P$ yields the price P_j of primitive security Π_j

Y: $F \times J \times \mathbf{R}^+{}_D \times \mathbf{R}_X \times \mathbf{R}^+{}_C \rightarrow \mathbf{R}^+{}_Y$ is the return to holders of debt D_f of every firm f in state j, where

$$Y_{fj}: \begin{cases} D_f \text{ for } D_f \leqslant X_{fj} \text{ (the firm "survived")} \\ X_{fj} - C_{fj} \text{ for } D_f > X_{fj} \text{ (the firm is bankrupt)} \end{cases}$$

Z: $F \times J \times \mathbf{R}^+{}_D \times \mathbf{R}_X \times \mathbf{R}_T[0,1] \rightarrow \mathbf{R}^+{}_Z$ is the return to holders of equities of f in state j, where

$$Z_{fj}: \begin{cases} X_{fj}(1-T_j) + T_jD_f - D_j \text{ for } D_f \leqslant X_{fj} \text{ (the firm "survived")} \\ 0 \text{ for } D_f > X_{fj} \text{ (the firm is bankrupt)} \end{cases}$$

---

[12] Wolfgang Balzer correctly suggests in recent correspondence that the types of the functions Y, Z, B, S and V can be simplified to functions from $F \times J$ into the real numbers.

The last three functions have again a different logical role:

B: $F \times J \times \mathbf{R}^+{}_Y \times \mathbf{R}^+{}_P \times \mathbf{R}^+{}_D \times \mathbf{R}_X \times \mathbf{R}[0,1]_T \times \mathbf{R}^+{}_C \rightarrow \mathbf{R}^+{}_B$ yields the present market value of the debt D_f of firm f

S: $F \times J \times \mathbf{R}^+{}_Z \times \mathbf{R}^+{}_P \times \mathbf{R}^+{}_D \times \mathbf{R}_X \times \mathbf{R}[0,1]_T \times \mathbf{R}^+{}_C \rightarrow \mathbf{R}^+{}_S$ yields the equities of firm f

V: $F \times J \times \mathbf{R}^+{}_S \times \mathbf{R}^+{}_B \times \mathbf{R}^+{}_P \times \mathbf{R}^+{}_D \times \mathbf{R}_X \times \mathbf{R}[0,1]_T \times \mathbf{R}^+{}_C \rightarrow \mathbf{R}^+{}_B$ yields the present total value of the firm, where $V_f{:} \equiv S_f + B_f$

Since B and S have only their domains and ranges specified, nothing is yet said about how they could be determined from the variables introduced earlier. This is all we do to specify the set *DETCp*. A thing x is a *potential* structure of the Kraus and Litzenberger theory, or a potential model iff it satisfies all requirements mentioned thusfar, and hence B_f, S_f and V_f can be, in an $x \in DETCp$, *any* nonnegative real number.

2.4. Models: introduction of the axioms on market forces

The set of models of the theory differs from the set of potential models by a specification of *how the present market value of debt and equity is determined*. This yields a subset $DETC \subset DETCp$ of structures:

x is a debt equity market system with corporate tax and bankruptcy cost (*DETC*) iff:

1) x is a *DETCp*.

2) P is such that primitive securities in $\Psi(\Pi_j,\ j \in J)$ have market equilibrium prices $P_j (j \in J)$. (An explicit definition of this as a defined function would require extension of *DETCp* with a set of investors, and functions mapping their probability beliefs on state $j \in J$, risk aversions, time preference and utility functions).

For convenient notation of the requirements on the functions B and S, Kraus and Litzenberger (re)number the states $j_1, j_2, ..., j_n$ in J for every firm in climbing order of the known return X_{fj} in each state. So we have, for every f:

$$X_{f1} \leqslant X_{f2} \leqslant ... \leqslant X_{fj} \leqslant ... \leqslant X_{fn}$$

3) B is such that for all firms f:

$$B(D) = \sum_{j=1}^{n} Y_{fj}P_j = \begin{cases} D_j \sum_{j=1}^{n} P_j \text{ iff } D_f \text{ is such that } D_f \leqslant X_{f1} \\ \sum_{j=1}^{k-1} (X_{fj} - C_{fj})P_j + D_j \sum_{j=k}^{n} P_j \text{ iff } D_f \text{ is such that} \\ \qquad \exists k > 1 \ (X_{f,k-1} < D_f < X_{fk}) \\ \sum_{j=1}^{n} (X_{fj} - C_{fj})P_j \text{ iff } D_f \text{ is such that } D_f > X_{fn} \end{cases}$$

The first of these three functions is meant for the case in which debt D_f is such that the firm survives (will not go bankrupt) in *every* possible state. The second function is meant for the cases where debt is such that the firm is bankrupt in state j = 1, .., $k-1$ and survives in the remaining states. The third function is meant for the case in which debt is such that in *all* states the firm will be bankrupt.

The present market value of debt is thus reduced to the present market value of primitive securities. The same is done for the equity of *f*:

4) S is such that for all *f*:

$$S(D) = \sum_{j=1}^{n} Z_{fj}P_j = \begin{cases} \sum_{j=1}^{n} [X_{fj}(1-T_j) + T_jD_f - D_f]P_j \text{ iff } D_f \text{ is such that } D_f \leqslant X_{f1} \\ \sum_{j=k}^{n} [X_{fj}(1-T_j) + T_jD_f - D_f]P_j \text{ iff } D_j \text{ is such that} \\ \qquad \exists k > 1 \ (X_{f,k-1} < D_f < X_{fk}) \\ 0 \text{ iff } D_f \text{ is such that } D_f > X_{fn} \end{cases}$$

The meaning of the tripartition is again bankruptcy in no/some/all possible end-of-period states.

2.5. *Interesting theorems: their exact shape*

This ends the list of additional requirements that a structure $x \in DETCp$ must meet in order to be an element of $DETC \subset DETCp$. The list is the result of a strategy meant to find the class of structures for which the following theorem *T-DETC* holds:

T-DETC: in all structures $x \in DETC$, for all firms *f*, if T_j is identical in all states *j* (dropping subscript *j*),

$$V(D_f) = V(0) + T \cdot B(D_f) - (1-T) \cdot \begin{cases} 0 \text{ iff } D_f \text{ is such that } D_f \leqslant X_{f1} \\ \sum_{j=1}^{k-1} C_{fj}P_j \text{ iff } D_f \text{ is such that } \\ \qquad \exists k > 1 \ (X_{f,k-1} < D_f < X_{fk}) \\ \sum_{j=1}^{n} C_{fj}P_j \text{ iff } D_f \text{ is such that } D_f > X_{fn} \end{cases}$$

Figure 1 depicts an example of a shape that $V(D_f)$ could take for some firm f:

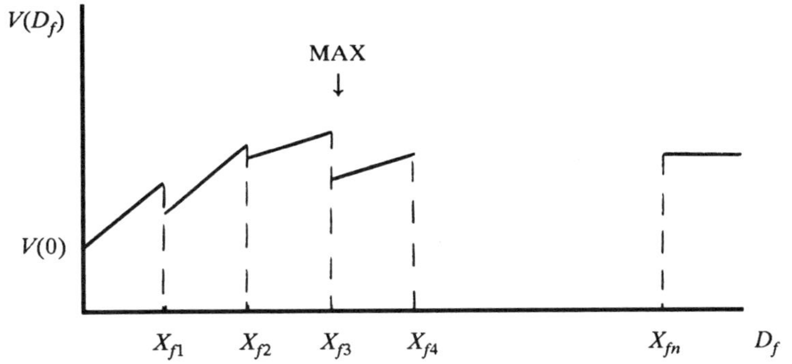

Figure 2: Typical shape implied by *T-DETC*

The slopes of the line segments are determined by T and P_j (Kraus and Litzenberger 1973, p. 916), and every time D_f passes the value at which it equals some state's total return of the firm, X_{fj}, the bankruptcy costs of that state kick down the value of the function $V(D_f)$.

T-DETC implies 1) that there *can* be a unique optimal amount of debt D_f, 2) this optimum amount of debt can be "interior", that is, larger than zero and smaller than the total return of the firm in the firm's most lucrative state (X_{fn}). Figure 2 is drawn as an example of this possibility.

This possibility arises as a result of the introduction of bankruptcy cost in the model. If bankruptcy costs are removed from the structures in *DETC* and *DETCp*, a poorer set of structures *DET(p)*, results, where $x \in$ *DET(p)* is called *(potential) debt equity market system with corporate tax.* This brings us back to the original paradoxical Modigliani-Miller theorem on the optimal amount of corporate debt in case of the existence of corporate tax; setting $C_{fj} \equiv 0$ in *T-DETC* immediately yields *T-DET*:

T-DET: in all structures $x \in DET$, for all firms f, if T_j is identical in all states j:

$$V(D_f) = V(0) + T \cdot B(D_f)$$

This is the typical shape of $V(D_f)$:

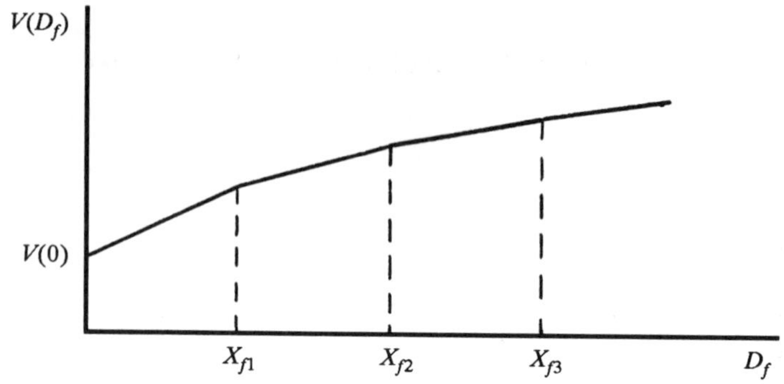

Figure 3: Typical shape implied by *T-DET*

T-DET implies, like *T-DETC*, the possible existence of a unique optimal amount of Debt D_f but if it exists, it is a "corner solution": the more debt, the higher the value of the firm, therefore 100% debt financing is optimal.

If, finally, tax T_j is removed from the structures, we obtain $DE(p)$, where $x \in DE(p)$ is called a *(potential) debt equity market system*. This yields the initial Modigliani-Miller Theorem *T-DE*.

T-DE: in all structures $x \in DE$, for all firms f, $V(D_f) = V(0)$

This means that the debt-equity ratio is irrelevant to the value of a firm. The graph becomes a horizontal line.

History would have been nice and simple if Modigliani and Miller had first discovered *T-DE* in the Kraus and Litzenberger framework presented above, then would have introduced tax to arrive at *T-DET*, and finally that Kraus and Litzenberger enriched the theory with bankruptcy cost to arrive at *T-DETC*.

However, Modigliani and Miller did not use the state preference framework. For what this example is meant to illustrate below, we do not need to go into the logical intricacies of reducing Modigliani and Miller's of introducing market forces to the method used by Kraus and Litzenberger.

Section 3

What the example illustrates: approximation of a provable interesting truth by concretization

3.1. Refined theorylikeness and concretization

Refined theorylikeness

As announced in the introduction, the refined definition of truthlikeness is based on the underlying ternary relation of structurelikeness. Let x, y, z etc. indicate members of a set of potential models Mp, and let $s(x,y,z)$ indicate that (structure) y is more similar to z than x is to z. (For technical reasons we will assume formally that $s(x,y,z)$ is slightly weaker, viz. at least as similar as). There is no general definition of structurelikeness. Every specification will depend on the type of structures involved. Structures x and z are said to be *related* when there is a structure y such that $s(x,y,z)$.

For what follows we only have to assume that s satisfies some very plausible minimal requirements:

centered: $s(x,x,x)$
centering: $s(x,y,x)$ implies $x = y$
conditionally reflexive: $s(x,y,z)$ implies $s(x,x,y)$, $s(x,x,z)$, $s(x,y,y)$, $s(x,z,z)$ and $s(y,z,z)$.

Refined *truth*likeness is conceived as a special case of a general relation of refined *theory*likeness (RTL) on the basis of s. For mutually non-overlapping subsets X, Y, Z of Mp, $RTL(X,Y,Z)$, Y is closer to Z than X, is defined by:

(i) for all x in X and z in Z if $r(x,z)$ there is y in Y such that $s(x,y,z)$
(ii) for all y in Y there are x in X and z in Z such that $s(x,y,z)$.

Informally speaking, $RTL(X,Y,Z)$ says (i) for every Z-model Y can improve upon any X-model related to that Z-model, and (ii) every Y-model improves upon some related X- and Z-model.

For technical reasons the definition formally allows the extreme situation that also $RTL(Y,X,Z)$ is true. Note that $RTL(X,Y,Z)$ reduces to the naive definition in the introduction when s is trivial, i.e. when $s(x,y,z)$ if and only if $x = y = z$.

Concretization
One specific notion of structurelikeness concerns concretization. We start with the definition of the constitutive binary relation: y is a concretization of x (and x an idealization of y), indicated by $con(x,y)$, if and only if y transforms into x, directly or by a limit procedure, when one or more constants and/or functions in y uniformly assume the value 0. On the basis of *con* we define the relevant ternary relation simply as follows: $\langle x,y,z\rangle$ is a concretization sequence, indicated by $ct(x,y,z)$, if and only if $con(x,y)$ & $con(y,z)$. It is easy to check that *con* is reflexive, antisymmetric and transitive, from which it follows immediately that *ct* satisfies the minimal requirements for a structurelikeness relation. Moreover, relatedness on the basis of *ct* trivially coincides with *con*.

Let *RTLct* indicate *RTL* based on *ct*. It is also plausible to define the following binary relation of concretization between theories: Y is a concretization of X, indicated by

$CON(X,Y)$ if and only if for all y in Y there is x in X such that $con(x,y)$ and for all x in X there is y in Y such that $con(x,y)$.

For mutually non-overlapping sets the following general concretization theorem (*GC*-theorem) is now easy to prove: if $CON(X,Y)$ and $CON(Y,Z)$ and if Y is convex and mediating then $RTLct(X,Y,T)$. Convexity and mediation are properties which are frequently and easily satisfied by a theory. Y is *convex* is the property that y is in Y when $ct(x,y,z)$ and x and z belong to Y. Y is *mediating* is the property that if $con(x,z)$ and if there are y and y' in Y such that $con(x,y)$ and $con(y',z)$ then there is y'' in Y such that $con(x,y'')$ and $con(y'',z)$, i.e. $ct(x,y'',z)$. It is important to note that convexity and mediation are properties of Y, independent of Y's relation to X and Z.

3.2. *Applications*

Now we are in the position to apply the above general notions to the case of capital structure theory. We will present the applications in three rounds. In the first application round we concentrate on the relations between the three theories, conceived as sets of models. In the second round we focus on interesting theorems and their domains of validity. Finally, in the third round we will characterize the heuristic strategy and hypotheses of the researchers which are typical for the present case of truth approximation. Only in the last round the application of the *GC*-theorem is of substantial importance, but we will mention its application also in the previous rounds.

Concretization of theories

Recall from Section 2 that *DE*, *DET*, and *DETC* are subsets of the set *DETCp* of potential Debt Equity market system with corporate Tax and bankruptcy Costs satisfying the extra conditions 2, 3 and 4 of section 2.4. Moreover, in the case of *DE*-models the bankruptcy cost function *C* and the corporate tax function *T* are uniformly zero, whereas in the case of *DET*-models only *C* is uniformly zero, and in the case of *DETC*, *T* nor *C* are uniformly zero. Note that by trivial consequence *DE*, *DET* and *DETC* are mutually non-overlapping.

Let *z* be a *DETC*-model. It is easy to check that there is a (unique) *DET*-model *y* and a (unique) *DE*-model *z* such that *con*(*x*,*y*) and *con*(*y*,*z*), and hence *ct*(*x*,*y*,*z*). From this it is a small step to prove directly *RTLct*(*DE*,*DET*,*DETC*), i.e. *DET* is closer to *DETC* than *DE* on the basis of concretization. This result is also easy to obtain *via* the *GC*-theorem from the fact that *DET* is convex and mediating and the combination of *CON*(*DE*,*DET*) and *CON*(*DET*,*DETC*).

Concretization of interesting theorems

In the second application round we introduce the interesting theorems in Hamminga's sense (section 2.1) and their domain of validity. Recall that theorems *T-DE*, *T-DET*, and *T-DETC* were associated with *DE*, *DET* and *DETC*, respectively. Let the consequents of *T-DE*, *T-DET* and *T-DETC* be indicated by *CT-DE*, *CT-DET* and *CT-DETC*, respectively. Let *VCT-DE*, *VCT-DET* and *VCT-DETC* indicate the subsets of *DEp*, *DETp* and *DETCp* for which these consequents are respectively provable, to be called their respective domains of validity. (For technical reasons we restrict *VCT-DE* and *VCT-DET* to *DEp* and *DETp*, respectively, assuring that the three domains of validity under consideration are mutually non-overlapping; extension to *DETCp* (only) meets some technical complications.)

The first crucial result of Modigliani and Miller can now be rephrased as the proof that *DE* is a subset of *VCT-DE*, i.e. *CT-DE* is provable for *DE*-models.[13] Their second result amounts to the proof that *DET* is a subset of *VCT-DET*. Finally, the crucial result of Kraus and Litzenberg is the proof that *DETC* is a subset of *VCT-DETC*.

Let us call in general, assuming some set of potential models *Mp*, a theorem *T** a concretization of *T* if and only if the domain of validity of *T** in *Mp* is a concretization of that of *T*, i.e. *CON*(*VT*,*VT**). This relation between two theorems may well be provable without the above mentioned type of subset proofs, as in the present case. That is, it is easy

[13] This can be strictly proven in the exposition of Kraus and Litzenberger (1973).

to check that *CON*(*VCT-DE*, *VCT-DET*) and *CON*(*VCT-DET*, *VCT-DETC*), and hence, by the *GC*-theorem and noting that *VCT-DET* is convex and mediating, that *VCT-DET* is closer to *VCT-DETC* than *VCT-DE* on the basis of concretization. Again, the latter result, i.e. *RTLct*(*VCT-DE*, *VCT-DET*, *VCT-DETC*), is also easy to prove directly. Recall that we arrived already in the first round to the conclusion *RTLct*(*DE*, *DET*, *DETC*).

The heuristic strategy of Kraus and Litzenberg

Why makes concretization sense? What further goals were Kraus and Litzenberg aiming at? Let us start from the basic result of Modigliani and Miller to the effect that *DE* is a subset of *VCT-DE*. We will omit further reference to the intermediate result concerning *(T-)DET* and use as much verbal formulations as possible.

The more or less explicit heuristic strategy of Kraus and Litzenberg which brought them to *(T-)DETC* can be characterized as follows. Look for *DE** and *CT-DE** such that *DE** is a convex and mediating concretization of *DE*, *CT-DE** is a convex and mediating (interesting) concretization of *CT-DE* and *DE** is a subset of *VCT-DE**.

The motivation for this strategy can be given in terms of an unknown set of (potential) economically possible systems *EP* (*EPp*), including of course the actual ones *EA*. To be precise, the following heuristic hypotheses form 'the good reasons' for this strategy.

- H1 it is possible to formulate a set of potential economically possible systems *EPp* such that there is a unique subset *EP* characterizing the economically possible systems and a unique subset *EA* of *EP* characterizing the economically actual systems,
- H2 all relevant sets can be reformulated as subsets of *EPp*,
- H3 *EP* is a concretization of *DE**,
- H4 there is an interesting theorem *CT-EP* such that
  - (a) *VCT-EP* is a concretization of *VCT-DE**
  - (b) *CT-EP* is provably true for *EP*-systems, and hence provably true for *AE*-systems.

If these hypotheses are true and if *DE** and *CT-DE** are in accordance with the explicit heuristic goals we may conclude that *DE** is closer to *EP* than *DE*, and that *VCT-DE** is closer to *VCT-EP* than *VCT-DE*. In both cases the application of the *GT*-theorem is crucial, as long as we do not dispose of *EP* and *CT-EP*.

The four hypotheses may or may not be true. There does not seem to be a reason why they are unlikely to be true, except for the fact that economic reality is infinitely complex. This objection however can be conceded by assuming only that the hypotheses are approximately true in some intuitive sense.

The other crucial point is H3: *EP* will only be a concretization of *DE** if the relevant factor(s) introduced in the concretization of *DE* to *DE** have been accounted for in an adequate way. Of course, it is impossible to evaluate the adequacy of the concretization of *DE* to *DE** in a conclusive way. Hence, we have to rely on good reasons, which may in general be of empirical and/or theoretical nature, leading to empirical and/or theoretical concretization. The example of Van der Waals is a clear case of theoretical concretization followed by empirical support. For Kraus and Litzenberger, the reasons to engage in concretization were empirical doubts about the validity of the original M&M-result for real world situations in general. The reasons to believe in the adequacy of the concretization were only of theoretical economic nature.

We may summarize the foregoing as follows. By concretizing a set of models (i.e. a theory) and a provable interesting theorem about them, we try to approximate a provable interesting truth about economically possible, and hence about economically actual, systems. The heuristic hypotheses guaranteeing the success of this attempt may well be true, provided the concretization of the theory is not an empirically empty gesture. Besides being a (convex and mediating) concretization in the logico-mathematical sense it has to be plausible on theoretical and/or empirical grounds.

Kees Cools
Jan Evertsenstraat 16
5021 RE Tilburg
The Netherland
The Netherlands

Bert Hamminga
Tilburg University
PO Box 90153
5000 LE Tilburg

Theo A.F. Kuipers
State University of Groningen
Department of Philosophy
A-weg 30
9718 CW Groningen
The Netherlands

REFERENCES

Arrow, K.J. (1969). The Role of Securities in the Optimal Allocation of Risk-Bearing. *Review of Economic Studies*, 91-96.

Arrow, K.J. (1971). *Theory of Risk Bearing*. Chicago: Markham.

Balzer, W. and B. Hamminga (Eds.) (1989). *Philosophy of Economics. Erkenntnis*, Vol. **30**, Nos. 1-2.

Baxter, N. and Nevins, D. (1967). Leverage, Risk of Ruin and the Cost of Capital. *Journal of finance*, **22**, September, 395-403.

Cools, K. and Zon, Liong (1992). Capital Structure under Financing and Investment Externalities. An Incomplete Contact Approach, Working Paper, CentER Discussion Paper, Tilburg University.

Debreu, G. (1959). *Theory of Value*. New Haven: Yale University Press.

Hamminga, B. (1983). *Neoclassical theory structure and theory development*. Berlin: Springer.

Harris, Milton and Artur Raviv (1988). Corporate Control Contests and Corporate Capital Structure. *Journal of Financial Economics*, **20**, 55-56.

Janssen, M. (1989). Structuralist Reconstruction of Classical and Keynesian Macroeconomics. In: Balzer and Hamminga (Eds.) (1989), pp. 165-181.

Janssen, M. and T. Kuipers (1989). Stratification of General Equilibrium Theory: A Synthesis of Reconstructions. In: Balzer and Hamminga (Eds.) (1989), pp. 183-205.

Jensen, M.C. and W.H. Meckling (1976). Theory of the Firm: Managerial Behavior, Agency Costs and Ownership Structure. *Journal of Financial Economics*, **3**, 305-360.

Kim, E.H. (1978). A Mean-Variance Theory of Optimal Capital Structure and Corporate Debt Capacity. *Journal of Finance*, **33**, March, 45-64.

Klamer, A. (1983). *Conversations with Economists*. Totowa: Rowman & Allanheld.

Kraus, A. and R.H. Litzenberger (1973). A State-Preference Model of Optimal Financial Leverage. *Journal of Finance*, **28**, September, 911-922.

Kuipers, T. (1982). Approaching descriptive and theoretical truth. *Erkenntnis*, **18**, 343-387.

Kuipers, T. (1987). A structuralist approach to truthlikeness. In: T. Kuipers (Ed.), *What is closer-to-the-truth? (Poznań Studies in the Philosophy of Sciences and the Humanities*, **10**). Amsterdam: Rodopi, pp. 79-99.

Kuipers, T. (1992). Naive and refined truth approximation. *Synthese*, 93.3 (December), 299-341.

Kuipers, T. (1992a). Truth approximation by concretization, In: J. Brzeziński, L. Nowak (Eds.), *Idealization III: Approximation and Truth* (*Poznań Studies in the Philosophy of Sciences and the Humanities*, **25**). Amsterdam: Rodopi, pp. 159-179.

Miller, M.H. (1977). Debt and Taxes. *Journal of Finance*, **32**, 261-275.

Miller, M.H. (1988). The Modigliani-Miller Propositions after Thirty Years. *Journal of Economic Perspectives*, **2**, 99-120.

Modigliani, F. and M.H. Miller (1958). The Cost of Capital, Corporation Finance, and the Theory of Investment. *American Economic Review* **48**, June, 261-297.

Modigliani, F. and M.H. Miller (1963). Corporate Income Taxes and the Cost of Capital: a Correction. *American Economic Review*, **53**, June, 433-443.

Scott, J.H. Jr. (1976). A Theory of Optimal Capital Structure. *The Bell Journal of Economics*, **7**, Spring, 33-54.

Titman, Sh. (1984). The Effect of Capital Structure on a Firm's Liquidation Decision. *Journal of Financial Economics*, **13**, 137-151.

Poznań Studies in the Philosophy of the Sciences and the Humanities
1994, Vol. 38, pp. 229-242

Daniel M. Hausman

PAUL SAMUELSON AS DR. FRANKENSTEIN: WHEN AN IDEALIZATION RUNS AMUCK*

ABSTRACT. This paper is concerned with relations between highly unrealistic or idealized models and the world, with how such models can be informative, with how they can be criticized, and with how their constituents can be incorporated into other models. It will focus on only one case, and its conclusions will be skeptical and suggestive.

Paul Samuelson's "Overlapping Generations" model

In 1958 Paul Samuelson published in *The Journal of Political Economy* a much celebrated and discussed paper entitled, "An Exact Consumption-Loan Model of Interest with or without the Social Contrivance of Money." The problem Samuelson addresses is the following: Suppose individuals want to save for their old age, when they cannot produce anything, and there is nothing imperishable that they can lay by. All people can do is to strike some deal with younger workers to support them later in exchange for some current consideration. What will the pattern of interest rates be? To avoid conflating the effect on interest rates of this desire to provide for one's old age, with the effects of technological productivity, of subjective preference for present consumption over future consumption and of expectations of improving or worsening economic circumstances (Böhm-Bawerk 1888; Kuenne 1971, pp. 25-34), Samuelson's model either assumes away these other factors or makes no mention of them at all.

Samuelson addresses this problem by inventing the device of overlapping generations. The utility functions and productive capabilities of all individuals are identical. But individuals are not all alive at the same time, and in any given time period, individuals will be of different ages, and their productive capacities and (in a more general setting than

* Parts of this essay derive from chapter 7 of *The Inexact and Separate Science of Economics* (1992).

Samuelson's) their tastes, may depend on their age. So one can combine in a non-arbitrary way human life-time uniformity with differences among contemporaries. In Samuelson's model, life has three periods. In the first two periods workers each produce one unit of a single completely perishable output — call it "chocolate". In the third period of their lives retired workers produce no output at all and consume only what younger producers transfer to them. All individuals have concave and increasing utility functions for consumption of chocolate in all three of the periods of their lives. As they mature, their tastes (and utility functions) do not change. Finally, productive activities take place in a closed competitive market economy. Nobody is a net creditor or debtor. Markets clear.

The basic model

Consider a person, P, born in period t. C_1, C_2 and C_3 are the amounts of chocolate consumed by P in the first, second and third periods of her life, which occupies periods t, $t + 1$, and $t + 2$ of the history of this economy. The value of P's consumption in the first period of her life (period t) in terms of chocolate in period t is simply C_1. The value in period t of P's consumption in the second period of her life (period $t + 1$) is $C_2/(1+i_t)$, and the value in period t of P's consumption in retirement (period $t + 2$) is $C_3/[(1+i_t)\cdot(1+i_{t+1})]$. So P faces the budget equation:

$$C_1 + C_2/(1+i_t) + C_3/[(1+i_t)\cdot(1+i_{t+1})] = 1 + 1/(1+i_t)$$

The left hand side of the equation is the total value in period t of P's lifetime consumption, while the right hand side is the total value in period t of P's lifetime production, which consists of one unit of output in each of periods t and $t + 1$, with the latter multiplied by the discount factor $1/(1+i_t)$ to get its value in period t.

It is, however, more convenient to work with each individual's *net savings* in each period — that is one or zero units of chocolate output minus the amount of chocolate consumed. So P's net savings in period t, S_1, the first period of her working life is $1 - C_1$. Similarly $S_2 = 1 - C_2$ and $S_3 = -C_3$. Restated in terms of net savings, the budget condition becomes:

$$(1) \quad S_1 + S_2/(1+i_t) + S_3/[(1+i_t)\cdot(1+i_{t+1})] = 0.$$

The condition that markets clear provides a second equation. Let B_t be the number of people first entering the labor force in period t. So in period t there are B_t people (Jacobs) in the first period of their life, B_{t-1}

people (Isaacs) in the second period of their lives and B_{t-2} retirees (Abrahams). Since markets clear, one has the equation:

$$(2) \quad B_t S_1(i_t, i_{t+1}) + B_{t-1} S_2(i_{t-1}, i_t) + B_{t-2} S_3(i_{t-2}, i_{t-1}) = 0.$$

The savings decision of those entering the workforce in period t depends on i_t and i_{t+1}, while the savings decision of those born in the preceeding periods depends on the interest rates they encounter in their lives. Knowing the utility functions, one could determine the savings if one knew the interest rates, but one has four unknowns and only two equations. If one adds the further equation stating that the market must clear in period $t - 1$ (or period $t + 1$), one picks up one equation, but one picks up another unknown, too. Without further constraints, there is no way to determine the rates of interest.

Stationary and constant growth cases

One drastic way to get some determinacy is to consider the case of an unchanging economy with a constant population, B, and a constant interest rate, i. Equations 1 and 2 become:

$$(1s) \quad S_1 + S_2(1/(1+i)) + S_3(1/(1+i))^2 = 0 \text{ and}$$

$$(2s) \quad BS_1 + BS_2 + BS_3 = 0.$$

Without considering the dependence of savings on the interest rate, one can see by inspection that one solution (and there are others!) is $i = 0$. Since Samuelson has placed no constraints at all on the extent to which individuals might prefer present to future consumption, this is (as Samuelson notes) a remarkable result. The terms of trade across periods are entirely equal. In every period t, individuals can secure exactly x units of the consumption good in a future period by surrendering x units of the consumption good in period t.

Suppose now that instead of a stationary population, population is growing at some constant exponential rate such that $B_{t+1} = (1 + m)B_t$. Suppose, as in the stationary case, that the rate of interest is constant through time. Equations 1 and 2 now become:

$$(1e) \quad S_1 + (1/(1+i))S_2 + (1/(1+i))^2 S_3 = 0 \text{ and}$$

$$(2e) \quad B_t S_1 + [B_t/(1 + m)]S_2 + [B_t/(1 + m)^2]S_3 = 0.$$

One can see that one solution (and again there are others!) is $i = m$. Samuelson thus proves the following theorem:

> Every geometrically growing consumption-loan economy has an equilibrium market rate of interest exactly equal to its biological percentage growth rate. (p. 472)

The stationary case is just a special case of an economy growing geometrically with a zero percentage growth rate. Having found this result, one might have expected Samuelson to consider whether equations (1e) and (2e) have other roots and to consider which of these are economically relevant, but first his discussion takes two interesting turns.

"Hump-saving" and social welfare

First Samuelson addresses the question of whether the biological interest rate maximizes the "lifetime (ordinal) well-being of a representative person, subject to the resources available to him (and to every other representative man) over his lifetime." (p. 472). (The answer is that it does.) Why would one ask this question here? One answer is that Samuelson (like economic theorists generally) has a deep and abiding interest in the welfare properties of competitive markets. He wants to know how well they would perform in hypothetical circumstances such as those envisioned. Note, however, how constrained the welfare question is by prior theoretical commitments.

But, before going further, Samuelson notes what he has known all along, which is that the mathematical solution $i = m$ is economically impossible. Samuelson suggests that we consider the two-period case where individuals work in the first period then retire. Although one can derive the same mathematical solution, $i = m$, voluntary saving is obviously impossible. Non-retirees have nobody with whom they can exchange who can support them in the next period. In the three (and n) period case, however, Isaacs can make repayable loans to Jacobs, but an extension of the two-period argument does, however, show that it is economically impossible (in the model as described) for workers to save in the first period of their lives. (Individual first period workers may, of course, arrange exchanges with other first period workers. All the argument shows is that there can be on average or in total no first-period savings.) For there is nobody who can repay consumption foregone in the first period with additional consumption later. Indeed in a numerical example of a stationary economy with completely symmetrical preferences for present as compared to future consumption, Jacobs consume more than they produce and the free-market rate of interest that arises is strongly negative — approximately $-2/3$. The Isaacs are giving up x units of consumption to the Jacobs in exchange for a retirement income next year of only $x/3$.

So two conclusions emerge. The biological interest rate is not an economically relevant solution to the model and whatever the economically relevant solution is, it is suboptimal (given the infinite time horizon). The invisible hand fails. The free market here leaves everybody worse off than they could have been.

This expository order, which is abbreviated and slightly altered in the retelling, is curious. Why make arguments for the economic plausibility of mathematical solutions that cannot arise through market transactions, except, perhaps, to anticipate objections that are bound to occur to readers?[1] The (theoretical) normative relevance of the discussion seems central. A large part of what makes the puzzle Samuelson poses interesting is the strong presumption that free markets are efficient.[2] The (positive) theoretical question, "What's going on here?" gets its interest and charge from these normative concerns.

Implications

Samuelson himself argues that the model is instructive positively, normatively and conceptually. Positively, it shows what interest rates *would be implied* if they were determined only by the desire to save for retirement. Normatively,

> it points up a fundamental and intrinsic deficiency in a free pricing system, namely, that free pricing gets you on the Pareto-efficiency frontier but by itself has no tendency to get you to positions on the frontier that are ethically optimal in terms of a social welfare function; only by social collusions – of tax, expenditure, fiat, or other type – can an ethical observer hope to end up where he wants to be. (p. 479)

Conceptually, it shows that zero or negative interest rates are in no sense logically contradictory, it helps to isolate the effects of separate causal influences on interest rates, and it gives one a new perspective on the importance of money as a store of wealth. For money now appears to be a sort of social compact that makes up for the perishability of goods. But

---

[1] There is a good deal more to be said in answer to this and other questions than I shall say here. What Donald McCloskey calls "the rhetoric of economics" (1985) is an interesting subject indeed. It seems evident that Samuelson is not only anticipating objections but also teasing and attempting to amuse the reader and hold his or her attention. He clearly wants the reader to see the intellectual attractions of the puzzles he has formulated.

[2] Although the free-market solution is inferior when confronted with an infinite horizon, it is in fact Pareto optimal for any finite time horizon, no matter how large. For the biological interest rate arrangement with S_1 greater than zero leaves the last generation of workers worse off during their productive years than does the free-market solution with S_1 negative.

how can "unrealistic" models such as this one be "instructive?" What sorts of relevance can they have to positive, normative, and conceptual issues?

The remainder of Samuelson's essay is devoted to the conceptual contributions the model supposedly makes. The causal questions concerning the effect on interest rates of the desire to save are dropped rather than answered. Samuelson points out that if individuals can make some sort of compact whereby the working Jacobs and Isaacs support the retired Abrahams in return for support from workers-to-be when the Isaacs and Jacobs are themselves retired, then (assuming an infinite horizon) everybody is better off and the biological interest rate can be attained. The contrivance of money has the same effect. By purchasing consumption goods from producers, retirees can pass on to them claims for the consumption goods which can be cashed in later. This feature of money depends, as Samuelson reminds us, on each generation agreeing to accept the notes of the previous generations.

Meckling's and Lerner's critiques

Notice how peculiar are Samuelson's normative conceptual concerns about optimality. Why should anybody care about the optimality of an impossible infinite economy? But Samuelson was not the only one who cared and cared deeply about these points. In the immediate aftermath of its publication there were two substantial critical discussions by Abba Lerner (1959a,b) and William Meckling (1960a,b). Both alleged that Samuelson made mistakes in his positive analysis, but both were in fact motivated by normative or ideological concerns.

This is not the occasion to discuss the details of Meckling's and Lerner's criticisms, which I have in any case scrutinized at length elsewhere. But one feature of criticisms is worth stressing in this context. Both claim that Samuelson has made some sort of *mistake*. Meckling objects that Samuelson has *misspecified* his model. Equation (2s) $S_1 + S_2 + S_3 = 0$ should be replaced with (2s') $S_3 = (1+i)S_1$. For, Meckling argues, Abrahams can only consume what they loaned last year to the Isaacs (plus interest). Meckling simply rules out the possibility of a social contract. Although Meckling's critique is mistaken for detailed technical reasons, it is worth thinking about the character of this criticism. In the case of a model that drastically misrepresents many features of reality, exactly what sense can one make of the distinction between correct and incorrect specification?

Similarly, Abba Lerner objects that Samuelson is wrong in his most fundamental claims about his model. Given a social contract or the acceptance of fiat money, what the overlapping-generations construction reveals are the possibilities for tax and gift programs, not for savings and repayments. For in Samuelson's model in which all goods are perishable, there can be no savings. Misconstruing the possibilities this way lends a superficial acceptibility to arbitrary and unpalatable redistribution programs. But how is it possible for Samuelson to *misconceive* of the transfers that take place in his model as savings and repayment? Can't Samuelson tell his fictitious story however he wants?

Thus far we have come across three puzzles concerning models such as Samuelson's which rely on extreme simplifications: what is their relevance? what are the critieria for correct specification? and what are the criteria for correct conceptualization of the relations they specify?

Overlapping generations on the loose

But overlapping-generations models present at least one further puzzle – a puzzle which inspired my title. For the history of overlapping-generations models had in 1960 scarcely begun. Samuelson's device comes to life and escapes from his model. Not only are there various extensions of Samuelson's model, which, for example, incorporate durable goods (Diamond 1965), but the device came to be a crucial feature in models that have virtually nothing else in common with Samuelson's. The notion of overlapping generations has come to be of particular importance to the "new classical" or "rational expectations" school of macroeconomics (see Begg 1982, Carter and Maddock 1984, Hoover 1988, and Minford and Peel 1983 for overviews of this school). Decisions to borrow and lend depend on expectations about what future generations will do and about what they will expect about the still more distant future. Determinate results can be obtained by assuming that everybody expects what actually occurs.

The overlapping-generations models that have turned out to be of great importance in contemporary macroeconomics owe little to Samuelson apart from the general overlapping-generations framework. For example Neil Wallace uses an overlapping-generations model to explain how fiat money (money that is inconvertible and of no intrinsic use) can have value.[3] Wallace argues,

---

[3] (1980b). For a more accessible exposition, see McCallum (1983).

> In order to pursue the notion that fiat money facilitates exchange, one must abandon the costless multilateral market clearing implicit in the Walrasian (or Arrow-Debreu) general equilibrium model. Since exchange works perfectly in that model, there can be no role for a device that is supposed to facilitate exchange. In order to get a theory of fiat money, one must generalize the Walrasian model by including in its some sort of *friction*, something that will inhibit the operation of markets. On that there is agreement.
>
> But what sort of friction? On that there is no agreement, which is to say that there is no widely accepted theory of fiat money. I will try to alter this situation by arguing that the friction in Samuelson's 1958 consumption loan model, *overlapping generations* gives rise to the best available model of fiat money. (1980b, p. 50)

Although Samuelson's essay does contain a suggestion of how fiat money may have value, Wallace's question is not Samuelson's. For Wallace gives members of both generations of his two-generation overlapping-generations models endowments of their own and is unconcerned with the problems of "hump" savings and with the hypothetical and normative issues that occupy Samuelson, Lerner and Meckling.

Although Wallace's account of fiat money has received serious criticism (see especially Tobin 1980, Hahn 1982 and McCallum 1983), it has been influential (see, for example, Sargent 1987). Indeed Cass and Shell argue that regardless of whether one endorses Wallace's particular model, dynamic and disaggregative theorizing is unavoidable in studies of money, government debt or intertemporal allocation. And, Cass and Shell argue, the only manageable framework for such theorizing is the overlapping-generations model (1980, p. 260).

But, as McCallum correctly points out, there is no necessary connection between the use of overlapping-generations models and new classical economics. And indeed Geanakoplos and Polemarchakis (1986) deploy overlapping-generations models to vindicate the consistency of Keynes' view that "animal spirits," that is, expectations of future economic performance, can have a dramatic effect on current economic activity. For the same infinity that Wallace relies on to find a value for fiat money, also leads to indeterminacies. Current prices can depend on prices expected next period which in turn depend on expectations then about the prices the period after and so on forever. In one of Geanakoplos and Polemarchakis's models there is a two-dimensional *continuum* of possible equilibrium paths depending on initial nominal wages and price expectations.

The appeal of the overlapping-generations framework is that it provides a relatively tractable way to begin to address the effects of the future on the present. It enables one to study an economy that is in competitive equilibrium with heterogeneous individuals who are changing over time. Yet the heterogeneity results from the effects of aging on an underlying homogeneity of taste and ability. The temporal constraints on the relations among different agents introduces complexities and frictions in a non-arbitrary way.

What this later history makes evident is that conceptual devices in models, such as Samuelson's overlapping-generations, are not chained within the models within which they appear. They are not like characters in works of fiction. One can employ them without referring back to the story in which they first appear. They are more like physical implements or, perhaps, characters in myths, who have at least apparent lives of their own. But since Samuelson's overlapping generations appear to be as fictional as is Hamlet, how is this possible?

Answers to the puzzles

Let us then sketch solutions to these four puzzles and to say something about how all this relates to issues concerning idealizations, which I have thus far intentionally not mentioned.

1. Relevance

In my view models are definitions of concepts or kinds of systems. One might, for example, say that Samuelson's model with a stationary population and a constant interest rate defines "a stationary Samuelson economy." Models do not themselves have any empirical implications. One *uses* them to make assertions that may be true or false. When one offers a "theoretical hypothesis" T maintaining that the concept defined by a model is true of some domain D, one recovers from the assumptions of the model a set of assertions, which in the case of very general theoretical hypotheses, can be called a theory. If M is a model, I shall denote as M_{TD}, the set of assertions implied by a theoretical hypothesis T, which asserts that M is true of D. The virtues of models themselves are conceptual and heuristic, not empirical, explanatory, or predictive. The relevance of a model clearly depends not only on the features of the model, but also on one's interests and questions.

To answer a question Q, M must be an essential part of an answer that stands in the right structural relation to Q and the answer must also satisfy semantic conditions. The structural relation depends on the nature of the question, and an extended discussion of so-called erotetic logic would be needed to elucidate the relations between questions and answers. Fortuntely, there is no need for me to enter into these knotty questions, and what I shall say is compatible with whatever the correct account of the relations between questions and answers may be. Notice that a model M can be relevant to a question Q by leading one to withdraw or to revise Q.

Let us say that M_{TD} provides *an exact answer* to Q if it stands in the right structural relation to Q and M_{TD} is true. Theoretical hypotheses asserting that a model is true of some domain will, of course, rarely by themselves provide answers to questions concerning individual events and states of affairs. The answers to such questions will also include statements concerning initial conditions. These further statements must also be true in order for answers to such questions to count as exact. An exact answer to a question is simply a set of true statements that answers the question.

The difficulty comes in seeing how highly unrealistic models (models in which M_{TD} is false for all T asserting that some real-world domain D satisfies the concept M defines) can help one to say anything other than that these models don't apply to anything. The easiest way, which seldom arises, is if the false statements in M_{TD} are not needed as premises in the derivation of P. So even though M_{TD} contains false statements, that part of M_{TD} needed to derive P is all true. In that unusual case a highly unrealistic model can still provide a exact answer to non-trivial questions. But models such as Samuelson's do not provide exact answers to any interesting questions.

I shall say that a model M helps provide a *correct* (but not exact) answer to a question Q if at least one of the following is true:

1. M_{TD}*, which "smears" what M_{TD} says, provides a exact answer to Q within some margin of error. M_{TD} might falsely say that that excess demand was zero, while M_{TD}* might truly say that that excess demand lay in some small interval $(-e,e)$. M_{TD}* might then no longer entail P, but it might entail that the values of certain variables are close to the values asserted in P.
2. There is a probabilistic variant of M_{TD} which provides a exact answer to a probabilistic variant of Q.
3. Subject to legitimate qualifications, M_{TD} provides an exact answer to Q. I've discussed "legitimate qualification" at great length elsewhere (1992, ch. 8). The idea is that, discounting the effect of disturbing causes, the relevant parts of M_{TD} are true and provide a exact answer.
4. The false claims in M_{TD} that are needed for the derivation of P could be replaced by true claims of the same kind, and within some margin of error P could still be derived. The vague "of the same kind" clause is crucial, for it is trivial to assert that P could

be derived by some other model in which all the falsities in M_{TD} were eliminated. The idea is, for example, that one might replace a false claim, such as that everyone lives exactly three periods, with a true claim about variable life spans and still be able to get much the same results. Investigations into the robustness of the implications of theories provide evidence for claims of the dispensability of falsehoods.

So unrealistic models can sometimes provide correct answers to questions even if they cannot provide exact answers. Samuelson's model is relevant to the various questions he raises insofar as it provides correct answers to them (or correctly leads to their reformulation or withdrawal).

2. Criteria for correct specification

There are several ways in which one might argue that a model is misspecified. Most simply, one might argue that the stated assumptions are logically inconsistent with one another. But this cannot be Meckling's view, since he does not believe Samuelson's axioms are literally logically inconsistent.

Somewhat more generally, one might object that the axioms as formulated are inconsistent with story that accompanies the model, that is with the informal implicit or explicit assumptions that the formal claims of the model are supposed to capture. When Meckling criticizes Samuelson's model on the grounds that self-interested agents could not get into a biological-interest rate equilibrium and would not remain in one if they got there, he is probably making this sort of criticism. But it is worth noticing that Meckling may be making a third sort of critique. He may be objecting that Samuelson's model is not so much internally inconsistent or inconsistent with its underlying story, as it is inconsistent with general principles common in orthodox economic modeling. Unlike agents as portrayed in many neoclassical models, Samuelson's hypothetical actors do not renege on the social contract when it is in their short-run self-interest to do so.

The misspecification charge might be understood in a fourth way, too. One might object that a model is misspecified in the sense that the assumptions employed in a particular model make it irrelevant to the questions to which it is intended to apply. The assumptions are inconsistent with some central facts or crucial generalizations that characterize the phenomena to which it is supposed to apply.

3. Criteria for correct construal

One easy way to spell out the notion of correct conceptualization is to maintain that one correctly conceptualizes the relationships within the model if and only if one has only true beliefs concerning which questions the model is relevant to. But it is not clear that this elucidation captures Lerner's meaning. When Lerner objects that Samuelson has misconstrued his model, he means that Samuelson is mistaken in conceiving of intergenerational transfers that are motivated solely by a desire to even-out lifetime consumption as savings and repayment. What is at issue is not whether Samuelson is correct about what phenomena his model applies to, but whether the explicit or implicit conceptual claims in the model are correct. Misconstrual is conceptual misspecification. The story and possibly also the formal model make a fundamental mistake. The alleged mistake in this case it seems to be misspecification of the fourth variety. Lerner maintains that Samuelson's model is mistaken in its classification and in its most fundamental descriptions of intergenerational transfers.

4. The autonomy of the notion of overlapping generations

Shakespeare's Hamlet may appear in other works of fiction, such as Stoppard's *Rosenkranz and Guildenstern Are Dead*, and he may apparently be referred to in works of non-fiction, such as this essay purports to be. But Hamlet cannot escape the play. Overlapping generations, on the other hand, can put in their appearance in many models, and although citations to Samuelson's work are almost always present, the device is on the loose. One need know nothing about Samuelson's work to appreciate fully most other works which involve overlapping generations. What's the difference?[4]

One possibility that comes to mind immediately is that overlapping generations were not invented by Samuelson. They are a fact of life, upon which he merely shined a spotlight. But Shakespeare based his play on a real person, too; and Samuelson's contribution is not merely to permit overlapping generations, but overlapping generations of identical individuals with identical life-spans.

It seems to me that what gives autonomous life to the device of overlapping generations is its thinness — its lack of character — coupled with the lucky circumstances that the device may be incorporated into many different axioms systems to address a variety of questions. Samuelson's creation, unlike Shakespeare's, is not a fictional individual. It is thinly characterized and none of its characterizations, apart from the

[4] Notice that the scientific realist has a ready answer to this question in the case of the postulation of theoretical entities. Physicists who accept very different theories can still talk of electrons, because they are referring to the same real entities. But there are, of course, no economies of identical agents with identical lifespans.

platitude that generations overlap, is more than a matter of convenience. Wallace may have gotten the idea of formulating a model of an infinite economy with overlapping generations from Samuelson, but what he is borrowing is a technique, as one artist might borrow a method of perspective from another. He is not concerned to probe further into any fictional entity or world Samuelson invented.

Overlapping generations and idealizations

The notion that there are overlapping generations is not an idealization: it is a fact. The notion that there are overlapping generations of identical individuals with identical life-spans is an idealization. For (a) it is false, (b) it is an exaggeration to a limit. Measures of the difference among utility functions, productive capacities and life-spans of different individuals are set to zero (c) its point is to "isolate" (Mäki, forthcoming) or separate the effects of overlapping generations on dependent variables such as the rate of interest from other relevant causal factors, (d) it can be combined with other idealizations such as zero time preference, unchanging tastes, no durable goods or an infinite economy, and (e) both it and the other idealizations with which it is combined can in principle at least be relaxed, and indeed many of the idealizations with which it was combined in Samuelson's original essay have been relaxed. Apart from the mathematical complexity, there is no reason why one cannot have overlapping generations with a distribution of different life-spans, tastes and productive capacities.

Having said all this, what is gained in called Samuelson's cunning device an idealization or an isolation? What simplifications cannot be called idealizations or isolations? What do the various conceptual categorizations offered by Nowak (1980) or Mäki have to contribute to our appreciation of this case? Is there anything interesting to be said about the logical structure or development of idealizations in economics? Are not all the interesting claims about idealizations to be made at a lower level of abstraction? I have doubts about whether any general theory of idealization can help appreciably to improve our understanding of the character of science.

Daniel M. Hausman
Department of Philosophy
University of Wisconsin, Madison
WI 53706 U.S.A.

REFERENCES

Begg, D. (1982). *The Rational Expectations Revolution in Macroeconomics: Theories and Evidence*. Baltimore: Johns-Hopkins University Press.

Böhm-Bawerk, E. (1888). *The Positive Theory of Capital*. Tr. W. Smart. rpt. New York: G.E. Stechert & Co., 1923.

Carter, M. and R. Maddock (1984). *Rational Expectations: Macroeconomics for the 1980's?* London: Macmillan.

Cass, D. and K. Shell (1980). In Defense of a Basic Approach. In: Kareken, J. and N. Wallace (Eds.), *Models of Monetary Economies*. Minneapolis: Federal Reserve Bank of Minneapolis.

Diamond, P. (1965). National Debt in a Neoclassical Growth Model. *American Economic Review*, **55**, 1126-50.

Geanakoplos, J. and H. Polemarchakis (1986). Warasian Indeterminacy and Keynesian Macroeconomics. *Review of Economic Studies*, **53**, 755-79.

Hahn, F. (1982). *Money and Inflation*. Oxford: Blackwell 1982.

Hausman, D. (1992). *The Inexact and Separate Science of Economics*. Cambridge: Cambridge University Press.

Hoover, K. (1988). *The New Classical Macroeconomics: A Sceptical Inquiry*. Oxford: Blackwells.

Kuenne, R. (1971). *Eugen von Böhm Bawerk*. New York: Columbia University Press.

Lerner, A. (1959a). Consumption-Loan Interest and Money. *Journal of Political Economy*, **67**, 512-18.

Lerner, A. (1959b). Rejoinder. *Journal of Political Economy*, **67**, 523-25.

McCallum, B. (1983). The Role of Overlapping Generations Models in Monetary Economics. In: K. Brunner and A. Meltzer (Eds.) *Theory, Policy and Institutions: Papers from the Carnegie-Rochester Conference Series on Public Policy*. Amsterdam: North-Holland, pp. 129-64.

McCloskey, D. (1985). *The Rhetoric of Economics*. Madison: University of Wisconsin Press.

Mäki, U. (1992). On the Method of Isolation in Economics. In: C. Dilworth (Ed.), *Intelligibility in Science* (*Poznań Studies in the Philosophy of the Sciences and the Humanities*, **26**). Amsterdam: Rodopi.

Meckling, W. (1960a). An Exact Consumption-Loan Model of Interst: A Comment. *Journal of Political Economy*, **68**, 72-76.

Meckling, W. (1960b). Rejoinder. *Journal of Political Economy*, **68**, 83-84.

Minford, P. and D. Peel. (1983). *Rational Expectations and the New Macroeconomics*. Oxford: Martin Robertson & Co.

Nowak, L. (1980). *The Structure of Idealization: Towards a Systematic Interpretation of the Marxian Idea of Science*. Dordrecht: Reidel.

Samuelson, P. (1958). An Exact Consumption-Loan Model of Interest with or without the Social Contrivance of Money. *Journal of Political Economy*, **66**, 467-82.

Samuelson, P. (1959). Reply. *Journal of Political Economy*, **67**, 518-22.

Samuelson, P. (1960). Infinity, Unanimity and Singularity: A Reply. *Journal of Political Economy*, **68**, 76-83.

Sargent, T. (1987). *Dynamic Macroeconomic Theory*. Cambridge, MA: Harvard University Press.

Tobin, J. (1980). Discussion. In: Kareken, J. and N. Wallace (Eds.), *Models of Monetary Economies*. Minneapolis: Federal Reserve Bank of Minneapolis, 1980, pp. 83-90.

Wallace, N. (1980). The Overlapping Generations Model of Fiat Money. In: Kareken, J. and N. Wallace (Eds.), *Models of Monetary Economies*. Minneapolis: Federal Reserve Bank of Minneapolis, 1980, pp. 49-82.

Poznań Studies in the Philosophy of the Sciences and the Humanities
1994, Vol. 38, pp. 243-254

Hugo A. Keuzenkamp

WHAT IF AN IDEALIZATION IS PROBLEMATIC? THE CASE OF THE HOMOGENEITY CONDITION IN CONSUMER DEMAND[1]

ABSTRACT. Discusses the econometric literature on testing the *a priori* plausible condition of homogeneity in consumer demand. Such usually disconfirming test did not lead to a rejection of this particular conditions, but to the rejections of other idealizations needed to perform the test. It is possible, but not necessary to describe this process in terms of idealization and concretization.

1. Introduction

The condition of homogeneity of degree zero in prices and incomes of Marshallian demand functions belongs to the core of microeconomic wisdom. Simply put, this condition says that if prices and income change proportionally, expenditure in real terms will remain unchanged. This has a strong intuitive appeal. Some economists call it the absence of money illusion, they claim that it is a direct consequence of rational behaviour.

The homogeneity condition results from an idealizing hypothesis, i.e. linearity of the budget constraint which, jointly with a set of idealizing hypotheses related to the preferences of individuals, implies an ideal law, the so-called Law of demand. The Law of demand states that (compensated) demand curves do not slope upward (see e.g. Hicks 1939, p. 35 and below). Another ideal condition that can be derived from the idealizing hypotheses is symmetry and negative semi-definiteness of the so-called Slutsky matrix of compensated price responses. Economists have tested these conditions, and, in many cases, they had to reject them statistically.

---

[1] This is a revised version of a paper presented at the conference on *Problems of Idealization in Economics*, Tilburg 1-3 July 1991. The paper is based on joint work with Ton Barten (Keuzenkamp and Barten, forthcoming). I would like to thank Bert Hamminga for useful comments.

In particular, the test reported in in Barten (1969) started an episode of embarrassment in microeconomics and econometrics. The test was repeated with different data and different models, with the same disconfirming result in most cases. Homogeneity itself remained widely accepted, due to the strong a priori appeal, its importance in (applied) microeconomics, and a lack of alternatives. This raises an important question: What does it mean to test an idealization, even if it turns out that the idealization appears wide off the mark? Should concretization be the consequence of a negative test result for a particular idealization, or were economists right to stick to the homogeneity condition? In this paper, I will investigate how the test of an ideal condition affects a research line, in particular the neoclassical theory of consumer behaviour.

2. The idealization of consumer behaviour

The economic theory of consumer behaviour is founded on a set of axioms and assumptions. Let preferences for consumption bundles q be denoted by the relations $\succcurlyeq$ and $\succ$, where $\succcurlyeq$ indicates 'is weakly preferred to', and $\succ$ indicates 'is strictly preferred to'. Then, the following requirements or 'axioms of choice' are imposed (see Deaton and Muellbauer 1980, pp. 26-29).

Axioms of choice

A1. Irreflexivity: for no consumption bundle q, it is true that $q \succ q$.
A2. Completeness: for any two bundles in the choice set, either $q^1 \succcurlyeq q^2$ or $q^2 \succcurlyeq q^1$ or both.
A3. Transitivity (consistency): if $q^1 \succ q^2$and $q^2 \succ q^3$, then $q^1 \succ q^3$.

In addition, we often find three more axioms: *A4.* continuity, *A5.* nonsatiation, and *A6.* convexity of preferences.

The first three axioms define what economists regard as rational behaviour. *A1* to *A4* imply the existence of a well-behaved utility function. The fourth axiom is not required for rational behaviour (it rules out lexicographic preferences which may be the taste of a perfectly rational individual) but is generally imposed for (mathematical) convenience. *A5* ensures that the solution is on the budget constraint instead of being inside the constraint (hence, there is no bliss point). *A6* allows to make use of standard optimization theory, but (though having strong intuitive appeal) is unessential for neoclassical demand theory.

An important additional restriction usually imposed on the consumer choice problem is linearity of the budget constraint:

$$R1. \quad \sum_{i=1}^{k} p_i q_i = y$$

where $p_1, p_2, ..., p_k$ is the set of prices of k different types of commodities q_k that a consumer likes to acquire, and y is the budget available for consumption. Yet another restriction that is needed if one wants to carry out empirical analysis, is to impose a particular functional form on the utility function or derived functions (in particular the indirect utility function, and the expenditure function), and to select an appropriate set of arguments that appear in the utility function. I will summarize these constraints in:

R2. Choice of a particular functional form.
R3. Choice of arguments.

To begin our analysis of the theory of consumer behaviour, we may ask whether these axioms and assumptions are idealizing hypotheses in the sense of Nowak (1980). Such idealizing hypotheses are false, in the sense that they are in conflict with reality. Most economists would agree that this is the case for *A1-A6* and *R1-R3*. Economic behaviour, it is argued, is explained by the set of restrictions and axioms stated here, but it is acknowledged that economic subjects do not always fit the straitjacket. This provides the food for psychologists.

Indeed, tests of the axioms (such as transitivity, and in particular tests in a situation of choice under uncertainty) have repeatedly shown that the axioms are violated by mortals – even by Nobel laureates in economics. The papers in Hogarth and Reder (1986) provide ample evidence against 'ideal' rationality as defined above.

Not only the axioms are 'false', also the additional restrictions are defective. We know, for example, that occasionally prices do depend on the quantity bought by a particular consumer. Either because the consumer is a monopsonist, or because of quantity discounts.[2] This would imply a non-linear budget constraint. However, such non-linearities are thought to be unessential in the case of choosing a consumption bundle.

---

[2] This is relatively unimportant in the ordinary consumer choice problem, which consists of choosing between goods q_i and q_j, but features prominently in the study of demand for leisure (i.e. the theory of labour supply). In that case, increasing marginal tax rates have an important impact on the budget constraint of the maximization problem.

Hence, the axioms and constraints are 'false', but still they are very useful for deriving economic theorems. One such theorem is the 'Law of demand', specified below. But the axioms and further restrictions are not just instrumental in deriving 'ideal laws', they also serve to interpret the 'real world'. It has even been argued that a researcher who obtains empirical findings or correlations that imply violations of any of *A1-A6* and *R1*, is not entitled to call such correlations 'demand functions' (Phlips 1974, p. 34, see also below). Such violations can be found by analyzing the properties of demand functions that can be deduced from the axioms and restrictions. I will now turn to this issue.

Given *A1-A6*, preferences can be represented by a utility function,

$$U(q_1, q_2, ..., q_n)$$

Note that, implicitly, it is assumed that prices are not arguments in the utility function. Furthermore, the function presented is a static one, independent of time. Both assumptions are examples of *R3*. The individual agent maximizes utility subject to the budget constraint, which is linear (*R1* repeated, for convenience):

$$\sum_{i=1}^{k} p_i q_i = y$$

Solving the optimization problem, by maximizing utility subject to the budget constraint, results in the Marshallian demand equations that relate desired quantities to be consumed to income and prices:

$$MD \quad q_i = f_i(y, p_1, p_2, ..., p_k)$$

Alternatively, it is possible to formulate demand functions in terms of a given level of utility, the so-called Hicksian or compensated demand functions:

$$HD \quad q_i = h_i(U, p_1, p_2, ..., p_k)$$

It is now possible to be more explicit about the properties of demand functions. There are four properties of interest (see Deaton and Muellbauer 1980, pp. 43-44):

P1. Adding up: the total value of demands for different goods equals expenditure.

P2. Homogeneity: the Marshallian demand functions are homogeneous of degree zero in prices and expenditure, the Hicksian demands are homogeneous of degree zero in prices.

P3. Symmetry: the cross price derivatives of Hicksian demand functions are symmetric.

P4. Negativity: the matrix of cross price derivatives of Hicksian demand functions is negative semi-definite.

It is *P4* in isolation which is often called the 'Law of Demand' (Deaton and Muellbauer 1980, p. 44). It is a typical example of an 'ideal law'. It implies downward sloping (compensated) demand functions (with the own price of the good on the vertical axis). Occasionally, the four properties taken together are interpreted as defining demand functions (Phlips 1974). Note that Hicks (1939, pp. 26, 32) shows that the downward sloping compensated demand curve is (using Nowak's terminology) a concretization of Marshall's original demand function. Marshall derived the condition that the (uncompensated) demand function is downward sloping by imposing that the marginal utility of money is constant. When this idealizing assumption is dropped, 'the remaining results are still of interest and, one might add, closer to reality (truth).

The homogeneity condition (*P2*) states that if y and all p_i are multiplied by the same factor, the quantity demanded of good i (or any other good) is not changed. Hence,

$$q_i = f_i(y, p_1, p_2, ..., p_k) = f_i(\alpha y, \alpha p_1, \alpha p_2, ..., \alpha p_k)$$

or $\partial q_i/\partial\alpha = 0$ which seems to be Nowak's condition to qualify as an idealizing assumption (Nowak 1980, p. 28). The price and income terms enter the demand equation *via* the budget constraint. It is clear that replacing p_i by αp_i and y by αy has no consequences for the composition of the set of quantities demanded satisfying the budget constraint. Prices do not appear in the utility function (1). Hence, the homogeneity condition is hardly more than a simple implication of the budget constraint and only a very weak condition of rational choice. Deaton (1974, p. 362) argues that it is hard to imagine any demand theory without the homogeneity and even identifies non-homogeneity with irrationality (in which case either *P2* or *R1* should be added to *A1-A3* in defining rational behaviour). Deaton is not alone in viewing *P2* as an indispensable condition. For example, Phlips (1974, p. 34) writes that "Every demand equation must be homogeneous of degree zero in income and prices. (...) In applied work, only those mathematical functions which have this property can be candidates for qualification as demand functions."

I will now turn to the question whether empirical work on estimating demand functions served a particular role in 'concretizing' the theory of consumer behaviour. In particular, I will focus on testing *P2*, the homogeneity condition.

3. Testing

If the homogeneity condition were beyond doubt, one might argue, there would be no reason for testing it. This would be the case if homogeneity belonged to the Lakatosian *hard core* of the neoclassical research programme of consumer behaviour. The statements of Phlips and Deaton, cited above, suggest that, indeed, homogeneity was seen as belonging to such a hard core. However, estimating demand systems and testing for the properties of demand functions, in particular *P2* and *P3* (homogeneity and symmetry), belonged to the most important activities within the neoclassical research programme during the 1970s. Keuzenkamp and Barten (forthcoming) suggest that the Lakatosian method of rational reconstruction does not fit the history of the neoclassical theory of consumer behaviour very well.[3]

In the 1960s, it became feasible to formulate systems of demand functions (one equation per good or category of goods), impose the properties *P1-P4* and estimate the system of equations (see in particular Barten 1969). A relatively minor additional effort was needed to test those properties. The results of the tests on homogeneity and symmetry caused turmoil: homogeneity and symmetry were rejected. In a large number of studies, using different data (for different countries, different time spans, different goods), different specifications and different statistical methods, the negative result was generally replicated. It was also found that homogeneity was more problematic than symmetry (see Deaton and Muellbauer 1980b, and Keuzenkamp and Barten, forthcoming, for overviews). How did this affect the idealizations in the theory of consumer behaviour, and did this induce a pattern of concretization in order to reconcile theory and data?

An outsider might think that the obvious response would be to drop homogeneity. Indeed, there are potential reasons for doubt on behalf of homogeneity. Some undermine homogeneity directly, others indicate that, even if homogeneity is valid in an ideal construction, it is invalid in the particular context of a specific empirical economic model. Below, I give a list of potential responses to the negative test result, i.e. the rejection of *P2*.

1. *A1-A6* are invalid, implying that subjects do not maximize utility. Such behaviour would result in 'money illusion'. In that case,

---

[3] A partial resolution would be to drop Lakatos' distinction between a hard core and the 'protective belt'. See Cross (1982) for such an approach to macro-economics.

changes in absolute (rather than relative) prices may not be recognized as such, and, therefore, induce changes in real expenditure patterns. It may also be the case that, although agents are willing to maximize utility, markets are imperfect. In disequilibrium outcomes, homogeneity may be violated. This response has been rare, Marschak (1943), an early tester of homogeneity, being an exception. The problem with the response is that, apart from 'anything goes', an alternative theory does not exist, at least in the microeconomic domain. Deaton (1974) is typical. He rejects this response, as it would require a hypothesis of irrational behaviour. This is not an attractive alternative (Deaton 1974, p. 362).

2. *R1* is invalid, i.e. the budget constraint is not linear. Prices may be a decreasing function of the quantity bought. This invalidates the homogeneity condition directly. However, there exists general agreement on the fact that in case of consumer behaviour, nonlinearities of the budget constraints are unessential. None of the investigators of consumer behaviour took this escape route.

3. *R2* is invalid. Since the pioneering work of Schultz, Stone and others, much work has been done to create more general functional forms for utility functions or demand equations. In addition, the system approach which takes advantage of the cross-equation restrictions meant a leap forward. During the 1970s, much effort was spent to inventing more flexible functional forms, inspired by Diewert's (1971) use of duality. It is not clear however, how the choice of a functional form affects tests of the homogeneity condition (apart from the fact that, for some functional forms, tests of homogeneity cannot be carried out). The increased subtlety of the specifications generally did not result in 'better' test results. More recently, non-parametric approaches to inference have been used to test the theory of consumer behaviour (see below).

4. *R3* is invalid. This is a case of omitted variables. The validity of an empirical test of homogeneity, symmetry and so forth is conditional on the correct specification of the model. Examples of omissions are:

   a. snob goods (goods that are more desirable if their prices go up, also known as Veblen goods). Their theoretical existence cannot be denied, which may invalidate the homogeneity condition. In general, though, economists are convinced that such goods are rare (this is on empirical as well as on theoretical grounds) and may therefore be legitimately omitted. Snob goods have never been invoked to explain the rejection of homogeneity;

b. the planning horizon. If consumers maximize lifetime utility rather than contemporary utility, the optimization problem should be formulated in lifetime terms. Demand equations derived from contemporaneous utility maximization are mis-specified and empirical rejections of any of *P1-P4* do not imply that the theory is wrong. At least, the savings decision should be incorporated in the model (more on this can be found in Deaton and Muellbauer 1980b);

c. goods not included in the goods bundle considered. In theory, the maximization problem should be formulated in the most general form possible, with all conceivable arguments that any consumer might be willing to consider. All conceivable qualities of goods should be specified in the choice set. This is impossible for the empirical economist. In applied work, goods are aggregated, the level of aggregation differs but it is impossible to do without aggregation. Conditions for aggregation over goods are spelled out in Hicks (1939). Most economists are not troubled by aggregation over goods, empirical deviations from Hicks' composite commodity theorem (if the relative prices of a group of commodities remains unchanged, they can be treated as a single commodity) are thought to be unessential;

d. apart from aggregating over goods, economists often tested demand theory by aggregating over individuals. Again, this may be inappropriate. Conditions for aggregating over individuals are sketched in Deaton and Muellbauer (1980a and 1980b). An interesting step has been the formulation of an *Almost Ideal Demand System* (note that the ideal is a very example of what Nowak would label 'concretized'), that takes care of flexible functional form and aggregation issues. Conditions for aggregation are so strong, that many doubt that findings for aggregate data have any implication at all for the theory of consumer demand, that deals with individual behaviour. Blundell (1988) discusses the merits of testing the theory using non-aggregated data. Still, even if individual's data are used, it is not always the case that the properties are not rejected by the data.

These explanations for a violation of the homogeneity condition can be supplemented by statistical reasons for the rejection of one of the properties *P1-P4*. First, measurement error is a possible source for rejecting homogeneity (for example, the income term in demand equations is usually obtained from the budget equation, not from independent sources). It is not clear, however, how measurement error could affect homogeneity. Furthermore, the rejection of homogeneity resulted from using a wide variety of data (different goods, periods and countries), and it is unlikely that there is a systematic bias in measurement that also systematically biases the test.

Secondly, small samples available for estimation and testing may be a problem, as many statistical tests do not have well understood small sample properties. Thirdly, statistical tests always pose a risk towards a wrong conclusion. A fluke cannot be precluded. In the econometric evaluation of consumer behaviour, investigators rely on two more 'axioms':

A7. Axiom of correct specification

A8. The sample size is infinite

The last axiom might also be labelled as the asymptotic idealization, i.e. sample size *N* goes to infinity. *A7* relates to the validity of the 'maintained hypothesis'. For tests to be meaningful, the maintained hypothesis should be correct. This is rarely the case, taken literally, but econometricians do *as if* their model is correctly specified. Furthermore, many tests are based on the assumption of the availability of an infinite amount of data. Again, no one would claim that a particular sample obeys this requirement, but a matter of dispute is, when 'large' is close enough to 'infinite'. In econometrics, it is clear that sample sizes are not quite as large as *A8* would require. This has been acknowledged early on. Haavelmo (1944), following R.A. Fisher, therefore relied on a weakened version of *A8*:

A8'. The sample is a random drawing from a hypothetical infinite population

The validity of these axioms has also been challenged by different researchers. The number of responses to rejections of homogeneity is naturally extended by the following two:

5. *A7* is invalid. This response is related to challenging *R2* and *R3*, but the purely statistical argument has been exploited by those who favour a non-parametric approach in inference. Varian

(1983) is an example of one who argues that a major drawback of parametric testing is the fact that a rejection can always be attributed to wrong functional forms or mis-specification.

6. *A8* is invalid. This response has been very effective, in particular since the finding by Laitinen (1978) that the tests employed in the 1970s episode were biased towards rejection, due to the need to estimate the variance-covariance matrix in finite (and rather small) samples. Econometricians were aware that the small samples available for investigating consumer demand were not large enough to neglect the resulting bias. Laitinen showed that the importance of the problem still had been underestimated. Testing homogeneity in a system of demand equations is dependent on the unknown variance-covariance matrix. In practice, this had to be replaced by an estimate, usually a least squares residual moment matrix. Laitinen showed with a Monte Carlo experiment that the correction of the test statistic for small samples had to be much larger than was generally believed. However, even after small sample correction of the test statistic, homogeneity is now and then problematic.

In short, it should become clear that a test of homogeneity involves a large number of auxiliary hypotheses. A rejection of homogeneity does not have to imply that *R1*, the source of the homogeneity property of demand functions, should be dropped or 'concretized'. Neither does it mean that homogeneity itself is in trouble. Economists are left empty handed if they give up the idealizing assumption of homogeneity. Paul Samuelson (1947, p. 117) declared that, if the basic conditions of microeconomic theory were ever to be tested, economists would not give up microeconomic theory even if the conditions would appear to be empirically untrue. Samuelson's prediction has proved right. The resulting inferences (econometric correlations) would be economically meaningless, as Phlips and others have argued. Economists who are willing to 'concretize' on part of homogeneity have to give up the link between data and economic theory. Kevin Hoover (in this volume) argues that scientists idealize because they lack a principled way of concretizing the idealized model. I interpret this as saying that it is not clear which auxiliary hypotheses should be amended if it appears that an idealization is problematic. This explains why during the 1970s econometricians and economic theorists directed their attention to *R2-R3* and *A7-A8*.

4. Conclusion: idealization, concretization and testing

Testing homogeneity and symmetry belonged to the favorite activities of leading econometricians during the late 1960s and 1970s. Theorists and empirical economists alike accepted homogeneity and symmetry as idealizations, knowing that they where literally false, but they were not willing to concretize by accepting the numerous rejections of homogeneity and symmetry as a step towards greater verisimilitude. Rather, the tests were interpreted as indications that the other idealizations employed where problematic. In particular, the test spurred interest in aggregation theory, duality theory and small sample theory in econometrics.

In this essay, I have viewed an episode in the development of applied microeconomics through the spectacles of Nowak's model of idealization. With a bit of phantasy, it was not hard to make use of the notions of idealization and concretization. Whether this really illuminates this particular episode in economics is not clear — the same story could have been told without using these words. The really interesting problem remains, that is, how a test of an essential (idealizing) statement affects the process of theory development (concretization). This problem of the choice of scrutinizing particular auxiliary assumptions is crucial. Which assumption is essential, and which assumptions may be fruitfully amended? There is no clear guidance where to go for the next concretizing step. This may be different in other disciplines, or perhaps in case of Marxism where essentialism (dogmatism?) is a virtue rather than lamentable.

If homogeneity is thought to be crucial for the theory of consumer behaviour, testing would seem senseless. The episode described in this paper shows that economists were not happy to give up demand theory. One might as well call this dogmatism or essentialism, but given the lack of a promising alternative that could do without *P2*, it seems to be the right attitude.

Instead, economists investigated which of the auxiliary hypotheses could be amended in order to save the theory of consumer demand. The problem that economists have to face is that it is very unclear into what direction one has to search for 'concretizations'. Hence, I would say, it is not idealizations and concretizations as such which are of key interest for an economic methodologist, but to get insight in the choice of auxiliary hypotheses that come under scrutiny if an essential proposition is in trouble. A Bayesian model of scientific development (see e.g. Earman 1992) may be helpful in this choice, even though economists will find it difficult to articulate prior probabilities of the different hypotheses that are made in a particular context. This latter approach is a source for future research.[4]

Hugo A. Keuzenkamp
Department of Economics
Tilburg University

REFERENCES

Barten, A.P. (1969). Maximum Likelihood Estimation of a Complete System of Demand Equations. *European Economic Review* Vol. **1**, 7-73.

Blundell, R. (1988). Consumer Behaviour: Theory and Empirical Evidence – a Survey. *The Economic Journal*, Vol. **98**, 16-65.

Cross, R. (1982). The Duhem-Quine Thesis, Lakatos and the Appraisal of Theories in Macroeconomics. *The Economic Journal* Vol. **92**, 320-340.

Deaton, A. (1974). The Analysis of Consumer Demand in the United Kingdom, 1900-1970. *Econometrica* Vol. **42**, 341-67.

Deaton, A. and J. Muellbauer (1980a). An Almost Ideal Demand System. *American Economic Review* **70**, 312-36.

Deaton, A. and J. Muellbauer (1980b). *Economics and Consumer behavior*. Cambridge: Cambridge University Press.

Diewert, W.E. (1971). An Application of the Shephard Duality Theorem: a Generalized Leontief Production Function. *Journal of Political Economy*, Vol. **79**, 481-507.

Earman, J. (1991). *Bayes or Bust? A Critical Examination of Bayesian Confirmation Theory*. Cambridge: MIT Press.

Haavelmo, T. (1944). The Probability Approach in Econometrics. Supplement to *Econometrica* **12**, July.

Hicks, J.R. (1939). *Value and Capital*. 2nd edition 1946. Oxford: Oxford University Press.

Hogarth, R.M. and Melvin W. Reder (1986). *Rational Choice, the Contrast Between Economics and Psychology*. Chicago: University of Chicago Press.

Keuzenkamp, H.A. and A.P. Barten (forthcoming). Rejection Without Falsification, *Journal of Econometrics*, Annals.

Laitinen, K. (1978). Why is Demand Homogeneity so often Rejected. *Economics Letters*, Vol **1**, 187-191.

Leamer, E.E. (1978). *Specification searches*. New York: John Wiley.

Marschak, J. (1943). Money Illusion and Demand Analysis. *The Review of Economic Statistics*, 40-48.

Nowak, L. (1980). The Structure of Idealization. Dordrecht: Reidel.

Phlips, L. (1974). *Applied Consumption Analysis*. Amsterdam: North Holland.

Samuelson, P.A. (1947). *Foundations of Economic Analysis*. Enlarged Edition 1983. Cambridge: Harvard University Press.

Varian, H. (1983). Nonparametric Tests of Consumer Behaviour, *Review of Economic Studies* **50**, 99-110.

---

[4] Some very cautious steps along those lines are made in Keuzenkamp and Barten (forthcoming), where some insights of Leamer (1978) are applied. We have not, however, attempted to make an explicit Bayesian account, including updating of priors (or Jeffrey conditionalization), of learning about consumer behaviour.

Poznań Studies in the Philosophy of the Sciences and the Humanities
1994, Vol. 38, pp. 255-264

Werner Diederich

NOWAK ON EXPLANATION AND IDEALIZATION IN MARX'S 'CAPITAL'*

ABSTRACT. Compares the Nowak model of concretization with another view, considered to be more appropriate, in which the categories for the concretized law arise during the development of the law, and thus are not, as in Nowak's reconstruction, present from the start in the idealized form of the law.

Twenty years ago L. Nowak investigated explanatory and idealizational patterns in Marx's *Capital*.[1] He claimed that these patterns fit into a model of explanation which

(i) differs considerably from Hempel's account,[2]
(ii) applies to all of empirical science.

Nowak mainly criticized Hempel's model of deductive nomological explanations as only insufficiently taking account of the role of idealization. He then analyzed the function of idealizing laws in Marx's *Capital*, exemplified by the explanation of the prices of agricultural products in a capitalistic economy.[3] From this example he developed a scheme for the explanation of facts by idealizing laws as follows:

$$T^k \dashv T^{k-1} \dashv \ldots \dashv T^0 \wedge I \Rightarrow K.$$

---

* The present paper is based on a lecture given in 1979 at the University of Bielefeld, Western Germany.

1 (Nowak 1971). Strictly speaking, I discuss only ideas of Nowak's which are expressed in this article. It seems, however, that with respect to the points I want to make, his views did not essentially alter in his later work on Marxist methodology, esp. his book (Nowak 1980) and (Nowak 1989).

2 The *locus classicus* for this 'deductive nomological (DN)' or – slightly more general – 'covering law' model is (Hempel/Oppenheim 1948). For Hempel's elaborations on this model cf. (Hempel 1965). Nowak mainly refers to the presentation (Hempel 1966).

3 A similar example is given in (Nowak 1980) and considerably elaborated on in (Hamminga 1989 and 1989a). These two papers discuss and elucidate some of the economical and methodological details of Marx's account and of Nowak's analysis thereof (what I am not focussing on in this paper) and "adds to Nowak's reconstruction, which is a qualitative analysis ...: it adds insight into the way in which, according to Marx, the economy *as a whole* completely determines prices ..." (Hamminga 1989a, p. 89). – My own attempt to reconstruct Marx's theory on prices may be found in (Diederich 1989).

This scheme – to be explained in a moment – would apply not only to Marx's *Capital*, but also to physics; indeed, we could regard it as "a general model of explanation, which correctly reconstructs that cognitive procedure commonly used in the empirical sciences".[4]

Although this seems to me a rather far-reaching extrapolation from an economic and some physical examples, in the following pages I am not going to dispute this general claim. Instead I shall mainly confine myself to a critique of Nowak's analysis of Marx's procedure in *Capital*. Marx's so-called method of ascent from the abstract to the concrete cannot, in my eyes, be adequately analyzed in Nowak's manner, but should be conceived of in a different way. I shall further argue that this analysis allows to draw some parallels to physics. But I am *not* thereby claiming to have found *the* explanatory pattern of all empirical science; on the contrary, I doubt that such a pattern exists.

1. Nowak on Marx explaining prices

In Nowak's scheme 'K' stands for the explanandum, a singular statement about a fact, 'T^0' for a not idealizing law (a 'factual law'), and 'I' for certain initial conditions, which, together with T^0, logically imply K.[5] T^1 through T^k are idealizing laws, where the indices give the numbers of idealizing conditions. T^1, with only one idealizing condition, comes closest to the factual law T^0; the removal of this condition already leads to T^0. Nowak calls such a removal a 'concretization' and symbolizes it by the inverse derivation symbol '$\dashv$'. Later on I shall discuss how idealizing conditions are removed by way of concretization.

According to Nowak, Marx deals with seven idealizing conditions in order to explain the prices of agricultural products in a capitalistic economy. I mention only four of them:

(1) perfect competition;
(2) the so-called organic composition of capital (i.e. the proportion of constant and variable capital) in the agricultural sector is not different from that in other sectors;
(3) there is no merchant profit;
(4) supply and demand are balanced.

---

[4] (Nowak 1971), p. 337.

[5] In his scheme of explanation Nowak uses '$\rightarrow$' instead of '$\Rightarrow$' for logical consequence. But since he elsewhere (in his examples of laws, e.g. in the formulation of the 'law of value', cf. T^7 below, and of Ohm's law, cf. O^0 below) evidently uses '$\rightarrow$' for something less than logical (material?) implication I have replaced '$\rightarrow$' by '$\Rightarrow$' in his scheme.

The conjunction of these four plus three more conditions forms the if-clause of a conditional statement, which expresses the most idealizing law, T^7; following Nowak, this runs as follows:

$$C^7(a,t) \rightarrow P(a,t) = V(a,t).$$

Here '*t*' is a time variable, '*a*' a variable for sorts of commodities, 'C^7' stands for the conjunction of idealizing assumptions mentioned above, '*P*' for price, and '*V*' for value; the arrow is to be read 'if-then' and symbolizes (material) implication. The idealizing law T^7 — the supposed final ground for explaining the prices of agricultural products and allegedly just the so-called *Wertgesetz* ('law of value')[6] — thus reads as follows:

> If the seven idealizing conditions are fulfilled, then prices equal values.

My present intent is not to dispute the above rendering of Marx's analysis on exegetical grounds. Instead I immediately focus on the process of concretization described by Nowak. Only by this process, it is said, does the law of value get some explanatory function. As an example I choose the removal of the assumption that supply and demand are balanced. For the sake of argument I follow Nowak in that supply and demand may be expressed by functions $S(a,t)$ and $D(a,t)$, respectively, such that the idealizing assumption may be rendered

$$D(a,t) - S(a,t) = 0.$$

In order to get rid of this assumption there has to be introduced, according to Nowak, a term

$$\beta[D(a,t) - S(a,t)]$$

into the price function, where β is a function which adds to or subtracts from the price a certain amount if demand should exceed supply or *vice versa*, respectively.

Skipping technical details I stress the point that, for Nowak, concretization means an explicit account of factors whose neglection amounts to the fulfillment of the respective idealizing conditions. All in all — by somewhat "idealizing" Nowak's analysis — every step of concretization

[6] Nowak thus conceives of the 'law of value' as a qualified correspondence between prices and values, while I would also explicitly include the determination of value by the respective durations of labour, cf. (Diederich 1982), p. 149; but this is only a - highly debatable - exegetical point.

consists in a weakening of the antecedent of the law of value while incidentally adding a term to the value function. Thus, a first concretization replaces — arguments omitted —

$$C^7 \rightarrow P = V$$

by

$$C^6 \rightarrow P = V + ...,$$

and so on, until finally the antecedent vanishes altogether and there remains, as the 'factual law' T^0:

$$P = V + ... + ... + ...,$$

one of the terms added on the right being '$\beta[D(a,t)-S(a,t)]$', as considered above.

2. Comparison with physics

Before critically discussing Nowak's scheme of explanation as applied to Marx's analysis (and, in outline, to natural science) I want to add one of Nowak's examples from physics, namely *Ohm's law*

$$IR = U,$$

in words: the intensity of an electric current times the resistance (of the conductor) equals the voltage. Nowak rightly remarks that in this form Ohm's law correctly applies only to homogeneous conductors in which the 'electromotive force' E vanishes. The above formulation therefore would stand for an idealizing law which more adequately should be rendered like this:

$$(O^1) \quad E = 0 \rightarrow IR = U.$$

In this case the respective concretization would simply consist in adding E to U:

$$(O^0) \quad IR = U + E.$$

Using Ohm's law for an explanation of a potential $U(a)$, measured at the ends of the conductor a, Nowak would proceed as follows: given the values of I and R for a, $I(a)$ and $R(a)$, a Hempelian explanation of $U(a)$, using the original formulation '$IR = U$', would essentially consist in calculating the product $I(a)R(a)$ and showing that this equals $U(a)$. But, supposed that (O^0) is correct, this cannot work, because, for a real conductor a, $E(a)$ does not vanish. Only by the concretized law (O^0), and measurement of $E(a)$, $U(a)$ may be explained.

No doubt, such an explanation would totally be in accord with the Hempelian pattern, as would be the explanation of prices by a 'factual law' (T^0) (and certain boundary conditions). More general: the last part of Nowak's scheme,

$$T^0 \wedge I \Rightarrow K,$$

simply satisfies Hempelian criteria for explanations. On the other hand, none of the idealizing laws $T^1, ..., T^k$ instead of T^0 would do the job. Nor would there be any help at all for a Hempelian explanation, once T^0 is at hand. In this case, they are simply redundant: they are consequences of T^0, and each of them is consequence of all less idealizing laws:

$$T^0 \Rightarrow T^1 \Rightarrow ... T^k.$$

(This, by the way, justifies Nowak's use of the inverse derivation symbol '$\dashv$'.) In the case of Ohm's law, for instance, if, in (O^0), you put $E = 0$, you at once gain $I \cdot R = U$, i.e. (O^1) is a consequence of (O^0). In the same manner, if in the totally concretized law on prices all disturbing terms vanish, you get back the consequence of the most idealized law (and by implication this law itself).

3. Back to explanation in Marx

Are the T^j, $j > 0$, then simply redundant for explanatory purposes? In order that they are not, Nowak should claim that the laws used in Hempelian explanations typically are gained by successive concretizations out of idealizing laws and that these chains of concretizations add to the explanations. Let us have a second look at the Marxian example for that reason. It seems to me that Nowak is right in seeing something like his explanatory pattern in Marx's account of prices in *Capital*. It is not by chance that only in the third volume of this work we find an explanation of prices which at least comes close to Hempel's pattern. Only there Marx has developed the categories necessary for his theory to become empirical, and quite consciously so. For this I may quote a passage from a letter of Marx to Kugelmann as of July 11, 1868, a passage to which Nowak himself refers,[7] although this passage, in my opinion, does not support his case:

---

[7] Nowak (1971), p. 335, with reference to K. Marx and F. Engels: *Briefe über "Das Kapital"*, Berlin 1954, p. 185; or cf. MEW 32, p. 553.

> The task of science consists exactly in explaining how the law of value manifests itself. Hence, should anyone wish to 'explain' in advance all those phenomena which are apparently at variance with that law, he would have to formulate science before science. Ricardo's error consists exactly in the fact that in the first chapter on value he adopts as given all the possible categories, which must only be deduced in order to prove that they are in agreement with the law of value.

Certainly Nowak is right in that Marx would not be content with a Hempelian explanation of prices by the concretized law as such and would stress that this law is developed from the (idealized form of the) 'law of value'. But at the same time Nowak does just what Marx blames Ricardo for: to presuppose the categories necessary for the concretized law already at the beginning of the development, namely in formulating the law of value in its original (idealized) version. As we have seen, in Nowak's account the respective categories already appear in the idealizing if-clause of this law. This is a crucial divergence from Marx's procedure. Nowak reconstructs only the *nomological* concretization, and presupposes the *conceptual* concretization, i.e. the explication of the eventually necessary categories, already at the beginning — contrary to Marx.

Marx's own theory development may more adequately be patterned by the following scheme (formulated as close as possible to Nowak's):

$$\overline{T}^k \ e \ \overline{T}^{k-1} \ e \ \dots \ e \ \overline{T}^0 \wedge I \Rightarrow K.$$

Here '$\overline{T}^i$', $i = 1,\dots,k$, stands for the then-clause of T^i, e.g. '$\overline{T}^k$' simply for '$P = V$', the unqualified identification of prices and values. (I would not, however, *identify* $\overline{T}^k$ with the law of value, but this is a minor point in the present context.[8]) Each of the k steps denoted by 'e' is what I would call an *expansion* (rather than 'concretization'): a refinement of both, a conceptual and a nomological nature.[9] Characteristically Marx introduces new categories only at a point of his theoretical development where the factors to be expressed by them really matter. Only the fully expanded theory $\overline{T}^0$, which is supposed to match the empirical findings, contains all the relevant concepts.

4. A paralleling example from thermodynamics

I do not want to elaborate on the reconstruction of the Marxian procedure in this paper,[10] but to go back to Nowak's claim to have found

---

[8] Cf. note 6 above.

[9] Cf. Diederich (1982), sec. 3.

[10] Cf. (Diederich 1989).

an explanatory pattern which is applicable not only to Marx's economic theory but more general to all empirical science.

A well-known law of thermodynamics (special cases of which Nowak deals with) states that the product of pressure p and volume v of a portion of gas is proportional to its (absolute) temperature T:

$$pv = RT,$$

the proportionality factor R being the so-called gas constant (if v is the volume of a mole of that gas). This law holds only approximately, or — as physicists use to say — only for *'ideal'* gases. (Ideal gases are just *defined* as gases for which this law holds.) *Real* gases behave in a different way. Within certain boundaries they more accurately obey the so-called van der Waals law

$$(p + a/v^2)(v - b) = RT,$$

where the empirically found constants a and b are susceptable of a molecular interpretation: the term a/v^2 accounts for the fact that the molecules of the gas are exerting forces upon each other and thus contribute to the inner pressure of the gas, while the term $-b$ expresses the finite volume of the molecules which detracts from the space available for the molecules to move around.

This interpretation was possible, of course, only *after* the molecular 'kinetic theory of gases' was developed. Only *then* it was possible to say that the law of ideal gases, $pv = RT$, holds for those cases where (or to the extent that) the intermolecular forces and the volume of the molecules are negligibly small: if in van der Waals's equation you can put $a = 0$ and $b = 0$ you get back the 'ideal gas law'.

However, it would be inadequate and anachronistic to formulate this law as a conditional with the conjunction of the two idealizing conditions as the if-clause. (Nowak does this for a special case of that law, the so-called law of Gay-Lussac.) The ideal gas law was essentially proposed prior to any knowledge of the possibility of its molecular interpretation. As far as I know, even the van der Waals law was originally put forward as an empirical law, i.e. the values of the constants a and b were determined in such a way that together with the triples (p, v, T) of actual gases they fit the van der Waals equation.

This episode in the history of thermodynamics could then be rendered as follows. First there was proposed a law, $pv = RT$, which only roughly fits the empirical data. Then there was a search for an analytical expression (comprising p, v, and T) which would better account for the data. Such an expression was found in van der Waals's equation. Finally, the additional ingredients in the latter formulation, the constants *a* and *b*, were interpreted within the framework of the kinetic theory of gases. Incidentally this interpretation explained why the behaviour of real gases deviated from that proposed by the ideal gas law.

The whole story shows that an explanation of the interplay of pressure, volume, and temperature of real gases by way of van der Waals's law as such, although perfectly in accordance with Hempel's scheme, is unsatisfying. Only in combination with the "idealized gas law" $pv = RT$ and the molecular reasons of the deviations from this law does van der Waals's law give a satisfying account of the behaviour of real gases. *Insofar* Nowak is right when arguing that Hempel's account of explanation needs some augmentation. However, Nowak's concepts of idealized law and the concretization procedure should be modified in the indicated way, i.e. by omitting the if-clauses in the idealizing laws and by conceiving of concretization as directly introducing new terms into these laws.[11]

5. The 'ideal' of factuality and the factuality of the 'ideal'

The proposed modifications have an additional advantage. In Nowak there is a sharp demarcation between 'factual' and 'idealizing' laws, the latter ones being conditional, the former ones not. However, one wonders whether, in scientific practice, there are any (interesting) cases of valid 'factual' laws at all!? Practically all laws in empirical science are (at most) only approximately true. Nowak does not deny this fact — nor does he claim that Marx has proposed an exactly true (quantitative) empirical law. Nowak's sticking to the idea (!) of factual laws ironically has the consequence that his *'factual' laws are fictitious* while his *idealizing laws* (because of their conditional formulation) *are* — if the counterfactual assumptions are completely stated — *factually true*!

With the modifications proposed above, however, all laws are on a par (in their unconditional formulations): all are ideal in that they are (at most) approximately true. And this is also what scientific practice tells us.[12]

---

[11] The idealizing assumptions may, however, play a role for the specification of the 'domains of intended applications', cf. (Diederich 1982), sec. 4.

[12] I just used the term "ideal" instead of "idealized" only in order to avoid the misleading impression that in the development of a theory of empirical science there typically is something like a process of idealization, the inverse of concretization. While the latter is a helpful concept for historians of science, the former is only useful in a systematic context, or in retrospect.

I suppose that Nowak and I focus on the same type of theoretical development. We differ in that he describes these developments as nomological *concretizations*, while I conceive of them as *expansions*, i.e. as nomological *and* conceptual refinements. I further suppose that Nowak – in spite of the paradoxical consequences of his formulations with respect to the actual applicability of 'idealizing' and 'factual' laws – would agree that there is the historical phenomenon that the *domain of application* of a developing theory typically *grows* (if one is willing to conceive of approximate applicability). Also for *this* reason, I would argue, one better avoids a sharp demarcation of 'factual' and 'idealizing' laws. On my account, the less expanded laws (less 'concretized' laws in Nowak's terms) may well have some real applications, i.e. a small domain, in which they hold fairly well. By way of refinement this domain may be more and more expanded, until finally (if such a final stage exists at all) all relevant phenomena are covered to an acceptable degree. This seems to me also the view of theory development underlying Marx's *Capital*.

Werner Diederich
Philosophisches Seminar
Universität Hamburg
Von-Melle-Park 6
D-20146 Hamburg
Germany

REFERENCES

Diederich, W. (1982). A Structuralist Reconstruction of Marx's Economics. In: W. Stegmüller, W. Balzer, W. Spohn (Eds.), *Philosophy of Economics*. Berlin/Heidelberg/New York: Springer, pp. 145-160.

Diederich, W. (1989). The Development of Marx's Economic Theory. *Erkenntnis*, **30**, 147-164.

Hamminga, B. (1989). Sneed Versus Nowak: An Illustration in Economics. *Erkenntnis*, **30**, 247-265.

Hamminga, B. (1989a). The Structure of Six Transformations in Marx's *Capital*, vol. III. In: J. Brzeziński, Fr. Coniglione, T.A.F. Kuipers and L. Nowak (Eds.). *Idealization I: General Problems* (*Poznań Studies in the Philosophy of the Sciences and the Humanities*, **16**), pp. 89-111.

Hempel, C.G. (1965). *Aspects of Scientific Explanation and other Essays in the Philosophy of Science*. New York: The Free Press.

Hempel, C.G. (1966). *Philosophy of Natural Science*. Englewood Cliffs, N.J.: Prentice-Hall.

Hempel, C.G. and Oppenheim, P. (1948). Studies in the Logic of Explanation. *Philosophy of Science*, **15**, 135-175. Reprinted in (Hempel 1965).

Nowak, L. (1971). The Problem of Explanation in Karl Marx's "Capital". *Quality and Quantity*, **V**, 2, 311-330.

Nowak, L. (1980). *The Structure of Idealization. Towards a Systematic Interpretation of the Marxian Idea of Science*. Dordrecht: Reidel.

Nowak, L. (1989). On the (Idealizational) Structure of Economic Theories. *Erkenntnis*, **30**, 225-246.

Poznań Studies in the Philosophy of the Sciences and the Humanities
1994, Vol. 38, pp. 265-275

Gérard Jorland

IDEALIZATION AND TRANSFORMATION

ABSTRACT. A critical evaluation of Nowak's application of the model of concretization to Marx's model of theory development in 'Capital'. It focuses on Nowak's account of transformation and of Marx's methods, and discusses the status of Nowak's method.

In his *Jokes and their relation to the unconscious* (1905), Freud tells the story of a man who borrowed a copper kettle from a neighbor, returned it with a big hole making it unusable, was sued for that and defended himself by claiming: "First, I never borrowed a kettle from B at all; secondly, the kettle had a hole in it already when I got it from him; and thirdly, I gave him back the kettle undamaged". I would like to argue — a bit differently in that I believe my claims not only valid in themselves but also taken together — that: First, Nowak's transformation of values into prices of production is not Marx's; secondly, Nowak's Marx's method is not Marx's; and thirdly Nowak's method is no method at all.

Nowak accounts for the transformation of values into prices of production as a case for "concretisation", namely of the law of value which is an "idealization". Put in words, his statement T^8 means that the law of value, according to which commodity price is proportional to its value, is valid only under eight conditions, i.e. provided : (x) is a commodity and (1) perfect competition prevails, (2) the economy producing (x) is closed, (3) the rate of surplus value is uniform, (4) the average organic composition of capital is the same in the agricultural and industrial sectors, (5) there is no merchant profit, (6) the average organic composition of capital is the same in the branch producing commodity (x) and in the overall economy, (7) demand for commodity (x) equals its supply, (8) the organic composition of capital of the firm producing commodity (x) is the same as the average of its branch.

Now, even if one could consider the way Marx establishes his law of value as a process of idealization, it would nevertheless not be the one Nowak describes. In the first chapter of book I, Marx does not abstract from economic, but from non-economic conditions, under the heading of use-value, in order to be entitled to claim that commodities exchange according to the quantity of labor embodied in them.

This is well known. It seems to me, therefore, that Nowak gave another account of Marx's process of idealization to describe the transformation of values into prices of production as a reverse process of concretization through relaxation of each condition in turn, starting with the last one, condition 8. Hence his statement T^7, which he called "the law of market value" and which is actually the first step of his transformation process, obtains through relaxation of the organic composition of capital uniformity condition within the given branch, while keeping the seven former conditions. It states that prices are equal to market values, i.e. values modified by an additive factor which is null, positive or negative if the organic composition of capital of the firm under consideration is equal to, lower or higher than the branch average. For higher organic composition means higher capital-labor ratio, thus higher productivity, thus less labor time embodied in unit commodity, thus less labor value, which is nevertheless worth more on the market if supply cannot match demand but at higher costs.

The second step of Nowak's transformation consists in relaxing condition 7 on demand and supply. Accordingly, his statement T^6, which he called "the law of market value under the consideration of demand and supply", states that, under all previous conditions but the equality of demand and supply and the uniformity of organic composition of capital within the branch, prices of commodities are equal to their market values modified by an additive factor which is null, positive or negative according to whether demand is equal to, greater or lower than supply.

The third step is the removal of condition 6 to take into consideration the difference of organic composition of capital between branches of the economy. But before, Nowak had to restate T^6 in terms of marxian cost prices: prices of commodities are equal to their cost price modified by two additive factors, one which is null, positive or negative according to whether demand is equal to, greater or lower than supply, the other one which is null, positive or negative if the organic composition of capital of the firm under consideration is equal to, lower or higher than the branch average. Now his statement T^5, which he called "a reconstruction of the law of production prices", runs as follows: under conditions 1-5 and if the branch average organic composition of capital is different from the social one, demand is unequal to supply, the firm organic composition is different from the branch average, then prices of commodities are equal to their cost price plus the general rate of profit on their cost price.[1]

---

[1] This formulation is not exact. The general rate of profit is always on the total capital invested, which is the same as the cost-price provided the constant capital is consumed in one production period.

Likewise, removing condition 5, i.e. taking account of merchant profit gives statement T^4, which Nowak called "the law of price production under the consideration of merchant profit", and which states that commodity price is equal to production price modified by a positive additive factor representing the share of the merchant in the social profit. Removing condition 4, i.e. allowing for a different average organic composition of capital in the agricultural sector from the average industrial one, Nowak comes to his statement T^3 which he called "the law of prices of production under the consideration of merchant profit and rent", and which states that the previous statement must be modified by a positive additive factor to take account of rent. Last, relaxing condition 3, i.e. introducing differences in rates of surplus value, leads to statement T^2, which Nowak called "the law of prices of production under the consideration of merchant profit, rent and fluctuations of rate of surplus value". It states that, if perfect competition still prevails and the economy remains closed, the previous statement must be completed by another additive factor, which is null, positive or negative according to a set of conditions that Nowak does not explain and that I fail to understand. Anyway, this condition 3 is already relaxed as soon as one assumes different organic compositions of capital but a uniform rate of profit. In that case, the rate of surplus value is greater the higher the organic composition of capital.

In order to show that Nowak's transformation of values into prices of production is not Marx's, it suffices to recall the latter. It consists in the transformation of value into wage, profit and rent and comprises four steps. The first one, taken in book I chapters 19-21, transforms the value of labor force in wages which appear as the value of labor. This transformation is made of two steps. The first one consists in an inversion subject-predicate carried out by time wages: "value of a day of labor force" becomes "value of the labor force for a day". The second one is a substitution, namely of the labor done to the labor force, carried out by piece wages: "value of the labor force for a day" becomes "value of the labor of a day".

Starting from the equation of value

$$(1) \quad w = c + v + m,$$

rewritten as

$$(2) \quad w = c + (v + m),$$

to stress the difference between dead and live labor, Marx denoted this first transformation by shifting the parenthesis to the left:

$$(3) \quad w = (c + v) + m.$$

Instead of the difference between dead and live labor, one has now another difference between what has cost something to the capitalist and what has not.

Marx comes now to his second step, the transformation of value into production cost, of surplus value into profit and of surplus value rate into profit rate. The difference between constant and variable capital changes into one between fix and circulating capital. Accordingly, only a portion of the invested capital is consumed during a single production period and constitutes the cost price k defined as $k = \alpha c + v$ (with $0 < \alpha < 1$). Thus (3) is transformed in

$$(4) \quad w = k + m.$$

Since the surplus value m cannot be related to the consumed capital k, which must appear again in the commodity price, it can only be related to the whole invested capital. It is changed in r and (4) is transformed in

$$(5) \quad w = k + r.$$

The transformation as a process of inversion is thus completed: it is no longer labor which creates surplus value, it is capital itself which gives a profit. Under this form, the capital relates to itself, it is, in hegelian terms, "for itself" (*für sich*).

Up to now, the transformation has preserved all quantities. It stops to be the case with the change of surplus value rate into profit rate, the latter being *ex definitione* always lower than the former. The most synthetic way of expressing this change is

$$(6) \quad \pi = \frac{\mu}{1 + \omega}$$

(where μ stands for the rate of surplus value and ω for the organic composition of capital).[2]

The next step is the formation of a general profit rate, supposedly brought about by competition since (6) shows clearly that, with a uniform surplus value rate, the profit rate is greater the lower the organic composition of capital. Therefore (6) becomes

$$(7) \quad \bar{\pi} = \frac{\bar{\mu}}{1 + \bar{\omega}}$$

(where $\bar{\pi}$, $\bar{\mu}$ and $\bar{\omega}$ means the respective average).

---

[2] The deduction of this form from the standard one – $\pi = m/(c+v)$ – is straightforward: it suffices to divide it through by v.

The last step is the transformation of value, as expressed in (5) into production prices

(8) $p = k + \bar{\pi}(c + v)$,

which reduces to

(9) $p = k(1 + \bar{\pi})$

if the whole capital invested does not last more than a single production period.

It is therefore crystal clear that Marx's transformation has nothing to do with Nowak's. Even if it were a process of concretization, it would not be the same assumptions which are removed. The notion of market value is introduced after the transformation far from being its starting point, it is nothing more than a transformation reduced to a branch which adds nothing new. Demand and supply are all along supposed to be equal, otherwise the formation of an average profit rate would be impeded. Consideration of merchant profit adds nothing but a new branch in the economy, contributing to the formation of the average rate of profit by its capital invested if not by its surplus value produced, and taking nevertheless its share of the total surplus value on the same grounds. On the other hand, it is true that identity of organic composition of capital is relaxed in order to introduce rent and that the uniformity of surplus value rates is removed but at the very beginning and not at the end. Taking Nowak's transformation as our basis, we see that no assumption concerning wages, fix and circulating capital and cost price are made.

It does not mean that Nowak's transformation is illegitimate; on the oppposite, it is perfectly legitimate, provided only that one does not take it for Marx's. But being legitimate does not entail being valid and Nowak's transformation does not seem to be valid because of three shortcomings: firstly, it gives no account of cost-price; secondly, it relaxes the condition of supply matching demand; thirdly, it removes the condition on surplus value rate too late in the process.

It can be shown moreover that Nowak's Marx's method is not Marx's method. Methodological issues were all-important to Marx who explained the mistakes of his fellow economists or philosophers by methodological blunders and his own reasoning by methodological analogy. And despite that, he left only three methodological texts of some extent: the 1857 *Introduction*, the 1859 *Preface* and the 1873 *Postface*. The first question they raise is the question of the substitution of the second text to the first in the *Critique* (my translation): "I drop a general introduction that I have sketched since, after all, anticipating results which must be demonstrated beforehand seems unfortunate to me, so the reader, who wishes to follow me, must accept to go from singular up to general." And so, to the 1857 *Introduction*, he substituted a preface in which he told how he came to imagine the links between productive forces and social relationships of production, and between infra- and superstructure. It can be shown that he denoted thus each part of his general introduction.

The first two parts of the 1857 *Introduction* — on production and on the relations between production, distribution, exchange and consommation — are those which seemed to him to anticipate results which remained to be established; to the method he advocated in the third part — "to go from abstract up to concrete", or Nowak's Marx's idealization method — he substituted another one, which consisted in "going from singular up to general"; last, the topics of the 1859 *Preface* — productive forces and social relationships or production, infra- and superstructure — were merely mentioned in the fourth part of the *Introduction*. All these changes are attested by the fact that in his index of his 1857-58 manuscripts, composed after the publication of his *Critique*, Marx mentioned only the first two parts, the third — on the method of idealization so to speak — having been abandoned and the fourth published.

The cause of this methodological change is not hard to find. The method that Marx advocated in 1857, the idealization method, had given him the wrong starting point of his *Grundriße*: the abstract category of exchange value. It was a wrong starting point since it led him to skip over the (concrete) category of use value. Now, Marx realized that he could not do without it in his theory of surplus value, since it is precisely the use value of labor power to produce net value, to produce more value than it consumes, if ever value is measured according to the quantum of embodied labor. So much so that Marx had to introduce use value at the very beginning of his *Critique* and to take a new starting point: commodity, as double-sided entity, altogether use value and exchange value. Therefore, the method that Nowak bestows on Marx had been explicitly rejected by the latter after it led him to a dead end.

But one cannot say either that the method consisting in "going from singular up to general" is Marx's method. At any rate, it strictly applies only to the *Critique* whose reader goes indeed from commodity to money, the latter being brought forward as the general form of the former. Therefore none of these texts teaches us what was Marx's method.

The only thing we know for sure is that it was a dialectical method. In other words, its essential feature is to account for contradictions instead of eliminating them. Now, Nowak's idealization method cannot be Marx's on the more substantial, and no longer factual, ground that it misses this most essential feature and contrives, on the opposite, to erase contradictions whenever they show up.

And the transformation of values into production prices is an instance where a contradiction did show up. According to Nowak, Marx acknowledged the contradiction between value and price, but as only apparent, and conceived of the intermediate terms that leads from the one to the other as concretizations. He writes: "the disagreement with facts is merely apparent: when law T^8 is concretized, additional factors are taken into account. They reduce the actual deviations between the price P and its successive sequences of determinants" (p. 122). If I do not err out of misunderstanding, the last sentence means that the additional factors reduce the deviations between the price supposedly equal to the value and the actual price, along a sequence of ever more realistic prices. So, concretization reduces the difference between the idealizational statement (commodity price is proportional to its value) and the empirical one (commodity price is proportional to production price) by showing how value changes into production price, namely by taking into account more and more additional properties that were discarded while idealizing.

Thus there can be no "Great Contradiction" within the Marxian system, between the law of value of book I and the law of equal rates of profit of book III, debated ever since Böhm-Bawerk's essay on the close of Marx's system. Indeed for Nowak, both laws are conditional statements which, stemming from terms to terms opposite conditions, cannot contradict one another and just exclude each other. He writes:

> Now one may easily observe that the statements do not contradict each other since they speak of different objects. The first one deals with an economy which, among others, contains an ideally balanced market (i.e. demand for each commodity equates supply of it), while the second one is concerned with an economy which, among others, contains a *realistic market* (i.e. it is allowed that supply is not equal to demand). (p. 247)

This instance of differing conditions is most unwelcome since, once again, the whole transformation of values into production prices is obviously based upon the implementation of the law of supply and demand.

However, it is not difficult to show 1) that the contradiction between value and price is not apparent and 2) that it cannot be explained away without losing a thorough insight into the historical trend of capitalism. As for the first point, it suffices to quote in full Marx's text that Nowak interpreted as acknowledging but an apparent contradiction. It is to be found in *Capital*, book I chapter 11 of the 1887 English edition, on the mass of suplus value:

> This law [that surplus value is proportional to variable capital, given the value of labour under uniform rate of exploitation] clearly contradicts all experience based on appearance. Every one knows that a cotton spinner, who, reckoning the percentage on the whole of his applied capital, employs much constant and little variable capital does not, on account of this, pocket less profit or surplus-value than a baker, who relatively sets in motion much variable and little constant capital. For the solution of this apparent contradiction, many intermediate terms are as yet wanted, as from the standpoint of elementary algebra many intermediate terms are wanted to understand that $^0/_0$ may represent an actual magnitude. Classical economy, although not formulating the law, holds instinctively to it, because it is a necessary consequence of the general law of value. It tries to rescue the law from collision with contradictory phenomena by a violent abstraction. It will be seen later how the school of Ricardo has come to grief over this stumbling-block. Vulgar economy which, indeed, "has really learnt nothing," here as everywhere stick to appearances in opposition to the law which regulates and explains them.

So, Marx speaks indeed of an "apparent contradiction", by which is meant, however, a contradiction with the appearance as is said in the first sentence. Moreover, the solution of this contradiction is not its elimination but its understanding: the intermediate terms bridge the gap between value and price and show how to pass from one to the other. In other words, thanks to these intermediate terms, the contradiction does not lead to an exclusion, to an "either ... or". In another instance – book I, chapter 3, at the very beginning of the paragraph on the metamorphosis of commodities – Marx stated that most clearly:

> We saw in a former chapter that the exchange of commodities implies contradictory and mutually exclusive conditions. The differentiation of commodities into commodities and money does not sweep away these inconsistencies, but developes a *modus vivendi*, a form in which they can exist side by side. This is generally the way in which real contradictions are reconciled. For instance, it is a contradiction to depict one body as constantly falling towards another, and as, at the same time, constantly flying away from it. The ellipse is a form of motion which, while allowing this contradiction to go on, at the same time reconciles it.

It is thus not question of reducing a contradiction but of reconciling its components, which makes sense only as hegelian terminology. Likewise, one could say that the contradiction between law of value and law of equal profit rates leads to transformation rather than exclusion.

One will have noticed in this last quotation, that Marx used the expression "real contradictions" (*wirkliche Widersprüche*) whereas in the former he used the expression "apparent contradiction" (*scheinbar widerspuch*). But, once again, both contradictions are real, their difference being in their ontological structures. In the one case, the entities contradicting each other are on the same ontological level, while in the other they are not. In book III, chapter 48, on the trinitary formula, Marx wrote at the end (my translation): "It does not only seem, but it is a fact that average commodity price is different from value, thus from embodied labor time, and the average profit of a particular capital is different from the surplus value that it has extracted from the workers it employs". In the same chapter, echoing the contrast drawn between classical and vulgar economists, Marx stressed that if classical political economists had had the merit of going through the appearance to grasp the essence of exchange value, i.e. embodied labor time, on the other hand vulgar economists, reflecting the common practice of economic agents, could not help sticking to the appearance. So, if himself leaned towards classical economists, neither them nor vulgar economists were able to solve the contradiction because they endeavored to eliminate it instead of letting it develop.

And it was all the more important not to eliminate the contradiction between value and price but, on the opposite, to let it develop, since it could then revealed a deeper contradiction within capitalism itself, a contradiction between private property and social production or, in more general terms, between relations of production and productive forces which points to the end of the capitalist mode of production and his replacement by what Marx considered a superior one. Since profit, evolved from the formation of a general rate of profit and the pooling of surplus value, appeared to him as communism among capitalists themselves.

It is also well known that Marx made a distinction, in his 1873 *Postface*, between investigation and exposition methods. By doing so, he was merely following the classical methodology which distinguished analytic and synthetic methods, as, for instance, Port Royal or Kant did. Marx's method of investigation corresponds to the analytic method, it consists in the analysis of an object, given as a complex entity, in order to break it as such and to isolate its constitutive elements. These must exhibit the property of belonging to a whole class of objects, so that the analytical method can be said to transform a concrete singularity into an abstract generality.

Marx's exposition method corresponds to the synthetic method, it consists in the inverse transformation of the abstract into concrete and aims at reconstituting the object as a synthesis of its several elements. The only difference between Marx's and classical methods is that the former are dialectic, i.e. they hold the constitutive elements as developmental moments.

One would be wrong to get the impression that Nowak's idealization and concretization methods are but other names for Marx's investigation and exposition ones. It can be shown that it is not the case. To Nowak, the idealization method "is able to reveal inner connections" (p. 95). It enables one to grasp the essence, which is, and on that point I wholeheartedly agree with him, the aim of whatever is Marx's method. But instead of showing how his method of idealization leads to the essence, Nowak describes in set-theoretical terms how it deals with it. He just calls the set of magnitude that have an influence upon a given magnitude "the space of essential magnitudes" and any element belonging to that set "an essential factor" for the given magnitude (p. 97).

His main task would be to give a criterion of "influence", in order to tell whether a magnitude belongs to the said set or not. Instead, Nowak shows that "the notion of influence is an ordering one" (ibid.), i.e. that the relation of being more influential gets all the required properties: it is antisymmetric and transitive. However, it is not reflexive; therefore, it is a strict order, not a total order. Now, since one does not know how to tell whether a magnitude has an influence or not, one does not know either how to tell that a magnitude has more influence than another.

Anyway, one can see the purpose of the definition of an order relation on the set of esential magnitudes: one can define a more essential factor, or if factors are equi-essential, a subset, of "principal factors". Now, "the essential structure" of the given magnitude is nothing more than the hierarchy of factors (p. 98). Adding to it the given magnitude and an object submitted to it, one gets "the complete phenomenal form" (p. 99) or "the phenomenon", whereas if one restricts the essential structure to the subset of principal factors and adds the given magnitude and the said object, one gets "the zero phenomenal form" or "the essence" (p. 101).

Turning at last to the question of discovering the essence by means of idealization, Nowak writes:

> In this sense the method of idealization makes possible the dicovery of the essence of facts of a given type, i.e., revealing the influence principal factors have upon the magnitude under investigation. Obviously, the method does not assure by any means that this influence will be in fact revealed. A researcher may be wrong in his recognition of factors which are in fact essential for the magnitude under consideration, for instance, he makes the idealizing condition disregarding the principal factor or he does not eliminate and takes into acount a factor which is not essential at all, etc. This problem will be discussed later. (p. 102).

When? It seems to be when one comes to the next chapter, under the heading "image of the essential structure": the investigator "aims at a reconstruction of the hierarchy ... of essential factors .... He does not, of course, know the (essential) structure, but he has various general schemes and patterns for tracing it, namely those expressed in the ontological perspective he presupposes consciously or tacitly" (p. 117). So, in order to discover the essence, the investigator would have to know it beforehand. What is thus the purpose of the method?

But if Nowak's idealization method turns out to be purposeless, is it not meaningless as well? I would not go that far. It seems to me that it is akin to the classical abstraction and determination operations as defined in John Neville Keynes' *Formal Logic*.

A last word about falsifiability and paradigms. First, it is not concretization which leads to falsifiability but, on the opposite, idealization. It's only idealized statements that are falsifiable, and it's precisely the reason why one constructs them; otherwise, one could always invoke more and more conditional clauses to make one's statement fit the facts. Or, put another way, idealized statements are correlated to experiments: the latter are nothing else but built in idealized statements. Concretized ones would seem to be correlated to experience, they would tend to be descriptive rather than predictive.

Second, Nowak's "assumption that paradigms are idealizational theories and their development consists in their concretization" (p. 81) misses the point about paradigms, that I'll try to pinpoint by means of an example. The history of classical mechanics is not the process of concretization of the gravitation law, but one of discovering new fields where a law of the same form obtains. Coulomb's law is a proper "development" of the Newtonian paradigm; it is by no means less abstract or more concrete than the latter's law of gravitation.

If that is so, production prices cannot be hold as vindicating labor values.

Gérard Jorland
Centre de Recherches Historiques
CNRS/EHESS
Paris

REFERENCES

G.Jorland (1993). *Les Paradoxes du Capital*, Paris: Gallimard-Le Seuil.
K. Marx (1872). *Das Kapital*, Erster Band, 2. Aufl. MEGA II.6.
K. Marx (1988). *Das Kapital*, Dritter Band, 14 Aufl. MEW XXV.
L. Nowak (1980). *The Structure of Idealization*, Dordrecht: Reidel.

Poznań Studies in the Philosophy of the Sciences and the Humanities
1994, Vol. 38, pp. 277-301

Jack Birner

IDEALIZATIONS AND THEORY DEVELOPMENT IN ECONOMICS SOME HISTORY AND LOGIC OF THE LOGIC DISCOVERY

ABSTRACT. How are idealized theories related to models that are closer to the reality of existing economics? Historical background of the method, and the problem, providing a framework for discussing some recent analyses, especially Nancy Cartwright's. The problem must be seen as a part of the context of the logic of discovery. The relation between idealizing theories and factual models can be fruitfully analyzed in terms of a presupposition relation.

1. Introduction

In the method of modern economic analysis highly idealized theories play a central part. But how are idealized theories related to models that are closer to the reality of existing economies? I will discuss some historical background of the method, and the problem, in order to provide a framework for discussing some recent analyses, one of which is Nancy Cartwright's. But she does not solve the problem. I will argue that a solution can be found by considering the problem as part of the context of the logic of discovery. The relation between idealizing theories and factual models can be fruitfully analyzed in terms of a presupposition relation, and I will discuss several attempts to formalize this relation logically. Two of these not only promise to offer prospects for solving the problem, they also appear to have some unintended methodological benefits.

2. Some history

The deductive systematization of economic knowledge by means of the construction and manipulation of idealized models of reality was introduced in the hope of promoting economics from the status of a collection of practical rules for public policy to the cognitive status of Euclidean geometry and Newtonian physics. According to Halévy, James

Mill was the first to advocate the Euclidean method in economics (in the Edinburgh Review of 1809).[1] Say had the similar purpose of improving upon the body of classical economics by systematizing it. His shining example was the Newtonian method, or what Say believed to be that method. He wanted to apply it with the dual purpose of bringing economic knowledge together in one system and discovering new economic knowledge. In the Preface to his *Principles of Political Economy* of 1809 Ricardo expresses his admiration for Say's method of the *Traité d'économie politique*. It is mainly through Ricardo that the new method gained a foothold in economics and that economics took a new turning in that it started looking for laws. In his approach to economics Ricardo was also influenced by James Mill, who had taken over the Newtonian principle of finding the smallest possible number of general laws to "enable all the detail of phenomena to be explained by a synthetic and deductive method" (Halévy 1972, p. 6) from Bentham, whose "Utilitarianism, or Philosophical Radicalism, can be defined as nothing but an attempt to apply the principles of Newton to the affairs of politics and of morals." (Halévy 1972, p. 6).

The so-called Newtonian method is part of a tradition that is much older than Newton. It is known as the method of analysis and synthesis (or resolution and composition).[2] The aim of the method was to discover fundamental causes and to gain conceptual or theoretical control of the complex world. According to Zabarella, a predecessor of Galilei,

> The end of the demonstrative method is perfect science, which is knowledge of things through their causes; but the end of the resolutive method is discovery rather than science; since by resolution we seek causes from their effects so that we may afterwards know effects from their causes, not so that we may rest in a knowledge of the causes themselves. (Quoted in Randall 1962, Book 2, p. 294)

Zabarella did not insist, however, that the principles of natural science be mathematical. It was not until Galilei that the method was put into practice in a mathematical form which actually allowed scientists to make calculations of the effects of various factors.

> With this mathematical emphasis added to the logical methodology of Zabarella, there stands completed the "new method" for which men had been so long seeking. By the mathematical analysis of a few simple instances we find the principle involved in them. From that principle we deduce further consequences, which we find illustrated and confirmed in experience. ... This is the method called by Euclid and Archimedes a combination of "analysis" and "synthesis", and by the Paduans and Galileo, "resolution" and "composition". (Randall 1962, Book 1, p. 307)[3]

---

[1] Cf. Halévy (1972), p. 272.
[2] Cf. Hintikka & Remes (1974), p. 110.
[3] Cf. also Koertge (1977).

Throughout its more than 2000 years of existence, the method of analysis and synthesis was considered not only a method of proof, but also a method of discovery.[4] It was only with the separation between context of discovery and context of justification, introduced by Reichenbach into modern philosophy of science, that the idea that proof and invention can be combined in one methodological framework was abandoned.

3. Carl Menger as the Galilei of the social sciences[5]

The first detailed description and defence of the new method in economics was given by the Austrian economist Carl Menger. Menger's objective in *Investigations into method* of 1883 was to show that the economic theory of his *Principles* of 1871 had succeeded in formulating a general, universally valid theory, i.e., a theory that is true without exceptions, because it follows the Galilean method. Both requirements, generality and universal validity, can only be met by idealizing theories of a particular kind, which Menger calls *exact* theories. Their laws govern *ideal* economic phenomena, as opposed to those belonging to the *realistic-empirical* branch of theoretical science, which study the regularities in the succession and coexistence of *real* phenomena. This distinction leaves Menger with the problem of clarifying the nature of the relationship between empirical and exact theoretical research.

Menger believes in the existence, in reality, of several fundamental motives for human behaviour: the economic drive, which he considers by far the most important, "Gemeinsinn", by which is meant "moral sentiments" in the sense of Adam Smith, altruism, and the sense of justice. These are ultimate causes in social affairs which provide the basis for causal explanations: "Scire est per causas scire" (Menger 1883, p. 87). The basic drives delineate the boundaries between scientific disciplines: economics, social philosophy (or perhaps sociology), ethics, and jurisprudence in the above cases. Each of these disciplines studies human behaviour under one of these different aspects to the exclusion of the others. Within each discipline, the influence of one fundamental drive can be studied in various degrees of purity, i.e. by abstracting to a greater or lesser degree from disturbing factors which are operative in reality.

---

[4] Cf. Hintikka & Remes (1974), p. 110. For an excellent history of the method, see Randall (1961) and Randall (1962), Vol. i, Book 2, II.

[5] The title is a variation on Nowak's claim that Marx is the Galilei of the social sciences. Cf. Nowak (1980), ch. 2 para. 5.

Following Wieser, we may call the separation of fundamental drives from one another *isolating abstraction* and omitting disturbing factors *emphasizing abstraction*.[6] This distinction is the foundation of Menger's analytic-compositive method. Through analysis or resolution one discovers single fundamental causes. But the mere isolation of a single fundamental cause is not sufficient for studying it in its pure form. For that purpose, we have to abstract from factors which inhibit the full working of that single cause. Exact theoretical science thus involves both types of abstraction.

The disturbing factors which are mentioned by Menger are ignorance, error, external force, and the measure in which people let themselves be guided by a specific fundamental drive (in the case of economics it is the degree to which people attend to their economic interests; I shall call the absence of it "neglect"). Thus we obtain the following classification:[7]

Disturbing factors (emphasizing abstraction)	Basic drives (isolating abstraction)				
	Economic drive	Morality	Altruism	Justice	etc.
Error	(Within each of the disciplines defined by one particular basic drive, the operation of that drive can be studied on various levels of emphasizing abstraction. Gradually abstracting from error, ignorance, etc., is something which recurs in each of the disciplines.)				
Ignorance					
Force					
Neglect					

Figure 1

The theoretical sciences study one or several aspects of reality or basic drives in isolation from others. Moreover, the exact theoretical sciences abstract from disturbing factors, whereas the empirical theoretical sciences do not. So, exact theories are even more idealized than empirical theories; they are about *isolated* aspects of *ideal* phenomena. According to Menger, attempting to test the predictions of exact laws empirically involves a category mistake and is a methodological absurdity.[8] Exact laws cannot be refuted by the results of empirical analysis. The consequence that has to be drawn from a negative test result must be not that the exact law is false, but that it is not applicable. This is an instrumentalist conclusion. Nevertheless, Menger is a scientific realist.

---

[6] These are my translations of Wieser's "isolierende" and "hervorhebende Abstraktion". See Wieser (1914), pp. 134-5.

[7] This classification cannot be found explicitly in Menger. It is the result of a reconstruction of his methodology. Cf. Birner (1990a).

[8] Menger (1883), p. 54.

He maintains that both empirical and exact theories are descriptions of reality, which is why *Principles* is put forward as a theory which is to provide practical men with a scientific foundation for their conduct by laying bare the real causal laws of economics.[9]

Though a major part of *Investigations* is devoted to the problem of the relation between exact and empirical theoretical analysis, Menger does not succeed in providing a solution. This is because he considers the problem as a problem of the *justification of knowledge*: how can empirical-theoretical and exact-theoretical knowledge be given a foundation that is true beyond doubt. The truth of one's knowledge is fully determined by the method used in obtaining it. The exact method guarantees the truth of exact laws.[10] Menger does not separate the context of discovery from the context of justification. In Menger's justificationist and inductivist theory of knowledge abstraction is conceived of as a *process* rather than as a set of hypotheses with particular properties. This creates the following dilemma: Either exact laws are about empirical reality, but then they must have been derived from it in some way that is not inductive, because Menger is well aware of the logical problem that arises if one maintains that general, universally valid laws can be derived from a finite number of observation statements.[11] Or they do not have an empirical basis, but then they cannot be about empirical reality. This leaves Menger with the problem of explaining how universal laws *are* to be justified. No matter how hard he tries, he fails to find a satisfactory way out of this justificationist dilemma.

4. The Polish Idealization Model

The analysis of the use of idealizing theories in science by Krajewski and Nowak[12] allows us to state the problem clearly. I have discussed their analysis extensively elsewhere,[13] and I will draw on that in what follows. In this approach, which I have called the Polish Idealization Model, or PIM, a theory or a model[14] is defined as a set of lawlike statements

$$(x)(C(x) \Rightarrow F(x)),$$

[9] Menger (1871), Preface.

[10] Cp. Menger (1883), p. 38.

[11] Cp. Menger (1883), pp. 34-5.

[12] Cp. for instance Krajewski (1977) and Nowak (1980).

[13] Birner (1989) and (forthcoming).

[14] As will become clear, the distinction between theory and model is relative, not absolute.

where $C(x)$ and $F(x)$ are statements about properties of x. It will be assumed that the properties of x can be fully described by mathematical functions assigning some numerical value to characteristic parameters of x. The antecedent $C(x)$ states the initial conditions or "assumptions", the consequent $F(x)$ the predictions or "theorems". I shall call F the characteristic parameter of a particular model. The antecedent may contain both factual and idealizing conditions. If it contains the latter, the model is an idealizing model. There is nothing in reality which corresponds to it; it is about ideal objects: "x is an ideal object (...) when it is an ideal limit of a sequence of real objects with diminishing value of some characteristic parameter p_i (usually there is a set of parameters). In other words, some of its parameters are equal to zero ($p_i = 0$), however we know that in all real objects they are positive ($p_i > 0$)." (Krajewski 1977, p. 23).

Economists follow several *strategies of theory development*, all of which can be described with the help of PIM.[15] *Factualization* or *concretization* amounts to replacing the model's idealizing assumptions that abstract from disturbing factors, $p_i(x) = 0$, one by one, by factual assumptions, $p_i(x) > 0$. The consequent may have to be adjusted as the idealizing assumptions are factualized. Thus, starting from a purely idealizing model M_I, we obtain a sequence of models with decreasing degrees of idealization which ends, in principle, with the purely factual model M_F.

$$M_I: \quad (x)(p_1(x) = 0 \;\&\; p_2(x) = 0 \;\&\; \dots \;\&\; p_n(x) = 0 \Rightarrow F(x) = 0)$$

$$M_1: \quad (x)(p_1(x) > 0 \;\&\; p_2(x) = 0 \;\&\; \dots \;\&\; p_n(x) = 0 \Rightarrow F_1(x) = 0)$$

$$M_{n-1}: \quad (x)(p_1(x) > 0 \;\&\; \dots \;\&\; p_{n-1}(x) > 0 \;\&\; p_n(x) = 0 \Rightarrow F_{n-1}(x) = 0)$$

$$M_F: \quad (x)(p_1(x) > 0 \;\&\; \dots \;\&\; p_n(x) > 0 \Rightarrow F_n(x) = 0)$$

The scheme shows the last link in the chain of factualizations to be a factual model that contains no idealizing assumptions at all. It is doubtful whether any model in any scientific discipline ever reaches this fully empirical status. The last step in the sequence may be an approximation. *Emphasizing abstraction*[16] operates in the opposite direction, and can be

[15] Only a brief characterization of the strategies can be given here. For a more detailed description see Birner (1990a) and (forthcoming).

[16] In Birner (1990a) this strategy was called idealization. The present expression reflects the insight (the elaboration of which is precluded by lack of space) that emphasizing abstraction is one type of idealization, the other being isolating abstraction.

shown in the above scheme as the transition from, for instance, M_F to M_{n-1}, where the prediction $F_{n-1}(x) = 0$ of M_{n-1} may be an approximation of $F_n(x) = 0$, the prediction of M_F. The *revealing of idealizing conditions* is another strategy of theory development. It amounts to discovering that the validity of a model or theory which was thought to be general is in fact conditional upon the assumption that a different factor, p_{i-1}, which was not included in the original model, influences the factor characterized by F. The discovery amounts to seeing that F is a function of p_{i-1} and that the older model is a special case which can be derived from the reconstructed, more general model plus the assumption that $p_i = 0$.[17] What all three strategies amount to, is that a particular relation is discovered or constructed between models of different levels of generality. In the case of the the third strategy this relation is known as *correspondence*.[18]

5. The correspondence relation

There is a correspondence relation between two theories if:[19]

1. The new theory is more general than the old one.
2. The new theory partly reconstructs the old one.
3. The new theory corrects the old one by replacing a parameter that was considered to be a constant by a variable.
4. The old theory is a limiting case of the new theory describing only what happens in a limited domain.
5. The new theory is logically incompatible with the old one.
6. The new theory explains why people holding the old theory thought their theory to be correct.
7. The new theory introduces a factor on which the value of the parameter that was considered a constant by the old theory depends.

The old theory is called the corresponded theory, the new one the corresponding theory.

---

[17] Cf. Krajewski (1977), par. 4.6.

[18] In PIM factualizations (and emphasizing abstractions) have the same logical structure as the correspondence relation. They are all a type of reduction relation. But whereas with correspondence reduction is associated with explanation, this is not the case with factualizations, cf. Krajewski (1984). This deserves more attention than can be given to it here. In the sequel, the analysis will concentrate on the more fundamental relation of correspondence. For examples of correspondence relations, see Birner (1993) and (forthcoming).

[19] For the following, cf. Watkins (1984), ch. 5 and Krajewski (1977).

6. The problem restated

In the framework of PIM, an idealizing model or law L_I is logically entailed by, or can be logically derived from the factualized model or law L_F plus an idealizing condition C_I:[20]

(1) L_F & $C_I \Rightarrow L_I$,

or, if, following Krajewski, we truncate the laws to their predictions and the relevant initial condition:

(2) $F_M(x) = 0$ & $p_i(x) = 0 \Rightarrow F_I(x) = 0$.

The logical structure of the relation between an idealized model and its factualization suggests that the relation is a reduction relation. But the symmetry that is commonly assumed to exist between reduction and explanation in the deducive-nomological model of explanation is not generally preserved.

> The reduction of L_I to L_F is obviously possible. It is not clear whether the opposite reduction of L_F to L_I is also possible. L. Nowak claims that it is, that L_F follows from L_I and some additional knowledge. Undoubtedly scientists in their theoretical reasoning usually start from L_I and pass to L_I, taking account of the factors disregarded earlier. But is it a deduction? (Krajewski 1977, p. 39)

Krajewski declares Nowak's claim undecided, and he continues rather casually to make an important observation.

> We see, by the way, that the concepts of reduction and explanation of theories should not be identified. Maybe Nowak is right and reduction is possible in both directions (of course, with different additional assumptions). Shall we then say that L_I explains L_F and L_F explains L_I? It would be a very strange conclusion.
> In practice we do not say that L_F explains L_I (...). Rather the opposite is true: in order to better understand a more complicated law L_F we start from a simpler law L_I and gradually add additional factors. We explain L_F by L_I though we are not sure whether there is a strict reduction here. We do not say that L_I is explained by L_F though there is an obvious strict reduction here. (Krajewski 1977, p. 39)[21]

I will summarize the relations as Krajewski states them.

	←correspondence →	
	←deduction ——	
idealizing nodel	— explanation ——→	factualized model
	— reduction ——→	

Figure 2

---

[20] Krajewski (1977), p. 39.

[21] When we take into account the conclusion of Krajewski (1984) that we do not speak of explanations anyway when dealing with factualizations, the argument in the text still applies to the correspondence relation.

There is clearly a clash between the analysis of PIM and a rather widespread and commonly-held intuition about the relations between idealizing and factualized laws and theories.

Krajewski does not stand alone in his questioning of the nature of the logical relation between idealizing and factualized laws, theories, or models. Rivett asks on what grounds theoretical and idealized hypotheses are applicable.[22] He rejects the answers given by Robbins ("because the assumptions of economic theory are (approximately) true") and Friedman ("because they are false"). He concludes:

> One is thus forced to the unattractive conclusion that though economic theory must always be used along with empirical observations, it seldom *entails* explanatory hypotheses. In most situations it merely *suggests* them. In consequence, the proven hypotheses of economics are not linked deductively. Its theory is best stated as a set of analytical propositions which *are* deductively linked and which suggest hypotheses, while also giving them support. (Rivett 1970, p. 128)

But he fails make clear how the suggesting is to be analyzed. According to Körner, idealization leads to a deductive disconnection between theory and empirical basis, and further idealization may even lead to disconnection within theories.[23] And Laymon observes: "Roughly, the choice is between true but vague descriptions or precise but false ones. But as Duhem already noted, if descriptions of natural phenomena are to logically attach to our theories, we must opt for the latter alternative." (Laymon 1980, p. 339). The problem of the relation between idealizing theories and empirical or factual models has been stated less roughly and more precisely by Worrall. He poses the dilemma: either an idealizing theory is a true theory about ideal phenomena, or a false theory about real or empirical phenomena, but not both.[24]

7. Truth *versus* the laws of nature

Cartwright[25] seems to make a clear choice for the option that idealizing laws are false descriptions of real phenomena. Their use lies in the fact that they organize and unify phenomenological laws, but "[t]here is no reason to think that the principles that best organize will be true, nor that the principles that are true will organize much." (Cartwright 1983, p. 53). Against the view that the fundamental laws of physics state the facts (the "facticity view"), she maintains that

---

22 Rivett (1970), p. 128.
23 Körner (1963) and (1966).
24 Cf. Worrall (1982), p. 218.
25 In Cartwright (1983) and (1989).

> nature is governed by a small number of simple, fundamental laws. The world is full of complex and varied phenomena, but these are not fundamental. They arise from the interplay of more simple processes obeying the basic laws of nature. ... This picture of how nature operates to produce the subtle and complicated effects we see around us is reflected in the explanations that we give: we explain complex phenomena by reducing them to their more simple components. ... [Following] Mill, ... [I] call this *explanation by composition of causes*. (Cartwright 1983, p. 58)

Simple laws do not state the facts, but they do have explanatory power. On the other hand, phenomenological laws do state the facts, but they are low-level laws without explanatory power.

> I think that the basic laws and equations of our fundamental theories organize and classify our knowledge in an elegant and efficient manner, a manner that allows us to make very precise calculations and predictions. The great explanatory and predictive power of our theories lies in their fundamental laws. Nevertheless the *content* of our scientific knowledge is expressed in the phenomenological laws. (Cartwright 1983, p. 100)

But then what are the logical relations between idealizing, fundamental laws or theories and descriptive, phenomenological laws or models? Are the latter derived from the former, or is it the other way around?

> Proponents of the D-N view tend to think that at least [when a model has been chosen] the generic-specific account holds good. But this view is patently mistaken when one looks at real derivations in physics or engineering. *It is never strict deduction* that takes you from the fundamental equations at the beginning to the phenomenological laws at the end. (Cartwright 1983, p. 104; emphasis added.)

Unlike Krajewski, Cartwright unhesitatingly draws the conclusion that the deductive-nomological account of explanation (or the generic-specific approach as Cartwright calls it) is wrong: "The generic-specific account fails because the content of the phenomenological laws we derive is not contained in the fundamental laws which explain them." (Cartwright 1983, p. 107). The point Cartwright is making is none other than the well-known logical principle that deductive inference cannot be ampliative, that is, that "one cannot deduce more from less".[26] In her second book the diagnosis of the logical relation is repeated in different words: "there is never any recipe for how to get from the abstract theory to any of the concrete systems it is supposed to treat." (Cartwright 1989, p. 185).

Despite her idea that fundamental laws are false descriptions of real phenomena, Cartwright still evades the dilemma stated by the scientific realist Worrall by introducing the mutual exclusiveness of truth and explanatory power. Following Duhem she chooses an intermediate position between realism and instrumentalism. That leaves her with the

[26] Cf. also Tietzel (1987), p. 319: "An idealized explanans is logically too weak to state a concrete, singular explanandum."

problem of explaining how fundamental laws are related to phenomenological laws. As part of her solution she introduces two different meanings of "realism", thus restoring the link between truth and explanatory power that she had severed earlier. Both models and fundamental laws are realistic, be it in a different sense.

> The two senses act at different levels. The first bears on the relation between the model and the world. The model is realistic if it presents an accurate picture of the situation modelled: it describes the real constituents of the system – the substances and fields that make it up – and ascribes to them characteristics and relations that acually obtain. The second sense bears on the relation between the model and the mathematics. A fundamental theory must supply a criterion for what is to count as explanatory. Relative to that criterion the model is realistic if it *explains* the mathematical representation. (Cartwright 1983, pp. 149-50, emphasis added.)

Instead of the D-N model of explanation, Cartwright proposes a theory that she calls the simulacrum account.

> The simulacrum account is not a formal account. It says that we lay out a model, and within the model we "derive" various laws which match more or less well with bits of phenomenological behaviour. But even inside the model, derivation is not what the D-N account would have it be, and I do not have any clear alternative. This is partly because I do not know how to treat causality. (Cartwright 1983, p. 161)

There is no strict deduction relation between fundamental equations and phenomenological models, but "a variety of different approximations." (Cartwright 1983, p. 104). Later this is replaced by the idea "that the method of Galilean idealization, which is at the heart of all modern physics, is a method that presupposes tendencies or capacities in nature." (Cartwright 1989, p. 188). The method is identified with "the logic that uses what happens in ideal circumstances to explain what happens in real ones; it is the logic of tendencies or capacities." (Cartwright 1989, p. 190). But it is not clear what logic that is, and Cartwright gets stuck at this point. Later, I will go into the kind of logic that may enable us to model the relation between idealizing theories and factualized models. For the moment, I will let the quoted passage continue, as it elucidates what Cartwright means by "ideal":

> What *is* an ideal situation for studying a particular factor? It is a situation in which all other "disturbing" factors are missing. And what is special about that? *When all other disturbances are absent, the factor manifests its power explicitly in its behaviour*. When nothing else is going on, you can see what tendencies a factor has by looking at what it does. This tells you something about what will happen in very different, mixed circumstances – but only if you assume that the factor has a fixed capacity that it carries with it from situation to situation. (Cartwright 1989, pp. 190-1; emphasis in the original.)

8. Is it better to be roughly accurate than precisely wrong?[27]

We have seen above that for Menger idealizing theories are true theories about ideal phenomena. However, he cannot solve the problem how the "exact" theories as he calls them are related to empirical reality. Against his will, he gets stuck between instrumentalism and realism. By separating truth from explanatory power, Cartwright chooses that position willingly. In his review of Cartwright's first book Krajewski argues that Cartwright's criticism of the facticity view of laws amounts to the idea that theoretical laws are C-false but M-true, a distinction that is made in his own "idealizational realism": "We state idealizational laws which are strictly fulfilled only in an ideal model but not in actual Nature. They are false in the simple classical sense (C-false) but they are true in a new, "model" sense (M-true)." (Krajewski 1987, p. 170). Moreover, the way in which Cartwright thinks fundamental laws are connected with phenomenological laws by being "amended to be true" (Cartwright 1983, p. 45) is identical to the procedure of what Krajewski has called factualization.[28] To this I add that Menger's idea of how exact laws may be related to empirical laws can be reconstructed in the same way with the scheme of PIM.

The parallels between Menger and Cartwright do not stop here. They both believe in the existence of causes which have to be separated on a theoretical level before being reassembled so as to obtain an explanation by composition of causes. And both distinguish between on the one hand abstraction (Cartwright) or isolating abstraction (Menger) and on the other hand idealization (Cartwright) or emphasizing abstraction (Menger). A major difference between Menger and Cartwright is the status they assign to idealizing laws. For Menger these are true descriptions of ideal phenomena. For Cartwright idealizing laws, if taken to be descriptive, are false. However, their real function is not to describe but to organize and unify phenomenological laws about surface phenomena and to allow scientists to calculate. Therefore, they must not be judged in terms of truth or falsehood, but rather by the extent to which they succeed in doing the job of organizing and unifying. Menger tries to maintain a consistent realism but fails to clarify the relation

---

[27] The paragraph title is suggested by Kamarck (1983), p. 2: "too often in economics, the choice is between being roughly accurate or precisely wrong." Of course, for applied science the answer is: we're satisfied when we're roughly accurate. The focus in this paper is on theoretical science, whose purpose it is to increase our understanding of reality.

[28] Surprisingly, Krajewski here abandons the fundamental distinction between factualization and correspondence that he had introduced in his (1984).

between idealizing theories and factualized models because of his justificationist epistemology. Cartwright identifies explanation with the subsumption of phenomenological laws under a fundamental, usually mathematical organizing scheme, yet at the same time she believes in the existence of causes which somehow or other are represented by the fundamental laws. The tension between the realism of the causes and the instrumentalism with respect to fundamental laws keeps her from formulating a satisfactory solution to the problem of the relation between idealizing laws and factualized models.

Bunge points the way to a solution. His answer to the question in the title of the present paragraph is: It is better to be precisely wrong, because "the failure of a precise idea is more instructive than the success of a muddled idea, for it may suggest the precise modifications producing more realistic (truer) models." (Bunge 1973, p. 95). What this amounts to is a view of idealizing theories as part of a heuristics, a rational method of theory development.[29] Despite the fact that both Menger and Cartwright stand in the tradition of the method of analysis and synthesis, neither looks for the solution to the problem of the relation between idealizing theories and factualized models in the direction of a logic of discovery. Menger, not because he does not believe in a logic of discovery, but because of his justificationism. And Cartwright, not because she is a justificationist, but because she concentrates on the static aspects of science rather than on its development. In the following I shall sketch how the function of idealizing theories and their relation with respect to factualized models may be better understood if one considers them as part of a logic of discovery.

9. On the logic of discovery

If a logic of discovery or a rational heuristics exists, what may we expect of it? Various demands may be formulated, for instance, that it be non-inductive, or more generally non-justificationist, non-trivial,[30] demonstrably more successful than rivals, or capable of accounting for real developments in science. But surely the most important demand is that it give direction to the development of a science. This is argued, for instance, by Nickles, who illustrates this with the example of chemistry.

---

[29] Cp. also Tietzel (1987), p. 315: "Idealized explanations are heuristic devices which, in the long run, ought to be transformed into adequate explanations." They do so by simplifying the explanatory argument, in the way described by Nowak, to whom the author refers.

[30] For this, cp. Musgrave (1989).

> [T]he model-building method of doing chemistry was and is also important in a *formal* sense (although not the usual logico-mathematical one) in that it induces a certain structural organization on the body of chemical knowledge, and provides a particularly concrete way to explore the space of possible chemical structures. Chemical knowledge imposes definite limits upon this space, hence, constraints on model building in general. Any specific structural problem imposes additional constraints, as does any hypothesized structural information; so model building is a way to represent the particular research problem with its full array of defining constraints. (Nickles 1990, p. 22)

In order to guide research, a heuristics must impose restrictions or constraints.

10. Presuppositions

The paradox that was noticed by Krajewski may be resolved if we distinguish the logic of explanation from the logic of priority or the logic of discovery. The intuition that idealizing theories are somehow prior to factualized models certainly seems correct. Idealizing theories are prior in the sense that they somehow provide heuristic guidance for factualizations. The intuition that idealizing theories explain factualized models seems equally right. But these correct intuitions have become conflated. The priority intuition was projected on the wrong relationship, the deductive logical relationship from idealizing theory to factualized model of which according to the received view explanation consists. Krajewski calls that received view into question. That, together with the distinction between explanation and heuristics removes the paradox. But is not the price we have to pay for the removal of the sense of paradox a weakening of what has long been considered the attraction of the standard view of science: that we can characterize the relations between theories and models in logical terms? Is the concept of a heuristics not uncomfortably vague?

Let us go back to the sense of paradox that may easily arise out of the confrontation of the logical relation between idealizing and factualized models that obtains according to Krajewski, and the idea that idealizing models are prior to factualized models. A comparable sense of paradox is the one that we feel when we are told by a logician that we can describe the presuppositions of a proposition as the logical *consequences* of that proposition, or, what is equivalent to this, that the presuppositions of a statement have the status of necessary conditions of that statement. For our intuition is that somehow presuppositions are prior to the propositions that they are presuppositions of. I suggest that we take the analogy literally:

Idealizing theories are among the presuppositions of factualized models, and the logical relation between idealizing and factualized models is a presupposition relation.

I will use an example taken from the debate in capital theory, also known as the Cambridge controversy, to illustrate that the idea of presuppositions as necessary conditions is not so counterintuitive as it may appear.[31] A particular neoclassical model predicted[32] that production techniques were a function of the rate of interest. If one ran through a monotonously increasing or decreasing sequence of interest rates one could never encounter the same technique more than once. To put the same thing in the received jargon, there could be no "reswitching of techniques". As was pointed out by several authors, first of all by Joan Robinson and D.G. Champernowne, the non-reswitching prediction rested on a hidden premise stating that production techniques were ordered according to capital intensity. Champernowne discovered that the ordering assumption was a *necessary condition* for ruling out reswitching.[33] Even in colloquial language this is equivalent to saying that non-reswitching *presupposes* that techniques are ordered in the way specified.

10.1 Bunge on priority and presuppositions

The idea that one theory or model acts as a presupposition of another has been advocated by Bunge. Bunge deals, *inter alia*, with the priority relation that may exist between pairs of theories. This relation is a pragmatic or psychological relation, while the logical relation between the theories is a presupposition relation which may "run in the opposite direction".

> Thus mathematics presupposes logic from a semantic point of view but mathematics usually comes first both historically and methodologically, in the sense that it has motivated most of modern logic and that it still provides the major control and the chief justification for it. Quite often, the semantic relation of presupposition runs counter to the pragmatic or historical direction. (Bunge 1970, p. 301)

An equivalent way of stating the relation between theories or disciplines such as mathematics and logic is to say that one is based on the other.

---

[31] An extensive methodological analysis is given in Birner (forthcoming).

[32] "Predicted" does not refer to an empirical prediction; the prediction was a logical consequence of the model.

[33] Champernowne (1953).

> To say that a theory A is *based on* another theory B means that A presupposes B ... And a theory A *presupposes* another theory B just in case the following conditions are met:
>
> (a) B is a necessary condition for the meaning or verisimilitude of A, because A contains concepts that are elucidated in B, or statements that are justified in B, and
>
> (b) B is not questioned while A is being built, worked out, criticized, tested, or applied ... (Bunge 1970, p. 300)

Condition (a) is said to capture the logical and semantic aspects of presuppositions, and (b) the methodological ones. Bunge observes that the concept of presupposition is to be kept distinct from the one of entailment, whether syntactic or semantic, which is why he rejects Van Fraassen's analysis. Bunge says it is counter-intuitive. This approach, initially proposed by Strawson, defines presuppositions as follows: a sentence A presupposes a sentence B iff both A and non-A semantically entail B. In what follows I will examine whether the semantic definition of presuppositions for the modelling of relations among theories is as counterintuitive as Bunge thinks.

10.2 Semantic entailment

Let p and q be sentences. The semantic definition of presupposition is:

p presupposes q iff $p \models q$ and $\sim p \models q$.

How could this be applied to the relation between an idealizing theory (T) and a factualized model (M)?

1. Consider a model to be a (set of) sentences(s).
2. Then M presupposes T iff $M \models T$ and $\sim M \models T$.
3. The model mentions relevant factors.
4. The theory T tells us what the (basic) relevant factors are.
5. The negation $\sim M$ of the model M mentions the same relevant factors as does M.

But what can the negation of a model possibly mean? Again, I take an example from the capital theory debate. The discovery that reswitching could occur was used by certain critics of neoclassical economics to conclude that neoclassical economics was refuted. To this Solow replied:

> Professor Robinson seems to think that the discovery of the logical reswitching phenomenon is destructive of "neoclassical economics". In this context I take neoclassical economics to be the working out of the logical consequences of the two principles of cost minimization and no pure profit, especially in steady states. It is certainly not the adoption of one-sector or two-sector models. In that sense – which may not be hers – the whole discussion *IS* neoclassical economics. The possibility of reswitching is a theorem of neoclassical economics, even if it was first pointed out by opponents of the theory. (Solow 1975, pp. 49-50)

Both reswitching and non-reswitching presuppose (the truth of) neoclassical economic theory (NCET). We may render the original neoclassical model and its prediction as[34]

M: $(x)((\text{Technique})x \; \& \; (\text{Ordering})x \rightarrow \text{no reswitching})$,

and the criticism as

$\sim M$: $\sim(x)((\text{Technique})x \; \& \; (\text{Ordering})x \rightarrow \text{no reswitching})$,

and both $M \models$ NCET and $\sim M \models$ NCET.

A well-known problem with the semantic-entailment view of presuppositions is that it is either trivial or leads to contradictions. If we hold on to the principle of bivalence (every sentence is either true or false), then the semantic definition states the triviality that every sentence presupposes only tautologies. However, in reality many sentences have false presuppositions. If the sentence q is the presupposition of a sentence p, from the falsity of q and the semantic definition of presupposition, it follows (by modus tollens and $p \models q$) that $\sim p$, and (by modus ponens and $\sim p \models q$) that q, so that we have the contradiction q & $\sim q$. Solutions have been proposed in terms of three-valued logics, but these have the disadvantage that many of the classical logical theorems are no longer valid. Van Fraassen has developed the so-called supervaluations approach,[35] which preserves all of the classical laws of logic except the law of bivalence. In Van Fraassen's system sentences may be neither true nor false. This is notably the case for sentences with presuppositions that are false: if one of the presuppositions of a sentence is false, then that sentence is neither true nor false.

The choice for the first horn of Worrall's dilemma, that idealizing theories are true theories of ideal phenomena, has in some cases given rise to the view that idealizing theories are tautologies (Mises, Hayek in his famous "Economics and Knowledge"[36]), or are at the very least very much like tautologies (Menger). Whatever the demerits of these positions, in these cases the semantic definition of presuppositions seems to model the relation between idealizing theory and factualized model adequately without the need to give up the principle of bivalence. If we choose the second horn of Worall's dilemma, that idealizing theories are false theories about real phenomena, Van Fraassen's system seems like a plausible way of modelling the relation between theory and model. When we read for "neither true nor false" "inapplicable", then from the falsity

---

[34] Assuming that the ordering assumption was implicitly made. If we do not assume this, we get a different model from the one of the critics.

[35] Cf. Van Fraassen (1968).

[36] Hayek (1937).

of the idealizing theory conceived of as being among the presuppositions of a factualized model we conclude that the model and its negation are inapplicable. A related intuition that seems to be captured by the supervaluations version of the semantic definition of presuppositions is the notion of "what it is like to do *X*" or "what it means that a particular model is a model of *X*", where *X* may be any discipline or theory. For instance, different geometries all share the axioms that constitute so-called natural geometry.[37] So it can be maintained that both Euclidean geometry and geometries that deny the axiom of parallels all presuppose natural geometry. Whether or not you maintain these axioms determines whether or not you are doing geometry. The same analysis seems to apply to neoclassical economics: whether or not one presupposes the truth of a maximizing hypothesis determines whether or not one is doing neoclassical economics. This is reminiscent of Menger's classification of the sciences according to fundamental factors. One places oneself outside a particular discipline if one abstracts by isolating abstraction from certain other fundamental factors.

10.3 Scientific explanations as answers to questions

Another proposal to apply the notion of presuppposition to the analysis of scientific theories and their relations is made by Sintonen.[38] He conceives of scientific explanations as answers to questions, and analyzes explanations with the means of erotetic logic. He distinguishes two types of presuppositions of questions. One type comprises logical (or syntactic) and pragmatic presuppositions. The second type is analyzed in terms of beliefs and subjective probabilities and I will not dwell upon these. The first type seems the more relevant to the present context: "presuppositions$_1$ of a question are logical entailments of the question sentences. Or rather, if only declarative sentences can have entailments, presuppositions$_1$ are logical entailments of the essentially syntactically chosen declarative counterparts of the question sentences." (Sintonen 1984, p. 45)

Sintonen (1985) contains a further discussion which relies on the so-called structuralist analysis augmented by elements from the traditional statement approach.[39] The questions a scientist asks are, in part at least,

[37] I owe this example to Henk Visser.

[38] Cf. Sintonen (1984).

[39] "because it best suits the intuition that problems are literally *questions*. (For this reason also I adopt the statement view for *theories*: theories must be linguistically formulated because we want (the presuppositions of) theories to make logical contact with certain presuppositions of questions.)" Sintonen (1985), p. 28.

defined by his theoretical framework, which in a structuralist analysis consists of so-called basic theory elements and specialized elements: "In a quite natural sense a scientist ... who holds a Kuhn-theory presupposes the basic theory-elements as well as the specialized elements at *t*, and these presuppositions provide the background for his questions in any problem contexts." (Sintonen 1985, p. 31).

Sintonen applies the logic of questions and answers to presuppositions, which act as constraints delimiting the space of admissible answers.

> In standard erotetic logic the notion of a presupposition is defined as follows: a proposition *p* is a presupposition of a question *q* if and only if the truth of *p* is necessary for the question to have a (direct) answer ... The presupposition of a question thus rules out as inappropriate all responses which violate the presupposition. (Sintonen 1985, p. 32)

This is consistent with the idea of a logic of discovery as a set of constraints,[40] and the example he gives expresses the same idea of the delimitations of a particular theory or group of theories that was discussed above.

> But even the Ptolemaic research tradition fits the model to some degree. There was a fundamental law or basic theory-core. Although there was no one single solution to the problem of the planets, all specific theories contained a system of earth-centered circles and major epicycles. ... A Ptolemaic astronomer thus *presupposed* the core, the Aristotelian physics and cosmology, the values as well as the theory-net specialization at hand." (Sintonen 1985, p. 34; emphasis added.)

Sintonen also addresses the analysis of the dynamics of theories and the correspondence relation. The latter is described in a manner that is very similar to the one in par. 5 above, augmented by the notion of idealizing theories as constraints or presuppositions: "The predecessor theory serves as a constraint on further theorizing: any potential theory T_n must have its predecessor theories T_{n-1} etc. as limit cases." (Sintonen 1985, p. 39).

Sintonen's analysis involves the notion of syntactic entailment. This may be a more suitable concept than semantic entailment for disciplines such as theoretical economics where the provability of theorems rather than the truth of predictions is important.[41]

---

[40] Cf. "What is crucial for a logic of discovery is the possibility of limiting the set of specific questions that arise in a problem context." Sintonen (1985), p. 36.

[41] For a discussion of provability versus truth in theoretical economics, cp. the paragraph "Empirical versus formal arguments: sleepwalking on the meta level" of the final chapter of Birner (forthcoming).

11. Presuppositions and the logic of discovery

The interpretation of the relation that obtains between idealizing theories and factualized models as a presupposition relation makes it susceptible to logical analysis and allows us to characterize the concept of idealizing theories (and other elements of the core of a research programme) acting as a heuristics in very definite terms. Their heuristic guidance consists of attempts on the part of theorists to construct their models in such a way that the idealizing theories and other hard-core elements be entailed by the conjunction of the models and the appropriate idealizing assumptions. In this way, the idealizing core acts as a constraint on factualized models. The semantic and the syntactic entailment views have this in common. The unity of the class of factualized models that is associated with a particular research programme resides in the fact that they all presuppose the same idealizing theories (and perhaps the same metaphysics). This is a feature that is also shared by the approach advocated by Bunge.

The introduction of presuppositions as crucial elements in the logic of discovery enables me to complete the scheme that was given above.

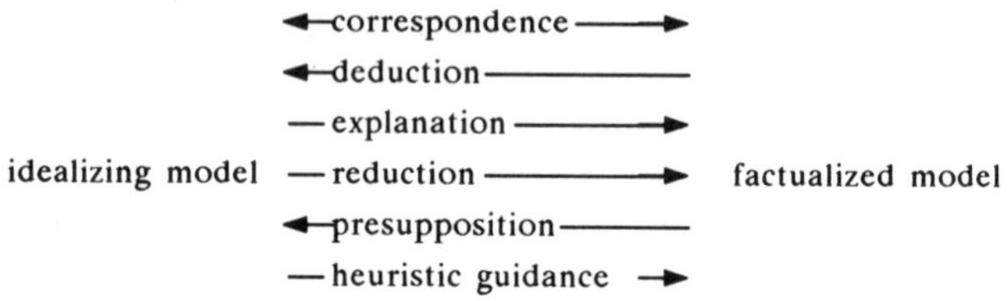

Figure 3

The heuristic function of an idealizing theory acting as a presupposition that must be related to factualized models by a logical entailment relation can be summarized in the methodological rule:

> *Construct models that are in a relation of correspondence to the basic theory.*

This regulative principle is central to the logic of discovery that has been called "conservative induction" by Post.[42] He and his student Koertge[43] present a number of case studies showing the operation of this rule. They

---

[42] Cf. Post (1971).

[43] In Koertge (1969).

advance the very strong empirical claim that in the history of science *all* successful theories, or successful parts of theories, were preserved in later theories.[44] This is called the General Correspondence Principle, and the similarities with the logic of scientific discovery that is described in the present paper warrant an extensive quotation.

> (a) There is a rationale of scientific discovery, over and above mere trial and error. There is a series of restrictions ... which render the activity of the scientist constructing new theories essentially different from that of a clueless rat trying one trapdoor after another (a remark probably also applying to any actual rat). "In der Beschränkung zeigt sich der Meister."
> (b) These restrictions are "theoretic", that is, based on internal analysis of available theory.
> (c) The procedure is inductive, in the sense of leading from a weaker to a stronger theory ("weaker" at least in the sense that the succesful part S^* of the old theory is less precise or less general than the succesful part of the new theory L).
> (d) It is also essentially inductive in retaining the old theory in a certain sense: it is conservative (as every good scientist is). (Post 1971, p. 218)[45]

12. Methodological spin-off

The conception of idealizing theories as presuppositions that are semantically or syntactically entailed by factualized models has two unintended advantages. First of all, it provides a reinforcement of one of the central ideas of Lakatos' methodology of scientific research programmes (MSRP). According to MSRP, the hard core of a theory is irrefutable *as a matter of convention*. In the present analysis, the hard core is irrefutable *as a matter of logic*. The only way in which idealizing theories could conceivably be tested empirically is via various factualized models (FM_i), but both the idealized theories presupposed by the factualized models and the empirical consequences of these models are among the consequences, not the premisses, of the models. If we depict entailment by arrows, the relations among different factualized models, their predictions, and the idealizing theory they are factualizations of, may be shown as follows.

---

[44] "Quite generally, the thesis may be put this way: no theory that ever "worked" adequately turned out to be a blind alley. Once a theory has proved itself useful in some respects, has shown its semantic simplicity or explanatory power, it will never be scrapped entirely. Even the phlogiston theory had features that were useful scientifically in its day, and those features translate smoothly into present theory." Post (1971), p. 237.

[45] It must be noticed with reference to item (c) that idealizing theories are less general but are more precise than factualized models in the sense that they make exact predictions for ideal domains. The factualized models may be more precise in that their predictions are closer approximations to empirical reality.

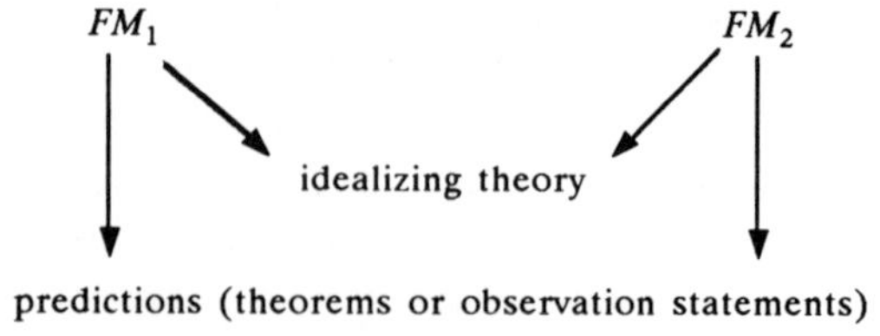

Figure 4

Another idea that is associated with Lakatos' MSRP, the hardening of the hard core, can likewise be analyzed and made more intelligible in terms of presuppositions. Scientists discover gradually that a collection of models has the same idealizing theory as their presupposition, and it may very well be the case that the idealizing theory is adapted over time so as to be in a relation of correspondence with a given collection of models.

13. Conclusion

In the above, I have sketched a way in which the idealizing theories of economics may act as part of a heuristics. That is my answer to the question how idealizing theories and factualized models are related. I have not analyzed the details of the process of theory development. This would involve, *inter alia*, an analysis of the role of mathematics, as mathematical arguments have become an integral part of the logic of economic discovery.[46] Yet the introduction of mathematics has not fundamentally changed the method of economic analysis that has become prominent since Ricardo. But it has enabled economists to apply the method more systematically. The method preceded the mathematics, as it had done much earlier in the scientific revolution.[47]

Jack Birner
Faculteit der Economische Wetenschappen
Rijksuniversiteit Limburg
Postbus 616
6200 MD Maastricht
The Netherlands

[46] This is argued in Birner (1993), and Birner (forthcoming) contains a further analysis that comprises case studies taken from the capital theory debate.

[47] Cf. Randall (1962), p. 66.

REFERENCES

Balzer, W., D.A. Pearce, H.-J. Schmidt (1984). *Reduction in Science*. Dordrecht: Reidel.

Birner, J. (1989). Idealizations and the Development of Capital Theory. In: J. Brzeziński *et al.* (Ed.) *Idealization I: General Problems (Poznań Studies in the Scieces and the Humanities*, **16**), pp. 127-49.

Birner, J. (1990). A roundabout solution to a problem in Menger's methodology and beyond. In: Caldwell (1990), pp. 241-61.

Birner, J. (1993). Testing Economic Theories Empirically: The Contribution of Econometrics, *Oekonomie und Gesellschaft*, **10**, 116-49.

Birner, J. (forthcoming). *Strategies and Programmes in Capital Theory; A Contribution to the Methodology of Theory Development*. Routledge.

Brzeziński, J., F. Coniglione, T.A.F. Kuipers, L. Nowak (Eds.). *Idealization I: General Problems* (Poznań Studies in the Philosophy of the Science and the Humanities, **16**). Amsterdam: Rodopi.

Bunge, M. (1970). Problems Concerning Intertheory Relations. In: Weingartner & Zecha (1970), pp. 293-315.

Bunge, M. (1973). *Method, Model and Matter*. Dordrecht: Reidel.

Caldwell, B. (Ed.) (1990). *Carl Menger and his Legacy in Economics*, special issue of *HOPE*, Duke University Press.

Cartwright, N. (1983). *How the Laws of Physics Lie*. Oxford: Clarendon.

Cartwright N. (1989). *Nature's Capacities and Their Measurement*. Oxford: Clarendon.

Champernowne, D.G. (1953). The production function and the theory of capital: a comment. *Review of Economic Studies*, **21**.

Gavroglu, K., Y. Goudaroulis & P. Nicolacopoulos (Eds.) (1989). *Imre Lakatos and Theories of Scientific Change*. Dordrecht: Kluwer.

Halévy, E. (1972). *The Growth of Philosophic Radicalism*. Faber.

Hayek, F.A. (1937). Economics and Knowledge. *Economica*, **IV**, 33-54.

Hintikka, J. & U. Remes (1974). *The Method of Analysis*. Dordrecht: Reidel.

Hintikka, J. & F. Vandamme (Eds.) (1985). *Logic of Discovery and Logic of Discourse*. Plenum Press.

Kamarck, A. (1983). *Economics and the Real World*. Oxford: Blackwell.

Koertge, N. (1969). *A Study of Relations Between Scientific Theories: a Test of the General Correspondence Principle*. Ph.D.-thesis, University of London.

Koertge, N. (1977). Galileo and the Problem of Accidents. *Journal of the History of Ideas*, **38**.

Körner, S. (1963). Deductive Unification and Idealisation. *The British Journal for the Philosophy of Science*, **14**.

Körner, S. (1966). *Experience and Theory*. London.

Krajewski, W. (1977). *Correspondence principle and growth of science*. Dordrecht: Reidel.

Krajewski, W. (1984). May we identify reduction and explanation of theories? In: Balzer et al. (1984).

Krajewski, W. (1987). Explanation, truth and idealization (Review of Cartwright 1983). *Dialectics and Humanism*, **2**.

Lakatos, I. (1978). *Mathematics, Science and Epistemology. Philosophical Papers, Volume 2*. Ed. by J. Worrall & G. Currie. Cambridge: Cambridge University Press.

Lakatos, I. (1978a). The method of analysis-synthesis. In: Lakatos (1978).

Laymon, R. (1980). Idealization, Explanation, and Confirmation. *PSA*, **1**, 336-50.

Menger, C. (1871). *Grundsätze der Volkswirthschaftslehre*. Vol. 1 of Menger (1968).

Menger, C. (1883). *Untersuchungen über die Methode der Sozialwissenschaften und der politischen Oekonomie insbesondere*. Vol. 2 of Menger (1968).

Menger, C. (1968). *Gesammelte Werke*. Edited by F.A. Hayek, Mohr.

Musgrave, A. (1989). Deductive heuristics. In: Gavroglu *et al.* (1989), 15-32.

Nickles, T. (1990). Logics of Discovery, *Philosophica*, vol. 35, 7-32.

Nowak, L. (1980). *The Structure of Idealization*. Dordrecht: Reidel.

Post, H. (1971). Correspondence, Invariance and Heuristics. In Praise of Conservative Induction. *Studies in the History and Philosophy of Science*, **2**, 213-255.

Randall, J.H. (1961). *The Career of Philosophy*. New York: Columbia University Press.

Randall, J.H. (1962). *The School of Padua and the Emergence of Modern Science*. Antenore.

Rivett, K. (1970). Suggest or Entail. *Australian Economic Papers*, **34**.

Say, J.-B. (1880). *A Treatise on Political Economy*. Kelley edition of the New American Edition.

Sintonen, M. (1984). *The Pragmatics of Scientific Explanation*. *Acta Philosophica Phennica*, Vol. 37.

Sintonen, M. (1985). Separating Problems from their Backgrounds: A Question-Theoretic Proposal. In: Hintikka & Vandamme (1985), pp. 25-49.

Solow, R.M. (1975). Brief Comments. *Quartely Journal of Economics*.

Tietzel, M. (1987). Idealisierte Erklärungen. *Zeitschrift für allgemeine Wissenschaftstheorie*, **17**, 315-21.

Van Fraassen, B. (1968). Presupposition, Implication, and Self-Reference. *The Journal of Philosophy*, **65**.

Watkins, J.W.N. (1984). *Science and Scepticism*. London: Hutchinson.

Weingartner, P. & G. Zecha (Eds.) (1970). *Induction, Physics, and Ethics*. Dordrecht: Reidel.

Worrall, J. (1982). Scientific Realism and Scientific Change. *Philosophical Quarterly*.

Discussions

Poznań Studies in the Philosophy of the Sciences and the Humanities
1994, Vol. 38, pp. 303-336

Leszek Nowak

THE IDEALIZATIONAL METHODOLOGY AND ECONOMICS*
Replies to Diederich, Hoover, Janssen, Jorland and Mäki

ABSTRACT. A reply to the papers by Kevin D. Hoover, Maarten C.W. Janssen, Werner Diederich, Gerard Jorland, Uskali Mäki, all in the present volume. It contains some additional explanations of various elements of the idealizational methodology and more detailed extensions and developments. Some of these extensions are avalaible only in the Polish writings of various authors from the Poznań milieu. However, there still remain some objections that challenge the conception as, even in its most developed forms, it does not contain a ready answer to them. These require new findings in the idealizational approach to science and in certain cases some conjectures are proposed.

The papers by Hoover and Janssen contain direct queries and/or objections concerning my writings and the papers by Jorland and by Diederich are extensive criticisms of my methodological proposals (all papers in this volume). Since all of them bring some interesting observations and sometimes innovative insights, I have asked the Editors to allow me to comment on them. On this occasion, I would also like to refer to some earlier criticism in another paper that appeared in this book series, Mäki (1992), the approach suggested there is continued in the paper by Mäki in this volume. Obviously, possible replies of the authors of the above contributions are welcome. Our book series will soon continue the problems of idealization in further volumes of *Idealization*-subseries and there will be certainly a place for continuing the discussion that the authors mentioned above have opened here.

Among comments and objections on the part of the above mentioned authors there are some which result from quite a different understanding of the task of methodology of science. In section 1 of the present paper I shall comment on them and discuss the status of methodology as I understand it. Some other objections result from the lack of clarity, likely also on my part. They will be analyzed in section 2. Other grievances find their solution in more detailed expositions of the idealizational methodology or in its extensions and developments. These will be

* Translation of this paper has been supported by the grant 2496 from the *Komitet Badań Naukowych*.

discussed in section 3. However, there still remain some objections that challenge the conception as, even in its most developed forms, it does not contain a ready answer to them. These will be discussed in section 4 of the present reply.

1. On Methodology

In the last two decades there appeared various trends in the philosophy of science that attempt to place the method of idealization at the center of the subject matter of methodology. Among others, the writings of Barr (1971), Suppe (1972), Wójcicki (1974, 1979), Ludwig (1981), Cartwright (1983, 1989), Niiniluoto (1986, 1990) give justice to the method hitherto practically neglected in our area. Moreover, and notably, a number of writings have appeared recently, which attempt to include the idea of idealization into the body of ideas of one of most powerful trends in the newest philosophy of science, viz. methodological structuralism. I mean in particular the writings of Kuipers (1985, 1992), Kuokkanen (1988, 1992), Hamminga (1989, 1992), Garcia de la Sienra (1992), Ibarra and Normann (1994), and others.

The idealizational conception of science is one of the above mentioned trends. It was initiated at the turn of the 60s and 70s (cf. my 1970a-b, 1971a-b, 1972a-b) being inspired by two orientations, Popper's hypotheticism and the Hegelian/Marxian dialectics. Here, I shall try to discuss the basic ideas of this approach in relation to its application to economics.

The role of the notion of essentiality. It is taken for granted from the methodological tradition that not all the methodological notions need to be defined; some notions may be introduced as conceptual primitives, it is only the rest which is to be defined with the aid of earlier terms, in the final instance with the aid of primitive notions. As has been noted (cf. my 1980, p. 97), the notion of influence is such a conceptual primitive whose legitimation is that it serves as a means to define other notions of the conception under consideration. That notion was only characterized formally (the relation: ... is more influential for .-.- than --- was supposed to be antisymmetric and transitive) in order to justify a construction of the notion of essential structure, and images of the essential structure, of a magnitude.

In sum, that is quite standard a way of constructing the conceptual apparatus of the idealizational approach to science. It is not quite clear for me why this fact worries G. Jorland (this volume, p. 176).

The notion of influence and the dialectics of definitions. More recently, I have attempted to define the notion of influence in more elementary terms (cf. my 1989). The initial idea is this: a magnitude *B* influences a magnitude *A* on an object *a* iff there is a subset *V* of values of *A* such that if *B* adopts a certain value for *a*, *A* takes no value from the set *V* for *a* (*V* is the area of exclusion of *A* relative to *B*, *a*). Such a notion of influence allows to introduce a comparative notion of essentiality: *B* is more essential for *A* on *a* than *C* iff the area of exclusion of *A* relative to *B* and *a* has a greater cardinality than the area of exclusion of *A* relative to *C* and *a*. This makes also possible to distinguish between isolated influences and interactions. Two factors, *B* and *C* are isolated in relation to *A* and *a* iff the area of exclusion of *A* in regard to *B* and *C* on *a* is the sum of the area of exclusion of *A* relative to *B* and *a* and the area of exclusion of *A* relative to *C* and *a*. *B* and *C* interact in relation to *A* and *a* iff they are not isolated in this respect. All this makes the definition of the essential structure (cf. my 1975), and its variations (Brzeziński 1977), and also of some other usual notions, possible.

The definition of essentiality plays an important role in a metaphysical conception for which it has been elaborated (cf. my 1991a, 1992a), but for the idealizational methodology, even if correct[1], it means much less than one could expect. It turned out that the primitive notions for the idealizational approach begin a bit earlier than expected, and that is all. Obviously, technically this means a lot — the conceptual structure of the theory becomes more clear and comprehensible — but its explanatory power does not profit very much from such an innovation. Such is the dialectics of definitions of the crucial notions of a theory: when they are lacking, everything in the theory appears to be unclear and dependent on the sense which is attached to the primitive notion. When such a definition is already given, it appears that the theory does not explain much more, if anything, than before.

Self-effective notions and methodology. One of the crucial, if not the crucial, of Jorland's objections reads: "[According to Nowak] in order to discover the essence, the investigator would have to know it beforehand. What is thus the purpose of the method [of idealization — L.N.]?" (this volume, p. 274).

This is understandable only on the supposition that, according to Jorland, the notion of influence (and hence of the essential structure of

[1] That is still far from being certain. Cf. the analyses of Paprzycka and Paprzycki (1992) and Kuokkanen and Tuomivaara (1992, pp. 93-95) which have amended my earlier formulation (1989). The formulation presented in the text makes use of these amendments.

a magnitude, etc.) is to be self-effective. A term is self-effective iff its intension provides a procedure to determine whether an arbitrary object belongs to the extension of that term or not. Now, it becomes clear why Jorland demands: Nowak's "main task" should be "to give a criterion of 'influence', in order to tell whether a magnitude belongs to the [mentioned] set [the space of essential magnitudes for a given magnitude – L.N.] or not" (*ibid.*, p. 274). Yet, the notion of influence, even if defined in the above way, is, obviously, not self-effective. The problem is whether this is a deficiency of the proposed approach or not. I do not have any elaborated metamethodology at my disposal, I must admit. Let us then try to see what the history of methodology teaches us.

Let us note that there was a methodological orientation which put forward the requirement that all concepts be self-effective. That was Bridgman's operationalism. However, the idea of reducing all concepts to mere bulks of operations failed entirely. It turned out, for instance, that this idea forces us to admit that there is not one notion of length measured in various way but as many as the (historically available) methods of measurement of distance.

Moreover, there are epistemological notions of undeniable significance which are overtly not-self-effective. Take, for instance, the semantic notion of truth: "*p*" is true iff *p*. This Tarski-condition does not give any imaginable procedure to decide whether a given statement is true or not. Is this bad? Imagine that it is possible to define truth as a self-effective concept. A general procedure enabling us to decide whether an arbitrary statement is true or false would follow from such a definition. What would be the use for human creative thinking in such a world then? Creativity would be utterly superfluous in this world: the question of truth would be in this world simply decided by philosophers applying such a definition to all possible statements. There, philosophy instead of understanding human creativity, would just eliminate it with the aid of its alleged "algorithm".

On a similar basis a self-effective definition of influence equipping us not only with the notion of essentiality but also with a general criterion to decide which factors are essential for which ones would make useless the building of empirical theories. For in order to know whether, say, the velocity of a body is essential for its length not the testing of the theory of relativity would be necessary but simply a verdict of a methodologist applying his general criterion.

Indeed, such a definition-and-criterion of influence would make a serious task of empirical sciences – putting forward what may be termed essentialist hypotheses (cf. my 1980, pp. 113ff) – entirely superfluous. To my understanding, it is not a deficiency but actually a merit of the idealizational methodology that it does not mix the notion and the criteria of essentiality. It is the task of methodology to explain the notion and the cognitive role of "essentiality" as it functions in science. But it is the task of empirical sciences to offer possibly many different criteria of influence of which they may make use building their theories.

The purpose of the idealizational methodology. If not to offer any workable criteria of essentiality, what is the purpose of the method of idealization? Simply: to reconstruct the way science works. According to the idealizational methodology, there are three main stages of scientific conduct:

I. pre-theoretical stage: postulation of essentialist hypotheses putting forward possible images of the essential structures of considered magnitudes;

II. theoretical stage: postulation of a body of idealizational hypotheses which subsequently undergo the process of concretization;

III. empirical testing of the theory.

Another claim of the conception is that the three stages are mutually tied in the sense that what is decided in one may be questioned on another which forces the theoretician to come back to the "earlier" stage (Brzeziński 1977, 1985, my 1980, p. 133). In other words, the "order of reconstruction" in methodology is not the "order of justification" in science. The latter is not, strictly speaking, order at all but a network of mutual connections. In particular, it is not so that "after" gaining the "knowledge" of what is essential for what (stage I) the theoretician builds an idealizational theory (stage II) and tests it (stage III). It is rather so that it is only the test of a hypothetical theory which confirms the essentialist hypotheses adopted at the very beginning.

Knowledge, suppositions, hypotheses. If the above point of view requires a philosophical legitimation, it is this. There have appeared three basic notions of cognition in the European epistemology (Marciszewski 1971). First one was that of Plato: to know something meant to be able to recognize for certain the hidden essence of things. Philosophy kept this notion of knowledge, and the belief that it is available for us, for more than one and a half thousand of years. This notion of knowledge is still present in Descartes. It was only Hume who called it into question and opened a new tradition. There is no knowledge in the Platonic sense, what is available for us is nothing more than a (far from being certain) supposition based on experience. The only thing we are able to realistically demand of ourselves is to increase the probability of our convictions. What is available to us are more or less probable suppositions, and that is all. Popper opened the third epistemological tradition: nothing is certain, that is correct, but we are not interested in increasing probability of our convictions at all. Were we, the most interesting for us would be tautologies which have the highest possible probability. Or stereotypes whose probability is, in our assessment, very high. Instead, claims Popper, we are interested in new, risky hypotheses whose initial subjective probability is always very low. It is novelty, or originality, of our hypotheses that matters to us.

The three ideas of human cognition — as knowledge, supposition, or hypothesis — are based on some metaphysical assumptions. The idea of knowledge presupposes essentialism, the ideas of supposition and hypothetical cognition deny it. Now, the idealizational methodology attempts to combine metaphysical essentialism — rather in the style of Hegel than of Plato (cf. my 1977a-b, 1978) — with the Popperian idea of hypothetical cognition. For it is not true that we cannot put forward hypotheses concerning the hidden essences of phenomena. We can, and science is the best example of that. This becomes even quite obvious, if we realize that science uses idealization and that the testing of a(n idealizational) theory is at the same time the main practical means to assess the reliability of the essentialist hypotheses underlying it. A final refutation of such a theory implies that the initial view of what is essential for the explained phenomena was doomed to failure from the very beginning. Therefore, new essentialist hypotheses and a new project of a theory must be tentatively proposed. Etc. The hidden essence is not something which can only be dogmatically believed in. Everything may be grasped hypothetically, for the hypotheticity lies in our attitude toward something, not in the nature of that something; empirical facts or God may be grasped either dogmatically or hypothetically. The hidden essences of phenomena may be treated as subject of hypotheses as everything else.

2. On the status of the idealizational methodology

Idealization about idealization. It is of importance for the correct understanding of the idealizational methodology that it is self-reflective. Not only does it focus on the method of idealization as it is used in science, it applies this method to itself. Not only does it claim that the method of idealization is the crucial method of scientific investigation (in the empirical sciences), but the idealizational approach to science itself is built as an idealizational theory. The remaining methods are to be understood as somehow related to the method of idealization. How? The structure of the (idealizational) theory of idealization gives some tentative answers to that question.

Consider, for instance, one of the presentations of the approach in question (cf. 1977d, 1980, Part III). It is composed of five models beginning with the most abstract one assuming of the investigator that (a) he attempts to build the first scientific theory in a given field (and hence the only available data for him are his philosophical presuppositions and empirical facts); (b) he is capable of conducting perfect experiments (that is, of annulling the influence of all the factors which he takes to be secondary for the given magnitude); (c) he is able to list all the factors considered to be secondary for the magnitude in question, etc. These are, obviously, idealizing conditions modeling the scientific investigation in a manner similar to the way in which the condition that a given economic system is in the state of perfect competition idealizes that system, for instance. Under these conditions some hypotheses are put forward:

(I.1) *the structure of a scientific law*: the idealizing conditions neglecting all the factors considered to be secondary are placed in the antecedent, the formula expressing the working of the factor(s) suspected to be principal for the given magnitude is placed in the consequent;

(I.2) *the structure of a scientific theory*: it begins with the law followed by all its concretizations;

(I.3) *the structure of explanation*: the explanatory chain begins with the idealizational law and contains all its concretizations including the final concretization which entails, with appropriate initial conditions, the explanandum;

(I.4) *the method of testing of idealizational theories*: it is the method of perfect experiments;

And so on.

Now, (I.1)-(I.4) etc. are formulae of idealizational statements which are true, if at all, under the idealizing conditions (a), (b), (c), etc. That is, the statements of model I are, strictly speaking, conditionals of the form: if (a), (b), (c), etc., then (I.1). These conditions are further waived and the formulae (I.1)-(I.4) etc. are modified (i.e., appropriate conditionals are concretized). The details are in my (1977d, 1980). Let me restrict myself here only to examples relevant for further discussion.

After the removal of (a) we obtain model II. In it, (I.1) still holds as well but (I.2) significantly changes and is replaced by the following claim:

(II.2) A scientific theory is a sequence of deductive systems (called models) $M^k, M^{k-1}, \ldots, M^0$, each composed of some axioms and theorems, such that, roughly, axioms A^{j-1} are concretizations of axioms A^j.

In model II it is not true any more that the structure of an explanatory chain overlaps with that of a scientific theory as was the case in model I. Instead of a simple, linear form it takes a bit more complicated shape:

(II.3) the explanatory chain begins with an idealizational law and its consequences in model M^k of the theory including the relevant one which is concretized in models $M^{k-1}, \ldots, M^0$ up to the final concretization entailing, with appropriate initial conditions, the explanandum.

In model II, claim (I.4) is slightly modified as well.

In model III, condition (b) is waived and the procedure of approximation is introduced. Now, the scientist may have no justified hypotheses concerning the working of at least some secondary factors. For the sake of simplicity assume he has confirmed hypotheses on none secondary factors. Thus the only thing which he can do is to approximate an appropriate idealizational statement, that is, to waive all the remaining idealizing conditions at once and to claim that in spite of this the joint deviation from the formula of that statement does not exceed the threshold adopted in advance. Approximation proves to be a subsidiary means in relation to the procedure of concretization. When a researcher is not in a position, or there is no cognitive need, to apply the latter, he resorts to approximating idealizational statements.

Thus, it turns out that in model III the notion of final concretization disappears altogether and all concretizations are completed not with strict factual statements but with approximations of the last chains in the appropriate sequences of concretizations. As a result, formula (II.2) is not valid any more and must be replaced by a new idea concerning the structure of the scientific theory as a sequence $M^k, M^{k-1}, \ldots, M^i, AM^i$. The claim (II.3) changes only slightly. In contrast to that, the claim (II.4) changes significantly. In models I-II the Popperian rule of falsification was kept in principle. In model III, it turns out that the discrepancy between the facts and the (last) idealizational concretization of the law may be diminished by continuing further the procedure of concretization and instead of (immediate) falsification, further corrections of the initial law are possible. The rule of falsification is not removed, however, but limited: it works only in the case when all the efforts to further concretize the law fail in the sense of not significantly diminishing the initial discrepancy (see also below).

In model IV, idealizational statements in the sense hitherto employed disappear almost altogether. It turns out that normally, apart from idealizing conditions, scientific hypotheses contain the semi-idealizing clause: "all the not yet recognized factors of a given type essential for a given magnitude do not work at all". In this case, apart from some factors which are identified by the researcher, he admits an open class of interferences which are treated by him *en bloc*. The removal of the semi-idealizing clause might be interpreted as generating probabilistic statements (my 1980, pp. 166ff).

Consequently, both the structure of a single statement, of the whole theory, the shape of the explanatory chain and the way of testing significantly change in model IV. Similarly in model V and in further models which will not be referred to here.

Concretizing the idealizational conception of science. Not only the structure of the idealizational methodology falls under its own theses but the same holds for the way in which this approach develops. The initial conception which may be roughly identified with the one outlined above (cf. my 1977d, 1980) has been criticized in numerous writings because of the inadequacy of its even most realistic models. The reasons normally given were various discrepancies from the actual scientific conduct. Such criticisms led to the introduction of new idealizing conditions, which had to be taken for the initial conception to be acceptable. Then those conditions have been waived and the theory modified accordingly so that the very aspect of the actual scientific conduct which had falsified the initial theory proved to be an argument confirming the modified version of that theory. It can be seen that analyses of the kind fall under the rule of dialectical correspondence put forward in Nowakowa (1975a-b, cf. also Nowakowa and Nowak, this volume). In other words, the idealizational approach to science evolves according to the rule of dialectical correspondence found in science of which it is a theory. Numerous undertakings of the kind have taken place. To mention just a few derivative constructions — *ceteris-paribus*-construction (Patryas 1975a, 1982), proto-idealization (Brzeziński 1978, 1985), stabilization (Chwalisz 1979, Zielińska 1981), para-idealization (Maruszewski 1983), aggregation (Łastowski 1987, 1990), normalization (Nowak 1991b). A brief survey of more important extensions of the original conception, up to 1991, is presented in my (1992b).

One should thus distinguish between the idealizational theory of science which may be, roughly, identified with the conception outlined in (1977d, 1980) and the idealizational approach to science developed by various authors who treat that conception as a mere starting point while extending in various directions and modifying it sometimes significantly. As I shall try to make clear, some of the objections posed by my critics may be correct as far as my own proposals are concerned but fail, if we consider the idealizational approach to science.

3. Some additional explanations

At first I would like, however, to deal with the objections that result from what I take to be a misunderstanding of my position. Likely, I was not clear enough on at least some of the points below and I take this opportunity to explain my position more clearly.

Idealization is not abstraction. The crucial point which follows from the proper understanding of the notion of idealization is that idealization is not abstraction (cf. my 1975, 1980, pp. 31ff, 1990). Roughly, abstraction consists in a passage from properties *AB* to *A*, idealization consists in a passage from *AB* to *A-B*. For instance, the move from the notion of an open capitalist economy (*CEO*) to the notion of a capitalist economy (*CE*) is an act of abstraction, whereas an act of idealization would consist, for instance, in a passage from *CEO* to the notion of a closed capitalist economy (*CE-O*).

G. Jorland claims that the method of idealization "is akin to the classical abstraction and determination operations" known from the textbooks of logic (this volume, p. 277). Not so. An abstract (general) statement:

(3.1) students are laborious

applies to our world directly, whereas, say, the statement:

(3.2) $(x)\ (ff(x)\ \&\ R(x) = 0 \rightarrow s(x) = 1\backslash 2gt^2(x))$

does not. Instead, (3.2) applies to the ideal world in which freely falling (*ff*) bodies do not meet any resistance (*R*) on their paths depending in the way shown in formula (3.2) on the gravitational constant (*g*) and the time (*t*) of free fall.

Idealization and the "rule of decreasing extension and increasing intension". Moreover, it is actually the "operation of abstraction and determination" which suffices to show why Jorland's claim fails. According to the famous classical formula, as the intension of a series of terms increases (they become more and more abstract), their extension decreases (they become more and more determinate) and, *vice versa*, as the intension decreases, their extension increases. We have already considered an example of such a series of terms: "open capitalist economy", "capitalist economy", "economy". Such a rule does not work, however, for the series of idealizational terms, that is, ones whose meaning characteristics (a set of meaning postulates, a partial definition, a definition, etc.) embraces at least one idealizing condition. The extension of the term "closed capitalist economy" is not narrower than the extension of the term "capitalist economy"; the two have no elements in common, that is, the intersection of these extensions is empty. The "law of decreasing extension and increasing intension" from the textbooks of elementary logic does not hold for idealizational terms.

Idealization and falsifiability. In the light of the outlined approach it is also obvious that idealizational statements are not directly falsifiable, only factual statements are. Indeed, to falsify (3.2) directly would mean to state that for a certain *a* such that $ff(a)$ & $R(a) = 0$, also $s(a) \neq 1/2gt^2(a)$ which is obviously impossible because of the falsity of the instantiation of the second condition of the law of free fall. How is, then, possible to claim that "[i]t's only idealized statements that are [directly – L.N.] falsifiable" (Jordan, this volume, p. 274)? It seems to me that the reason for that lies in a confusion about the relation between idealization and abstraction. Abstract statements are factuals and are directly falsifiable, indeed.

And what about falsifiability of the idealizational statements? Here, K.D. Hoover poses one of his queries: "Can we test idealized models?" (this volume, p. 49; bold in the original). We can, although with some peculiarities. The main thing to be said here is that in case they meet counterexamples they are yet not falsified but further concretized.

Let the idealizational statement be given:

$$\text{t:}\quad (x)\ (G(x)\ \&\ p(x) = 0\ \&\ q(x) = 0\ \&\ r(x) = 0 \rightarrow F(x) = f(H(x)))$$

which undergoes a one-step concretization:

$$\text{Ct:}\quad (x)\ (G(x)\ \&\ p(x) = 0\ \&\ q(x) = 0\ \&\ r(x) \neq 0 \Rightarrow \Rightarrow F(x) = f'(H(x), r(x)))).$$

Assume that for one reason or another already the latter statement is approximated:

$$\text{ACt:}(x)\ (G(x)\ \&\ p(x) \neq 0\ \&\ q(x) \neq 0\ \&\ r(x) \neq 0 \Rightarrow \Rightarrow F(x) \underset{\varepsilon}{\approx} f'(H(x), r(x))))$$

and that it is proved to be false for an object a:

$$\text{(3.3)}\quad G(a)\ \&\ r(a) = \text{R}\ \&\ H(a) = \text{H}\ \&\ F(a) = \text{F}\ \&\ \text{D} = |f'(\text{H}, \text{R}) - \text{F}| > \varepsilon.$$

Following the rule of hypotheticism we should falsify thesis t. Yet, this would be obviously irrational since the source of deviation D may well lie in the fact that, e.g., the working of the factor q on F is yet not accounted for. Therefore, the first thing to be done is to concretize t further:

$$\text{CCt:}\quad (x)\ (G(x)\ \&\ p(x) = 0\ \&\ q(x) \neq 0\ \&\ r(x) \neq 0 \Rightarrow \Rightarrow F(x) = f''(H(x), r(x), q(x)))$$

and then approximate it:

$$\text{ACCt:}\ (x)\ (G(x)\ \&\ p(x) \neq 0\ \&\ q(x) \neq 0\ \&\ r(x) \neq 0 \Rightarrow \Rightarrow F(x) \underset{\varepsilon}{\approx} f''(H(x), r(x), q(x))).$$

If the results of observation of the object a will be this time:

$$\text{(3.4)}\quad G(a)\ \&\ q(a) = \text{Q}\ \&\ r(a) = \text{R}\ \&\ H(a) = \text{H}\ \&\ F(a) = \text{F}\ \&\ \text{D}' = |f''(\text{H}, \text{R}, \text{Q}) - \text{F}| < \varepsilon,$$

then actually the same fact which falsified (in the sense of hypotheticism) t at present confirms it.[2] That is why it would be absurd to reject t on the basis of the former observation.

That does not mean, contrary to what Hoover suspects (this volume, p. 49), that idealizational statements are not falsifiable at all. Assume that the results of the second observation are different:

$$\text{(3.5)}\quad G(a)\ \&\ q(a) = \text{Q}\ \&\ r(a) = \text{R}\ \&\ H(a) = \text{H}\ \&\ F(a) = \text{F}\ \&\ \text{D}'' = |f''(\text{H}, \text{R}, \text{Q}) - \text{F}| > \varepsilon.$$

The same rule of testing forces the researcher to continue the process of concretization of t:

$$\text{CCCt:}\ (x)\ (G(x)\ \&\ p(x) \neq 0\ \&\ q(x) \neq 0\ \&\ r(x) \neq 0 \Rightarrow \Rightarrow F(x) = f'''(H(x), r(x), q(x), p(x))).$$

---

[2] This is the rule applied by Marx in *Capital*. Hence Hamminga and De Marchi (this volume) correctly observe that Marx would manage with counterexamples in that style (p. 38). It is not clear, however, on what basis they distinguish McCulloch's rule of dealing with counterexamples ("Whereas you – erroneously – 'see' a counterexample, I teach you to recognize that it is actually an example" – *ibid.*) and contrast it with the Marxian one. I would say that the Marxian rule actually consists in revealing to the critic that where he sees a counterexample (to a too early approximation of the idealizational law) it proves to appear (after further steps of concretization) actually an example confirming the law.

This time he gets the final concretization of t with which to set directly the outcomes of observation. If these are the following, however:

$$(3.6)\ G(a)\ \&\ p(a) = \mathrm{P}\ \&\ q(a) = \mathrm{Q}\ \&\ r(\mathrm{a}) = \mathrm{R}\ \&\ H(a) = \mathrm{H}\ \&\ F(a) = \mathrm{F}\ \&\ \mathrm{D}''' = |f'''(\mathrm{H, R, Q, P}) - \mathrm{F}| > \varepsilon,$$

then t is finally falsified. That is, there are no possible concretizations programmed in its form any more and the verdict of experience must be finally accepted.[3] In sum, the above rule of testing — first try to correct a statement, falsify it as late as all the attempts to remove the discrepancies with facts finally fail — may be termed the rule of delayed falsification.

Reification of idealization and *ad hoc* idealization. Given the idealizational statement t, one thing is forbidden: to relate t directly (i.e. without concretization or approximation) to reality using the following reasoning pattern:

$$(3.7){:}\quad \frac{\begin{array}{l}(x)\ (G(x)\ \&\ p(x) = 0\ \&\ q(x) = 0\ \&\ r(x) = 0 \Rightarrow \\ \qquad\qquad \Rightarrow F(x) = f(H(x)))\\ G(a)\end{array}}{F(a) = f(H(a)).}$$

This is the fallacy of reification of idealization. The reason for considering this reasoning pattern fallacious is obvious. In inference (3.7) the conclusion does not follow from the premisses. On the other hand, if the enthymematic premisses, $p(a) = 0$, etc. will be added to the scheme (3.7), the body of premisses will prove to be contradictory. For, according to the knowledge on which our idealizational statement t is based, $p(a) \neq 0$, $q(a) \neq 0$ and $r(a) \neq 0$.

Let us add for the sake of symmetry that, given the factual statement:

$$(3.8)\ (x)\ (G(x) \Rightarrow F(x) = f(H(x))),$$

which is falsified by finding such a that $G(a)\ \&\ F(a) \neq f(H(a))$, it is forbidden to add an idealizing condition *ad hoc*, that is, without making an effort to remove it and to correspondingly correct the formula of the statement. In other words, passage from (3.8) to t is forbidden as long as it is merely a means of saving a threatened theorem.

---

[3] Hoover claims that the rule of testing outlined in the text makes of the initial, most idealized model something similar to "a Lakatosian hard core" (this volume, p. 49). In a sense – yes. But still there is a significant difference. The hard core is immune from the negative outcomes of experience due to adoption of the additional hypotheses making possible a reinterpretation of those outcomes. Not so in case of the rule in question. For it results from what is inherent in a model without any additional statements.

Idealization and explanation. W. Diederich claims that in the model of explanation (let us take for the sake of simplicity its non-approximativist version) which I defend:

$$T^k \; concr \ldots concr \; T^1 \; concr \; T^0 \; \& \; I \Rightarrow E$$

the whole story with concretization is redundant because what actually explains the fact E under the initial conditions I is the factual law T^0. Two arguments are given for this supposition.

First, we use in explanation only the final expression $T^0 \; \& \; I \Rightarrow E$ which is to perfectly agree with Hempel's model because we cannot apply the idealizational laws to the real conditions. Second, all the idealizational statements are consequences (the limiting cases) of the factual presumption T^0.

I do not agree with the first argument. The legitimation for the use of idealizational statements in explanation is their role in deriving the factual statement T^0 *via* concretization. They legitimate T^0, not E directly. It will be useful to employ the well-known distinction between "explaining laws" and "explaining the facts". One could say that the idealizational premisses, including the first of them, i.e. the law T^k, explain the (general) factual statement T^0, whereas the latter explains the (singular) statement about the fact E.

The second argument is much more subtle for it refers to a controversial problem (cf. Birner, this volume) of the logical relationship between an idealizational statement and its concretizations. That is really a serious problem and it may be solved in various ways. One is them is what Diederich claims: *concr* is the relation of entailment. But that position is not mine. Here is the form of the nomological elements of an explanatory chain:

$$\mathrm{T}^k\colon \; (x) \; ([G(x) \; \& \; p_1(x) = 0 \; \& \ldots \& \; p_{k-1}(x) = 0 \; \& \; p_k(x) = 0] \Rightarrow \\ \Rightarrow F(x) = f_k(H(x)))$$

. . . .

$$\mathrm{T}^i\colon \; (x) \; ([G(x) \; \& \; p_1(x) = 0 \; \& \ldots \& \; p_i(x) = 0 \; \& \; p_{i+1}(x) \neq 0 \; \& \\ \ldots \& \; p_{k-1}(x) \neq 0 \; \& \; p_k(x) \neq 0] \Rightarrow \\ \Rightarrow F(x) = f_i[H(x), p_k(x), \ldots, p_{i+1}(x)])$$

. . . .

$$\mathrm{T}^0\colon \; (x) \; ([G(x) \; \& \; p_1(x) \neq 0 \; \& \; p_2(x) \neq 0 \; \& \ldots \& \; p_{k-1}(x) \neq 0 \; \& \\ \& \; p_k(x) \neq 0] \Rightarrow \\ \Rightarrow F(x) = f_0[H(x), p_k(x), \ldots, p_2(x), p_1(x)]).$$

It is visible that T^{i+1} is not more general than T^{i}: their ranges of application do not intersect. That is so obvious that it should be explained how it is possible that the prominent methodologist does not acknowledge this very fact. The reason, I conjecture, is that concretization is (mis)conceived (cf. also Krajewski 1977) as an operation of deleting an idealizing condition, not as one of replacing it with an appropriate realistic condition. For instance, if concretization is understood as a passage from t to

(3.9) $(x)\ (G(x)\ \&\ p(x) = 0\ \&\ q(x) = 0 \Rightarrow F(x) = f'(H(x), r(x)))$

and then to

(3.10) $(x)\ (G(x)\ \&\ p(x) = 0 \Rightarrow F(x) = f''(H(x), r(x), q(x)))$

and, in the final case, to:

(3.11) $(x)\ (G(x) \Rightarrow F(x) = f'''(H(x), r(x), q(x), p(x)))$,

then it is obvious to claim that concretization consists in generalization. However, (3.9) differs from Ct, and so do statements (3.10) and CCt. In the final case, (3.11) does not fall under the scheme T^0. The statement (3.11) is neither factual, as T^0 is, nor idealizational, as $T^k, \ldots, T^1$ are. (3.11) is a more general statement applying both to the ideal worlds deprived of factors p_k and/or,..., and/or p_1 and the actual world in which all these factors operate.

How to interpret this metaphysically is another matter, and my present views on that subject, I would like to add, differ from those of the seventies, i.e. ones underlying the writings W. Diederich deals with. At present, I am rather inclined to think that D. Lewis's doctrine of modal possibilism requires a significant strengthening and to admit the existence of the ideal worlds including the empty world ("nothingness") in which all the magnitudes are idealized (reduced — cf. below). But the outlining of this metaphysical proposal (cf. some elements of it in my 1991a, 1992a) would lead us too far here. For the task of this discussion it suffices to say that what I have not changed are the above schemes of an idealizational statement and its concretization. And those schemes imply that the former is not a special case of the latter. It is only the formula (consequent) of the idealizational statement which is — if taken in itself — a special case of the formula of its concretization. But the unit of science are, I am still inclined to think, not the formulae themselves — let alone the formulae treated formally, without a substantive (e.g. economical) interpretation — but the conditionals.

The form of a law of science. But this is what Diederich calls in question as "anachronic". Well, that is really a rather traditional point of view. What matters, however, are arguments. My arguments would run as follows.

It is notoriously true that scientists use not the conditionals but the formulae, e.g. equations, calling them scientific laws. *Prima facie* then, my critic is in a better position as what he claims does agree with the linguistic custom in science. However, the way in which an expression is used often does not matter too much: sometimes it is of significance, sometimes it is confused; think, for instance, of a biologist who would be inclined to classify plants according to the natural language – a crucial category for him would be one of "vegetables" which is an absurd notion from a genetic standpoint.

A proper criterion for such a discussion would be, I think, the following: assuming a given linguistic stipulation, try to explain from your standpoint the reasons underlying the contrary one adopted by your protagonist. The problem from my point of view is, then, to understand why the scientists call the formulae the scientific laws. The answer is that they spontaneously look for the factors considered to be principal for the investigated magnitudes. The way such a factor influences a given magnitude is grasped in the formula of the appropriate idealizational law; the antecedent of it abstracts instead from the working of factors treated to be secondary for this magnitude. The list of those factors always changes and is never considered to be complete. In case of finding counterexamples for the formula, the scientist normally assumes that the formula is correct, it is only the list of secondary factors which is incomplete and attempts to find a source of the discrepancy, i.e. an hitherto unknown secondary factor causing the deviations. As a result, the antecedent of the conditional changes with the formula which is kept in force (cf. 1980, pp. 201ff, Nowakowa and Nowak, this volume). Therefore, the conditional T^k, quite "symmetric" from the methodologist's point of view is for the scientist evidently "non-symmetric" – the consequent of it is for him much more important than its antecedent. It is not surprising that in his linguistic custom he focuses on what is crucial for him.

If I am not mistaken, given my assumptions it is possible to explain why science applies the terminology contrary to mine. I cannot, however, imagine how Diederich could explain the fact that sometimes scientists explicitly formulate idealizational conditionals calling them the laws of nature. For instance: Kittel et al. (1969, p. 77) expresses the law of inertia as follows: "$\mathbf{a} = 0$, when $\mathbf{F} = 0$". Marx formulated the law of value in the following manner: "*if* demand and supply balance each other, *then* the market prices of commodities correspond to their natural prices, that is, their values defined by the corresponding amounts of labor indispensable for the production of these commodities" (Marx 1845, p. 141; italics of the original); etc. Is it really permissible for a methodologist to make the law of inertia "shorter" distorting the original formulation?[4]

When a theory is realistic? Obviously, I do not take arguments of this kind as "decisive" in any sense. What can be seriously said is simply this: in the respect analyzed above the conception of law as an idealizational conditional agrees with scientific facts better than one identifying the law with a formula. I am perfectly aware that there are also respects under which the latter prevails the former. If the history of philosophy of science teaches us anything at all, it teaches us that no "decisive arguments" in our domain exist. Everything is instead a matter of balancing arguments and counterarguments in order to keep the basic idea that underlies the whole conception working. And I guess that it is in this respect that Diederich and the present writer disagree. The idea in question is that of realistic interpretation of a scientific theory. For him "realistic" in science means "sufficiently close to the empirical facts"; this is an empiricist tradition or, rather, what remained out of it in the so sophisticated approach as one W. Diederich adheres to. For me, "real" means in science "essential", that is, "not disturbed by the accidentalities"; this is the Hegelian tradition in which "real" stands in an intimate relation with "essential" (and "true"). How to decide between the two without engaging in an open metaphysical discussion which I want to avoid here? As philosophers of science we should not develop

[4] I shall not comment on Diederich's objections derived from the "episode in the history of thermodynamics" as they arise from his negligence of the dynamics of idealization (cf. my 1980, pp. 201ff, Nowakowa 1975, 1994) and the present volume contains a paper of mine and I. Nowakowa's devoted entirely to this subject.

Another matter which I leave aside here has to do with Diederich's remark that "idealizing laws (because of their conditional formulation) are – if the counterfactual assumptions are completely stated – factually true!" (this volume, p. 264). It is correct that, for example, (3.2) is factually true. The point is, however, that for the same reason it is also true that:

$$ff(x)\ \&\ R(x) = 0 \Rightarrow s(x) \neq 1/2\,gt^2(x).$$

To my understanding this proves that the notion of truthfulness that allows for such a qualification is a very weak one for the goals of methodology and requires a significant strengthening. There are various ways to strengthen the classical notion of truth. Nowakowa's (1977, 1992) proposal of the essentialist notion of truth is one of them. In (1980, pp. 134ff) I have accepted it, but now I am rather inclined to think of the matter in different terms (cf. a tentative proposal in 1991a). Still, what is required is, I believe, a conception of truth which would be able to do justice rather to idealizational laws than to claims of the "It is snowing"-type.

an overt metaphysics, we are instead obliged to respect the metaphysical assumptions accepted in science. My conjecture is that science respects an ontology which is closer to Hegel rather than to Bacon. The most straightforward reasons are these.

a. Consider the current terminology in science. It is Newton's most idealized laws for the mass points, inertial systems etc. that are termed "principles" not their numerous concretizations much closer to the empirical world. The closer is a statement to the empirical facts the lesser chance it has to gain the dignity of a "principle", "basic law", etc. Also proper names ("Ohm's law", "Lorenz's transformations", "Domar-Harrod's model" etc.) are attached most often to idealizational laws (i.e., the most abstract idealizational statements), not to their concretizations closer to the actual facts.

b. The quite spontaneous criteria of evaluation in science incline us to name a crucial discovery (an interesting or innovative idea etc.) a new proposal of the idealizational law in the given domain, and not any concretization of the already established law; the terminological custom noted above is only a manifestation of this. Were the attitude of scientists close to the one adopted by my critic, one could rightly expect the reverse to be true. For the new idealizational law as such does not contribute to the diminishing of the discrepancies with facts (sometimes the opposite holds true), it is the concretizations of the old idealizational law that do.

c. Most important changes in science, sometimes referred to as revolutionary, consist actually in replacing one idealizational law by another (e.g., the Aristotelian principle of inertia by the Galilean-Newtonian one), not in their concretizations although it is actually the former, not the latter, which make the whole machinery closer to empirical facts.

And so on, and so forth. All this testifies not to any negligence of the empirical testing in science but, I would risk saying, to a better understanding of its role. First and foremost, nobody knows in advance what is essential for what. That is a matter of theoretical hypotheses which undergo constant tests eliminating less adequate images of the hidden, essential sides of reality.

The problem of the "conceptual concretization". Diederich points out that the process of concretization as it is reconstructed in my writings lacks an important dimension which is the "conceptual concretization, i.e. the explication of the eventually necessary categories" (this volume, p. 260). That is certainly true. All the considerations concerning the procedure of concretization and of its changes presuppose that the conceptual apparatus is ready made which obviously need not be true. This simplification underlying the idealizational conception of science has not been waived and the problem what should appropriately be changed in the standard notions of the conception (concretization, dialectical correspondence, dialectical refutation etc.) still waits for its author. I must admit, both the idealizational methodology and its concrete applications, including my analyses of Marx referred to by Diederich, suffer because of this limitation.[5]

Some Marxian themes. The main misunderstanding underlying G. Jorland's critique is, if I am not mistaken, this. He does not account for the fact that my reconstruction of Marx's scientific practice is partial. I take only one theorem from only one of Marx's numerous theories in order to reconstruct the changes it undergoes throughout his three-volume book. The only formula which was a subject of my interest in (1971a-b, 1980) is this: $P(x) = V(x)$ and I collected its transformations[6] depending on the removal of the idealizing conditions initially underlying it. And that is all. Jordan instead takes my modest work as a systematic reconstruction of the whole economic content of *Das Kapital*. That is why he may object, e.g., "that no assumptions concerning wages, fix and circulating capital and cost price are made" (this volume, p. 269). These subjects, so important as they are, are subsequent steps in the process of reconstruction of the system of the capitalist economy but they do not seem to be variables to be straightforwardly introduced into the formula of prices.

To be sure, my intention was to reveal on the example of the law of value and its concretizations how Marx does the scientific job in the whole. But one thing is to pretend to give a typical case of the job and the other is to claim that the case is actually the whole job. I was, and I still am, of the opinion that the law of value and its "logical history" throughout *Das Kapital* is a typical application of Marx's "method of ascending from the abstract to the concrete". Perhaps the same method is also a clue to the understanding of the way in which the bunch of various theories (of value, of the surplus value, of profit, of reproduction

---

[5] There are only two partial attempts to undertake the problem in idealizational terms (Tuchańska 1980 and Łastowski 1987) but they do not do that in all its complexity as it undoubtedly deserves. The point is that the idealizational methodology presupposes quite a standard theory of the scientific language. Thus, the releasing of these assumptions and making use of the structuralist ideas, including those developed by Diederich, would likely open new possibilities of enriching the idealizational approach to science.

[6] These transformations were mainly of a qualitative nature. A systematic and quantitative reconstruction of the concretizations of the law of value in *Das Kapital* is presented, with all the economic subtleties, by Hamminga (1990).

etc.) is structured in *Das Kapital*. But of the two subjects only the former was mine. I did not write about the latter because I did not, and until today I do not, understand the methodological rules with which these theories relate one to another. I did not make any further progress in this direction simply because several years after my work on Marx's theory of value I have started to criticize Marx trying to find an alternative to his historical materialism (1979, 1983); non-Marxian historical materialism is made, however, according to what I had earlier found in the Marxian method (1983, pp. 3-16). As a result of this work, to be frank, I lost an interest in deepening the earlier reconstruction of the contents of *Das Kapital*. On the other hand, it is obvious that my private biography has nothing to do with the cognitive import of the problem. And it is a real problem how, methodologically speaking, Marx tied his theories in order to reconstruct the whole capitalist mode of production. Marx was a great scholar and such a problem certainly deserves to be undertaken. Yet, that was not the problem I was trying to solve in the writings analyzed by Jorland.[7]

4. Problems with the idealizational nature of the theory of idealization

Presently, I would like to discuss objections which I take to result from not realizing the methodological nature of the idealizational approach to science. I will argue that since this metascientific conception is idealizational itself, the counterarguments do not undermine it.

The case of final concretization. Since the idealizational methodology is an idealization in itself, some (meta-)methodological conclusions follow. First and foremost, it is inadmissible to relate an idealizational methodological statement directly to actual scientific facts, if a concreti-

[7] Jorland also charges me for "eliminating the contradictions instead of accounting for them". I must admit, I do not understand what the "contradictions" mean in terms of variables introduced to a given simple formula and what Jordan takes to be the "elimination" of "contradictions" in the same context.

One more minor point about contradictions, this time in a well-defined sense of logical contradictions. I tried to show that the famous Böhm-Bawerk's criticism of Marx's vol. III of *Das Kapital* does not hold true if one realizes that the method applied by Marx was the concretization of the idealizational law of value (1980, pp. 246ff). Jordan claims that "the contradiction between value and price is not apparent". Maybe he is right. Assume he is. Then, it is his job to explain how one of the greatest minds in the history of social sciences could have committed a childish contradiction: price = value (in vol. I), price = price of production ≠ value (in vol. III).

zation of the claim under scrutiny is made within the criticized conception. Such is the case with one of the theses of M.C.W. Janssen's paper: "In the above I have criticized the relevance of Nowak's model of idealization and concretization for economics. I have not argued that concretization is not something to be wished for, but instead that fully concretized models are far beyond reach" (this volume, p. 113). It is the thesis (I.2) which claims that final concretization is possible — for the ideal science fulfilling conditions (a), (b), (c), etc. Already in model III it turns out that practically final concretization is impossible and it is approximation which is the last word of the more realistic (although still very abstract) theoretician from model III.

The internal and external concretization. Another of Janssen's objections is also based on not realizing the difference between what is claimed in model I and in further models of the idealizational conception of science. The objection reads: "Nowak's model of concretization should allow for the possibility of concretization by means of adding equations, not only by means of adding variables to *one* [italics of the original — L.N.] equation" (this volume, p. 112). In model I concretization consists in "adding variables to one equation", indeed. In model II, however, apart from such an internal concretization, new idealizational statement with new formula appears at a lower model of the idealizational theory. This statement tells us what the magnitude introduced at a given level of concretization depends on itself (cf. my 1980, model II, examples may be also found in Nowakowa and Nowak, this volume, pp. 139-40).

Idealization and the *ceteris paribus* clause. The replies to the above objections were based on what I term the idealizational conception of science. Now we pass to objections which, I must admit, correctly reveal some weaknesses of my initial proposal but, at the same time, the problems noted are already solved in some later writings by various authors.

M. Janssen (this volume, pp. 111ff) considers the relation between the two formulae:

(4.1) $PT = \alpha'_0 + \alpha'_1 I + \varepsilon'$

(4.2) $PT = \alpha_0 + \alpha_1 I + \alpha_2 W + \varepsilon$

and claims that the latter is a concretization of the former. Not so. The formulae may be reconstructed either as semi-idealizational statements or as *ceteris paribus* statements (Patryas 1976, 1982). Since I have already had an occasion to present a semi-idealizational interpretation of the econometric model (1972, 1980, pp. 170f), here I would like to present an interpretation in terms of the *ceteris paribus* clause.

Referring to our simplified scheme considered above, the statement of such a type may be formulated thus:

$$\mathrm{t}^{\mathrm{cp}}\colon \quad (x)\ (G(x)\ \&\ p(x) = 0\ \&\ q(x) = 0\ \&\ r(x) = 0\ \&\ \forall_n F(x) = 0 \Rightarrow F(x) = f(H(x)))$$

This statement, in comparison to the standard idealizational statement considered above, t, possesses only one component more, the *ceteris paribus* clause. The clause $\forall_n F(x) = 0$ is read: "all the remaining factors influencing F take on value 0 for x"; n is the level of admissible deviations adopted in advance. To simplify, the clause postulates that the difference between the space of essential factors or F and its image, as composed of $\{H, r, q, p\}$, is empty and that the influence of all those other factors essential for F, i.e. not (yet) identified disturbances, leads to deviations in the values of F at most by n.

The procedure of concretization leads to the sequence of statements, the final of which is of the form:

$$\mathrm{CCCt}^{\mathrm{cp}}\colon (x)\ (G(x)\ \&\ p(x) \neq 0\ \&\ q(x) \neq 0\ \&\ r(x) \neq 0\ \&\ \forall F_n(x) = 0 \Rightarrow F(x) = f'''(H(x), r(x), q(x), p(x))).$$

As is visible, this formula is not an idealizational statement any more, but it is not a factual statement either. It is a pure statement with a *ceteris paribus* clause. It does not describe the phenomena (we are fully aware of the fact that apart from H, r, q, p there are other factors influencing F) but it does not abstract from any definite magnitude (we are unable to identify the disturbances, or not interested in doing so).

According to Patryas (1976, 1982), $\mathrm{CCCt}^{\mathrm{cp}}$ is factualized, that is, the influence of the disturbances is accounted for as responsible for the deviations at most by n:

$$\mathrm{FCCCt}^{\mathrm{cp}}\colon (x)\ (G(x)\ \&\ p(x) \neq 0\ \&\ q(x) \neq 0\ \&\ r(x) \neq 0\ \&\ \exists F_n(x) \neq 0 \Rightarrow F(x) \underset{n}{\approx} f'''(H(x), r(x), q(x), p(x))).$$

Factualization is thus a procedure more similar to approximation than to concretization. However, it cannot be identified with approximation. When approximating we are able to identify the factors whose global influence is accounted for. In contrast, when factualizing we are only aware of the rough fact that there are some disturbances whose nature is unknown to us.

Passing to the example discussed by Janssen, it may appear that two procedures are to be disentangled there. First is the usual concretization, second is factualization. Roughly, we have to do with two pairs of statements connected by factualization:

$$(4.3) \quad W = 0 \ \& \ \forall_{\varepsilon'} PT = 0 \Rightarrow PT = \alpha'_0 + \alpha'_1 I$$

$$(4.3f) \quad W = 0 \ \& \ \exists_{\varepsilon'} PT \neq 0 \Rightarrow PT \underset{\varepsilon'}{\approx} \alpha'_0 + \alpha'_1 I;$$

$$(4.4) \quad W \neq 0 \ \& \ \forall_{\varepsilon} PT = 0 \Rightarrow PT = \alpha_0 + \alpha_1 I + \alpha_2 W$$

$$(4.4f) \quad W \neq 0 \ \& \ \exists_{\varepsilon} PT = 0 \Rightarrow PT \underset{\varepsilon}{\approx} \alpha_0 + \alpha_1 I + \alpha_2 W.$$

At the same time (4.4) is a concretization of (4.3). The question arises what is the relation between (4.2) and (4.1). It seems that the closest reconstruction of it would be to claim that it holds between (4.3f) and (4.4f). These two are not, however, self-sustained units of scientific knowledge, they are derivative forms of more elementary units (4.3) and (4.4). Hence our analysis must be continued.

In order to deepen it, let us notice that in (4.4f) there occurs a new threshold ε, instead of ε'. Normally, the change of the threshold of admissible deviations is a symptom of a decomposition of the set of disturbances, that is, of the fact that one additional essential factor has been identified and may be made explicit in an appropriate idealizing condition (see also below). This shows that (4.4) is perhaps too hastily conceptualized as a concretization of (4.3). One may suspect that what matters is perhaps the connection of dialectical correspondence (Nowakowa 1975a-b, 1994). Here is the paradigmatic scheme of the relation in question:

$$(4.5) \quad (x)\ (G(x) \Rightarrow F(x) = f(H(x)))$$

$$(4.6) \quad (x)\ (G(x)\ \&\ p(x) = 0 \Rightarrow F(x) = f(H(x)))$$

$$(4.7) \quad (x)\ (G(x)\ \&\ p(x) \neq 0 \Rightarrow F(x) = f(H(x), p(x))).$$

The relation, to put it briefly, expresses a certain historical tendency: a factual statement is falsified; a source of discrepancy between (4.5) and the facts is identified as the working of an additional essential factor for F, viz. p; this new factor is abstracted in the idealizational statement (4.6); its influence is assessed in the concretization (4.7) of (4.6). In sum, the dialectical correspondence consists in the fact that the formula from (4.5) is made more abstract in (4.6) and then more concrete in (4.7). That tendency may be treated as an explication in idealizational terms of the phenomenon of puzzle-solving peculiar to what Kuhn has called "normal science".

One may conjecture now that (4.2) is not a factualization of (4.1) but that what is involved here is what is termed dialectical-correspondence-accounting-for-*ceteris-paribus*-clause (Patryas 1976, 1977). Applying this for the case under consideration, (4.1) may be analyzed as

(4.8) $\forall_{\varepsilon'} PT = 0 \Rightarrow PT = \alpha_0' + \alpha_1' I.$

A step further toward the decomposition of the set of disturbances is made when a new essential factor for *PT* is identified, *W*. This may be reconstructed as a putting forward the following claim:

(4.9) $W = 0 \ \& \ \forall_{\varepsilon'} PT = 0 \Rightarrow PT = \alpha_0' + \alpha_1' I,$

and concretizing it:

(4.10) $W \neq 0 \ \& \ \forall_{\varepsilon} PT = 0 \Rightarrow PT = \alpha_0 + \alpha_1 I + \alpha_2 W;$

the set of disturbances (4.10) refers to is diminished in comparison to the one presupposed by (4.8), hence $\varepsilon < \varepsilon'$. Then (4.10) is factualized:

(4.11) $W \neq 0 \ \& \ \exists_{\varepsilon} PT \neq 0 \Rightarrow PT \underset{\varepsilon}{\approx} \alpha_0 + \alpha_1 I + \alpha_2 W.$

And the this statement may be claimed to reconstruct (4.2). So, the relation taken by Janssen to be "concretization" is in fact the dialectical-correspondence-accounting-for-*ceteris-paribus*-clause.

Certainly, this analysis is not a full reconstruction of the relation in question. There is an additional element of the example responsible for this deviation: the parameters contained in the two formulae may be different. This, however, can be hardly explained in idealizational terms as the question of the methodological characterization of parameters is analyzed in these terms only partially.

Stabilization. I must admit that my (1971a/1980) book does not do justice to the following observation of K.D. Hoover:

> Idealizing steps for Nowak are ones that set parameters to extreme values: zero or infinity.... In contrast, ... economic models in general often involve simplified or stylized features that result from stipulating definite values or forms, and not from removing features altogether by setting characteristics to extreme values (Hoover, this volume, p. 45).

Quite so. However, one of the papers by P. Chwalisz contains an outline of an appropriate correction of the idealizational methodology which seems to satisfy this objection at least in part. Chwalisz (1979) generalizes the notion of idealizing condition as to the form. He so terms the condition $p(x) = c$, where c is an arbitrary but definite value of the magnitude *p* provided there is no member of the range of *p*, for which this magnitude takes on exactly the value c. In an extreme case, c may be zero. If c differs from zero, the above condition is termed a stabilizing assumption. In consequence, the schemes of an idealizational law, of concretization etc. are somewhat modified. The new ones allow, for instance, for understanding the role played by the so-called constants in the formulae of laws and their concretization (Chwalisz 1979, cf. also Nowakowa 1994, Chap. V).

On the other hand, the conception of stabilization (Chwalisz 1979, Zielińska 1981, 1990) is still too general to handle another of Hoover's queries, one referring to the role of empirical coefficients (this volume, p.48).

Idealization as a combination of reduction and ideation. Another accurate point of Hoover is this: "Is there a difference between setting aside a disturbing factor ... and setting an essential factor to a stipulated value?" (this volume, p. 45; original emphasis). Indeed, Zielińska (1981, 1990) has shown that my formulation of the notion of an idealizing condition covered two different ideas. One is to neglect the very existence of a given magnitude by postulating counterfactually that the range of it is empty. The other is to admit the existence of a magnitude but to neglect its influence on other magnitudes by postulating that this magnitude takes on the value of zero. These two, claims Zielińska, are conceptually independent counterfactual procedures. The former may be termed reduction, the latter – ideation. Combining this with Chwalisz's idea we easily find that stabilization is a generalization of ideation, and not of reduction.

In my (1990) there is an attempt to systematically outline all the deformative (counterfactual) procedures involved. The construction is of some metaphysical import (cf. my 1991a, 1992a), but one conclusion is also of methodological interest: what we intuitively call idealization is a composition of ideation (with respect to some magnitude) and reduction (with respect to all the other magnitudes).

5. *Some new challenges*

How to empirically discriminate among idealizations? K.D. Hoover doubts the cognitive usefulness of the rule of delayed falsification. He asks the following question. Assume that there are two competing idealizational theories each developing according to the rule of delayed falsification. There will then take place progress in explaining empirical facts better and better – within each theory taken separately. But what about their commensurability? How could we decide which of them is better not internally but externally, that is, by reference to empirical facts? The author provides us with a decisional procedure in econometric terms. That is really an important problem for the idealizational methodology and I would like to reconstruct such a procedure in general terms.

Let us consider a simple conceptual structure called, in the idealizational approach to science, a linear approximative explanatory chain:

T: $T^k, \ldots, T^i, AT^i$,

where $T^k, T^{k-1}, \ldots, T^i$ are of the standard form explained in section 3 and AT^i is an approximation of T^i:

$$AT^i\text{: } (x)\ ([G(x) \ \&\ p_1(x) \neq 0 \ \&\ \ldots \ \&\ p_i(x) \neq 0 \ \&\ p_{i+1}(x) \neq 0 \ \&\ \ldots \ \&\ p_{k-1}(x) \neq 0 \ \&\ p_k(x) \neq 0 \Rightarrow \Rightarrow F(x) \underset{\varepsilon}{\approx} f_i[H(x), p_k(x), \ldots, p_{i+1}(x)]).$$

Let also the competing approximative explanation of the same facts be given:

S: $S^n, S^{n-1}, \ldots, S^j, AS^j$.

It invokes another image of the essential structure of the magnitude F, composed of $K, q_n, \ldots, q_{j+1}, \ldots, q_i$. Assume also that both T and S develop according to the rule of delayed falsification and that they have reached their maximally concretized statements, T^i and S^j, correspondingly. How can we decide which is cognitively better?

The answer may be given by reference to the following criterion which is, as far as I understand, a generalization of the criterion proposed by Hoover for economic models:

(a) Take an arbitrary object a from the range of the investigated magnitude F and measure the intensity $F(a)$. That explanation which gives smaller discrepancy with $F(a)$ is cognitively better for the object a; e.g. if $\varepsilon = |F(a) - f_i[H(a), p_k(a), \ldots, p_{i+1}(a)]| < |F(a) - g_j[K(a), q_n(a), \ldots, q_{j+1}(a)]|$, then the explanation T is better than S for a.

(b) Take the whole range of the magnitude F and impose ε as the level of approximation. That explanation which retains the level ε for a larger fraction of objects from the range of F is cognitively better.

(c) If the level ε does not discriminate between T and S, impose $\varepsilon_1 < \varepsilon$ as the level of approximation and continue the procedure until such ε_m is found which allows to discriminate in the sense (b) between T and S.

So, if I am not mistaken, the conceptual apparatus of the idealizational approach can reconstruct the criterion put forward by Hoover for economic models.

Empirical and theoretical concretizations. The same author writes:

> Nowak's account ... assumes that the ramifications of each idealizing step – or of the correlative sequence of concretizing steps – can be worked out from some principles. ... In practice, however, we idealize – at least in the context of quantifying models – precisely because we lack a principled way of concretizing the idealized model. We generally do not know all the factors that are relevant or in just what way they are relevant (Hoover, this volume, pp. 47-48).

"Quantified idealized models" in the sense of Hoover may be likely interpreted as possessing, apart from standard idealizing conditions, the *ceteris paribus* clause (see above). Let the initial statement of this type will be of the following shape:

$$t^{cp}: \quad (x)\ (G(x)\ \&\ p(x) = 0\ \&\ q(x) = 0\ \&\ r(x) = 0\ \&\ \forall_n F(x) = 0 \Rightarrow F(x) = f(H(x)))$$

Assume that t^{cp} is concretized three times resulting in:

$$CCCt^{cp}: (x)\ ([G(x)\ \&\ p(x) \neq 0\ \&\ q(x) \neq 0\ \&\ r(x) \neq 0\ \&\ \forall_n F(x) = 0] \Rightarrow F(x) = f'''(H(x), r(x), q(x), p(x))),$$

but it still does not approximate the facts sufficiently well. Then, one of possible ways to cope with this is to decompose the set of the remaining influences identifying a certain factor s as essential for F. Such a procedure is of an empirical character as there is no general theory of this set; to have such a theory would mean to possess knowledge on everything that influences F whereas we have assumed that we do not have one. Decomposition of the *ceteris paribus* clause leads to a new version of the initial statement:

$$t^{cp'}: \quad (x)\ ([G(x)\ \&\ s(x) = 0\ \&\ p(x) = 0\ \&\ q(x) = 0\ \&\ r(x) = 0\ \&\ \forall_{n'} F(x) = 0] \Rightarrow F(x) = f(H(x)))$$

which is then concretized anew. If this time a (better) agreement with the facts is reached, the procedure of decomposition of the *ceteris paribus* clause proves to be successful. If not, it must be repeated.

It is of importance that such a procedure cannot be theoretical in nature. The procedure of decomposition must be based on empirical research both in identifying a given factor s out of the set of "essential residuals" and in recognizing the way in which s influences F. No theory is able to decompose the set of factors of which it does not speak at all. The paraphrase of Hoover's suggestion into the idealizational language allows to fully confirm it. One should distinguish theoretical concretization based on some general principles (e.g. the principle of superposition in physics, the so-called method of disturbances in astronomy, etc.) and empirical concretization. Above, following Hoover's suggestion we have identified a certain type of empirical concretization. It is possible that there are more of them, so that the problem is still open.

This is not to fully agree with Hoover. For sometimes he exaggerates the significance of empirical concretizations. His "assertion [that] the bridge between quantified idealized models and the real world is atheoretical" (*ibid.*, p. 48) leaves no room for theoretical concretization at all. Moreover, his claim that "[w]hen theoretical understanding of the implications of various complications is relatively complete, idealization would appear to be a fairly sterile formal relationship" (*ibid.*) does not do justice to theoretical concretization. By analogy, one would claim that when the proof of a certain theorem from a given system of axioms is known "deduction would appear to be a fairly sterile formal relationship." Perhaps it would, but the problem is that the proof was waiting for the discoverer, sometimes for a long time. That the general methodological scheme of a certain procedure is formal does not imply that the concrete discoveries falling under that scheme are trivial. This simply varies from one case to another, similarly as in case of empirical studies which sometimes are bright and penetrating and sometimes quite banal. And there are cases of undoubtedly creative theoretical concretizations as becomes clear when one looks at, for instance, the sophisticated reconstruction of the concretization of the ideal gas law by Kuipers (1985), or Hamminga's reconstruction of the concretization of the Marxian law of value (1990).

Technical and essentialist idealizations. K.D. Hoover makes the following remark:

> Bert Hamminga has suggested to me that one needs to distinguish, as Nowak does not, between technical idealizations made for reasons of tractability (mathematical or statistical) and essentialist idealizations made to isolate the fundamental from the secondary. Clearly both simplifications occur. The issue is whether there is enough of a family resemblance between them to class them both as idealizations (this volume, p. 46, n. 6).

That is correct. The distinction is necessary and I did not make it.[8] Science uses "technical idealizations" when deforming a given domain of objects as to make possible the adoption of the mathematical apparatus, e.g., we adopt the assumption of continuity of a given domain in order to employ the differential calculus. Even superficial look reveals that there is a serious difference between such assumptions and idealizing assumptions. When we adopt an idealizing condition we are certain that a given

---

[8] It is only a paper by Zielińska (1992) which deals with the subject but on a rather limited terrain. She considers the role of the assumptions of linearity of a given dependency adopted contrary to one's empirical knowledge.

factor acts in reality, so it is excluded that the condition is fulfilled in the world. In case of "technical idealization" the matter is not decided. It may be that a given field is continuous or not. On the strength of the assumption of continuity we lead reasonings as if the given domain were continuous, independently of whether this is really the case.

Whether such differences between normal idealizing conditions and assumptions underlying the application of mathematics allow to speak of idealization in both cases, it is difficult to say. The problem is open. And it is of considerable importance.

Isolation as idealization. U. Mäki puts forward a view that

> any theory is bound to isolate a small slice of the world from the rest of reality. Therefore, any theory is bound to violate the whole truth (this volume, p. 148). [Therefore] the method of isolation is a central method employed in economics, and ... many other methods such as that of idealization are subservient for it (1992, p. 318).

First of all, one should distinguish here the terminological and the substantive question. Obviously, it is possible to say that by idealization we "isolate" something (e.g., the principal factors for a given magnitude) from something else (e.g., the secondary factors for this magnitude) but that is not too rich a metaphor. In order to use it the author must introduce a convention according to which what is usually termed 'idealization' (a composition of reduction and ideation — see above) is named 'isolation' whereas the term 'idealization' is used "in a narrow sense in which idealizations are formulated in terms of limiting concepts designated ... by variables with the value of 0 or $|\infty|$" (Mäki 1992, p. 324), that is, in the sense of our "ideation". Were this the whole story, it would be of terminological nature.

Mäki puts forward, however, also a substantive problem here. For even if we accept the view that all phenomena (the facts that magnitudes take on some of their values) have their essential structures and the basic role of science is to discover the structures by trial and error, that is, by putting forward idealizational hypotheses and concretizing them, there is still something lacking. Nothing has been said about the way in which those essential structures are tied. That is certainly a substantive problem which is worth being posed. And, leaving the whole terminological affair aside, Mäki's intuitions, I think, point actually to that.

Call a categorial system a set of magnitudes S iff, for every $F \in S$, the set of all factors principal for F is a subset of S (cf. my 1978, 1989). A categorial system is thus one which includes all the principal determinants of all its members. Assume that the world (roughly, the universe of all individuals and its characteristics constituted by all the magnitudes defined on subsets of the universe) is a set of categorial systems. This entails that the characteristics of the universe splits into sets $X, Y, Z, \ldots$ of magnitudes such that for every member of X all the principal factors are included in X and the appropriate conditions are satisfied for $Y, Z, \ldots$ Add to a categorial system all the factors which are secondary for at least one member of that system; such a set of magnitudes will be termed an essential system. We shall say that the categorial system is submerged in an appropriate essential system.

One may conjecture that it is the final goal of a scientific theory to reconstruct a definite essential system and that the first, most idealized, model of such a theory is to reconstruct the core of the essential system, that is, the appropriate categorial system. It might well be that one and the same factor is secondary for magnitudes from different categorial systems. Here is a schematic illustration. Let two categorial systems be given:

$$X = \{A, B, C\}$$
$$Y = \{a, b, c\}.$$

Let the essential structures of the above magnitudes of systems X and Y be the following:

S_A:	B, C	S_a:	b, c
	B, C, p		b, c, p
S_B:	A, C	S_b:	a, c
	A, C, q		$a, c, r.$
S_C:	A, B	S_c:	a, b
	A, B, s		$a, b, t.$

X and Y are disjoint whereas one and the same secondary factor p is essential (viz. secondary) for two magnitudes A and a from systems X and Y, respectively. We shall say that p is the connection between the essential systems X and Y.

Consider now the problem of isolation. First and foremost, isolation consists in adopting an idealizing condition that neglects a magnitude which is a connection between at least two essential systems. Its point is to create a model of the world in which essential systems that are connected in the actual world are separated one from another. An isolating condition is thus an idealizing assumption of a special sort. One may term the isolational statements statements equipped with some isolating assumptions. De-isolation is thus a concretization of a kind: it consists in the waiving of an isolating condition and introducing corresponding correction (that is, corrective function – see my 1980, p. 103) to (at least) two idealizational statements from different theories.

In this way de-isolation reconstructs the two essential systems connected to one another by the appropriate secondary factor.

Such a procedure certainly deserves to be distinguished from the "standard" procedures analyzed in the idealizational approach to science. That is why, the intuitions put forward in Mäki's writings are interesting and worth analyzing. However, isolation/de-isolation proves to be a special sort of idealization/concretization procedure if the latter terms are understood as they are in the idealizational approach to science.

* * *

As will have become obvious for a reader of the present reply, the idealizational approach to science profited very much from the criticisms analyzed above. All methodological theories should be tested against actual scientific practice and I am obliged to all the authors for creating an opportunity for such a test for the approach under consideration.

REFERENCES

Balzer, W. and B. Hamminga (1989), Eds. *Philosophy of Economics*. Dordrecht/Boston/London: Kluwer.

Barr, W.F. (1971). A Syntactic and Semantic Analysis of Idealizations in Science. *Philosophy of Science*, **38**, 258-72.

Brzeziński, J. (1977). *Struktura procesu badawczego w naukach behawioralnych* (The structure of research process in the behavioural sciences). Warszawa-Poznań: PWN.

Brzeziński, J. (1978). *Metodologiczne i psychologiczne wyznaczniki postępowania* badawczego w psychologii (The Methodological and Psychological Determinants of the Research Practice in Psychology). Poznań: Poznań University Press.

Brzeziński, J. (1985a). The Protoidealizational Model of the Investigative Process in Psychology. In: Brzeziński (1985b), pp. 36-57.

Brzeziński, J. (1985b), Ed. *Consciousness: Methodological and Psychological Approaches* (*Poznań Studies in the Philosophy of the Sciences and the Humanities*, **8**) Amsterdam: Rodopi.

Brzeziński, J., Fr. Coniglione, T.A.F. Kuipers and L. Nowak (1990a), Eds. *Idealization-I: General Problems* (*Poznań Studies in the Philosophy of the Sciences and the Humanities*, **16**). Amsterdam/Atlanta: Rodopi.

Brzeziński, J., Fr. Coniglione, T.A.F. Kuipers and L. Nowak (1990b), Eds. *Idealization-II: Forms and Applications* (*Poznań Studies in the Philosophy of the Sciences and the Humanities*, **17**). Amsterdam/Atlanta: Rodopi.

Brzeziński, J. and L. Nowak (1992), Eds. *Idealization-III: Approximation and Truth* (*Poznań Studies in the Philosophy of the Sciences and the Humanities*, **25**). Amsterdam/Atlanta: Rodopi.

Cartwright, N. (1983). *How the Laws of Physics Lie?*. Oxford: Oxford University Press.

Cartwright, N. (1989). *Nature's Capacities and Their Measurement*. Oxford: Oxford University Press.

Chwalisz, P. (1979). Stałe w idealizacyjnej koncepcji nauki (Constants in the idealizational conception of science). In: Klawiter and Nowak (1979), pp. 99-104.

Dilworth, C. (1992), Ed. *Intelligibility and Science* (*Poznań Studies in the Philosophy of the Sciences and the Humanities*, **26**). Amsterdam/Atlanta: Rodopi.

Eells, E.L. and T. Maruszewski (1991), Eds. *Rationality in Reasoning. Studies on L. Jonathan Cohen's Philosophy of Science* (*Poznań Studies in the Philosophy of the Sciences and the Humanities*, **19**). Amsterdam/Atlanta: Rodopi.

Garcia de la Sienra, A. (1992). *The Logical Foundations of the Marxian Theory of Value*. Dordrecht/Boston/London: Kluwer.

Hamminga, B. (1989). Sneed versus Nowak: An Illustration in Economics. In: Balzer and Hamminga (1989), pp. 247-65.

Hamminga, B. (1990). The Structure of Six Transformations in Marx's Capital. In: Brzeziński *et al.* (1990a), pp. 89-111.

Hamminga, B. (1992). Idealization in the Practice and Methodology of the Classical Economics. In: Brzeziński and Nowak (1992), pp. 103-114.

Hartkamper, A. and H.-J. Schmidt (1981), Eds. *Structure and Approximation in Physical Theories*. New York/London: Plenum Press.

Kittel, C., W.D. Knittel and H.A. Ruderman (1969). *Mechanics* (Polish translation). Warszawa: PWN.

Klawiter, A. and L. Nowak (1979), Eds. *Odkrycie, abstrakcja, prawda, empiria, historia – a idealizacja* (Discovery, Abstraction, Truth, Experience, History – and Idealization). Warszawa-Poznań: PWN.

Kmita, J. (1974), Ed. *Metodologiczne implikacje epistemologii marksistowskiej* (Methodological Implications of the Marxist Methodology). Warszawa-Poznań: PWN.

Krajewski, W. (1977). *Correspondence Principle and the Growth of Science*. Dordrecht: Reidel.

Krajewski, W. (1982), Ed. *Polish Essays in the Philosophy of the Natural Sciences* (*Boston Studies in the Philosophy of Science*, **68**). Dordrecht/Boston/London: Reidel.

Kuipers, T.A.F (1985). The Paradigm of Concretization: the Law of van der Waals. In: Brzeziński (1985b), pp. 185-99.

Kuipers, T.A.F. (1987), Ed. *What is Closer-to-the-Truth?* (*Poznań Studies in the Philosophy of the Sciences and the Humanities*, **10**). Amsterdam: Rodopi.

Kuipers, T.A.F. (1992). Truth Approximation by Concretization. In: Brzeziński and Nowak (1992), pp. 159-79.

Kuokkanen, M. (1988). The Poznań School Methodology of Idealization and Concretization from the Point of View of a Revised Structuralist Theory Conception. *Erkenntnis* **28**, 97-115.

Kuokkanen, M. and T. Tuomivaara (1992). On the Structure of Idealizations. Explorations in the Poznań School Methodology of Idealization and Concretization. In: Brzeziński and Nowak (1992), pp. 67-102.

Kupracz, A. (1990). Concretization and the Correction of Data. In: Brzeziński *et al.* (1990b), pp. 61-75.

Ludwig, L. (1981). Imprecision in Physics. In: Hartkämper and Schmidt (1981), pp. 7-19.

Łastowski, K. (1987). *Rozwój teorii ewolucji* (The Development of the Theory of Evolution). Poznań: Poznań University Press.

Łastowski, K. (1990). On Multi-Level Scientific Theories. In: Brzeziński *et al.* (1990b), pp. 33-59.

Mäki, U. (1992). On the Method of Isolation in Economics. In: Dilworth (1992), pp. 317-51.

Marciszewski, W. (1971). *Podstawy logicznej teorii przekonań* (Foundations of the Logical Theory of Beliefs). Warszawa: PWN.

Markus, R.B., G.J.W. Dorn and P. Weingartner (1986), Eds. *Logic, Methodology and Philosophy of Science VII*. Amsterdam: North-Holland.

Maruszewski, T. (1983). *Procesy poznawcze jednostki w świetle idealizacyjnej teorii nauki* (The Cognitive Processes of Individual in the Light of the Idealizational Theory of Science). Poznań: Poznań University Press.

Marx, K. (1845). *Wages, Prices and Profit* (quoted after the Polish translation). *Dzieła* (Works), vol. XVI. Warszawa: KiW 1968.

Niiniluoto, I. (1986). Theories, Approximations and Idealizations. In: Markus *et al.*, pp. 255-89.

Niiniluoto, I. (1990). Theories, Approximations and Idealizations. In: Brzeziński *et al.* (a revised and enlarged version of the 1986 paper), pp. 9-57.

Nowak, L. (1970a). Analiza logicznej struktury modelu ekonomicznego (An Analysis of the Logical Structure of Economic Models). *Ekonomista*, **6**, 1231-51.

Nowak, L. (1970b). Teorie racjonalnego zachowania jako teorie modelowe (Theories of Rational Behaviour as Modeling Theories). *Studia Metodologiczne*, **7**, 59-89.

Nowak, L. (1971a) *U podstaw Marksowskiej metodologii nauk* (Foundations of the Marxian Methodology of Science). Warszawa: PWN.

Nowak, L. (1971b). The Model of Explanation in Marx's Capital. *Quality & Quantity* **V**, 2, 311-30.

Nowak, L. (1972a). Theories, Idealization and Measurement. *Philosophy of Science*, **39**, 4, 533-547.

Nowak, L. (1972b). *Model ekonomiczny. Studium z metodologii ekonomii politycznej* (Economic Models. A Study from the Methodology of the Political Economy). Warszawa: PWE.

Nowak, L. (1975). Abstraction and Idealization. *Teoria a Metoda*, **VII**, 4, 23-36.

Nowak, L. (1977a). *U podstaw dialektyki Marksowskiej. Próba interpretacji kategorialnej* (Foundations of the Marxian dialectics. An Attempt at a Categorial Interpretation). Warszawa: PWN.

Nowak, L. (1977b). On the Structure of Marxist Dialectics: An Attempt at a Categorial Interpretation. *Erkenntniss*, **11**, 3, 341-63.

Nowak, L. (1977c). The Classic and the Essentialist Conceptions of Truth. In: M. de May, R. Pinxten, H. Poriau, F. Vandamme (Eds.), *The Cognitive Viewpoint*. Ghent: Ghent University, Press, pp. 344-53.

Nowak, L. (1977d). *Wstęp do idealizacyjnej teorii nauki* (An Introduction to the Idealizational Theory of Science). Warszawa: PWN.

Nowak, L. (1978). *U podstaw ontologii kategorialnej* (Foundations of the Categorial Ontology). Poznań, mimeo.

Nowak, L. (1979). Historical Epochs and Historical Momentums. An Attempt at a non-Marxian Historical Materialism. *Analyse und Kritik*, **1**, 60-76.

Nowak, L. (1980). *The Structure of Idealization. Towards a Systematic Interpretation of the Marxian Idea of Science*. Dordrecht/Boston/London: Reidel.

Nowak, L. (1983). *Property and Power. Toward a non-Marxian Historical Materialism*. Dordrecht/Boston/Lancaster: Reidel.

Nowak, L. (1989). On the (Idealizational) Nature of Economic Theories. In: Balzer and Hamminga (1989), pp. 225-46.

Nowak, L. (1990). Abstracts Are Not Our Constructs. The Mental Constructs Are Abstracts. In: Brzeziński *et al.*, pp. 193-203.

Nowak, L. (1991a). Thoughts Are Facts of Possible Worlds. Truths Are Facts of a Given World. *Dialectica*, **45**, 273-87.

Nowak, L. (1991b). The Method of Relevant Variables and Idealization. In: Eells and Maruszewski (1991), pp. 41-63.
Nowak, L. (1992a). Myśl o czymś jest tym właśnie (A Thought of Something Is Actually This Something). *Poznańskie Studia z Filozofii Nauki*, **12**. Warszawa/Poznań: PWN, 17-63.
Nowak, L. (1992b). The Idealizational Approach to Science: A Survey. In: Brzeziński and Nowak (1992), pp. 9-63.
Nowakowa, I. (1975a). *Dialektyczna korespondencja a rozwój nauki*. Warszawa/Poznań: PWN.
Nowakowa, I. (1975b). Idealization and the Problem of Correspondence. *Poznań Studies in the Philosophy of the Sciences and the Humanities*, **I**, 1, 65-70.
Nowakowa, I. (1982). Dialectical Correspondence and Essential Truth. In: Krajewski (1982), pp. 135-46.
Nowakowa, I. (1992). A Notion of Truth for Idealization. In: Brzeziński and Nowak (1992), pp. 181-213.
Nowakowa, I. (1994). *Idealization-V: The Dynamics of Idealizations* (*Poznań Studies in the Philosophy of the Sciences and the Humanities*, **34**). Amsterdam/Atlanta: Rodopi.
Paprzycka, K. and M. Paprzycki (1992). A Note on the Unitarian Explication of Idealization. In: Brzeziński and Nowak (1992), pp. 279-81.
Patryas, W. (1975a). An Analysis of the *Ceteris Paribus* Clause. *Poznań Studies in the Philosophy of the Sciences and the Humanities*, **1**, 1, 59-64.
Patryas, W. (1975b). Approximation and Idealization. *Poznań Studies in the Philosophy of the Sciences and the Humanities*, **1**, 4, 83-85.
Patryas, W. (1976). *Eksperyment a idealizacja* (Experiment and Idealization). Warszawa-Poznań: PWN.
Patryas, W. (1977). When Do Two Theorems Correspond? *Poznań Studies in the Philosophy of the Sciences and the Humanities*, **4**, 253-55.
Patryas, W. (1982). The Pluralistic Approach to Empirical Testing and the Special Forms of Experiment. In: Krajewski (1982), pp. 127-34.
Popper, K.R. (1945). *Open Society and Its Enemies*, vol. ii. London: Routledge and Kegan Paul 1966.
Popper, K.R. (1965). *Conjectures and Refutations*. London: Routledge & Kegan Paul.
Popper, K.R. (1973). *Objective Knowledge. An Evolutionary Approach*. Oxford: Oxford University Press.
Popper, K.R. (1982). *The Undended Quest. An Intellectual Autobiography*. Glasgow: Fontana.
Suppe, F. (1972). What's Wrong with the Received View on the Structure of Scientific Theories? *Philosophy of Science*, **39**, 1-19.
Tuchańska, B. (1980). *Czynnik – wielkość, związek – zależność. Przyczynek do idealizacyjnej koncepcji nauki* (Factor – Magnitude, Regularity – Correlation. A Contribution to the Idealizational Conception of Science). Poznań-Warszawa: PWN.
Wójcicki, R. (1974). *Metody formalne w problematyce teoriopoznawczej* (The formal methods in the epistemological problematics). In: Kmita (1974), pp. 15-44.
Wójcicki, R. (1979). *Topics in the Formal Methodology of Empirical Sciences*. Dordrecht/Boston/London: Reidel.
Zielińska, R. (1981). *Abstrakcja, Idealizacja, Uogólnienie* (Abstraction, Idealization, and Generalization). Poznań: Poznań University Press.
Zielińska, R. (1990). A Contribution to the Characteristics of Abstraction. In: Brzeziński *et al.* (1990a), pp. 9-22.

LIST OF AUTHORS OF THIS VOLUME

Wolgang Balzer, Seminar fuer Philosophie, Logik und Wissenschafsttheorie, Universitaet Muenchen, Ludwigstrasse 31, 8000 Muenchen 22, Germany

Jack Birner, Faculteit der Economische Wetenschappen, Rijksuniversiteit Limburg, Postbus 616, 6200 MD Maastricht, The Netherlands

Nancy Cartwright, Department of Philosophy, London School of Economics, Houghton St. London WC2A 2AE, United Kingdom

Steven Cook, Institute of Economics and Statistics, Nuffield College OX1 1NF, United Kingdom

Kees Cools, Jan Evertsenstraat 16, 5021 RE Tilburg, The Netherlands

Werner Diederich, Abteilung Philosophie, Universität Bielefeld, Postfach 8640, D-4800 Bielefeld 1, Germany

Adolfo Garcia de là Sienra, Instituto de Investigaciones Filosóficas, Universidad Nacional Autónoma de México, Circuito Mario de la Cuerva, CU 04215, Mexico DF

Bert Hamminga, Department of Philosophy, Tilburg University, P.O.Box 90153, 5000 LE Tilburg, The Netherlands

Daniel W. Hausman, University of Wisconsin-Madison, WI 53706, USA

David Hendry, Nuffield College, Oxford OX1 1NF, United Kingdom

Kevin Hoover, Department of Economics, University of California, Davis, CA 95616 U.S.A.

Maarten Janssen, Faculteit der Economische Wetenschappen, Erasmusuniversiteit Rotterdam, Postbus 1738, 3000 DR Rotterdam, The Netherlands

Gerard Jorland, Centre de Recherches Historiques, Ecole des Hautes Etudes en Sciences Sociales, 54, Boulevard Raspail, 7527 Paris Cedex 06, France

Hugo Keuzenkamp, Department of Economics, Tilburg University, P.O. Box 90153, 5000 LE Tilburg, The Netherlands

Theo A.F. Kuipers, Filosofisch Instituut, Rijksuniversiteit Groningen, A-weg 30, 9718 CW Groningen

Uskali Mäki, Department of Economics, University of Helsinki, P.O. Box 33, SF 00014, Helsinki, Finland

Neil B. de Marchi, Department of Economics, Duke University, Durham, NC 27706, U.S.A.

Leszek Nowak, ul. Cybulskiego 13, 60-247 Poznań, Poland

Bernard Walliser, C.E.R.A.S., Ecole Nationale des Ponts et Chaussees, 28 Rue des Saint-Peres, 75007 Paris, France

POZNAŃ STUDIES IN THE PHILOSOPHY OF THE SCIENCES AND THE HUMANITIES

Contents of back issues

VOLUME 1 (1975)

No. 1 (Sold out)

The Method of Humanistic Interpretation – J. Kmita, *Humanistic Interpretation*; W. Ławniczak, *On a Systematized Interpretation of Works of Fine Arts*; J. Topolski, *Rational Explanation in History*. **The Method of Idealization** – L. Nowak, *Idealization: A Reconstruction of Marx's Ideas*; J. Brzeziński, *Interaction, Essential Structure, Experiment*; W. Patryas, *An Analysis of the "Caeteris Paribus" Clause*; I. Nowakowa, *Idealization and the Problem of Correspondence*. **The Application: The Reconstruction of Some Marxist Theories** – J. Topolski, *Lenin's Theory of History*; J. Kmita, *Marx's Way of Explanation of Social Processes*; A. Jasińska, L. Nowak, *Foundations of Marx's Theory of Class: A Reconstruction*.

No. 2 (Sold out)

Articles – J. Kmita, L. Nowak, J. Topolski, *Against the False Alternatives*; É. Balibar, *Dialectique, Contradiction, Lutte des Classes*; J. Burbelka, *Historical Materialism: Its Essence and Forms*; S. Magala, *Dialectics and Praxis*. **Discussions** – A. Feenberg, *Notes on Methodology and Ontology in Lenin's Thought*; J. Kmita, *The Controversy About the Principles of the Development of Science*; I. Nowakowa, *On the Notion of Correspondence*; A. Klawiter, *Kuhn and Feyerabend on a Scientific Fact and Its Interpretation*.

No. 3 (Sold out)

Articles – K. Zamiara, *Pavlov's Theory and Marx's Directive of the Functional-Genetic Explanation in the Humanities*; J. Hilpelä, *Factors Determining Theory Formation and Methods in Sociology*; A. Klawiter, *The Category of Generation in Historical Materialism*; L. Nowak, *The Anatomy of Anti-Marxist Criticism*. **Discussions** – W. Mejbaum, *Standard and Non-Standard Concept of Social Praxis*.

No. 4 (Sold out)

Articles – J. Agassi, *Between Metaphysics and Methodology*; T. Czeżowski, *Definitions in Science*; P. Materna, *Frege Revised (on a New Concept of Semantics)*; W. Marciszewski, *The Cartesian Concept of Conviction*; M. Bunge, *Meaning in Science*. **Discussions** – J. Misiek, *On the Concept of Matter*; D.A. Rohatyn, *Why "Internal Relations" Cannot be True*; J. Kmita, *Methodological Proposals of Claude Lévi-Strauss*; W. Patryas, *Idealization and Approximation*.

VOLUME 2 (1976)

No. 1 (Sold out)

Articles – W. Mejbaum, *Value and Conceptualization*; J. Kmita, *On Axiological Heterogeneity of Evaluating Predicates*; P. Buczkowski, *The Marxian Category of Bourgeois Scientist*; L. Nowak, *Evaluation and Cognition*; T.M. Jaroszewski, *The Peculiarity of Man*. **Discussions** – M. Franklin, *Professor Topolski on Lenin's Theory of History*; F.J. Fleron, *Comments on "Lenin's Theory of History" by Jerzy Topolski*.

No. 2 (Sold out)

Articles – M. Przełęcki, *On Possibility and Possible Worlds*; Z. Augustynek, *Relational Becoming*; T. Kubiński, *On Foundations of Deontic Logic*; Z. Ziembiński, *Factual Assumptions of Normative Utterances*; J. Agassi, *On Spontaneity in the Arts*; B. Tuchańska, *A Phenomenon, the Essence of the Phenomenon, a Theory*; T. Pawłowski, *Indicators in Comparative Research. The Problems. Introductory Remarks.* **Discussions** – F. J. Vandamme, *Theory Change, Incompatibility and Non-Deducibility*; D.H. DeGrood, *Dialectical Method and "Idealizations"*; I. Supek, *Boscovich's Philosophy of Nature*.

No. 3 (Sold out)

Idealizational Concept of Science – L. Nowak, *Essence – Idealization – Praxis. An Attempt at a Certain Interpretation of the Marxist Concept of Science*; B. Tuchańska, *Factor versus Magnitude*; J. Brzeziński, *Empirical Essentialist Procedures in Behavioral Inquiry*; J. Brzeziński, J. Burbelka, A. Klawiter, K. Łastowski, S. Magala, L. Nowak, *Law and Theory. A Contribution to the Idealizational Interpretation of Marxist Methodology*; P. Chwalisz, P. Kowalik, L. Nowak, W. Patryas, M. Stefański, *The Peculiarities of Practical Research*. **Discussions** – T. Batóg, *Concretization and Generalization*; R. Zielińska, *On Inter-Functional Concretization*; L. Nowak, *A Note on Simplicity*; L. Witkowski, *A Note on Implicational Concept of Correspondence*.

No. 4 (Sold out)

Categorial Interpretation of Dialectics – L. Nowak, *On the Categorial Interpretation of History*; I. Nowakowa, *The Principle of Universal Nexus in the Categorial Interpretation of Dialectics*; S. Magala, *The Phenomenon of Complementarity in the Categorial Dialectics*; I. Nowakowa, *Partial Truth – Relative Truth – Absolute Truth. An Attempt at a Construction of the Ordering Concept of Essential Truth.* **Discussions** – J. Witt-Hansen, *Reflections on Marxian Dialectics*; A. Pałubicka, J. Kmita, *Some Remarks on the Dialectical Method of Karl Marx*, D.W. Felder, *Contradiction and Conflict*; M.A. Amer, *Contradiction: Dialectical and Logical*; O.A. Wojtasiewicz, *The Concept of Effect in Autodynamic World*; A. Miś, *Remarks on a Certain Interpretation of the Marxist Methodology*.

VOLUME 3 (1977)

Nos. 1-4 (Sold out)

Aspects of the Production of Scientific Knowledge (Edited by J. Witt-Hansen) – J. Witt-Hansen, *Marx's Method in Social Science, and Its Relationship to Classical and Modern Physics and Mathematics*; S.A. Pedersen, *Logic and Ontology in Study of Theory Change*;

H.S. Jensen, *On the Production of Scientific Knowledge.* **Articles** – R. Arthur, *The Empiricist Account of Scientific Knowledge – A Polemic Evaluation*; S. Shibata, *Die Moderne Wissenschaft und marxistische Philosophie. Zur Problematik der Methodologie der Wissenschaft*; W. Patryas, *The Sense of Empirical Testing*; K. Łastowski, *The Method of Idealization in the Populational Genetics*; B. Tuchańska, *An Idealizational View on Measurement and Indicator-Based Reasoning*; J. Topolski, *On the Class Approach to History.* **Discussions** – W. Patryas, *When do Two Theorems Correspond?*; E. Paszkiewicz, *Context of Discovery and Context of Justification – Opposition or Complementarity?*; J. Woleński, *Jörgensen's Dilemma and the Problem of the Logic of Norms.*

VOLUME 4 (1978)

Nos. 1-4 (Sold out)

Aspects of the Growth of Science (Edited by W. Krajewski) – W. Krajewski, *Preface*; I. Szumilewicz, *The Postulate of Simplicity*; E. Pietruska-Madej, *Anomalies and the Dynamics of Scientific Theories*; A. Motycka, *Kuhn's Sociological Principle of Demarcation*; A. Lewenstam, *Models of Atom. Remarks on the Development of Science.* **Articles** – J. Agassi, *Logic and Logic of*; E. Köhler, *Observation Established by Artificial Intelligence and the Solution to Goodman's Paradox*; M. Przełęcki, *Some Approach to Inexact Measurement*; S. Bartlett, *Lower Bounds of Ambiguity and Redundancy*; J. Such, *Idealization and Concretization in Natural Sciences*; J. Pogonowski, J. Wiśniewski, *A Formal Approach to Causality*; S. Richmond, *Polanyi's Critique of Methodology and Liberalism*; M. Nowakowska, *Towards a Formal Theory of Group Action*; K. Zamiara, *The Problem of Psychologistic Reduction*; M.A. Finocchiaro, *Theory and Practice in the Philosophy of Science. Comments on Galileo and Clavelin*; M.J. Siemek, *Lukács' Dialectical Epistemology*; I. Nowakowa, L. Nowak, *Marxism and Positivism: The Idea of a Scientific Philosophy.* **Discussions** – E. Kronthaler, *Induction und Gesetzsartigkeit. Zu einer Theorie von Nelson Goodman*; E. Kronthaler, *Marginalie zu G.H. von Wright's "The Logical Problem of Induction".*

VOLUME 5 (1979)

Nos. 1-4 (Sold out)

Methodological Problems of Historical Research (Edited by J. Topolski) – J. Topolski, *The Basic Problems of the Methodology of History*; G. Castellan, *Histoire et Psychologie*; G.G. Iggers, *History as an Historical Science*; L. Canfora, *Epic and Historical Claim to Totality*; A. Pałubicka, *The Positivist and Instrumentalist Concepts of the So-called Archeological Culture*; T. Kostyrko, *On the Concept of Historical Sources.* **Articles** – W. Marciszewski, *Epistemological Foundations of Democratism in Cartesian Philosophy*; G. di Bernardo, *Thetic and Prohairetic Normative Systems*; J. Wróblewski, *The Theory of Law – Multilevel, Empirical or Sociological?*; T. Maruszewski, *On Humanist Interpretation in Psychology: The Case of Investigations of the Defence Mechanisms*; K. Nielsen, *On Marx and Moralizing Social Science*; H. Skolimowski, *Space in Architecture: A Phenomenological Analysis*; B. Dziemidok, *On Cathartic-Compensatory Function of Art*; W. Ławniczak, *On Different Concepts of a Model*; K. Łastowski, *On Possibility of Adaptive Interpretation of Dialectics*; I.S. Narski, *The Functions and Structure of Dialectical Logic.* **Discussions** – K. Berka, *Critical Remarks on the Axiomatized Expected Utility Theory*; J. Ławniczak, *Anti-Individualism, Scientific Discovery and Third World*; R. McCleary, *Remarks on Historical Materialism and Dialectics.*

VOLUME 6 (1982)

SOCIAL CLASSES ACTION & HISTORICAL MATERIALISM

On Classes – I. Fetscher, *Some Theories on the Role of Intellectuals in the Revolutionary Labour-Movement. Brecht and Sartre*; R.P. Sieferle, *Class Consciousness in Marx's Theory of Revolution: Some Remarks*; M. Franklin, *On the Magic of Meritocracy*; O.A. Wojtasiewicz, *Status and Social Structures.* **On Action** – J. Ritsert, *"Wertbeziehung" to the Societal Basis – Two Lines of Argument in Max Weber's Theory of Action?*; A. Klawiter, *Structure and Praxis*; W. Patryas, *The Form of the Principle of Rationality.* **The Adaptive Interpretation of Historical Materialism** – L. Nowak, *The Theory of Socio-Economic Formations as a Theory of Adaptation Processes*; K. Łastowski, *The Theory of Development of Species and the Theory of Motion of Socio-Economic Formation*; P. Buczkowski, *Toward a Theory of Economic Society. An Attempt at the Adaptive Interpretation*; J. Burbelka, *Historical Materialism: General Theory and Forms*; P. Buczkowski, A. Klawiter, L. Nowak, *Historical Materialism as a Theory of Social Whole*; A. Klawiter, *The Theory of Social Formation in Historical Materialism*; P. Buczkowski, *International Relations in the Adaptive Interpretation of Historical Materialism.* **Contributions to Historical Materialism** – J. Ritsert, *Totality, Theory and Historical Analysis. Remarks on Critical Sociology and Empirical Research*; L. Nowak, *Adaptation and Revolution. The Problem of Motion of Socio-Economic Formations in the Adaptive Interpretation of Historical Materialism*; J. Ritsert, *On Horkheimer's and Adorno's Concept of Ideology*; P. Buczkowski, *Imperialism: On the Possibility of Reinterpretation of Lenin's Concept.*

VOLUME 7 (1982)

DIALECTICAL LOGICS FOR THE POLITICAL SCIENCE
(Edited by Hayward R. Alker, Jr.)

L. Nowak, *Marxian Methodology Leads to the Generalization of Historical Materialism*; D. Mefford, *A Comparison of Dialectical and Boolean-Algebraic Models of the Genesis of Interpersonal Relations*; C. Roig, *Leninist Dialectic Seen From the Point of View of Kenneth Burke's Dialectic: Theory, Analysis and Ideology in Lenin's Speech*; H.R. Alker Jr., *Logic, Dialectics, Politics: Some Recent Controversies*; F. Loeser, *What is Dialectical Logic?*

VOLUME 8 (1985)

CONSCIOUSNESS: METHODOLOGICAL AND PSYCHOLOGICAL APPROACHES
(Edited by Jerzy Brzeziński)

Editor's Introduction; A. Klawiter, *A Scientific Theory versus Theoretical Program. A Contribution to the Problem of a Social Character of Cognition*; S. Magala, L. Nowak, *The Problem of Historicity of Cognition in the Idealizational Concept of Science*; J.Brzeziński, *The Protoidealizational Model of the Investigative Process in Psychology*; M. Gaul, *The Problem of Interaction in the Protoidealizational Model of Investigative Process. Modifications and Developments*; J. Kmita, *A Humanistic Coefficient of Activity and the Psychology-Humanities Relation*; K. Zamiara, *In Support of Psycho-Physical Parallelism*; M. Ziółkowski, *Some Remarks on the Notion of Social Consciousness*; S. Kowalik, *The Psycho-*

Social Problem and Modern Psychology; J. Topolski, *On the Concept and Structure of Methodological Consciousness of Historians*; T. Maruszewski, *Are the Idealizational Procedures Used within the Scope of Common Sense Knowledge?*; T. Zgółka, *Stylistic and Sociolinguistics*. **Discussions** – T.A.F. Kuipers, *The Paradigm of Concretization: The Law of van der Waals*; N. Ziv, *The Paradoxical Nature of Bloor's Strong Program in the Sociology of Knowledge*.

VOLUME 9 (1986)

THEORIES OF IDEOLOGY AND IDEOLOGY OF THEORIES
(Edited by Piotr Buczkowski and Andrzej Klawiter)

I. Theories of Ideology – P. Buczkowski, *The Levels of Consciousness: Some Remarks on Sociology of Knowledge*; L. Nowak, *Ideology versus Utopia. A Contribution to the Analysis of the Role of Social Consciousness in the Movement of Socio-Economic Formation*; J. Kmita, *The Antagonism of Art and Science as a Worldview Component*. **II. Ideology of Theories** – J. Kmita, *Scientism and Anti-Scientism*; L. Nowak, *Science, that is, Domination through Truth*; J. Sensat, *Recasting Marxism: Habermas's Proposals*. **Discussions** – J. Brzeziński, *A Statistical Model of Data Analysis in Interactional Psychology. Comments on the Quantitative Analysis of the Scores of the "S-R" Inventory of Anxiousness*.

VOLUME 10 (1987)

WHAT IS CLOSER-TO-THE-TRUTH ?
A PARADE OF APPROACHES TO TRUTHLIKENESS
(Edited by Theo A.F. Kuipers)

Introduction. **Part I: Four Approaches to Truthlikeness** – I. Niiniluoto, *How to Define Verisimilitude*; G. Oddie, *The Picture Theory of Truthlikeness*; G. Schurz, P. Weingartner, *Verisimilitude Defined by Relevant Consequence-Elements*; T.A.F. Kuipers, *A Structuralist Approach to Truthlikeness*. **Part II: Eight Aspects of Truthlikeness** – J. van Benthem, *Verisimilitude and Conditionals*; J. Cohen, *Verisimilitude and Legisimilitude*; R. Festa, *Theory of Similarity, Similarity of Theories, and Verisimilitude*; T.A.F. Kuipers, *Truthlikeness of Stratified Theories*; I. Niiniluoto, *Verisimilitude with Indefinite Truth*; G. Oddie, *Truthlikeness and the Convexity of Propositions*; G. de Vries, *Explaining 'Truth' in a Relativist Way*; H. Zandvoort, *Verisimilitude and Novel Facts*.

VOLUME 11 (1988)

NORMATIVE STRUCTURES OF THE SOCIAL WORLD
(Edited by Giuliano di Bernardo)

Editor's Introduction; H.-N. Castañeda, *Ought, Reasons, Motivation, and the Unity of the Social Sciences*; G.H. von Wright, *Action Logic as a Basis for Deontic Logic*; S. Galvan, *Über den Begriff von möglicher Welt in den Anwendungen der Modallogik*; G. di Bernardo, *The Formal Model M of the Game of Chess as a Type of Social Context*; R. Guastini, *Constitutive Rules and the Is-Ought Dichotomy*; H.J. Heringer, *Not by Nature nor by Intention. The Normative Power of the Language Signs*; A. Kasher, *Justification of Speech, Acts and Speech Acts*; Z. Ziembiński, *Le contenu et la structure des normes concédant les compétences*; K. Opałek, *Directives, Norms, and Performatives*; G. Kalinowski, *Les performatifs en droit. Sur la distinction entre le langage prescriptif et le langage performatif*; J. Wróblewski, *Cognition of Norms and Cognition through Norms*; A.G. Conte, *Eidos. An Essay on Constitutive Rules.* **Discussions** – A. Wiśniewski, *On Some Consequences of the Postulate of an Empirical Falsifiability of Logical Theorems*; H. Gipper, *Die Sprachphilosophie Adam Schaffs.*

VOLUME 12 (1987)

POLISH CONTRIBUTIONS TO THE THEORY AND PHILOSOPHY OF LAW
(Edited by Zygmunt Ziembiński)

Editor's Introduction. **Part I** – S. Czepita, *Leon Petrażycki and Czesław Znamierowski – Founders of the Polish Theory of Law*; K. Opałek, *Normativism against the Background of the Methodological Inquiries in Polish Legal Theory*; C. Znamierowski, *The Basic Concepts of Theory of Law. Introductory Remarks.* **Part II** – Z. Ziembiński, *The Methodological Problems of Theory and Philosophy of Law: a Survey*; J. Wróblewski, *Paradigm of Legal Dogmatics and the Legal Sciences*; J. Woleński, *Jurisprudence, Science, Philosophy*; T. Gizbert-Studnicki, *Is an Empirical Theory of Language of Law Possible?* **Part III** – L. Nowak, S. Wronkowska, M. Zieliński, Z. Ziembiński, *Conventional Acts in Law*; L. Nowak, *A Concept of Rational Legislator*; S. Wronkowska, *The Rational Legislator as a Model for the Real Lawmaker*; M. Zieliński, *Decoding Legal Text.* **Part IV** – S. Wronkowska, M. Zieliński, Z. Ziembiński, *The Methodological Problems Concerning the "Principles of Law"*; S. Pałczyński, *The Concept of Human Act in the Legal Sciences.* **Discussions** – Fr. Castellani, *Some Remarks on the Semantic Interpretation of Intensional Logic.*

VOLUME 13 (1988)

DIMENSIONS OF THE HISTORICAL PROCESS
(Edited by Leszek Nowak)

Editor's Introduction. **I. Analyzing the Dimensions of the Historical Process** – A. Klawiter, *Historical Materialism and the Visions of Social Development. A Study of Transformations of Marxian Periodization Formula*; L. Kreisberg, *The Role of Consensus in Social Conflicts*; I.C. Jarvie, *Objective versus Mentalist Conceptions of Social Class.* **II. Individual/Civilizational/Transformational Approach** – A. Honneth, *Work and Instrumental Action*; P. Buczkowski, *Rationality and the Levels of Organization of Society*; A. Bartoszek, E. Bogalska-Czajkowska, W. Czajkowski, A. Małkiewicz, *The Social Division of Labor.* **III. Globalistic/Civilizational/Adaptive Approach** – A. Klawiter, K. Łastowski, L. Nowak, W. Patryas, *Adaptation, Learning, Praxis. Some Applications of the Adaptive Conceptual Apparatus*; A. Klawiter, *Adaptation and Competition. A Contribution to the Classification of Adaptive Relationships*; M. Witkowski, *On Adaptive and Functional Dependencies. An Attempt at Categorial Approach*; K. Niedźwiadek, *The Structure and Development of the Society's Modes of Spiritual Production.* **IV. Globalistic/Conflict/Transformational Approach** – T. Söderqvist, *The Macro- and Micro-Conflict Structure of the Information- and Knowledge Society*; D. Pels, *Towards a Non-Hegelian Conception of the "New Class"*; L. Nowak, *An Idealizational Model of Capitalist Society*; G. Tomczak, *The Economic Collapse in Two Models of Socio-Economic Formation*; M. Niewiadomski, *Toward a Model of Economic Institutions*; A. Falkiewicz, *The Anatomy of Utopia*; K. Paprzycka, L. Nowak, *On the Social Nature of Colonization.*

VOLUME 14 (1990)

ACTION AND PERFORMANCE: MODELS AND TESTS. CONTRIBUTIONS TO THE QUANTITATIVE PSYCHOLOGY AND ITS METHODOLOGY

(Edited by Jerzy Brzeziński and Tadeusz Marek)

I. Philosophical Problems of Quantitative Modeling in Psychology – L.J. Cohen, *What is the Role of Mathematical Models in Psychology?*; F. Coniglione, *Models and Ideal Concepts in Contemporary Epistemological Approaches*; L. Nowak, *On Theories, Half-Theories, One-Fourth-Theories, etc. The Requirement of Formalization and the Results of the Inability to Fulfil It*; R. Stachowski, *On Pythagorean Roots of the Quantitative Psychological Thought*; H. Wottawa, *Idiographic versus Nomothetic Methodology.* **II Modeling Human Actions** – G. van den Wittenboer, *Decision Making in Scheduling Interventions*; E. Sommerfeld, *Systematization and Formalization of Cognitive Structure Transformations on the Basic of Graph Transformations*; F. Sobik, *An Approach for the Comparison of Cognitive Structures by Similarity Measures on the Basis of Graph Matrices*; B. Krause, *Non-Metric Measuring Change in Learning Processes.* **III Modeling Human Performances** – M. Gaul, *Interactional Models in Behavioral Research. Testing Interaction on Non-Interval Level of Measurement*; T. Marek and C. Noworol, *A Sequential Quasi-Measure in Questionnaire Research*; J. Brzeziński, *The ANOVA Approach to Evaluation of Psychometric Test. The New Solution of an Old Problem*; C. Nosal and Z. Piskorz, *Category Width and its Role in Human Cognitive Cycles*; W. Karwowski and A. Mital, *Fuzzy Models in Human Factors Research: Review and Appraisal.* **IV. Applications** – E.Z. Rothkopf and P. Grambsch, *Statistical Inference of Individual Eye Movement. Styles in Purposeful Reading*; J. Lindell, H. Wos and B. Samuelson, *Subjective Ratings – Comparisons Between Different Modalities.*

VOLUME 15 (1989)

VISIONS OF CULTURE AND THE MODELS OF CULTURAL SCIENCES

(Edited by Jerzy Kmita and Krystyna Zamiara)

Part I: Methodological Orientations in the Studies on Culture – J. Grad, *Theories of Culture and Studies of Participation in Culture in Polish Sociology*; E. Rewers, *The Image of the Literary Work in Present Day Sociological Studies*; T. Jerzak-Gierszewska, *Theoretical and Methodological Context of the Differentation between Magic and Religion in the Conception of Hubert, Mauss and Durkheim*; A. Grzegorczyk, *Reconstruction of Myth in the Semantics of A. J. Greimas*; B. Kotowa, *Antinaturalistic Principles of Systematizing Statements in Art Studies*; A. Szahaj, *Reflection on the Methodology of Social Sciences in the Critical Theory of Jürgen Habermas*; E. Kobylińska, *From Critical Theory to a Theory of Communicative Action: A Change of Paradigm?*; Z. Gierszewski, *Types of Cognitive and Moral Relativism and Herskovits' Cultural Relativism*; W. Ławniczak, *Theoretical Problems of Reinterpretation*; M. Piotrowski, *On Two "Intrinsic" Meanings of Music.* **Part II: Science as a Domain of Culture** – J. Kmita, *The Legacy of Magic in Science*; J. Sójka, *Theory of Science in the Light of Recent Methodological Discussions*; W. Burszta, *The Epistemological Aspects of the Controversy over Cultural Relativism*; M. Buchowski, *Ethnocentrism, Eurocentrism, Scientocentrism*; A. Pałubicka, *Structuralist Overdetermination and Historical Materialism.* **Part III: On Culture and Cultural Participation** – K. Zamiara, *Psychological versus Cultural Approaches to Participation in Culture*; A. Pluta, *On Application of the*

Notion of Pedagogical Culture; P. Ozdowski, *Logical Semantics and Psychology of Cognitive Processes*; T. Zgółka, *Study of Language as a Form of Symbolic Culture: Methodological Foundations*; G. Banaszak, *Contemporary Musical Consciousness in the Perspective of the Socio-pragmatic Theory of Culture*; A. Zeidler, *Valorization of Tradition as a Means of Preserving the Continuity of Culture.*

VOLUME 16 (1990)

IDEALIZATION I: GENERAL PROBLEMS

(Edited by Jerzy Brzeziński, Francesco Coniglione, Theo A.F. Kuipers and Leszek Nowak)

Introduction – I. Niiniluoto, *Theories, Aproximations, and Idealizations.* **Historical Studies** – F. Coniglione, *Abstraction and Idealization in Hegel and Marx*; B. Hamminga, *The Structure of Six Transformations in Marx's "Capital"*; A.G. de la Sienra, *Marx's Dialectical Method*; J. Birner, *Idealization and the Development of Capital Theory.* **Approaches to Idealization** – L.J. Cohen, *Idealization as a Form of Inductive Reasoning*; C. Dilworth, *Idealization and the Abstractive-Theoretical Model of Explanation*; R. Harré, *Idealization in Scientific Practice*; L.Nowak, *Abstracts Are Not Our Constructs. The Mental Constructs Are Abstracts.* **Idealization and problems of the philosophy of science** – M. Gaul, *Models of Cognition or Models of Reality?*; P.P. Kirschenmann, *Heuristic Strategies: Another Look at Idealization and Concretization*; T.A.F. Kuipers, *Reduction of Laws and Theories*; K. Paprzycka, *Reduction and Correspondence in the Idealizational Approach to Science.*

VOLUME 17 (1990)

IDEALIZATION II: FORMS AND APPLICATIONS

(Edited by Jerzy Brzeziński, Francesco Coniglione, Theo A.F. Kuipers and Leszek Nowak)

Forms of Idealization – R. Zielińska, *A Contribution to the Characteristic of Abstraction*; A. Machowski, *Significance: An Attempt at a Variational Interpretation*; K. Łastowski, *On Multi-Level Scientific Theories*; A. Kupracz, *Concretization and the Correction of Data*; E. Hornowska, *A Certain Approach to Operationalization*; I. Nowakowa, *External and Internal Determinants of the Development of Science: Some Methodological Remarks.* **Idealization in Science** – H. Rott, *Approximation versus Idealization: The Kepler-Newton Case*; J. Such, *The Idealizational Conception of Science and the Law of Universal Gravitation*; G. Boscarino, *Absolute Space and Idealization in Newton*; M. Sachs, *Space, Time and Motion in Einstein's Theory of Relativity*; J. Brzeziński, *On Experimental Discovery of Essential Factors in Psychological Research*; T. Maruszewski, *On Some Elements of Science in Everyday Knowledge.*

VOLUME 18 (1990)

STUDIES ON MARIO BUNGE'S TREATISE

(Edited by Paul Weingartner and Georg J.W. Dorn)

Section I: Semantics – M. Dillinger, *On the Concept of 'a Language'*; J. Ferrater-Mora, *On Mario Bunge's Semantical Realism*; A. Bartels, *Mario Bunge's Semantical Realism. An*

Antidote against Incommensurability?; J.-P. Marquis, *Partial Truths about Partial Truth*; I. Nowakowa and L. Nowak, *Approximation and the Two Ideas of Truth.* **Section II: Ontology** – J. M. Bocheński, *On the System*; J Agassi, *Ontology and Its Discontent*; Y. Wand and R. Weber, *Mario Bunge's Ontology as a Formal Foundation for Information Systems Concepts*; D. Blitz, *Emergent Evolution and the Level Structure of Reality*; M. Espinoza, *The Four Causes*; B. Dubrovsky, *A Comment on Three Topics in Volume 7 of the 'Treatise': Teleology, the Mind-Body Problem, and Health and Disease*; W. R. Shea, *Tackling the Mind*; H. Kurosaki, *Mario Bunge on the Mind-Body Problem and Ontology. Critical Examinations.* **Section III: Epistemology** – R. Boudon, *On Relativism*; G. Vollmer, *Against Instrumentalism*; M. Kary, *Information Theory and the 'Treatise': Towards a New Understanding.* **Section IV: Philosophy of Science and Technology** – F. Miró-Quesada-Canturias, *Mario Bunge's Philosophy of Logic and Mathematics*; M. Paty, *Reality and Probability in Bunge's 'Treatise'*; M. García-Sucre, *On the Relationship Between Mathematics and Physics*; B. Kanitscheider, *Does Physical Cosmology Transcend the Limits of Naturalistic Reasoning?*; M. Stöckler, *Realism and Classicism, or Something More? Some Comments on Mario Bunge's Philosophy of Quantum Mechanics*; M. E. Burgos, *Projections Are a Law of Nature*; A. Barceló, *Are there Economic Laws?*; R. Mattessich, *Mario Bunge's Influence on the Administrative and Systems Sciences*; Y. Gingras and J. Niosi, *Technology and Society: A View from Sociology*; D. A. Seni, *The Sociotechnology of Sociotechnical Systems: Elements of a Theory of Plans*; P. Weingartner, *The Non-Statement View. A Dialogue between Socrates and Theaetetus.* **Section V: Ethics** – E. Garzón-Valdes, *Basic Needs, Legitimate Wants and Political Legitimacy in Mario Bunge's Conception of Ethics*; F. Forman, *Virtue, The Missing Link to the Last Volume of the 'Treatise'*; G. Zecha, *Which Values Are Conductive to Human Survival? A Bunge-Test of Bunge-Ethics.* **Section VI: The Treatise as a Philosophy** – A. Cupani, *The Significance of the 'Treatise' in the Light of the Western Philosophical Tradition*; E. Rosenthal, *Scientific Philosophical and Sociopolitical Aspects of the Work of Mario Bunge.* **Section VII: Mario Bunge Replies. Section VIII: Mario Bunge's Life and Work** – M. Bunge, *Instant Autobiography*; D. Blitz, *Bibliography of Mario Bunge's Publications 1939-1989.*

VOLUME 19 (1990)

NARRATION AND EXPLANATION.
CONTRIBUTION TO THE METHODOLOGY OF THE HISTORICAL RESEARCH

(Edited by Jerzy Topolski)

G. Iggers, *Historical Studies in the 1980's. Some Observations*; I. Nowakowa, *Historical Narration and Idealization*; J. Pomorski, *On Historical Narration. A Contribution to the Methodology of a Research Programme*; G. Zalejko, *On Cognitive and Extra-Cognitive Components of the Historical Narrative*; J. Topolski, *Historical Explanation in Historical Materialism*; A. Zybertowicz, *Technological Determinism and Historical Materialism Revisited. Some Preliminary Notes*; J. Burbelka, *Types of Historical Processes in Ethnology*; W. Wrzosek, *In Search of Historical Time. An Essay on Time, Culture and History*; A. Ponzio, *Humanism, Philosophy of Language and Theory of Knowledge in Adam Schaff*; J. Rüsen, *Was ist historische Methode?*; A. Constanzo, *Several Remarks on Principles of Law.*

VOLUME 20 (1990)

Jürgen Ritsert
MODELS AND CONCEPTS OF IDEOLOGY

Chapter 1: *Preface – Enterprise and Experiment*; Chapter 2: *Some Theoretical Problems of Theories of Ideology*; Chapter 3: *Base and Superstructure – On the Generality of Some Marxian Models*; Chapter 4: *Action, Interest and Reflection – Weber and Weberian Models of Scientific Knowledge*; Chapter 5: *Analysis of Social Content and the Debate about Internalism and Externalism*; Chapter 6: *French Connections in Models of Ideology – Or: Des idées Franco-allemandes*; Chapter 7: *Critical Theory of Ideology – On Adorno's Dialectical Model of Appearance and Ideology.*

VOLUME 21 (1991)

PROBABILITY AND RATIONALITY
STUDIES ON L. JONATHAN COHEN'S PHILOSOPHY OF SCIENCE
(Edited by Ellery Eells and Tomasz Maruszewski)

Part I: Setting the Stage – L. J. Cohen, *From a Historical Point of View*; **Part II: The Method of Relevant Variables and Other Modes of Scientific Reasoning** – L. Nowak, *The Method of Relevant Variables and Idealization*; M. Fisch, *Learning from Experience*; M. A. Finocchiaro, *Induction and Intuition in the Normative Study of Reasoning.* **Part III: Subjective Probability: Pascalian and Baconian Conceptions** – D.A. Schum, *Jonathan Cohen and Thomas Bayes on the Analysis of Chains of Reasoning*; J. Logue, *Weight of Evidence, Resiliency and Second-Order Probabilities*; C.S. Nosal, *Neurobiology of Subjective Probability*; R. Stachowski, *On Standard and Non-Standard Models in Theories of Psychological Measurment.* **Part IV: Rationality and Methodological Pluralism** – L.L. Lopes and G.C. Oden, *The Rationality of Intelligence*; G. Gigerenzer, *On Cognitive Illusions and Rationality*; J.E. Adler, *An Optimist's Pessimism: Conversation and Conjuction*; T. Maruszewski, *Human Rationality – Fact or Idealizational Assumption*; I.T. Ścigała, *Are People Programmed to be Normal? Psychological Determinants of Human Normality.* **Part V: Conclusion** – L. Jonathan Cohen, *Some Comments by L.J.C.*

VOLUME 22 (1991)

THE SOCIAL HORIZON OF KNOWLEDGE
(Edited by Piotr Buczkowski)

J. Ritsert, *The Wittgenstein-Problem in Sociology or: The "Linguistic Turn" as a Pirouette*; D. Jary, *Beyond Objectivity and Relativism: Feyerabend's "Two Argumentative Chains" and Sociology*; L. Nowak, *The Defence of a Social System Against its Ideology. A Case Study*; P. Buczkowski, *Remarks on the Structure of Social Consciousness*; A. Falkiewicz, *The Individual's Horizon and Valuation*; F. Lövenich, *Heiligsprechung des Imaginären. Das Imaginäre in Cornelius Castoriadis' Gesellschaftstheorie*; T. Maruszewski, *Everyday Knowledge as Representation of Reality.*

VOLUME 23 (1991)

ETHICAL DIMENSIONS OF LEGAL THEORY
(Edited by Wojciech Sadurski)

W. Sadurski, *Introduction*; J. Wróblewski, *Moral Values and Legal Reasoning: Some Aspects of Their Mutual Relations*; H. Tapani-Klami, J. Sorvettula and M. Hatakka, *Moral Reasoning and Evidence in Legal Decision-Making*; T. Gizbert-Studnicki, *Conflict of Values in Adjudication*; M. Krygier, *Thinking Like a Lawyer*; A. Peczenik, *Prima-facie Values and the Law*; R. Wacks, *Judges and Moral Responsibility*; Z. Ziembiński, *The Concept of Morality in Philosophy of Law*; G. Haarscher, *Law, Reason and Ethics in the Philosophy of Human Rights*; T.D. Campbell, *Unlawful Discrimination*; H. Ph. Visser' Hoft, *Intergenerational Justice: Some Reflections on Methodology*; Ch. Sampford and D. Wood, *Tax, Justice and Priority of Property.*

VOLUME 24 (1991)

ADVANCES IN SCIENTIFIC PHILOSOPHY
ESSAYS IN HONOUR OF PAUL WEINGARTNER ON THE OCCASION OF THE 60TH ANNIVERSARY OF HIS BIRTHDAY
(Edited by Gerhard Schurz and Georg J.W. Dorn)

Section I: Advances in Philosophical Logic – R. Sylvan and R. Nola, *Confirmation without Paradoxes*; B. Smith, *Relevance, Relatedness and Restricted Set Theory*; G. Schurz, *Relevant Deductive Inference: Criteria and Logics*; M.L. Dalla Chiara, *Epistemic Logic without Logical Omniscience*; P. Gochet and E. Gillet, *On Professor Weingartner's Contribution to Epistemic Logic*; H. Festini, *An Application of Weingartner's Logical Proposal for Rational Belief, Knowledge and Assumption*; L. Åquist, *Deontic Tense Logic: Restricted Equivalence of Certain Forms of Conditional Obligation and a Solution to Chisholm's Paradox*; E. Orlowska, *Relational Formalization of Temporal Logics*; W. Lenzen, *What Is (or At Least Appears to Be) Wrong with Intuitionistic Logic?* **Section II: Current Challenges in Philosophy of Science** – Ch.P. Enz, *Quantum Theory in the Light of Modern Experiments*; P. Mittelstaedt, *An Inconsistency between Quantum Mechanics and Its Interpretation: The "Disaster" of Objectification*; E. Scheibe, *Substances, Physical Systems, and Quantum Mechanics*; M. Stockler, *Reductionism and the New Theories of Self-Organization*; B. Kanitscheider, *Unification as an Epistemological Problem*; R. Haller, *Atomism and Holism in the Vienna Circle*; M. Przełęcki, *Is the Notion of Truth Applicable to Scientific Theories?*; T.A.F. Kuipers, *Structuralist Explications of Dialectics*; C.U. Moulines, *Pragmatics in the Structuralist View of Science*; K.R. Popper, *A World of Propensities. Two New Views of Causality*; G.J.W. Dorn, *Inductive Support*. **Section III: Recent Debates in Semantics and Ontology** – F. von Kutschera, *Kripke's Doubts about Meaning*; I. Bellert, *A Linguistic Approach to Frege's Puzzles*; P.M. Simons, *Inadequacies of Intension and Extension*; E. Morscher, *Inadequacies of Peter and Paul*; J. Brandl, *Some Remarks on the "Slingshot" Argument*; A. Hieke, *Real Facts*. **Section IV: Epistemological and Ethical Problems with Society** – E. Klevakina, *The Case against Value-Free Belief*; R. Tuomela, *Mutual Beliefs and Social Characteristics*; H. Lenk nad M. Maring, *A Pie-Model of Moral Responsibility? Remarks Concerning Ethical Dilutionism*; O. Neumaier, *Are Collectives Morally Responsible?*; E. Bencivenga, *The Electronic Self*. **Section V: Analytical Philosophy of Religion** – J.M. Bocheński, *Faith and Science. A Logical Commentary on the First Question of the*

Summa; E. Nieznański, *The Beginnings of Formalization in Theology*; H. Ganthaler, *Some Comments on Paul Weingartner's Concept of Scientific Theology.* **Section VI: Methods of Philosophy** – G. Kreisel, *Suitable Descriptions for Suitable Categories*; M. Bunge, *Why We Cherish Exactness?*; L. Koj, *Exactness and Philosophy.* **Section VII: Life and Work of Paul Weingartner** – G. Zecha, *Paul Weingartner: Philosophy at Work. A Biographical Sketch*; E. Stieringer, *Bibliography of Paul Weingartner's Publications 1961-1991.*

VOLUME 25 (1992)

IDEALIZATION III: APPROXIMATION AND TRUTH
(Edited by Jerzy Brzeziński and Leszek Nowak)

Introduction – L. Nowak, *The Idealizational Approach to Science: A Survey.* **On the Nature of Idealization** – M. Kuokkanen and T. Tuomivaara, *On the Structure of Idealizations*; B. Hamminga, *Idealization in the Practice and Methodology of Classical Economics: The Logical Struggle with Lemma's and Undesired Theorems*; R. Zielińska, *The Threshold Generalization of the Idealizational Laws*; A. Kupracz, *Testing and Correspondence*; K. Paprzycka, *Why Do Idealizational Statements Apply to Reality?* **Idealization, Approximation, and Truth** – T.A.F. Kuipers, *Truth Approximation by Concretization*; I. Nowakowa, *A Notion of Truth for Idealization*; I. Nowakowa, L. Nowak, *"Truth is a System": An Explication*; I. Nowakowa, *The Idea of "Truth as a Process". An Explication*; L. Nowak, *On the Concept of Adequacy of Laws. An Idealizational Explication*; M. Paprzycki, K. Paprzycka, *Accuracy, Essentiality and Idealization.* **Discussions** – J. Sójka, *On the Origins of Idealization in the Social Experience*; M. Paprzycki, K. Paprzycka, *A Note on the Unitarian Explication of Idealization*; I. Hanzel, *The Pure Idealizational Law – The Inherent Law – The Inherent Idealizational Law.*

VOLUME 26 (1992)

IDEALIZATION IV: INTELLIGIBILITY IN SCIENCE
(Edited by Craig Dilworth)

C. Dilworth, *Introduction: Idealization and Intelligibility in Science*; E. Agazzi, *Intelligibility, Understanding and Explanation in Science*; H. Lauener, *Transcendental Arguments Pragmatically Relativized: Accepted Norms (Conventions) as an A Priori Condition for any Form of Intelligibility*; M. Paty, *L'Endoréférence d'une Science Formalisée de la Nature*; B. d'Espagnat, *De l'Intelligibilité du Monde Physique*; M. Artigas, *Three Levels of Interaction between Science and Philosophy*; J. Crompton, *The Unity of Knowledge and Understanding in Science*; G. Del Re, *The Case for Finalism in Science*; A. Cordero, *Intelligibility and Quantum Theory*; O. Costa de Beauregard, *De l'Intelligibilité en Physique. Example: Relativité, Quanta, Correlations EPR*; L. Fleischhacker, *Mathematical Abstraction, Idealization and Intelligibility in Science*; B. Ellis, *Idealization in Science*; P.T. Manicas, *Intelligibility and Idealization: Marx and Weber*; H. Lind, *Intelligibility and Formal Models in Economics*; U. Mäki, *On the Method of Isolation in Economics*; C. Dilworth, R. Pyddoke, *Principles, Facts and Theories in Economics*; J.C. Graves, *Intelligibility in Psychotherapy*; René Thom, *The True, the False and the Insignificant or Landscaping the Logos.*

VOLUME 27 (1992)

Ryszard Stachowski

THE MATHEMATICAL SOUL.
AN ANTIQUE PROTOTYPE OF THE MODERN MATEMATISATION OF PSYCHOLOGY

Chapter 1: *The Pythagorean "Number of Man"*; Chapter 2: *The Soul as a (Self-Moving) Number*; Chapter 3: *The Soul as Harmony*; Chapter 4: *The Soul as Originative of Relational Concepts*; Chapter 5: *The Faculty of the Soul as Intensive Psychological Quantity*; Chapter 6: *Soul Equals Mathematicals*; Chapter 7: *Soul to a Greater or Lesser Degree*; Epilogue; *Why Did Aristotle Call Psychology an Exact Science?*; Conclusion

VOLUME 28 (1993)

POLISH SCIENTIFIC PHILOSOPHY:
THE LVOV-WARSAW SCHOOL
(Edited by Francesco Coniglione, Roberto Poli and Jan Woleński)

Preface. **Background and Influence** – L. Albertazzi, *Brentano, Twardowski, and Polish Scientific Philosophy*; K. Schuhmann, *Husserl and Twardowski*; G. Küng, *Phenomenology and Polish Scientific Philosophy*; F. Coniglione, *Scientific Philosophy and Marxism in Poland.* **History and Systematics** – T. Kwiatkowski, *Classification of Reasonings in Contemporary Polish Philosophy*; A. Dylus, *The Problems of Ethics of Science in the Lvov-Warsaw School*; J.J. Jadacki, *Kazimierz Twardowski's Descriptive Semiotics*; P.M. Simons, *Nominalism in Poland*; T. Rzepa, R. Stachowski, *Roots of the Methodology of Polish Psychology*; K. Trzęsicki, *Łukasiewicz on Philosophy and Determinism*; A. Jedynak, *Conventionalism in Ajdukiewicz*; A. Siemianowski, *On Certain Consequences of the Radical Empiricism Hypothesis*; J. Woleński, *Tarski as a Philosopher*; R. Poli, *The Dispute over Reism: Kotarbiński – Ajdukiewicz – Brentano.*

VOLUME 29 (1993)

Zdzisław Augustynek and Jacek J. Jadacki

POSSIBLE ONTOLOGIES

Possible Ontologies – J.J. Jadacki, *Preface*; Z. Augustynek, *Point Eventism. An Outline of a Certain Ontology*; J.J. Jadacki, *Ontological Minimum.* **Discussions** – K. Paprzycka, *Carnap and Leibniz on the Problem of Being*; P. Przybysz, *Polish Discussions about Reism.*

VOLUME 30 (1993)

GOVERNMENT: SERVANT OR MASTER?
(Edited by Gerard Radnitzky and Hardy Bouillon)

G. Radnitzky, *Introduction: The Ominous Growth of the Monstrous Leviathan.* **Part I: Theory** – A. Seldon, *Politicians for or against the People*; G. Radnitzky, *Private Rights against Public Power: The Contemporary Conflict*; A. de Jasay, *Is Limited Government*

Possible?; H. Bouillon, *Mastering the Growth of Government: A Muzzle for Leviathan*; A. de Jasay, *Ownership, Agency, Socialism.* **Part II: Case Studies** – P. Bernholz, *Necessary and Sufficient Conditions to End Hyperinflations*; G. Schwarz, *The Deterioration of Switzerland's Economic System Policy*; H.O. Lenel, *Three Turns in West Germany since 1948 – Considered from the Viewpoint of the Theory of Economic Systems*; A. Flew, *Educational Services: Abuses of State Monopoly*; J.W.F. Sundberg, *Revenue-Only Taxes vs. Multipurpose Taxes: Philosophy and Implementation in Swedish High Tax Society*; S. Pejovich, *Political and Economic Reforms in Eastern Europe: The Case of Yugoslavia.* **Part III: The Limiting Case. The Totalitarian Order** – P. Bernholz, *Necessary Conditions for Totalitarianism: Supreme Values, Power and Personal Interest.*

VOLUME 31 (1993)

CREATIVITY AND CONSCIOUSNESS. PHILOSOPHICAL AND PSYCHOLOGICAL DIMENSIONS

(Edited by Jerzy Brzeziński, Santo Di Nuovo, Tadeusz Marek and Tomasz Maruszewski)

Introduction. **Part I: What Do Philosophers Say about Creativity and Consciousness?** – K. Zamiara, *Psychological Approach to Creativity. A Critical Approach*; R.L. Franklin, *Creativity and Depth in Understanding*; Z. Piątek, *Creating of Life and F. Nietzsche's Idea of Superman*; J. Janousek, *Dialogue and Joint Activity: A Psychological Approach*; K. Zamiara, *Some Remarks on Piagetian Notion of "Consciousness" and Its Importance for the Science of Culture*; A. Gałdowa, A. Nelicki, *Attitudes Toward Values as a Factor Determining Creativity.* **Part II: The Role of Creativity in Theory-Building** – L. Nowak, *Creativity in Theory-Bulding*; I. Nowak, *Discovery and Correspondence*; J. Brzeziński, *Factors Disturbing Validity of Experimental and Non-Experimental Psychological Research – Context's Analysis of Researcher's Psychologists Methodological Consciousness*; A. Falkowski, *Cognitive Similarity in Scientific Discovery: An Ecological Approach.* **Part III: Consciousness in Historical Perspective** – K.V. Wilkes, *Inside Insight*; F. di Maria, G. Lavanco, *Conscious/Unconscious and Group-Analysis.* **Part IV: Between Expression and Projection** – M. Stasiakiewicz, *Creativity and Projection: Paradigm Opposition and Implicit Correspondence*; A. Brzezińska, *Creative Expression versus Projection.* **Part V: The Role of Psychophysiological Components in Explanation of Phenomena of Consciousness and Creativity** – M. Bunge, *Explaining Creativity*; P. Wolski, *Hemispheric Asymmetry and Consciousness. Is there Any Relationship?*; A. Kokoszka, *A Rationale for Psychology of Consciousness*; M. Fąfrowicz, T. Marek, *Creativity and Attention.* **Part VI: Psychological Explanations of Creativity and Consciousness** – S. Di Nuovo, *Consciousness and Attention*; T. Maruszewski, *Some Remarks about Consciousness*; M. Kowalczyk, *On the Question of Functions of Consciousness*; D.K. Simonton, *From Childhood Giftedness to Creativity Genius*; M. Fąfrowicz, T. Marek, Cz. Noworol, K. Żarczyński, *Creativity and Organization*; M.A. Runco and J. R. Gaynor, *Creativity and Optimal Development.*

VOLUME 32 (1993)

FROM ONE-PARTY-SYSTEM TO DEMOCRACY

(Edited by Janina Frentzel-Zagórska)

J. Frentzel-Zagórska, *Introduction.* **Part I: Theoretical Approaches** – Z. Bauman, *A Postmodern Revolution*; L. Holmes, *On Communism, Post-communism, Modernity and Post-*

modernity; L. Nowak, *The Totalitarian Approach and the History of Socialism*; J. Pakulski, *East European Revolutions and 'Legitimacy Crisis'*. **Part II: The Transitional Period** – A. Czarnota, M. Krygier, *From State to Legal Traditions? Prospects for the Rule of Law after Communism*; M. Szabó, *Social Protest in a Post-communist Democracy: Taxi Drivers' Demonstration in Hungary*; Z. Bauman, *Dismantling Patronage State*; E. Mokrzycki, *Between Reform and Revolution: Eastern Europe Two Years after the Fall of Communism*; J. Frentzel-Zagórska, *The Road to Democratic Political System in Post-communist Eastern Europe*. **Part III: The Case of Yugoslavia** – R.F. Miller, *Yugoslavia: The End of the Experiment*.

VOLUME 33 (1993)

SOCIAL SYSTEM, RATIONALITY, AND REVOLUTION
(Edited by Marcin Paprzycki and Leszek Nowak)

Introduction. **On the Nature of Social System** – U. Preuss, *Political Order and Democracy. Carl Schmitt and his Influence*; K. Paprzycka, *A Paradox in Hobbes' Philosophy of Law*; S. Esquith, *Democratic Political Dialogue*; E. Jeliński, *Democracy in Polish Reformist Socialist Thought*; K. Paprzycka, *The Master and Slave Configuration in Hegel's System*; M. Godelier, *Lévi-Strauss, Marx and After. A Reappraisal of Structuralist and Marxist Tools for Social Logics*; K. Niedźwiadek, *On the Structure of Social System*; W. Czajkowski, *Social Being and Its Reproduction*. **On Rationality and Captivity** – M. Ziółkowski, *Power and Knowledge*, L. Nowak, *Two Inter-Human Limits to the Rationality of Man*; M. Paprzycki, *The Non-Christian Model of Man: An Attempt at Psychological Explanation*; R. Egiert, *Toward the Sophisticated Rationalistic Model of Man*. **On Social Revolution** – L. Nowak, *Revolution is an Opaque Progress but a Progress Nonetheless*; K. Paprzycka, M. Paprzycki, *How do Enslaved People Make Revolutions?*; G. Tomczak, *Is it Worth Winning a Revolution?*; K. Brzechczyn, *Civil Loops and the Absorption of Elites*; R. McCleary, *What Makes Marxist Historical Materialism Objective?*; G. Kotlarski, *Classes and Masses in Social Philosophy of Rosa Luxemburg*. **On Real Socialism** – E. Gellner, *The Civil and the Sacred*; W. Marciszewski, *Economics and the Idea of Information. Why Socialism must have Collapsed?*; L. Nowak, K. Paprzycka, M. Paprzycki, *On Multilinearity of Socialism*; A. Siegel, *The Overrepression Cycle in the Soviet Union. An Operationalization of a Theoretical Model*; K. Brzechczyn, *The State of the Teutonic Order as a Socialist Society*. **Discussions** – R. McCleary, *Socioanalysis and Philosophy*; W. Heller, *Methodological Remarks on the Public and the Private in Hannah Arendt's Political Philosophy*; K. Brzechczyn, *On Unsuccessful Conquest and Successful Subordination*.

VOLUME 34 (1994)

Izabella Nowakowa

IDEALIZATION V: THE DYNAMICS OF IDEALIZATIONS

Introduction; Chapter I: *Idealization and Theories of Correspondence*; Chapter II: *Dialectical Correspondence of Scientific Laws*; Chapter III: *Dialectical Correspondence in Science: Some Examples*; Chapter IV: *Dialectical Correspondence of Scientific Theories*; Chapter V: *Generalizations of the Rule of Correspondence*; Chapter VI: *Extensions of the Rule of Correspondence*; Chapter VII: *Correspondence and the Empirical Environment of a Theory*; Chapter VIII: *Some Methodological Problems of Dialectical Correspondence*.

VOLUME 35 (1993)

EMPIRICAL LOGIC AND PUBLIC DEBATE. ESSAYS IN HONOUR OF ELSE M. BARTH

(Edited by E.C.W. Krabbe, R.J. Dalitz, and P.A. Smit)

Part I: Interpersonal Reasoning: Conflicts and Fallacies – T. Govier, *Needing Each Other for Knowledge: Reflections on Trust and Testimony*; J. Woods, *'Secundum quid' as a Research Programme*; G. Nuchelmans, *On the Fourfold Root of the 'argumentum ad hominem'*; F.H. van Eemeren, R. Grootendorst, *The History of the 'argumentum ad hominem' Since the Seventeenth Century*; L.S. van Epenhuysen, *Debate in a Bermuda Triangle of Medical Ethics*; E.C.W. Krabbe, *Reasonable Argument and Fallacies in the Kok-Stekelenburg Debate*; **Part II: Linguistic and Conceptual Tools** – J.D. North, *Some Weak Links in the Great Chain of Being*; A. Næss, *'You assert this?' An Empirical Study of Weight Expressions*; R. Wiche, *Gerrit Mannoury on the Communicative Functions of Negation in Ordinary Language*; J. Hoepelman, T. van Hoof, *Default and Dogma*; Ch. Goossens, *On the Logic of Nonmoral Commitment*; W. Marciszewski, *Arguments Founded on Creative Definitions*; R. Jorna, *Cognitive Science and Connectivism: Friend and Enemy or Move and Counter-Move, an Application of Empirical Logic*; **Part III: Dialectical Climates and Tempests** – R.H. Johnson, *Dialectical Fields and Manifest Rationality*; P. du Preez, *Reason Which Cannot Be Reasoned With: What Is Public Debate and How Does it Change?*; M.A. Finocchiaro, *Logic, Democracy, and Mosca*; P.A. Smit, *The Logic of Virtue and Terror*; G. van Benthem van den Bergh, *On Obstacles to Public Debate*; J.P. van Bendegem, *Real-Life Mathematics versus Ideal Mathematics: The Ugly Truth*; **Part IV: The Disempowernment of Woman: Strategies and Counter-Moves** – V. Songe-Møller, *The Road of Being and the Exclusion of the Feminine. An Analysis of the Poem of Parmenides*; R.J. Dalitz, *The Subjection of Women in the Contractual Society. An Analysis of Thomas Hobbes' Theory of Agreement*; H. Schröder, *Anti-Semitism and anti-Feminism Again: The Dissemination of Otto Weininger's 'Sex and Character' in the Seventies and Eighties*; J.R. Richards, *Traditional Spheres and Traditional Logic.*

VOLUME 36 (1994)

MARXISM AND COMMUNISM: POSTHUMOUS REFLECTIONS ON POLITICS, SOCIETY, AND LAW

(Edited by Martin Krygier)

M. Krygier, *Introduction*; A. Flis, *From Marx to Real Socialism: The History of a Utopia*; P. Marciniak, *The Collapse of Communism: Defeat or Opportunity for Marxism in Eastern Europe*; J. Clark, A. Wildavsky, *Chronicle of a Collapse Foretold: How Marx Predicted the Demise of Communism (Although He Called It "Capitalism")*; L. Nowak, *Political Theory and Socialism. On the Main Paradigms of Political Power and Their Methodological and Historical Legitimation*; E. Mokrzycki, *Marxism, Sociology, and "Real Socialism"*; R. Bäcker, *The Collapse of Communism and Theoretical Models*; A. Zybertowicz, *Three Deaths an Ideology: The Withering Away of Marxism and the Collapse of Communism. The Case of Poland*; M. Krygier, *Marxism, Communism, and the Rule of Law*; A. Czarnota, *Marxism, Ideology, and Law*; G. Skąpska, *The Legacy of Anti-Legalism*; A. Sajo, *Law and the Legal Scholarship in the Happiest Barrack and Among the Hungry Liberated: Personal Recollections.*

VOLUME 37 (1994)

THE SOCIAL PHILOSOPHY OF AGNES HELLER
(Edited by John Burnheim)

J. Burnheim, *Introduction*; M. Vajda, *A Lover of Philosophy – A Lover of Europe*; P. Despoix, *On the Possibility of a Philosophy of Values. A Dialogue within the Budapest School*; M. Jay, *Women in Dark Times: Agnes Heller and Hannah Arendt*; J.P. Arnason, *The Human Condition and the Modern Predicament*; R.J. Bernstein, *Agnes Heller: Philosophy, Rational Utopia and Praxis*; Z. Bauman, *Narrating Modernity*; P. Beilharz, *Theories of History – Agnes Heller and R.G. Collingwood*; P. Wolin, *Heller's Theory of Everyday Life*; P. Harrison, *Radical Philosophy and the Theory of Modernity*; A.J. Jacobson, *The Limits of Formal Justice*; P. Murphy, *Civility and Radicalism*; P. Murphy, *Pluralism and Politics*; V. Camps, *The Good Life: A Moral Gesture*; L. Boella, *Philosophy Beyond the Baseless and Tragic Character of Action*; G. Márkus, *The Politics of Morals*; A. Heller, *A Reply to My Critics*; *The Bibliography of Agnes Heller.*

MAURO ANTONELLI

Die experimentelle Analyse des Bewußtseins bei Vittorio Benussi

Amsterdam/Atlanta, GA 1994. 218 pp. + XIV.
(Studien zur österreichischen Philosophie 21)
ISBN: 90-5183-650-3 Hfl. 75,-/US-$ 44.-

Inhaltsverzeichnis: Vorwort. I. Einleitung. II. Vittorio Benussi: Eine Skizze seines Lebens. III. Die Phänomenologie der Wahrnehmung. 1. Die inadäquate Gestaltauffassung. 2. Die Zeitauffassung. 3. Die Phänomenologie des latenten Subjektes. IV. Die Benussi-Koffka Kontroverse. Produktionstheorie und Gestalttheorie. V. Die "psychische Realanalyse" der Wahrnehmung: Wahrnehmung, Vorstellung und Überzeugung; Gestalt und Assimilation. VI. Zur Nachwirkung Vittorio Benussis: Die italienische Gestaltpsychologie. Anhang: Verzeichnis der Lehrveranstaltungen Benussis. Literatur- und Quellenverzeichnis. Namensverzeichnis.

HEINZ KIMMERLE

Die Dimension des Interkulturellen
Philosophie in Afrika – afrikanische Philosophie
Zweiter Teil: Supplemente und Verallgemeinerungsschritte

Amsterdam/Atlanta, GA 1994. 198 pp.
(Studien zur interkulturellen Philosophie 2)
ISBN: 90–5183–694–5 Hfl. 60,–/US–$ 35.–

Dieses Buch sucht den Diskurs über afrikanische Philosophie, der in früheren Veröffentlichungen des Autors begonnen wurde, fortzusetzen. Wichtige neue Themen sind: 1. Die Situation der Philosophie in den französisch–sprachigen afrikanischen Ländern, insbesondere der Einfluß des Islam auf die afrikanische Weisheitslehre; 2. Die Arbeit afrikanischer Philosophen in der amerikanischen Diaspora; 3. Das wichtige Buch von K.A. Appiah: *In My Father's House. Africa in the Philosophy of Culture* (1992). – Von diesen Untersuchungen aus wird die Bedeutung der Beschäftigung mit afrikanischer Philosophie für die interkulturelle Philosophie oder – genauer gesagt – für die Notwendigkeit der Dimension des Interkulturellen innerhalb der heutigen Philosophie überhaupt in drei Schritten herausgearbeitet: 1. Afrika in der Philosophie Hegels; 2. Eine nicht mehr eurozentrische Neubestimmung des Verhältnisses der Kulturen zueinander. 3. Der Status universaler Erkenntnis aus der Perspektive kulturanthropologischer Forschungen. – Schließlich wird in zwei Zwischenbetrachtungen die Kritik am hier vertretenen Ansatz einer interkulturellen Philosophie gegenkritisch behandelt.

INTERNATIONAL SOCIETY FOR UNIVERSALISM
invites you to our journal *DIALOGUE AND HUMANISM*
published quarterly by Warsaw University

SOME OF THE PROMINENT AUTHORS FEATURED IN *DIALOGUE AND HUMANISM*:

John Paul II — "The Address Delivered at a Meeting with Governmental Authorities and the President of the Republic of Poland at the Royal Castle in Warsaw", No. 3–4/1991
Evandro Agazzi — "Hermeneutic and Referential Aspects of Comparing Theories", No. 2/1991
Eugene Kamenka — "Marx and Hegel", No. 1/1991
A Conversation with Professor Zbigniew Brzeziński — "Do We Have Now a Beginning of Universal History?"
Janina Kotarbińska — "Tadeusz Kotarbiński's Independent Ethics", No. 3–4/1992
Leszek Kołakowski — "Even When the Devil Says He Is Telling the Truth, He Is Lying", No. 3–4/1992
Michael H. Mitias — "Toward a Concept of Universal Justice", No. 3–4/1992
James Sterba — "Reconciling Conceptions of Justice: A Path to Universal Justice", No. 3–4/1992
Arthur McGovern — "John Paul II's Social Thought and U.S. Responses", No. 2/1992
Gert Hummel — "*Media vita in morte sumus* — Life and Death in Christian View", No. 2/1992
Relations between JUDAISM, CHRISTIANITY AND ISLAM IN THE QUEST FOR A METAPHILOSOPHY OF UNIVERSALISM, Discussion initiated by the Ambassadors of Egypt and Israel, No. 2/1992

TOPICS WE WOULD LIKE TO BE DISCUSSED IN THE FORTHCOMING ISSUES:

★ The development of universalism as a metaphilosophy in response to post-modernism, and the crisis in all philosophies.
★ Universalism as an approach to the integration of the sciences and humanities; theory and practice, leading towards an open synthesis.
★ The university as a model of interdisciplinarity; the integration yet differentiation of disciplines — unity and particularity.
★ University as a forerunner and present implicit form of universalism: potentialities of revitalizing a dialogue among autonomous disciplines in joint scholarly tasks (co-teaching, co-research...)
★ Universalism and philosophy of science.
★ The categories and interpretations of universalism: dialogue, pluralism, multi-level identification, conjunctive thinking, synergy.
★ Universalism as an area of common fundamental, transcendental and crowning values, as methodology, as metaphilosophy, as an attitude.
★ Inter-cultural relations, including the supposedly-religious justifications of such conflicts as those in the Middle East, former Yugoslavia and the former Soviet Union.
★ The emergence of a new European consciousness, supplementary to national identification — in the global context.
★ The growing role of non-Western traditions in the dialogical development of humanity for itself, as global community.
★ Metaphilosophical anthropology: Homo universalis.

Subscription rates:	Before Aug. 31, 1993.	Later.
Individuals	$ 25	$ 40
Same, for 3 years in advance	$ 60	$ 100
Institutions	$ 50	$ 80
Same, for 3 years in advance	$ 120	$ 200

ADDRESS:
Centre of Universalism/**Dialogue and Humanism**
Philosophy, U.W., Krakowskie Przedmieście 3
00-047 WARSAW 64, POLAND

FAX: 4822/267-520
Tel.: 4822/264-567

E-mail in Europe: Kuczynsk@PLEARN.BITNET
E-mail in North America: CY59@MusicA.McGill.ca

SIDNEY AXINN

The Logic of Hope
Extensions of Kant's View of Religion

Amsterdam/Atlanta, GA 1994. XI,313 pp.
(Value Inquiry Book Series 15)
ISBN: 90-5183-693-7 Hfl. 100,-/US-$ 58.50

This book is a thorough study of the question posed by Kant, *For what can a human being rationally hope?* It offers a detailed commentary on Kant's seminal work, *Religion Within the Limits of Reason Alone,* as well as an original development of the logic of three of Kant's basic ideas: ambivalence, ignorance, and hope. Sophisticated analytic techniques, including symbolic logic, are applied to this conceptual matrix. The result is a striking case for the transformation of world society into a Kingdom of Ends of individuals and a peaceful League of Nations.

USA/Canada: Editions Rodopi, 233 Peachtree Street, N.E., Suite 404, Atlanta, GA 30303-1504, Telephone (404) 523-1964, Call toll-free 1-800-225-3998 (U.S. only), Fax (404) 522-7116

And Others: Editions Rodopi B.V., Keizersgracht 302-304, 1016 EX Amsterdam, The Netherlands. Telephone ++ (0) 20 622 75 07, Fax ++ (0) 20 638 09 48

JOSEPH P. DEMARCO

A Coherence Theory in Ethics

Amsterdam/Atlanta, GA 1994. XIV,270 pp.
(Value Inquiry Book Series 10)
ISBN: 90–5183–670–8 Hfl. 90,–/US–$ 52.50

This book offers a comprehensive approach to moral experience. It respects the many dimensions of our moral life which elude the traditional philosophical theories that deal exclusively with principles, consequences, virtues, or some other single dimension. Working from a critique of such traditions, the book shows how to integrate their values in a dynamic coherence. Thus, it is not just another ethical theory, but a new level of philosophizing in ethics which rewards the reader with an enlarged and enriched vision of our complexity as moral beings.

WILLIAM GERBER

The Meaning of Life
Insights of the World's Great Thinkers

Amsterdam/Atlanta, GA 1994. XVII,282 pp.
(Value Inquiry Book Series 12)

ISBN: 90-5183-691-0 Bound Hfl. 125,-/US-$ 73.50
ISBN: 90-5183-680-5 Paper Hfl. 45,-/US-$ 26.-

The book aims to present the wisdom of sages, great thinkers, renowned writers, and philosophers, of many countries and time periods, in their own words, regarding life. The book also aims to place the numerous quotations from these sources in a structured organization, with introductory and explanatory comments and comparisons.

Main Topics or Fields – See Organization or Principal Parts.

Organization or Principal Parts – Part 1, The Deepest Questions About Life in General (whence *came* life? what *is* life? what is the nature of plants and animals? etc.); Part 2, The Deepest Questions About Human Life in Particular (what is unique about humanity? who am I and what am I? do humans have free will?); Part 3, The Deepest Questions About the Quality, Meaning, and Span of Our Lives (are we more like angels or like devils? what meaning if any do our lives have? how do we march from infancy to old age and death?); and Part 4, The Deepest Questions About Living in Society (what are the basic truths about sex, love, marriage, civilization, and religion?).

Special Features – An appendix shows the source of every quotation included in the book. An index of authors lists the quotations taken from each author.

FRANK G. FORREST

Valuemetrics$\aleph$: The Science of Personal and Professional Ethics

Amsterdam/Atlanta, GA 1994. XVIII,179 pp.
(Value Inquiry Book Series 11)
ISBN: 90–5183–683–X Hfl. 60,–/US–$ 35.–

Valuemetrics is an elaboration of Robert S. Hartman's innovative development in the application of an abstract system to the study of ethical problems. The system used for this purpose is a branch of logic called set theory. Set theory fulfills this role because goodness, the fundamental phenomenon of ethics, is defined axiomatically in terms of sets. The similarity of structure between certain elements of set theory and the various types and degrees of goodness makes mathematical accounting of goodness phenomena possible. In the valuemetrics context, value judgments are considered as an assessment of the goodness of something. Therefore, the mathematical system for the accounting of goodness serves as a tool for objectively making many kinds of value judgments and possible attendant ethical decisions. One of the results of this conception, attributable to Hartman, is the birth of the science of ethics.

The first half of the book elucidates the theory, terminology, and mathematical system used in valuemetrics, known as Hartmanean algebra. The second half is devoted to the application of this system to the measurement and development of a person's value vision, and the solution of various problems in ethics using the case study technique. Hartmanean algebra will resolve several types of problems such as the determination of right and wrong, good and bad; determining how to redress and amend instances of wrongs and badness; and how to determine when, if ever, wrongs and badness are justified.

USA/Canada: Editions Rodopi, 233 Peachtree Street, N.E., Suite 404, Atlanta, GA 30303–1504, Telephone (404) 523–1964, Call toll–free 1–800–225–3998 (U.S. only), Fax (404) 522–7116

And Others: Editions Rodopi B.V., Keizersgracht 302–304, 1016 EX Amsterdam, The Netherlands. Telephone ++ (0) 20 622 75 07, Fax ++ (0) 20 638 09 48

GEORGE DAVID MILLER

An Idiosyncratic Ethics Or, the Lauramachean Ethics

Amsterdam/Atlanta, GA 1994. VII,140 pp.
(Value Inquiry Book Series 9)
ISBN: 90-5183-682-1 Hfl. 45,-/US-$ 26.-

This book is an original synthesis of four elements: (1) the phenomenology of value, (2) caring, (3) the moral imagination, and (4) Kant's formula of humanity. The striking result is an ethics of caring that develops our shared humanity. The probing analysis and pungent argument are assisted by imaginative forms of dialogue, narration, and parable. This lively contribution to our ethical fulfillment concludes with a case for student-centered education that is democratic, creative and caring.

SABINE DOYÉ

J.G. Fichte-Bibliographie (1968–1992/93)

Amsterdam/Atlanta, GA 1993. 383 pp.
(Fichte–Studien Suppl. 3)
ISBN: 90–5183–443–8Bound Hfl. 180,–/US–$ 105.50

Inhaltsverzeichnis: Vorwort. **A. SCHRIFTEN FICHTES**. I. Gesammelte Werke. II. Einzelausgaben. III. Fremdsprachige Ausgaben. **B. LITERATUR ZU FICHTE.** I. Publikationen zu Leben und Werk im allgemeinen. II. Untersuchungen zu einzelnen Sachgebieten. III. Fichte und andere Denker. C. **REGISTER. ZEITSCHRIFTENVERZEICHNIS. NACHTRAG.**

USA/Canada: Editions Rodopi, 233 Peachtree Street, N.E., Suite 404, Atlanta, GA 30303–1504, Telephone (404) 523–1964, Call toll–free 1-800–225–3998 (U.S. only), Fax (404) 522–7116

And Others: Editions Rodopi B.V., Keizersgracht 302–304, 1016 EX Amsterdam, The Netherlands. Telephone (020) 622.75.07, Fax (020) 638.09.48